PASSAGES FROM THE LIFE

OF

CHARLES KNIGHT.

"PAST and FUTURE are the wings,
On whose support, harmoniously combined,
Moves the great spirit of human knowledge."
WORDSWORTH.

NEW YORK:
G. P. PUTNAM'S SONS.
1874.

LANGE, LITTLE & Co.,
PRINTERS,
108 TO 114 WOOSTER STREET, N. Y.

PREFACE.

N 1862 I received an intimation from the proprietor of the "Windsor and Eton Express," that, on the following first of August, the newspaper so called would have completed the fiftieth year of its publication. The fact was an interesting one to me. That newspaper was established by my father and myself; my proprietary interest in it lasted for fourteen years; and I continued to be its editor till the end of 1826, as I had been from its commencement.

Looking back upon the August of 1812, at which time my working life really commenced, it occurred to me that there were passages of that working life of fifty years which might have an interest for a wider circle than that of my family and my immediate friends, if presented without the tedious egotism of a formal Auto-Biography. During that period my social position has not materially altered, and I have not had the advantage of seeing "life in many lands." I have therefore no startling incidents to relate, and no great variety of scenes to describe. My occupation has been that of a publisher and a writer. But, in the course of my long connection with the Press (I use this word in its most extended meaning), I have been brought into communication with many eminent persons, and have been somewhat extensively mixed up with vast changes in the social condition of the people, in the progress of which elementary education and popular literature have been amongst the most efficient instruments of amelioration.

But before I start upon a long journey—broken, however, into several stages,—it may give a completeness to my narrative if I put together some earlier Reminiscences of circumstances by which I was surrounded, from the beginning of the century, in my childhood and my advance to manhood. The first steps of self-formation are, I think, always interesting to follow, however uneventful may be the subsequent career of an individual. But my early days at Windsor have a wider interest, as they made me familiar with the outward manifestations of the simple life of George the Third and his Court—an old-fashioned life of publicity, which wholly passed away in the seclusion of the next reign, when the King was seldom seen by his people, much less living among them in a sort of family intimacy, such as I had looked upon from my humble point of observation. In 1810, the regal aspect of Windsor was wholly changed by the illness of the King. In 1812, when I put on the responsibilities of full age, the Regent was invested with unrestricted power. There never was a more eventful period in the history of our country than the first twelve years of the Nineteenth Century. They were calculated to produce a strong and abiding impression upon the mind of a thoughtful youth, whose local associations were suggestive of past dangers and triumphs—of the Blenheim of Anne and the Crecy of Edward. Moreover, as I advanced towards manhood, there was an outburst of literature, which stirred my spirit with a new power. If, in recording my impressions of this memorable era, I should be able to recal some of the enthusiasm of the passing time, I may not be without the hope of imparting an interest to the Reminiscences of a solitary boy and an obscure young man.

The half-century of active employment which I look back upon is divided, in my retrospection, into three epochs. I shall regard them as stages in my journey of life; not always caring thus to measure my progress by any extreme nicety of dates; and not suddenly halting when the interest of a subject carries me forward to its natural close.

I. From 1812 to the end of 1822, my chief occupation was that of a journalist at Windsor. But my duties were not wholly limited to that narrow range, although in tracing my course as the editor of a local paper I may regard some circumstances as of peculiar interest. The political aspects of that period are not pleasant to review; when the thoughtful man saw as much to be apprehended from an unsympathising Government as from a discontented people. In 1820 I made my first attempt in publishing a Cheap Miscellany; and I have to estimate what Popular Literature was, at a period when the majority looked upon Books for the Many as a very dangerous experiment in giving a direction to the newly-diffused art of reading. At this period, also, of strong political excitement, I was induced to accept the editorship of a London Weekly Newspaper. My area of observation was thus somewhat enlarged. My aim was to make "The Guardian" as much a literary as a political paper; and I thus incidentally acquired a familiarity with the Periodical Literature of a time when Magazines were becoming more original and more influential. I also gained some insight into the general commerce of books in that closing era of high prices. During this period one of the pleasantest occupations of my Windsor life opened to me, as the printer and publisher of "The Etonian." This circumstance led to my intercourse with that most remarkable knot of Cambridge students who became the chief contributors to "Knight's Quarterly Magazine." It may be sufficient to mention the names of Macaulay, Praed, Sidney Walker, Henry Nelson Coleridge (of these I may, unhappily, speak without reserve), and add those of Derwent Coleridge, Henry Malden, and John Moultrie, to give an abiding interest to such remembrances. "The Quarterly Magazine" chiefly led to my establishment as a London publisher in the season of 1823. Through this year, and in 1824, I was occupied in the literary and commercial management of that work, which was concluded after the publication of six numbers. A second series was subsequently undertaken; but this attempt at a revival was of too solid a character fitly to succeed its brilliant predecessor.

II. I had been gradually extending my field of business as a publisher of Miscellaneous Books, and was not without the support of persons of reputation and influence. Yet my experience of the risk of miscellaneous publishing became in a year or two somewhat discouraging. In 1826, I had to struggle, in common with many others of my craft, against the depression in value of all literary property. But in this period of difficulty I was endeavouring to mature several plans for wholly and systematically devoting myself to cheap Popular Literature. Some of the seed thus prepared was ultimately sown.

In 1827 I became connected with the Society for the Diffusion of Useful Knowledge; and soon after edited and published "The British Almanac" and "Companion," and "The Library of Entertaining Knowledge." Through twenty years—until, indeed, the Society thought that the time was come when individual enterprise would accomplish all that they had attempted—I was more or less connected with this memorable Association. My remembrances will embrace whatever, without violation of confidence, may be related of this connection. I need not here particularise the eminent persons with whom I was brought into contact, in carrying forward the works which were entrusted to my care as Publisher, and in several cases as Editor. Other important works were undertaken by me without the support of the Society's reputation. I availed myself—perhaps more than most of the publishers of that period—of the revived process of wood-engraving, to diffuse popular Art as well as popular Literature. In this species of enterprise "The Penny Magazine" led the way. "The Pictorial Bible" was the most successful of the more permanent class of such publications; the "Thousand and one Nights" was the most beautiful. The "Pictorial History of England" was followed by the "Pictorial Shakspere," which was the most congenial undertaking of my literary life; and then by the "London." This series of years, which brought with them unabated literary labour and most anxious commercial responsibility, were not without their enjoyments of pleasant and remunerating work. They afforded me the consolation that I was performing a public good, when I bore up, unaided, under the heavy load of "The Penny Cyclopædia," overweighted by taxation. This was the most busy and the most interesting period of my working life; and its interest is heightened beyond measure to myself by the consideration that this epoch was the great turning-point in our political and social history; that it was a period of wonderful progress; and that many of the distinguished men with whom I was associated can never be separated, by the future historian, from the course of that peaceful revolution which has made the institutions of the country in harmony with the advance of intelligence, and has identified the interests and the wishes of the rulers and of the nation. In this period, also, I became officially connected, as a Publisher, with those who originated and carried forward the Amendment of the Poor-Law and other cognate reforms; and I was thus necessarily called upon to give a close attention to the principles and practical working of measures which have so materially improved the Condition of the People.

III. My third epoch is one of comparative repose. I edited and published the extensive series of the "Weekly Volume." I had opportunities of seeing much of the actual condition of the country in editing "The Land we Live in," during the transition period of Free Trade. I assisted as Publisher in the great sanitary measures which had assumed fresh importance. Gradually I withdrew from any novel undertakings involving considerable risk; for I found that the new competition of excessive cheapness, without regard to the quality of the reading made cheap, was not suited to the habits in which I had been so long trained. But I had still to look for happiness in work. I had to become more a writer and editor than a publisher. A few separate volumes were published for me by Mr. Murray. Larger undertakings, connected with copyrights which I had retained, or was to create, were published by Messrs. Bradbury & Evans. I was thus relieved from the minor cares of business, and, having a just confidence in those to whom my interests were committed, I could work more efficiently at my responsible duties as author and conductor. The nature of my writings was such that I had to look upon the various phases of Society in the Past, and so, by comparison, to estimate the Present more accurately and impartially than a view mainly directed to current things might attain. Whilst engaged in writing the History of my Country, I had also to keep a steady eye upon the general characteristics of its progress—political, social, scientific, and literary; for I was occupied in reproducing, with large additions, that Cyclopædia of which I had been the proprietor and publisher under the Society for the Diffusion of Useful Knowledge. In this evening of my life I had the happiness to become intimate with many who were eminent in the imaginative walks of Literature; and I learnt, more completely than I knew before, that it is not only the scientific and the philosophical who are advancing, by their writings, the moral and intellectual developments of a nation.

In thus producing my memorials of Men and Books, of Social Progress and Changing Manners, I may be considered as risking the indulgence of the garrulous egotism of advanced years. I hope that the form of "Passages" will keep me from many of the usual faults of Auto-Biography. I shall prefer to speak of others rather than of myself. I shall endeavour to deal with public realities rather than with transient moods of my own mind. I have undertaken a survey of a "long tract of time," and, having often to rely upon my memory, may have to ask the indulgence of the reader if he discover any mistakes in dates, or any confusion in the relation of one circumstance to another. I never kept a diary. I am not sure that I should have had a clearer view of the leading Passages of my life if I had done so. I was not always careful in preserving letters. Yet somehow I feel as if I could find my way through labyrinths which might be impenetrable in their obscurity, were it not for associations which conduct me onward, even as the Indian can see his road by old footmarks which he alone can recognise.

CHARLES KNIGHT.

November 11, 1863.

PREFACE OF THE AMERICAN EDITOR.

IN placing before American readers Charles Knight's modest and manly record of his most fruitful and earnest work, the editor would feel himself at variance with the whole spirit of the Autobiography, if he should endeavor to add to it any words of his own that could seem like the attempt to point its very noble moral. The creed on which Knight's life was based, was as simple as the acts resulting from it were beneficial and useful in the highest sense. It comprehended two leading articles—first, a most hopeful and unshaken belief in good and in the great power of good; and secondly, a complete sacrifice of selfish aims, to the endeavor to benefit and elevate other men. Perhaps, after all, it is not often that a creed comes nearer than this to the simplest rendering of a law, formulated some twenty centuries ago, wherein are set forth a man's duty to God and to his neighbor.

The regret which the editor feels at finding himself compelled to omit from this abridgment many things which have been of great interest to him and would be equally interesting to the reader, is partly atoned for by his hope that in this smaller form the Autobiography will reach many to whom the larger English edition in three volumes would be less accessible. In making omissions, the editor has endeavored to leave out such passages as were rather descriptive of outside events than of Mr. Knight's own life, or of subjects intimately connected with his career. Summaries of political affairs in Europe, descriptions of journeys and places visited, and Mr. Knight's quotations (if of great length) from the published writings of other authors, have often been omitted; and opinions expressed upon matters foreign to the general topics of the book have sometimes shared the same fate. The account in the English edition, of Knight's experiences with the company of amateur actors, among whom Dickens was the leading spirit, could be spared from this volume better than many other passages, since the subject is treated of in Mr. Forster's widely-read biography of the great novelist.

Mr. Knight's words have in no case been changed. A sentence has here and there been inserted to restore the connection, where this has been interrupted by the omission of a passage; but the language, with these exceptions, remains precisely that of the author. It has been thought better that this should be preserved, even at the cost of a possible abruptness of transition in a few exceptional cases. While the editor is prepared for the inevitable differences of opinion that must exist with regard to what should be retained and what omitted in the abridgment of a book, he ventures to hope that in the plan he has pursued he has avoided any actual injustice to the author's clear and vivid presentation of his life's history.

NEW YORK, *March*, 1874.

CONTENTS.

INTRODUCTORY.

THE book, for the new issue of which I have undertaken to write an Introductory Note, is strictly what its title indicates—the record of 'Passages of a Working Life during Half a Century.' The Worker has ceased from his labours and entered upon his rest. But it is too soon yet to add the final chapter to his 'Passages.' All that will be attempted here will be to carry on the record till the goal was reached. I have called the note Introductory, but its more fitting place would, perhaps, be at the end rather than at the beginning of the book, and the reader may, if he please, defer the reading of it till he has read the 'Passages.'

In the Preface Mr. Knight tells us that it was in the August of 1812 his "working life really commenced;" but nowhere, I think, has he mentioned the year when life itself began, though, from various incidental references, it may readily be inferred.

But in considering the closing years of his working life it is well to keep in mind his actual age.

He was born at Windsor on the 15th of March, 1791. The Dedication, which terminates the 'Passages' (vol. iii. p. 328), is dated January 16, 1865. He had thus, as we see, nearly completed his seventy-fourth year when he wrote the last pages of his book: he had quite completed it when the book was published. To pass in review half a century of such varied and active occupation, and to produce his 'Memorials of Men and Books, of Social Progress, and Changing Manners,' was a toilsome and arduous undertaking at such an age; and it might have been thought that its author would feel that, having accomplished it, he had at length fairly earned repose. But old habits could not be so easily cast off. Work had long been necessary to his enjoyment of life. The love of literature had coloured his business transactions when he was most active as a publisher: when he withdrew from direct participation in trade, the pursuit of literature became his chief occupation. As he wrote in the Preface to the volume now in the reader's hand, he "had still to look for happiness in work." Before he had completed the present book, he had, in fact, been laying down the lines of a new one.

The subject of this lay close to his hand, and the research it involved was a congenial and pleasant labour. Various references in the 'Passages' had vividly recalled the images of one and another of the bygone generations of booksellers—many of them writers, printers, publishers, as well as booksellers. Dryden's quaint old publisher, "left-legged Jacob," Pope's "huge Lintott," and "dauntless Curll," Johnson's first London friend, Edward Cave, and folio-smitten Osborne, Grandison-Richardson, and the philanthropic old curmudgeon, Thomas Guy, sitting in his odd little shop at the corner of Lombard Street, "over against the Stocks Market," were more than mere names to him; and, as one and another of their shadows crossed his path, there recurred an old, half-formed fancy that a pleasant gossiping volume might be written about them, their doings, and their associates, such as years before had led him to collect books and prints that served to illustrate the history of the Trade. More than once we had talked the subject over, and having often had occasion, during the quarter of a century we had worked together, to admire how quickly performance followed on conception, I was little surprised at receiving, a month or so after the publication of the third volume of the 'Passages,' the first proof-sheets of a Memoir of the Founder of Guy's Hospital, and learning that it was to form the opening chapter of a volume to be entitled 'Shadows of the Old Booksellers.' On some of the more out-of-the-way points of a topographical and antiquarian kind, respecting which he was unsatisfied, and which he was, of course, unable personally to investigate, I was able to throw a little additional light, and to indicate some collateral sources of information which he had overlooked. The new materials entailed fresh toil, but he at once cheerfully engaged on it, recast the memoir, and made it the best, the most interesting, and the most appreciative biography that had been written of one well entitled to commemoration.

Once fairly started, the work advanced smoothly and rapidly. With his life-long acquaintance with the theme in all its parts and bearings, his knowledge of the men, his fondness for picturesque details, and tact in selecting and grouping them, and his never-failing facility of expression, the mere writing was comparatively easy, and printing, as was his custom, chapter by chapter as each was written, by the end of the year the volume was finished.

The Old Booksellers had been a congenial theme, and he parted from them unwillingly. He had told the story, more or less fully, of a goodly number of them—from Thomas Guy to James Lackington—and thus traversed, in a desultory but not unconnected manner, the history of bookselling and publishing during the entire eighteenth century, at the same time illustrating on the way many a by-path of literary and social life. But then, how many had he been forced to exclude whose claims to a place seemed scarcely inferior to those he had admitted, and of whom, as representatives of special phases of art or literature, of the trade or of the times, so much might have been told that would have given life and freshness to the book, and amused and interested the reader! Lingering thus over their memories, he, in the Introduction to the volume, enumerates and characterises many of those he has omitted, and, noting some of the associations evoked by their names, observes that the more prominent among them might "fitly form the subject of a separate series," and, "without pledging himself to such an attempt," states that he "may probably employ his leisure in collecting some of the necessary materials, which, like those upon which the present volume has been based, have to be sought for in odd corners, as well as in open spaces accessible to all."

Research such as this was, however, more than could be entered upon immediately, and, as a lighter exercise, he undertook the preparation of a volume entitled 'Half-hours with the best Letter-Writers and Autobiographers,' a selection of short but always interesting extracts, with introductory notices of the writers, and usually some apt comments. 'Shadows of the Old Booksellers' was completed in October 1865; the 'Half-hours' occupied him till November 1866. But already he had a new work on the anvil. Sight was fast failing; the fingers could not guide the pen; the memory no longer responded as of old to the calls made upon it. But there was the old craving for work, and, as the readiest means of satisfying it, he set about the composition of an historical romance, led thereto, probably, by the circumstance that he had been once again reading through Scott's novels—or, rather, had listened to them, for his eyes no longer permitted him to read for himself. The story was, however, suggested by a passage in a letter from the Rev. George Garrard to Sir Thomas Wentworth, Lord Deputy of Ireland, dated January 8th, 1635-6, telling how a man of mean estate, succeeding unexpectedly to a large fortune, "was so overjoyed that he fell mad," when, under the vicious action of the Court of Wards, "instantly he was begged at Court," but died two days after. 'Begg'd at Court,' as the novel was called, is the story of this "poor rich man's" daughter, who, in place of her father, has been given as a ward to a certain Captain Blackman. It is a "Legend of Westminster," and referring to the Commonwealth period, affords room for some interesting local historical gossip. The story is told in a single volume, and a reader old-fashioned enough to enjoy a plain unsensational historical novelette will peruse it with pleasure; but its chief interest will probably be found in the time and the circumstances in which it was composed. The last lines of it were written on the 15th of March, 1867, the author's seventy-sixth birthday:

The story itself, owing to the failure of sight, was "dictated to a kind helper." It would not be easy to find a parallel to this in literary history.

The novel finished, his thoughts were still at work. As lying within the compass of his now limited means of research, he undertook a second series of 'Half-hours with the best Letter-Writers and Autobiographers;' and I see by the dates on the proof-sheets now lying before me, that he had completed it by the beginning of June 1868. But his vigour was by this time greatly abated, and he acknowledges in the Preface the help for which he had been indebted to a member of his family. Still, as in the earlier series, the examples are well selected; the introductions and interchapters are written in a cheerful and kindly spirit; there is shrewd characterisation, genial criticism, a healthy moral tone; and, as in the sketch of Sir John Dinely, some pleasant personal reminiscences.

With these Half-hours ended his career as an author. His career as editor continued a few months longer. In the second volume of the 'Passages' (pp. 58-64) he narrates at length the circumstances which led him to originate in 1827 the 'British Almanac,' and the associated volume, the 'Companion to the Almanac,' and he remarks with evident, and very justifiable, satisfaction that "the pair have travelled on together for thirty-seven years under my direction, through many changes of times and men," while "the general features of these publications have undergone very little change during this long period." For yet five years more he continued to edit the pair, and he brought his literary labours to a close by preparing during the last autumn days of 1868, the volume of the 'Companion to the Almanac' for 1869. This was the forty-second of the annual series, each volume of which had been produced under his direct supervision. He could not have undertaken the labour another year, and the work was transferred, with its high character unimpaired, to other hands. Mr. Knight's latest literary contribution to the 'Companion' was a lively and interesting paper in the volume for 1867 on 'Mural Records of Pedestrian Tourists'—the pedestrian tourists being the professional tramps who infest the country workhouses, and the mural records the scribblings they leave behind them on the walls of the "Tramp-wards" in which they make their temporary abode.

For a while longer he continued to select, or to talk of selecting, books to be read to him with a view to some new work; but day by day it became more and more clear to those who watched so tenderly over him, that at length his working days were past, and gradually, but tacitly, he seemed himself to acquiesce in that conviction. When, however, he ceased to read, or be read to, with a view to writing, he remained as eager as ever in acquisition. At this time, and indeed as long as his strength held out, he was an almost insatiable listener. Still, as of old, he watched with unfailing interest the course of public events, still liked to know what new books were published, and in his general reading, whilst following the current literature, mingled therewith the good old favourites, alternating with the lighter works, whether old or new, those of a higher and graver purpose. Thus, for example, in these last years he found in the Life, but still more in the Sermons, of the Rev. W. F. Robertson, of Brighton, a perennial source of pleasure, refreshment and support.

And so, becoming constantly feebler, more and more entirely dependent on those around him, slowly wore away these latter days. For change of air and scene, and brighter skies and warmer winter climate, Ventnor, St. Boniface, with its pleasant grounds, and Bonchurch, were successively chosen for residence (1869-71); and when it was thought advisable to be nearer London, Esher, Weybridge, and finally Addlestone in Surrey (1871-73). But he had become indifferent now to place or scene; the days of his fourscore years were in "their strength but labour and sorrow," and fast "coming to an end, as it were a tale that is told."

The end came gently, solemnly. About half-past two in the afternoon of Sunday, the 9th of March, 1873, tended and supported still, as ever, by Her to whom, eight years before, he had dedicated these

'Passages,' and by the Daughters who constantly shared in the pious duty, he passed away peacefully, and, as it seemed to those who watched by him, painlessly, to his rest. He was laid in the family vault in the old burial-ground at Windsor on the following Friday: the morrow would have been his eighty-second birthday.

This is neither the place nor the occasion to consider the rank of Charles Knight as a writer, or to attempt to estimate the work which he undertook and that which he achieved. What he did is told in the following pages. These few supplementary lines are simply a notice of the occupations of his last years. What he aimed to bring about, and what he more than any one else aided in effecting, was, "the *general* diffusion of sound popular literature." He from the first longed to see "the wide fields of knowledge become the inheritance of all;" or, as he expressed it in one of the last pages which he wrote with his own hand,* in the outset of life he formed the "desire to make knowledge a common possession instead of an exclusive privilege," and to the end, through good and evil fortune, he steadily prosecuted his purpose.

JAMES THORNE.

April, 1873.

* Dedication to 'Shadows of the Old Booksellers.' October, 1865.

EARLY REMINISCENCES.

A Prelude.

EARLY REMINISCENCES:

A PRELUDE.

SECTION I.

N the night of the thirty-first of December, 1800, I had gone to bed with a vague fear that I should be awakened by a terrific noise which would shake the house more than the loudest thunder-clap, and would produce such a concussion of the air as would break every window-pane in Windsor town. The house in which my father lived, and in which I was born, was close to the great entrance to the lower ward of Windsor Castle, called, after its builder, Henry the Eighth's gateway. I crept down in the dawning of that first day of the year to a sitting room which commanded a view of the Round Tower. The aspect of that room was eastern. I watched the gradual reddening of the sky; and I momently expected to see a flash from one of the many cannon mounted on the Tower, and to hear that roar from those mighty pieces of ordnance which was to produce such alarming consequences. I knew not then that these guns were only four-pounders, and that if all the seventeen had been fired at once the windows would most probably have been safe. I watched and watched till the sun was high. It was then reported that the King had ordered there should be no discharge of the cannon of the keep, for the new painted window by Mr. West, at the east end of St. George's Chapel, might be broken by the concussion. There was no boom of artillery; but the bells of the belfry of St. George's Chapel and the bells of the parish church rang out a merry peal—not so much to welcome the coming of the new year and beginning of the new century (for the learned had settled, after a vast deal of popular controversy, that the century had its beginning on the 1st of January, 1801, and not on the 1st of January, 1800), but to hail the legal commencement of the Union with Ireland. The sun shone brilliantly on a *new* standard on the Round Tower. I had often looked admiringly upon the old standard, tattered and dingy as it sometimes was; but I now beheld that this new standard was not only perfect in its shape and bright in its colours, but was wholly of an unaccustomed pattern. There were the arms of England in the first and fourth quarterings; the arms of Scotland in the second quartering; and the arms of Ireland in the third. But where had vanished the *fleur-de-lys?* Was his gracious majesty no longer King of Great Britain, France, and Ireland, as his style had run in all legal instruments in the memory of man, and a good deal beyond? The newspapers said he was now to be styled "George the Third, by the grace of God, of the United Kingdom of Great Britain and Ireland, King, Defender of the Faith." The good folks of Windsor argued that the change was ominous of the departing glory of Old England.

It is not to be supposed that I knew much of such matters in this tenth year of my life; but, nevertheless, I knew something of what was going on in my little world of Windsor, in connexion with the doings of the great world beyond the favoured home of the king. I was the only child of a widowed father; his companion in his few leisure hours; the object of his incessant solicitude. I cannot remember myself as I was painted at two years old, in a white frock with a black sash—the indication that I had lost my mother. She was, as I was told by those who knew her and loved her, a most amiable woman, whose society my father had enjoyed only for a few years—the daughter of a wealthy yeoman, of Iver, in Buckinghamshire. The "yeoman" of those days, although a landed proprietor, did not aspire to be called "esquire." He would now be recognised as "gentleman-farmer." My white frock and black sash had given place to jacket and trowsers. But still I can call to remembrance the unjoyous head of the desolate household; his passionate caresses of his boy; his long fits of gloom and silence. We had little talk of childish things. Of his own childhood he never spake to me. I came to know, in after years, that he had been brought up by his relative, the Rev. James Hampton, who subsequently earned an honourable fame as the translator of Polybius. This learned man died in 1778. In 1780, my father was settled at Windsor; for I have heard him relate with some complacency how he had asserted his political independence, by voting for Admiral Keppel in that year; "though," according to Horace Walpole, "all the royal bakers, and brewers, and butchers voted against him." My father had qualified himself for his trade of a bookseller, by his experience in the house of —— Horsfield, the successor of the Knaptons, both of which publishers were very eminent in their day. He had moreover a taste for literary composition, which he professionally indulged in the useful labour of compiling a little work which held its place in many editions for half a century as "The Windsor Guide." I find copper-plate views accompanying this handbook which bear the inscription: "Published as the Act directs by Charles Knight, Windsor, March 31st, 1785." In 1786 and 1787 he published the first celebrated periodical written by Etonians. I possess an interesting document, being the receipt to Charles Knight for fifty guineas "in full for the copyright of 'The Microcosm,' a periodical work carried on by us, the undermentioned persons, under the name and title of Gregory Griffin. Received for John Smith, Robert Smith, John Frere, and self, George Canning." Of this school-boys' production, remarkable for its intrinsic merits, but more so for the subsequent eminence of its writers, Canning was the working Editor. He was thus brought into friendly communication with my father. It was not only when the brilliant supporter of Pitt was rising into political importance, but when he had taken his place among the foremost men of his time, that he had a kindly feeling towards his first publisher, often calling upon him with a cordial greeting when he visited Windsor.

As I recollect my father when I was a child of seven or eight years, he was much occupied by his business, for he had become a printer in addition to his trade of stationer and bookseller. A considerable portion of his time was also spent on public affairs, first of the Parish, and then of the Corporation. I was left much to myself, except when I listened to the old-world stories of the faithful servant to whose charge I was committed by my dying mother —how like she was to the Peggotty of Dickens! It was fortunate, therefore, that I acquired very early a taste for reading. I had access to a large collection of books, and I quickly found abundant consolation for my solitary hours in that reading which, somewhat unwisely I think, has now been supplanted by what is held to be directly instructive. To the child, Robinson Crusoe is, happily, not a sealed book in an educational age; but the "Seven Champions of Christendom," the "Arabian Nights," the "Arabian Tales," with their wonders of the "Dom Daniel" (which, looking back upon, seem to me to have as much poetry in them as "Thalaba"), the "Tales of the Genii," "Gulliver's Travels," "Philip Quarll," "Peter Wilkins," and a dozen others, now vanished, were not then superseded, either in their original seductions or in safer abridgments, by the tamer fictions in which moral and religious truths are inculcated. My avidity for reading, and, perhaps, the dangerous locality in which I lived—an open sewer from the Castle creeping at the back of my father's house—made my constitution feeble; and the feebleness ended in typhoid fever. I recovered slowly, and was taken for the establishment of my health to a farm which was tenanted by the father of my good nurse. I have described what was the life of a small farmer when I was playing at "Farmer's Boy" at Warfield—one of the parishes comprised in Windsor Forest.* My host was a

* "Once upon a Time."—The Farmer's Kitchen.

shrewd Yorkshireman, from whom I learnt more than I could have obtained from many books. He was a tenant on the Walsh estate, having been placed in this farm as a reward for his faithful service with the Governor of Pennsylvania, Sir John Walsh, before the War of Independence. He would discourse to me of the wonderful man who drew lightning from the skies—the friend of his own scientific master (whose papers about the Torpedo and other curious matters may be read in the Philosophical Transactions), and he told how Benjamin Franklin became a great instrument in accomplishing that change which had separated the American States from their parent country. He would relate to me incidents of the war about taxing the colonists, speaking rather from the revolutionist than the loyal point of view. Altogether, a plain good man of simple habits and large intelligence. He and his bustling wife lived in the usual style of the southern farmer of the days of Arthur Young, before he was pampered by war-prices into luxury and display. The greater war-time of the French Revolution had in twenty years extinguished much of the immediate interest of the half-forgotten era of the American war. My experienced friend would make the stirring passing events of the week known to his household, in reading aloud the "Reading Mercury," which was duly delivered at his door by an old newsman on a shambling pony. How eagerly we looked for this messenger, whose budget would provide occupation for many a dull evening! Pitt and Fox, Nelson and Bonaparte, were familiar names. Dibdin's songs had found their way to this solitary inland place. Invasion was a threat we despised; for within a couple of miles of our farm was a summer-camp of regular soldiers. I have walked wonderingly through the lines of tents which stretched across the sandy plain near Swinley, and have lingered among the pickets till the evening gun warned us to move homeward. But our country had other protectors from our great enemy. It was satisfactory to learn, from a popular song which our ploughmen trolled out, that—

> "Should their flat-bottoms in darkness come o'er,
> Our brave Volunteers would receive them on shore."

There were, indeed, Volunteers before the close of the eighteenth century, and though they were somewhat disparagingly called "Loyal Associations," as though they were not soldiers, I can bear my testimony that at Windsor in their blue coats, black belts, and round hats with a bear-skin over the crown, they looked very formidable, although perhaps not quite equal to suppress a riot for cheap bread.

My pleasant months at Brock Hill Farm came to an end; and I went home to begin the dreary life of a day-school. Dreary, indeed, it was; for the education was altogether rote-work; without the slightest attempt to smooth over the difficulties that presented themselves in geographical names held together by no thread of description, and in rules of arithmetic, to be regularly worked through without the slightest endeavour to explain their *rationale*. The beginning of the century found me at this school. I was one of the few who learnt Latin and French. The same *emigré* of the Revolutionary times taught both tongues. I have no doubt his French accent was perfect; but his Latin, if I may judge from the way in which he read the first line of the Æneid, was not the Latin of Eton "I do trow."

"Arma veeroomque cano, Trojæ quee preemus ab orees."

My language-master was a pleasant gentlemanly person who hated England thoroughly. I have looked with him upon our illuminations of tallow candles for some naval victory, and have been dashed in my confident belief that our town guns, and our bells, and the "Reading Mercury" told the truth, when he assured me that this rejoicing was only a false pretence; that it was vain to expect that a trumpery island would ever be able to contend against France; and that assuredly George III. would soon resign Windsor Castle to the First Consul. Nevertheless, he prayed that he might not see the downfall of another monarchy.

The misery of the poor in my native town at the beginning of the century was sufficiently visible even to my childish apprehension. On an evening of the previous autumn, when I was returning homeward from a game in the Park, I heard the distant shouts of a multitude, and saw a furious mob gathering at the junction of the streets near the market-place. I got into the safety of my home not too soon, for the mob was coming towards the baker's shop that was next door. They had smashed the windows of several bakers in the lower part of the town. They believed, as the greater number of people everywhere believed, that the high price of corn was wholly occasioned by combinations of corn-factors, meal-men, millers, and bakers; and that if these oppressors of the nation could be compelled to bring their stores to market, there would be abundance and cheapness, and no possible chance of the supply falling short. Our neighbour the baker hid himself. He cared little if his door were forced, and his loaves stolen, provided the heavy box under his bed were safe. That box, as he more than once showed me, was full of crowns and half crowns, with some bright guineas, which he had long hoarded. The reputed money-hoarders were many in our town—men and women who had no faith in the Funds or the Bank of England. The baker hid himself in the back bed-room where his treasure was. My father from his window exhorted the people to go home. I stood trembling behind him, and was somewhat astonished to see how powerful was the influence of firmness and kindness in turning aside the wild but unpremeditated excitement of unhappy and ignorant men, who were not without a sense of justice even in their anger. There were a few more outbreaks as the winter drew on; for the price of bread continued to rise. In January the price of the quartern loaf of 4 lbs. 5½ ozs. was 1*s.* 9*d.* Windsor was always famous for its charities, which, no doubt, were often improvidently bestowed; but this, at any rate, was not a time in which the rich could shrink from helping the poor, even if they had known that the gratuitous distribution of provisions had really a tendency to raise the price of food. And so I looked upon crowds bringing daily their tickets to a great empty house, which had been fitted up with coppers, wherein unlimited shins of beef became reduced into savoury soup, and bushels of rice were boiled into a palatable mess. The work of distribution was performed under the inspection of a committee, who laboured with zeal, if not always with judgment. One benefit they effected in addition to that of saving the humbler population from the pains of hunger. They gave time for them to ask themselves whether any good would be accomplished by threatening millers and bakers with summary vengeance if they did not lower the price of meal and bread. It was a hard lesson to learn, when there were few sound teachers. Not many of the working people could then read the newspapers; but some who did read them might tell their neighbours that it was argued that the excessive price of meal and bread was a hard thing to bear, but that it was less terrible than the famine which would ensue, if farmers and millers and bakers could be compelled to sell from their small stores at a price at which every mouth could be fed as in years of plenty. Nevertheless, the educated and the ignorant would equally learn from the newspapers, that great peers and wise judges did not altogether disapprove of the principles that led to mill-burning and window-breaking. They would learn how a corn-factor named Rusby had been found guilty of the crime of having purchased by sample in the corn-market at Mark Lane 90 quarters of oats at 41*s.* per quarter, and sold 30 of them in the same market, on the same day, at 44*s.*; and how the Lord Chief Justice Kenyon had said to the jury, "You have conferred, by your verdict, almost the greatest benefit on your country that ever was conferred by any jury." They would learn how this wicked corn-factor met with his deserts, even before his sentence for the crime of regrating had been passed upon him; for that his house in Blackfriars Road had been gutted by an enraged populace. They would learn how the earl of Warwick in the House of Lords had recommended the adoption of a *maximum*, by which no wheat should be sold at a higher price than ten shillings the bushel; and how his lordship had rejoiced that no less than four hundred convictions had taken place throughout the country for forestalling, regrating, and monopolising. And why did he rejoice? When the man Rusby, he said, was convicted, the price of oats was fifty-two shillings per quarter; but such was the effect of his conviction, that the price of oats fell from day to day till it came as low as seventeen shillings and sixpence. Such were the economic doctrines proclaimed sixty years ago in high places! Can we wonder that the ignorance of the people was in perfect concord?

It was a gloomy season, but nevertheless we went on with our usual course of social observances. Valentine's Day was well kept amongst us. It was a serious affair then for a bachelor to send a letter embellished with hearts and darts to a lady; for it was held to have a solemn meaning. But children innocently played at Valentines. I have been led blindfolded to the mistress of my affections in the early morn, that no meaner divinity might meet my eyes: no vulgar chance should interfere with our deliberate choice. On St. Valentine's eve some would draw lots, to determine which pair should be registered in "Cupid's Kalendar." Old customs linger about my early memories, like patches of sunlight in a sombre wood. On the Saturday before midlent Sunday, the farmers' wives who kept their stalls in our market would exhibit their well-known preparation of boiled wheat, which few old housewives would neglect to purchase. On that fourth Sunday in Lent, I regularly feasted on Furmety, with a lady who was carefully observant of ancient usages. Does any one in the southern counties now know the taste of this once famous dish, made of boiled wheat prepared in the farmer's household, and having been a second time boiled in milk with plums, was served sugared and spiced in a tureen? In the West, the custom is still as duly regarded as the rite of the pancake on Shrove Tuesday. The first of May was scarcely saluted "with our early song." But in this May of 1801, there was a great ceremony at Windsor, in which I bore a humble part. On the 10th of May the custom of perambulating the parish, which had been in disuse since 1783, was revived, with wondrous feastings. The printed record of these doings for three days takes me back into the scenes of my childhood. There, still, my "little footsteps lightly print the ground." The population of Windsor gave themselves up for three days to singing psalms at boundary oaks, and carousing at boundary houses. A good deal of the winter's gloom was passing away. The spring was fine. The price of the quartern loaf had been rapidly falling from the 1*s.* 10½*d.* of the 5th of March (the highest price it ever attained), to the 1*s.* 6¼*d.* of the 7th of May. The king,—who had been shut up in the queen's lodge from the 14th of February to the 16th of March, with what the physicians called "cold and fever," but which we now know to have been insanity,—was again trudging early to the dairy at Frogmore; or riding at a very gentle pace after his harriers; or travelling once a week to London to meet his Council, where Mr. Pitt was no longer the presiding genius. Our loyal people said that the minister had justly forfeited the favour of "the best of kings," by trying to make him violate his coronation oath. To me, as to much older persons, the removal of a great statesman from the government of the kingdom was less important than the things which concerned our borough and parish; and of such was our Perambulation.

Great were the preparations for our "Rogation days of Procession." Mindful of the order of Queen Elizabeth, that the curate on such occasions "shall admonish the people to give thanks to God in the beholding of God's benefits," our vicar and churchwardens were solicitous that there should be unusual store of benefits to behold. And so it is recorded in the churchwardens' "Book of Benefactions and Charities,"* how sundry letters were written to the owners and occupiers of boundary houses, to remind them that, in former times, entertainment, whether of a barrel of ale and bread and cheese, or a "genteel" dinner, with wine to correspond, was provided for the wayfarers, rich and poor, who thus laboured to preserve their parish rights and liberties. Generous were the answers from all, except from the treasurer to the College of Windsor, "who cast a damp upon the business, observing that it was a waste of victuals and viands when everything was dear." The chronicle of the perambulation was duly printed for the edification of those who were partakers of the solemnity, and for the bewilderment of all future topographers. It was a glorious tenth of May, when, after morning service at our old church, we marched from the Town Hall — mayor, vicar, curate, charity children, inhabitants—two and two; boys like myself clinging to their fathers' skirts.

* "Annals of Windsor;" by Mr. Tighe and Mr. Davis Vol. II., pp. 556 to 563.

We came to the first boundary house, at the bottom of Peascod Street. The psalm was sung; the wine was drunk "by the respectable parts of the company," according to the record. Then comes an entry, which, even at this distance of time, produces a qualm in my stomach: "We proceeded northward, along the west side of the ditch; crossed the road in Goswell Lane and the ditch at the bottom of George Street on planks, and kept the drain that runs from the houses in Thames Street." All the lower parts of Windsor were then drain or ditch. The ditch—the black ditch—predominated. Never was there such a sink of impurity as my native town. Those pleasant fields, the Goswells, which in winter were flooded, were in spring, summer, and autumn, pestilent with black ditches. The railroad has there swept away these horrors. The authorities have also found out that the smaller black ditches of every alley have a tendency to increase the poor's rate. But in my early days these things were unheeded. In the Bachelor's Acre the "little victims" played by the side of a great open cesspool, kept brimming and overflowing by drains disgorging from every street. The Court sniffed this filthy reek. In the fields around Frogmore it tainted the cowslip and the hawthorn blossom. Municipal or royal dignitaries never interfered to abate or remove the nuisance. In truth, the word nuisance had scarcely then found a place in our language in a sanitary sense. Foul ditches, crossed on planks, scarcely disturbed the usual complacency of the perambulators, for there was a dinner in prospect, at her majesty's house at Frogmore. I was with my father, as one of the favoured guests in the "state parlour," where Major Price presided. The churchwardens' book records that "a gentleman who accompanied us sung a song or two, by permission." How well I remember that facetious song of the "learned pig;" how often has it been brought to my mind in recent years, in the acquaintance of the very gentleman who sang a song or two—the indefatigable, good-tempered, self-satisfied, pushing and puffing John Britton, who, then in his thirtieth year, was at Windsor, occupied in a topographical work which was commencing to be published, "The Beauties of England and Wales." He is gone, having done good service in his day by wedding archæology to a high style of illustrative art. The Frogmore dinner was over. I was tired; but perambulating was too pleasant to be readily relinquished. The next day I was tramping by the side of a "bosky bourn" to Cranbourn, then a lodge, which I had been told had as many windows as there are days in the year. How changed is all this forest scene! The lodge has been demolished. Many of the grand old sapless oaks have been hewn down. New plantations cover the plain which was sixty years ago a wilderness of fern. The beauty of the district is more ornate than of old. But nothing can destroy the noble features of the site of Cranbourn, whether called Great Park or Forest. Another royal dinner solaced our second day's march. The third day's perambulation took us to Surly Hall and The Willows—familiar scenes to every Etonian. The Church was not as bountiful as the Crown when we had returned to the boundary house at the foot of the Hundred Steps. The dean and canons had provided, it is chronicled, "a dinner and a dozen of wine."

Our way to the Town Hall was up the narrow Thames-street, the whole castle side of the road from the Hundred Steps to Henry the Eighth's gateway being then, and long after, crowded with houses. Some of the meanest character, and with the most disreputable occupiers, were the property of no one, but were tenanted under what was termed "key-hold." They have all been swept away. The rubbish that grew up under the castle walls has been cleared, even as the social rubbish has been cleared which hid a good deal of the grandeur of our Constitutional Monarchy.

About this period my father took me to London. The journey from our town to the White Horse Cellar in Piccadilly was satisfactorily performed in the usual time of five hours, and a little more. As the night had closed in, I stood at the door of the well-accustomed hotel, and looked with unspeakable wonder upon the long line of brilliancy to the east and to the west. Our lamps, few and far between, were as farthing rushlights compared to this blaze from patent reflectors. I knew not that even this radiance would, like the glowworm in the matin light, "pale its uneffectual fire," by the side of the illumination without oil or wick. I saw the sights which most boys were then taken to see, such as the jewels in the Tower, and the wax-work in the Abbey. But for one sight I was unprepared. I was led along a somewhat dark passage up a narrow stair; and there—(oh! that my mind could ever again feel, at the contemplation of the most sublime or the most beautiful object of nature, as it felt at that moment)—there lay my beloved Windsor, stretched at my feet. I screamed with an agony of pleasure. I knew that I was in London ; but *there* were spread before me the park, where I was wont to play; the terraces, where I had used to gaze upon the distant hills; the river, whose osier bowers were as familiar to me as my own little garden ; the steep and narrow streets, which I then thought the perfection of architecture; the very house in which I was born. I rubbed my eyes ; I was awake; the scene was still there. I strained my ears, and I fancied I could hear the cawing of the rooks in those old towers. It was with difficulty that I could be dragged away; and when I came out into the garish sunshine of Leicester Square, and saw the bustling crowds, and heard the din of the anxious city, I was reluctantly convinced that I had looked upon a picture, called a panorama. The bird's-eye representation, in one compact grouping, of objects which I had previously looked upon singly, has left an impression upon my memory which will assist me in tracing one of my own boyish perambulations about Windsor Castle.

It is the Saturday half-holiday at my day-school. The afternoon is bright and frosty. The rains which have flooded the low lands of the Thames have ceased. I can again ramble in the upper park. Castle Street, in which I live, has a continuation of houses up to the Queen's Lodge, in which the King dwells at his Castle foot. There is nothing to separate the Castle Hill from the town but a small gateway, which bears the inscription, "Elizabethæ Reginæ, xiii., 1572." Beyond the gate are substantial houses, inhabited by good families. In one of those near the Lodge once dwelt Mrs. Delany, at whose door the King would unceremoniously enter, as he entered in a December twilight and caught Fanny

Burney playing at puss-in-the-corner. This house is shut up in these my early school days. It is haunted, and the fact is proved by a broken window-pane, through which the sentry had thrust his bayonet when he saw the apparition. I pass the railings which enclose the lawn before the Lodge, and I reach the iron gates which terminate the road. No gate-keeper is there to bar the entrance even of beggars and vagrants. There is an old half-crazy woman in an oil-skin coat, who opens the gate in the hope of a halfpenny. Such is the "state and ancientry" upon which the inmates of the royal Lodge look out. School boys, with their kites and hoops and cricket-bats, have free admission through these gates. It is the common footpath to Datchet. There is another footpath which leads to the dairy at Frogmore, of which I may hereafter speak. I walk by the well-trodden Datchet path to the edge of the table-land forming the north side of the upper park, and I reach the descent, winding amidst old thorns and oaks, called Dod's Hill. My onward walk is stopped, for the lower park is flooded. I turn back and mount the broad flight of steps which lead to the south terrace. This is no privileged region for maids of honour and lords of the bedchamber alone to enjoy. The entire terrace is free to the commonalty. The town boys here play at follow my leader, and fearlessly run along the parapet, whether on the south, the east, or the north sides. No one looks out of windows draperied or undraperied, for no one dwells there, except, on the north side, Mr. James Wyatt, the Surveyor-General. He has been busy about the Castle for a year or two. A few of the mean circular-headed windows—by which the upper court was deformed, when Wren, at the command of Charles II., tried to obliterate the old fortress character of the buildings—are being gothicised. The Star building on the north terrace is undergoing the same process. The patchwork system of improvements which is going forward, a window at a time, appears very unlike the exercise of a royal will. The war absorbs the revenues of the State, leaving little or nothing for art. I come up the paltry wooden stairs that lead from the north terrace. I look into the Quadrangle, which is solitary and silent, except where a stonemason or two are at work. I pass through the Norman gateway, by the brick wall of the Round Tower garden, to a pile of ugly buildings—the guard-house, and its canteen, the Royal Standard. Adjoining the Deanery is a ruinous building called Wolsey's Tomb-house. St. George's Chapel has been restored and beautified; but this building has been neglected since the days of James the Second, when it was a Roman Catholic Chapel. I come home through Henry the Eighth's gateway, the rooms of which, then, or a little before, were used as a Court of Record, whose jurisdiction extended over the forest of Windsor comprising many parishes. Here, under the arch, was the prison of this "Castle Court," which in 1790 was described as a disgrace to the sight and to the feelings. I have seen the grated windows of this prison, which was called "the Colehouse." At the beginning of the century it was converted into a guard-room.

From the circumstance that there was no carriage-road from the Castle or the Queen's Lodge, except through the town, it resulted that the King and his family were for ever in the public eye. There was a lawn behind the Lodge in which their privacy would be undisturbed; but there was no other place in which strangers or neighbours might not gaze upon them or jostle them. The propinquity of the town, and the constant passage of the royal carriages through the town, made every movement of the Court familiar to the lieges. Royalty lived in a glass house. There was no restraint in these movements. What the gossiping and inquiring gentleman who dwelt up the hill said and did; how his daughters were dressed, and how they nodded to their friend, the linen-draper, as he bowed at his shop-door; how the good man's lady was somewhat more reserved, but always gracious —these matters mixed themselves up as familiarly with the town talk as if the personages were the squire of the village and his family, who sat in the great pew every Sunday. Out of the observation of this antiquated publicity was Peter Pindar made.

"The works of the sublime bard are sold publicly at Windsor." Thus writes this once-famous Dr. Wolcott of his own ribald lyrics, which he says "are now in the library at the Queen's palace;" adding, "his Majesty has written notes on the odes." As I remember, there was no secresy observed in the sale of these popular satires, although they might, perchance, come under the notice of the illustrious objects of their ridicule,

> "Who down at Windsor daily go a-shopping,
> Their heads, right royal, into houses popping."

In my boyish experience I never saw the King accompanying the Queen and Princesses in their frequent visits to the shops of Windsor. The prints in which the royal pair are represented as haggling with their tradesmen, and cheapening their merchandise, were the productions of fifteen years before the opening of the nineteenth century. But I have often bowed to George III. in the upper park, as he walked to his dairy at Frogmore, and passed me as I was hunting for mushrooms in the short grass on some dewy morning. He had an extraordinary faculty of recognizing everybody, young or old; and he knew something of the character and affairs of most persons who lived under the shadow of his castle. There was ever a successor to the famous court barber,

> "Ramus, called Billy by the best of kings,"

who could retail the current scandal of our "Little Pedlington," as he presided over the royal toilet. The scandal was forgotten with the laugh which it excited.

My early familiarity with the person of George III. might have abated something in my mind of the divinity which doth hedge a king; but it has left an impression of the homely kindness of his nature, which no subsequent knowledge of his despotic tendencies, his cherished political hatreds, and his obstinate prejudices as a sovereign, can make me lay aside. There was a magnanimity about the man in his forgetfulness of the petty offences of very humble people, who did not come across his will, although they might appear indiscreet or even dangerous in their supposed principles. Sir Richard Phillips, with somewhat of a violation of confidence, printed in his "Monthly Magazine" an anecdote of George III. which was told him by my father. Soon after the publication of Paine's "Rights of Man," in 1791, —before the work was declared libellous,—the King was wandering about Windsor early on a summer morning, and was heard calling out "Knight, Knight!" in the shop whose shutters were just opened. My father made his appearance as quickly as possible, at the sound of the well-known voice, and he beheld his Majesty quietly seated, reading with marked attention. Late on the preceding evening a parcel from Paternoster Row had been opened, and its miscellaneous contents were exposed on the counter. Horror! the King has taken up the dreadful "Rights of Man," which advocated the French Revolution in reply to Burke. Absorbed Majesty continued reading for half an hour. The King went away without a remark; but he never afterwards expressed his displeasure, or withdrew his countenance. Peter Pindar's incessant endeavours to represent the King as a garrulous simpleton were more likely to provoke the laughter of his family, than to suggest any desire to stifle the poor jests by those terrors of the law which might have been easily commanded. It was the same with the people. The amusements which the satirist ridiculed, when he told of a monarch

> "Who rams, and ewes, and lambs, and bullocks fed,"

were pursuits congenial to the English taste, and not incompatible with the most diligent performance of public duty. The daubs of the caricaturist provoked no contempt for "Farmer George and his Wife." The sneers of the rhymester at "sharp and prudent economic kings,"—at the parsimony which prescribed that at the breaking up of a royal card party "the candles should be immediately blown out,"—fell harmless upon Windsor ears. Blowing out of wax candles, leaving the guests or congregation in the dark, was the invariable practice of royal and ecclesiastical officials. At St. George's Chapel, the instant the benediction was pronounced, vergers and choristers blew out the lights. Perquisites were the law of all service. The good-natured King respected the law as one of our institutions. He dined early. The Queen dined at an hour then deemed late. He wrote or read in his own uncarpeted room, till the time when he joined his family in the drawing-room. One evening, on a sudden recollection, he went back to his library. The wax-candles were still burning. When he returned, the page, whose especial duty was about the King's person, followed his Majesty in, and was thus addressed, "Clarke, Clarke, you should mind your perquisites. *I* blew out the candles." The King's savings were no savings to the nation. In 1812 it was stated in the House of Commons that the wax lights for Windsor Castle cost ten thousand a year.

There were abundant opportunities for every stranger to gaze upon the King and his family. The opportunities were so abundant that his Majesty's neighbours of Windsor did not manifest any great solicitude to look upon the royal person. Duly every Wednesday his travelling carriage passed down the Castle Hill, preceded and followed by some twenty light horse. A council or a levée at St. James's demanded the royal presence. I remember that his Majesty's saddler stood at his door in a cocked hat and bowed most reverentially, on these weekly journeyings. Once a month the King went to receive the recorder's report,—that awful duty of which great statesmen and lawyers then thought so lightly.

Seldom were there fewer than four or six convicts, male and female, left for execution. That all should be respited is chronicled as a rare occurrence. The severe administration of the law produced no diminution of crime. In those days we lived in fear of highwaymen and footpads. Three gentlemen from the City—bearing the well-known names of Mellish, Bosanquet, and Pole, potentates in the money market—were flattered by his Majesty's attention to them in commanding that a deer of much speed and bottom should be turned out for their diversion at Langley Broom. The party hilariously dined at Salt Hill, after a glorious run. On their return, when near the Magpies on Hounslow Heath they were robbed by three footpads. Not content with their plunder, one of the robbers fired a pistol into the carriage. The ball entered the forehead of Mr. Mellish, and he died at the Magpies. Hounslow Heath, Maidenhead Thicket, Langley Broom, were the resorts of desperadoes, who clustered round Windsor as brigands still cluster round Rome. At the root of the evil in England was the inefficient and corrupt administration of the lesser functionaries. In the Papal States brigandage is only a part of the general misrule. Robbers, with us, escaped till the police-officer could obtain his "blood-money," the measure of the marauder's iniquity being full. Terror had no permanent influence. In the "Annual Register" for 1799 is this record: "Haines has been hung in chains on Hounslow Heath between the two roads." In 1804, as I was riding home from school, the man who accompanied me proposed to show me something curious. Between the two roads, near a clump of firs, was a gibbet, on which two bodies hung in chains. The chains rattled; the iron plates scarcely held the gibbet together; the rags of the highwaymen displayed their horrible skeletons. That was a holiday sight for a schoolboy, sixty years ago!

The most attractive of all the gatherings of crowds to gaze on royalty was the Terrace. Before the Castle was inhabited by the King and his family, the music-room on the eastern side had been fitted up, and here the Court repaired on Sunday evenings. Dr. Burney, writing to his daughter Fanny (then Madame D'Arblay) in July, 1799, has a most enthusiastic appreciation of the joys of Windsor Terrace. "I never saw it more crowded or gay. The Park was almost full of happy people—farmers, servants, tradespeople, all in Elysium." On the Terrace he walked amidst a crowd of "the first people in the kingdom for rank and office. . . . . All was cheerfulness, gaiety, and good humour, such as the subjects of no other monarch, I believe, on earth enjoy at present." Thus "*voir tout couleur de rose*" makes life move pleasantly even to such as Dr. Burney, who had been doomed "in suing long to bide." He was perhaps seeking no advancement in 1799; but in 1786 he had been sagaciously advised to walk upon the Terrace. "The King will understand." The crowd of "the first people in the kingdom" had many of them the same belief in the sagacity of the King. The dean was there, looking for a bishopric; the rich incumbent was there, looking for a deanery; the pluralist was there, looking for a richer benefice than his smaller one of poor five hundred a year. It was a time when the Crown had more to say in the choice of church dignitaries, and in the mode of disposing of rich livings, than in the present degenerate times, when the chancellor and the prime minister have advisers to regulate their patronage upon parliamentary principles. The Terrace, at the beginning of the present century, was not strictly an institution that was in accordance with the ordinary religious habits of the King's life. As carriage after carriage rolled up the Castle Hill, until a file of carriages, having discharged their aristocratic occupants, filled the space from the Terrace steps to the centre of the town, there were unquestionably such violations of Sunday observances as Bishop Porteus remonstrated against and Wilberforce groaned over. There were many anomalies in those days, and this was one of them. I thought little then of such matters. I sat upon the low Terrace wall; listened to the two bands—the Queen's and that of the Staffordshire Militia; wondered at garters upon gouty legs, and at great lords looking like valets in the Windsor uniform; saw the sun go down as the gay company dispersed, and was gratified, if not altogether "in Elysium."

On one of these occasions—it was in 1804—I saw Mr. Pitt. He was waiting among the crowd till the time when the King and Queen should come forth from a small side-door, and descend the steps which led to the level of the Eastern Terrace. A queer position this for the man who was at that moment the arbiter of European affairs; who was to decide whether continental kings were to draw their swords at the magical word "Subsidy;" upon whom a few were looking with sorrow in the belief that he had forfeited the pledge he had given when England and Ireland became an United Kingdom, and whom the many regarded as the pilot who had come to his senses, and who could now be trusted with the vessel of the state in the becalmed waters of intolerance. Soon was the minister walking side by side with the sovereign, who, courageous as he was, had a dread of his great servant till he had manacled him. It was something to me, even this once, to have seen Mr. Pitt. The face and figure and deportment of the man gave a precision to my subsequent conception of him as one of the realities of history. The immobility of those features, the erectness of that form, told of one born to command. The loftiness and breadth of the forehead spoke of sagacity and firmness—the quick eye, of eloquent promptitude—the nose (I cannot pass over that remarkable feature, though painters and sculptors failed to reproduce it), the nose, somewhat twisted out of the perpendicular, made his enemies say his face was as crooked as his policy. I saw these characteristics, or had them pointed out to me afterwards. But the smile, revealing the charm of his inner nature—*that* was to win the love of his intimates, but it was not for vulgar observation.

Loudly and rapidly did his Majesty always talk as the royal *cortége* moved up and down, amidst the double line of his subjects duteously bowing or curtseying, and graciously rewarded with nods and smiles from Queen and Princesses when any familiar face was recognised. "How do you do, Dr. Burney?" said the King, "Why, you are grown fat and young! Why, you used to be as thin as Dr. Lind." What mattered it to Dr. Lind, who was close at hand, that crowds, noble or plebeian, should then direct their eyes to the tall gentleman, who is described by Dr. Burney as "a mere lath"? From my early years was the person well known to me of that good physician. He interested me, as I learnt that he had been round the world with Captain Cook. He had stood at my bedside with another friend, Mr. Battiscomb, the royal apothecary, as I hovered between life and death; when, as my good nurse afterwards told me, she thought it was all over, for they shook their heads and talked Latin. Miss Burney writes of Dr. Lind, in 1785, "He is married and settled here, and follows, as much as he can get practice, his profession; but his taste for tricks, conundrums, and queer things, makes people fearful of his trying experiments upon their constitutions, and think him a better conjuror than physician." He has often charmed me with a sight of his "queer things." Mr. Hogg has, within the last few years, given currency to a somewhat incredible story that Shelley imputed to Dr. Lind his initiation, when an Eton boy, into the reasons for hating kings and priests, even as the Windsor physician hated them. Perhaps Shelley, who was credulous in worldly matters, as are most sceptics in religion, believed that the mysterious little books which Dr. Lind printed from characters which he called "Lindian Ogham," cut by himself into strange fashions from battered printing types which my father gave him, were the secret modes by which the illuminati corresponded, even under the very eye of the Court. I doubt whether he were conjuror enough to make the shrewd George III. mistake covert Jacobinism for ostentatious loyalty.

There were eminent men living at Windsor and in the neighhourhood, from whom I occasionally obtained glimpses of knowledge beyond my ordinary routine of imperfect school instruction. My father took me to see the great telescope of Dr. Herschel at

Slough. The clear explanations of the celebrated astronomer filled me with wonder, if they went beyond my comprehension. The venerable philosopher, Jean André de Luc (I believe it was somewhat later), showed me a galvanic pile which he had constructed, and astonished me by causing the mysterious agency to ring a little bell. M. Porny, who had been French master at Eton, and whose grammar and exercises my father printed for the London publishers, would occasionally come to see us, and would talk with a kindly interest about my small acquirements. I have an earlier remembrance of another amiable foreigner, the Rev. Charles de Guiffardière, for whom my father was printing a French work on Ancient History for the private use of the Royal Family—a gentleman whom Miss Burney held up to ridicule in her Diary, as Mr. Turbulent. But—must I confess it?—I am inclined to believe that the stage did for the enlargement of my mind something more than school lessons—something more than these rare opportunities of listening to the conversation of men of learning and ability. From my eighth year upwards, I could always obtain a free admission to that smallest of playhouses, the Theatre Royal of Windsor, where Majesty oft was delighted to recreate itself with hearty laughs at the comic stars of sixty years since. Tragedy was not to the King's taste. Miss Burney has recorded how he appreciated the dramatist whose Hamlet and Benedick were sometimes here personated by Elliston; and whose Richard III. Cooke coarsely but powerfully enacted on this stage: "Was there ever such stuff as great part of Shakspere? only one must not say so! But what think you? What? Is there not sad stuff? What? What?" George III. has had supporters in this opinion where we might scarcely look for them. I have heard one such heretic, whose intellectual dimensions would appear gigantic in comparison with those of the King, say of the writer of the sad stuff, "D—— and I always call him Silly Billy." The publicity of which I have spoken was, in the Windsor Theatre, carried to its extremest limit. That honoured playhouse no longer exists. The High Street exhibits a dissenting chapel on its site, whose frontage may give some notion of the dimensions of that cosy apartment, with its two tier of boxes, its gallery, and its slips. It was not an exclusive theatre. Three shillings gave the entrance to the boxes, two shillings to the pit, and one shilling to the gallery. One side of the lower tier of boxes was occupied by the Court. The King and Queen sat in capacious arm-chairs, with satin playbills spread before them. The orchestra, which would hold half a dozen fiddlers, and the pit, where some dozen persons might be closely packed on each bench, separated the royal circle from the genteel parties in the opposite tier of boxes. With the plebeians in the pit the Royal Family might have shaken hands; and when they left, there was always a scramble for their satin bills, which would be afterwards duly framed and glazed as spoils of peace. As the King laughed and cried, "Bravo, Quick!" or "Bravo, Suett!"—for he had rejoiced in their well-known mirth-provoking faces many a time before,—the pit and gallery clapped and roared in loyal sympathy: the boxes were too genteel for such emotional feelings. As the King, Queen, and Princesses retired at the end of the third act, to sip their coffee, the pot of Windsor ale, called Queen's ale, circulated in the gallery. At eleven o'clock the curtain dropped. The fiddles struck up "God save the King;" their Majesties bowed around as the house clapped; and the gouty manager, Mr. Thornton, leading the way to the entrance (carrying wax-lights and walking backward with the well-practised steps of a Lord Chamberlain), the flambeaux of three or four carriages gleamed through the dimly lighted streets, and Royalty was quickly at rest.

Our theatre was only open at the Eton vacations. But there, whether the King and Queen were present or not, I obtained something like a peep into the outer world—the world beyond the little orb of my country town. For the Royal Windsor was essentially a country town of the narrowest range of observation, and the tiniest circle of knowledge. The people vegetated, although living amidst a continual din of Royalty going to and fro—of bell-ringing for birthdays—of gun-firing for victories—of reviews in the Park—of the relief of the guard, with all pomp of military music—of the chapel bell tolling twice a day, unheeded by few besides official worshippers—of crowding to the Terrace on Sunday evenings—of periodical holidays, such as Ascot races and Egham races—of rare festivities, such as a fête at Frogmore. The "loyal," or the "independent" voters of Windsor, as they were styled in election bills by rival candidates, were fierce in their partisanship, but there was no real principle at the root of their differences. Through 1801 they were preparing, by rounds of treating, for an expected election, which occurred in 1802; when the Court candidate was returned by a large majority, and the one who bribed highest of two "independent" candidates was also returned, but was finally unseated by a parliamentary committee. Those who did not receive bribes were never scrupulous about administering them. Corruption was an open and almost a legitimate trade, as I occasionally learnt from the talk of those around me. The Court was an indirect party to the corruption, by installing two of the most influential of the plebeian partisans into the snug retirement of the ancient foundation of the Poor Knights of Windsor. The institution had lost its character of "Milites Pauperes;" and tailors and victuallers were not held to desecrate it. In spite of all this laxity of political morals, the people amongst whom I was thrown were, for the most part, of honourable private character. It was a period when there was less competition amongst tradesmen than in the present day. There were, consequently, fewer of what we now regard as the common tricks of trade. They sold the article which they professed to sell; and were offended if they were asked to abate their price. The few gentry were patronising, with a certain friendliness. The many clergy of the two colleges had somewhat haughty brows under their shovel hats, but were charitable and not very intolerant. The distinction between the trading and the professional classes was not so nicely preserved as it is now. Respectability was the quality more aimed at by the attorney and the doctor than what we call gentility; and respectability did not mean the pretension of keeping a gig or a footman—display for the world, and meanness for the household.

One of the most vivid of my recollections of this period, and indeed of some years after, is that of the extremely easy mode in which the majority of the trading classes struggled with the cares of obtaining a livelihood. It is not within my remembrance that anybody worked hard. The absence of extreme competition appeared to give the old settlers in the borough a sort of vested interest in their occupations; and if sometimes a stranger came amongst them, with lower prices and lower bows, he would be regarded as an intruder on the fertile close, who would soon come to the end of his tether. It was the same with the attorneys and the apothecaries. Those who had to preserve a genteel appearance spent an hour each day under the hands of the hair-dresser. Every morning the hair was powdered, the queue was unrolled and rolled up again, the gossip was talked, the evening paper was glanced at, and by eleven the good man was behind his counter. There were a few of the oldest school who closed their hatch when they went to their noonday dinner, and no importunity would induce them to open it. When the baker had drawn his afternoon batch, he took off his red cap and washed his bald head, put on his flaxen wig, and sallied forth to spend his long evening in his accustomed chair at the ale-house, which had become his second home. Some had a notion that they secured custom to the shop by a constant round among the numerous hostelries. I knew a most worthy man, occupying a large house which his forefathers had occupied from the time of Queen Anne, who, when he gave up the business to his son, who, recently married, preferred his own fireside, told the innovator that he would infallibly be ruined if he did not go out to make friends over his evening glass. The secret of these worthy people keeping their heads above water, in this *laissez faire* sort of existence, was, that their ordinary habits were frugal, that they rarely drank wine; never occupied the best room except on Sunday, and on that day alone had the "added pudding" of time immemorial. The frugal habits of all of the middle classes, and the want of education of many, did not abate anything of their importance when they were chosen to fill public offices. Under the guidance of the Town Clerk, corporate magistrates generally got through their business decently. Sometimes they made little slips. Late in the evening an offender was brought before one of our mayors, having been detected in stealing a smock-frock from a pawnbroker's door. "Look in 'Burn's Justice,'" said his worship to his son; "look in the index for smock-frock." "Can't find it, father. Not there." "What! no law against stealing smock-frocks? D—— my heart, young fellow, but you've had a lucky escape." (Even justices in those times might incur the penalties against profane oaths.) The constable demurred at the discharge of the prisoner. "Well, well! Lock him up, and we'll see the Town Clerk in the morning."

Peter Pindar wrote an ode on "Frogmore Fête," in which he describes the "Pair of England" with "The family of Orange by their side." This would take us to 1796 or 1797. It was about the beginning of the century that I was present at one of these fêtes, at which, as on previous occasions, however sneered at, there was a real desire to promote the pleasures of their neighbours and dependents on the part of the Royal Family. Amongst other delights of that occasion, there was a play, or rather scenes of a play, acted before the mansion, in the colonnade of which the Court stood, whilst the common spectators were grouped on the lawn below. The scenes were from the "Merry Wives of Windsor." The critical faculty had not then been developed to stand in the way of my perfect enjoyment. I believed then in the real existence of Slender and Anne Page; of the French doctor and the Welsh parson; of mine host of the Garter, who was undoubtedly the host of the White Hart. I then knew an old house at the corner of Sheet Street (alas! it is pulled down) where Mr. and Mrs. Ford once dwelt, and whence Falstaff was carried in the buck-basket to Datchet Mead. I could then tell the precise spot where the epicurean knight went hissing hot into the Thames. Herne's Oak was then to me an undeniable memorial of centuries past. Forty years afterwards, I went over the footsteps of my childhood with Mr. Creswick, and we tried to verify the sites of these immortal scenes. The pencil of my eminent friend has shadowed forth some aids to the imagination of the readers of the "Merry Wives of Windsor," in my "pictorial" edition. But to my mind there were no realities such as I had pictured when, after the Fête at Frogmore, I wandered about, book in hand, to the fields where Sir Hugh Evans sang "To shallow rivers," and looked for the "oak with great ragg'd horns," near the pit where the fairies danced. Diligent antiquarianism has pointed out a mistake or two in my conjectural sites. It is of little moment. It was with a pang that I gave up my boyish conviction that I had gathered acorns beneath "Herne's Oak," and yielded to the evidence that it had been cut down. The "undoubting mind" is a youthful possession beyond all price; and though the Winter of scepticism may have come, it is still pleasant to look back upon the Spring of belief.

There are some things that are prominent among the recollections of my nonage, in which the faith of my inexperience and the doubts of my small knowledge, were curiously blended. I was a frequent visitor to the State Apartments and the Round Tower. I sometimes accompanied friends who came to see Windsor; sometimes was permitted by the kind and intelligent keeper of the pictures in the Castle to linger about and look my fill. The State Rooms now are very different from the State Rooms as I remember them. There had been little change, I apprehend, in the architectural character of the rooms since the period of Anne and George I., when Sir James Thornhill painted new allegories to supplement the old flatteries of Charles II. by Verrio. We entered by a staircase under a dome gaudily decorated with the story of Phaeton and with lady-like representatives of the four elements, Fire, Air, Earth, and Water. The pictures in the apartments had received a large addition to their number after George III. came to reside at Windsor. Amongst these additions were the Cartoons. At the period of which I speak, and during several succeeding years, an artist was employed in making the most elaborate pencil-drawings of these bold designs for tapestry, which, perpetuated in the most exquisitely finished engravings, gave a very adequate notion of the skill of Mr. Holloway, but very little of the grandeur of Raffaelle. That grandeur I could even then comprehend in the Ananias, and Paul Preaching at Athens; I could feel the exquisite tenderness of the charge to Peter; but I could not quite understand the large men in the little boat in the Miraculous Draught of Fishes. The most interesting room, at the beginning of the century, was that known as Queen Elizabeth's, or the Picture Gallery. In a few years it was dismantled of its somewhat choice collection, and became a lumber-room, into which no one looked. There I once gazed upon the Misers of Quintin Matsys—well-fed misers, gloating over their money-heaps, with a joyous expression quite incompatible with the ordinary notion of the self-denying misery of avarice. At the end of this long and narrow room, looking out on the North Terrace, hung a wonderful Boy and Puppies, by Murillo. In this gallery were the three grand ancient paintings of the Battle of Spurs, the Embarkation of Henry the Eighth, and the Field of the Cloth of Gold. They first went away to the Society of Antiquaries, who were forced to acknowledge that they were only a loan; and they are now among the heir-looms of the people at Hampton Court. I hope that I had not faith enough in the ideal of Lely and Wissing to believe that the profuse display of their charms by most of King Charles's "beauties" was an adequate representation of female loveliness. In the same spirit of incredulity I was not quite content to believe that the Roman Triumph which Verrio had painted in St. George's Hall—in which Edward the Black Prince and his royal prisoner of France were the principal personages—was a faithful representation of the costume and manners of the fourteenth century. The Round Tower, whose rooms, now private, were then open to the public gaze at the price of a shilling, was a miserably-furnished, dreary place, which had little charm for me, except in the noble view from its leads. One of these dingy rooms was hung with faded tapestry, delineating the piteous story of Hero and Leander. Long ago I related the discourse of the fair guide, who aroused my critical scepticism in my boyhood, and who was a perpetual source of enjoyment to me when I could beguile some unsuspecting stranger into a patient attention to her learned volubility. "Here, ladies and gentlemen, is the whole lamentable history of Hero and Leander. Hero was a nun. She lived in that old ancient nunnery which you see," &c., &c. We have gained many great and good things through the Education of the People; but what have we not lost, in losing the humorous contrasts of society which were presented in the days of the Horn-Book.

At the age of twelve a new life opened upon me. I was sent to a somewhat famous classical school—that of the Rev. Dr. Nicholas, at Ealing. Here, for the first time, I was stimulated into the ambition to excel. I had read a good deal for my own pleasure; but I had read little for solid improvement. My command of books had given me advantages over other boys; for, although it might have been deemed a waste of time that I had been devouring plays and novels without stint, I had thus acquired some command of my own language, and could write it with ease and correctness. But I soon found that my desultory knowledge would stand me in little stead when I had to construe Cæsar or Horace. There was a kind friend at hand in one of the masters—Joseph Heath, a Fellow of St. John's, Oxford—whose memory I shall ever cherish. He helped me over the first difficulties of my advance in the routine of my class. I soon did my exercises quickly, and did them well; but the system of the school was not favourable to steady and continuous exertion in climbing heights by other than beaten tracks. My memory enabled me readily to accomplish tasks which to others were severe labours. But I was very young and very small, so that I was kept too long amidst slow class-fellows. Whilst I should have been learning Greek, I was construing easy Latin authors, writing a weekly theme, and making verses which required little talent besides the careful use of the "Gradus ad Parnassum." Nevertheless my school-life was a real happiness. My nature bourgeoned under kindness, and I received unusual favours from the friend I have mentioned. He treated me in some degree as his companion. At his house on a Saturday afternoon I have been admitted to the privilege of taking a glass of wine with scholars from London, who came to renew the associations of their Oxford undergraduate days. One of these was Mr. Ellis, of the British Museum—the Sir Henry Ellis of the present time—whose genial courtesy still reminds me of the sixty years ago when, as a boy, I first made an acquaintance which I have never ceased to appreciate as a man. I was happy at Ealing school, and if I had been permitted to stay there long enough, I might have fought my way to some sound scholarship. After little more than two years I was uprooted from this congenial soil, to be planted once more in the arid sands of Windsor, my father's apprentice; to become my own instructor; and, like too many self-teachers, to dream away the precious years of youth in desultory reading—purposeless, almost hopeless.

Section II.

At the midsummer of 1805, I was taken altogether from my school. It did not appear to me that I was changing restraint for freedom. I left with bitter feelings, for I had imbibed such a tincture of learning as made me desirous to be a scholar. My father's determination to put me to business, at the early age of fourteen, did not pass without some remonstrance from my schoolmaster. His answer was that I had acquired enough knowledge to fit me for my station in life; and if I became a bookseller I was not likely to be treated as Johnson treated Osborne, when he knocked him down with a folio, saying, "Lie there, thou lump of lead." My destiny was sealed when I signed my indenture of apprenticeship. My life, however, was not altogether without opportunities of mental improvement. My first occupation interested me greatly. M. Porny, of whom I have spoken, died in 1804, leaving my father one of his executors. The co-executor declined to act. With the exception of a few legacies, all M. Porny's property, of which the residue exceeded 4000*l.*, was bequeathed to a small charity school at Eton. Upon his decease, letters which he had prepared were forwarded to his surviving relatives at Caen, and they manifested an intention to dispute his chief bequest, under the Statute of Mortmain. A friendly suit in Chancery was accordingly commenced; and it being necessary that a somewhat voluminous French correspondence should be laid before the Master in Chancery to whom the matter was referred, my first literary task was to translate the letters which had been sent and received during the half century in which M. Porny had found a refuge in England from the alleged unkindness of his family. The probability is that the Master never read either the originals or my translation; but these letters were read by me with intense interest. In them there was a mystery gradually unfolded, as in some enchaining narrative of fiction. The real name of the French teacher at Eton College—the author of many elementary books, and of a well-known volume on Heraldry, that bear the name of A. Porny—was Antoine Pyron du Martre. Here were depicted the undying memories of early wrongs; the strong will which had scorned all fellowship of his kinsmen when the solitary native of Normandy was struggling for bread in a foreign land; the triumphs of his pride in rejecting the proffered kindness which came too late; the determination that he would leave his hard-earned riches for the benefit of the land in which he had gathered them. From fourteen to seventeen I was learning the printer's trade, more, as it were, for recreation than for use; set no task-work, but occasionally working with irregular industry at some self-appointed tasks. The indulgence of my father was meant, I may believe, to compensate me for his opposition to my desire for a higher occupation than that which he pursued. Thus I was often galloping my pony along the glades of the forest; or watching my float, hour after hour, from the Thames bank at Datchet or at Clewer; or wandering, book in hand, by the river-side in the early morning; or plunging into "the shade of melancholy boughs" on some "sunshine holiday." I read the old novels and the old poems again and again. Miss Porter and Mrs. Opie gave me fresh excitement when I was tired of Mrs. Radcliffe. "The Pleasures of Hope" and Beattie's "Minstrel" had long been my familiar favourites. At this time there were published charming little volumes of verse and prose, as "Walker's Classics," one of which was generally in my pocket. But in 1805 a new world of romance was opened to me by "The Lay of the Last Minstrel." The old didactic form of poetry now seemed tedious compared with the adventures of William of Deloraine, and the tricks of the Goblin Page. Meanwhile my small Latin and less Greek were vanishing away. The newspaper, too, occupied much of my reading time. It was a period of tremendous interest, even to the apprehension of a boy. What an autumn and what a winter were those of 1805, in which I was enabled, day by day, to read the narratives of such deeds as stirred the heart of England in the days of the great Armada! Napoleon had broken up the camp at Boulogne, and was marching to the Rhine. Nelson had gone on board the "Victory" at Portsmouth, and had joined the fleet before Cadiz. On the 3rd of November came the news of the surrender of the Austrian army to the French Emperor at Ulm. On the 7th we were huzzaing for the final naval glory of Trafalgar, and weeping for the death of Nelson. Pitt rejoiced and wept when he was called up in the night to receive this news, as the humblest in the land rejoiced and wept. Before I saw the funeral of Nelson, on the 9th of January, Pitt had received that fatal mail which told of the destruction at Austerlitz of all his hopes of a triumphant coalition against France. It broke his heart. He died on the 23rd of January. Tame, by comparison, as were the great public events which followed these mighty struggles, they were perhaps more exciting in the conflicting opinions which they provoked. England was still heart-whole. She was not dismayed, even when Napoleon had the Prussian monarchy at his feet, and Alexander of Russia had exchanged vows of friendship with him on the raft at Tilsit. Though she became isolated in her great battle for existence, her resolution was not exhausted. But she was humiliated by the events of the Dardanelles and of Buenos Ayres. She blushed when Copenhagen was bombarded, and she fancied that the abstraction of the Danish fleet was a wanton robbery. In this case, as in many others, journalism was not history. The secret articles of the Treaty of Tilsit had not then come to light for the vindication of the Government.

The people at this time, even at Windsor, grew gloomy and discontented. Public affairs were unprosperous; parties ran high; the taxes increased with the expenses of the war and the yearly additions to the interest of the debt. It was not only the actual amount of taxation of which the middle classes complained, but of the oppressive and insulting mode of their assessment. The excisable trader had too long been familiarised with the presence of the revenue officer to complain. He walked into the tallow-chandler's workshop without ceremony, put a seal upon his copper and his dipping vat, and locked up his moulds. He looked over the grocer's wares of tobacco, pepper, and tea, at his good pleasure; and this process, which he called taking stock, was insulting and troublesome to the honest, and no real check upon the fraudulent. The liquor-merchant did not dare to send out a dozen of wine or a gallon of spirits without a permit. The Income-Tax was truly inquisitorial, for the local Commissioners had no hesitation in ordering a tradesman to produce his ledger and cash-book. If there was an error in the return of Assessed Taxes the resident officer of revenue, called an Inspector, immediately made a surcharge, which it was extremely difficult to get off by appeal. I was once horror-struck by witnessing a scene between an apoplectic innkeeper and the tax-collector, who had no alternative but to insist upon the payment of a confirmed surcharge. The unhappy man, doubly red with passion, slid out of his arm-chair in the bar, and, falling upon his knees, exclaimed, "May the curse of God light upon you all. Now I'll pay it."

And yet, amidst much grumbling and disaffection, the majority of my townsmen went on in the light-hearted course which was habitual to them. There were few fluctuations of fortune amongst us, as in a manufacturing district; no sudden prostrations of the capitalist; no exceptional miseries of the labourer. There was amusement and excitement for us in the invariable round of the weeks and months. The 4th of June was a great day of bell-ringing, and reviews, and the regatta of the Eton boys, which closed with fireworks. There were Ascot Races, to which the Royal Family came in state up the course, their carriages preceded by the master of the buck-hounds, with his huntsman and his yeomen prickers. Ascot was too distant from London for a multifarious assemblage from Tottenham Court Road and St. Mary Axe to be there. The neighbouring gentry came in their carriages, and the farmers came in their taxed carts. A few Bow Street officers stood around the royal booth, but they were not installed in the preventive duties of suppressing E. O. tables, and of overturning the stools of the numberless professors of "the thimble-rig" and "prick in the garter." If a pickpocket were detected, he had Lynch law. He was conducted to a pond at the rear of the booths, and there, with a long rope fastened round his waist, was dragged through the water till he was half dead. There was the weekly meet of the hounds, who duly went forth to some neighbouring common from the kennel at Swinley, with the deer in the cart. It was not necessary to give the poor animal much law, for the stag-hound of that day was slow, and there were more hacks than hunters in the field. The King walked as usual on the Terrace, but loyalty was not so demonstrative as in the earlier days. The Marquis of Thomond knocked off a man's hat when it was not lifted as the King passed, and the suspected democrat knocked down the Marquis of Thomond.

Left much to my own thoughts, young as I was, I gradually grew into a chronic state of suspicion as to the general excellence of our political and social system. I saw a vast deal of wretchedness around me, and I saw no attempt to relieve it except by doles of bread at the church door on Sundays, with an indiscriminate alms-giving to vagrants every night by the overseer, and a driving of them out of the borough by the beadle the next day. There was no education, except at the Free School for some thirty boys and twenty girls. The national school of Eton, which the good old Frenchman founded, preceded our Windsor national school by fifteen years. Out relief to the poor was voted every week by a committee with a lavish hand. The assistant overseer insulted the weak, and was bullied by the strong. The parish gravel-pit was the specific for want of employment, continuous or temporary. The poor's rate was enormous, for there was destitution everywhere through sickness and death, produced by the contempt of sanitary laws. There was no dispensary, and the parish doctor was hard worked and ill paid. It is difficult, in these happier times of fiscal enlightenment, to estimate what the poor had to endure in the incidence of taxation. The great burden which they had to bear was in the dearness of food. Without mentioning the effect upon their means of living by the laws for the protection of agriculture—which told upon the market-price not only of bread, but of meat, bacon, butter, cheese—there was excessive direct taxation for the purposes of revenue upon sugar, upon tea, upon coffee, upon soap, upon candles, upon salt. They lived in miserable hovels, for there were duties of enormous pressure upon bricks, upon foreign timber, upon glass. The cost of a cotton gown was enhanced by the duties upon raw cotton and upon printed calicos. Worst of all, the effect of this vast mass of injudicious taxes was to arrest the profitable employment of capital, and thus to reduce the labourer to the lowest condition. The oppression and the neglect which I witnessed all around me,—evils of which I did not see the causes or anticipate the remedies,—drove me into those socialistic beliefs which it is a mistake to think did not exist in young and incautious minds long before the present day. I was a sort of Communist in 1808. In a satirical poem (whose MS. has turned up with other rubbish of verse and prose stored in an old box) I poured out my indignation against the indifference and pride, lay and clerical, which I saw around me. I find there these lines, which I give, believe me, not as evidence of poetical talent but of a jaundiced imagination. Many have written much of the same stuff at a riper age than mine, who have in time learnt the worth of more practical philanthropy. But surely that youth is to be pitied who begins by setting up for a political economist.

"Hail happy days, primeval ages hail,
Which deck the warm enthusiast's glowing tale,
When simple Nature, pure and unconfined,
With equal gifts ennobled all mankind;
When hardy energy and rugged toil
Alone could snatch the blessings of the soil,
And wearied diligence return'd to seize
The cup of pleasure in the lap of ease!
Now when the hand of unsubstantial worth
Grasps every treasure of the teeming earth,
And Nature vainly spreads her equal store
Whilst millions, heirs of plenty, still are poor,
Say, shall the glittering pomp of pride despise
The humble toil that taught the proud to rise?
Say, shall the wretched, all-laborious hind
In vain demand the bread he gives mankind?"

I fear that in this unwatched time of morbid thoughts my religious principles were in as great danger of running wild as my political. I had read some of the old divines—Hall, and Barrow, and Jeremy Taylor—with real benefit. I fear that I acquired a sceptical humour from such defences of the faith as Watson's "Apology for the Bible," and

Lyttelton's "Conversion of St. Paul." They attempted to prove too much to satisfy my reason, which they addressed exclusively. They did not marshal their proofs with the consummate skill displayed by Sherlock in his "Trial of the Witnesses;" nor did they charm away the mists of doubt by the tolerant and fearless candour of Berkeley in his "Alciphron." Beattie's "Essay on Truth" did not sink deep into my heart, although the King and Queen had lauded it as the greatest of all theological triumphs, as if there had been no such book as Butler's "Analogy." The service at our church was too cold and formal—often too slovenly—to satisfy me. There was no congregational singing. Chaunts and musical responses were unknown. I got away from it, whenever I could, to find a seat in St. George's Chapel, where the cathedral service was exquisitely performed. On Sunday the choir was full; but I could stand by the iron gates of the south aisle, and hear every note of the rich harmonies of Boyce and Handel breathed from the lips of Sale or Vaughan. On a frosty winter evening of the week-day it mattered little to me that the choir was empty and cold. I yielded up my whole heart to the soothing influences. I was sometimes glad to be admitted into a stall by a good-natured verger; for at times my attention was sadly distracted by the tricks and grimaces of the young choristers, who, as they knelt in apparent prayer, were occupied in modelling hideous figures out of the ends of their wax candles. Such were the secrets disclosed to me as I commonly sat on the free bench by the side of the sportive lads. These practices were gradually extinguished by a better discipline; but there was one practice which no discipline could control, for it was an institution as old as the days of James I. Decker, in his "Gull's Horn-book," thus ironically advises the lounger in Paul's: "Be sure your silver spurs clog your heels, and then the boys will swarm about you like so many white butterflies; when you, in the open quire, shall draw forth a perfumed embroidered purse, and quoit silver into the boys' hands." Thus have I seen a stranger civilian stalk into the choir of St. George's Chapel. The spur was instantly detected; and when the bewildered man was surrounded by a bevy of white surplices as he loitered in the nave, there was no help for him but to pay the spur-money.

Such interruptions to the beauty and solemnity of the service were not sufficient to prevent their abiding impressions; and thus the salt of devotion was not wholly washed out of me. I was, however, well nigh rushing into the desert, in going through the ceremony which was to keep me in the fold. I had diligently prepared myself for Confirmation. Dr. Fisher, Bishop of Salisbury, was to perform the rite. There was an absence of all solemnity, and even of decency, upon which I look back with disgust. I still see the bishop's officers driving the young people to the altar-rails as if they were sheep going to the fair; the monotonous formality of the imposition of hands upon the huddled batches who knelt for a few minutes, and then were chased back to their seats by the impatient ministers of the solemnity. Its failure altogether to satisfy my excited feelings compelled me into a passion of tears, and I went home and told my father that I would be a Quaker or a Unitarian. I think that Confirmation confirmed whatever was sceptical in my composition; and I had to escape into the region of natural piety, and long dwell there, before I could become reconciled to the establishment which could endure such profanations.

Up to my sixteenth or seventeenth year I had found little in my professional pursuits to interest me. But I then became what Mr. Hill Burton terms a "Bookhunter." My father was always a great buyer of second-hand books. He attended sales. He purchased private libraries. He bought many more books than he sold. Many of his rare volumes had been heaped up in cupboards till I routed them out, and made a complete catalogue of some thousands. This occupation was of lasting advantage to me, in widening my horizon of knowledge. I was led to study and abstract, not only Dibdin and De Bure, but the catalogues of great London booksellers, such as those of White and Egerton and Cuthell (the predecessors of the later and greater authorities). These enlightened my provincial estimate of value by "scarce," "rare," "very rare." To hunt in brokers' shops; to attend sales, and sometimes bid for volumes that I carried home in triumph at a small price; to talk with gusto to an old apothecary at Slough about black-letter treasures; this was a pursuit that weaned me from many of my idle reveries, and was not without its use in later life. The remembrance of that worthy book-collector of the then small village of Slough fills me, even now, with a sort of pride at the honour of having been regarded by him with a feeling that we were fellow-travellers upon the same road—he with his large experience and superb acquisitions, I with my newly-developed bibliomania and small store of treasures. Often have I peeped into his little shop on the high road,—strong in many odours among which rhubarb prevailed,—to see if my master was at liberty to discourse to a pupil on his favourite theme. He would suspend his labours, if he were not too busy, and hand over the pestle to his attendant boy. We then went up his narrow staircase into his sanctum. His first words invariably were, "What have you got?" I remember to have found upon a stall in Windsor market two black-letter pamphlets of the early English Reformers. They were not much to his taste when I produced them; nor did he care for a rare Elzevir which I brought out of my pocket. He would then unlock the casket where he kept his jewels, and would delight my eyes with something rich and rare that he had recently obtained in a hasty visit to London, made for the especial purpose of a book-hunt. How well do I recollect the glow of his honest face as he placed before me a Wynkyn de Worde, torn and dirty, but nevertheless a fit companion for the imperfect Caxton on his most sacred shelf. Missals he had, and early English Bibles. They ranged harmoniously side by side. I soon grew to laugh at Dr. Peckham's enthusiasm; but better thoughts would suggest to me how good it was that an old man who had no cares of children to engross him,—one who had little aptitude for the acquirement of real knowledge, scientific or literary—should have a pursuit which was intensely gratifying to him, and had a semblance of learning to the world as well as to himself.

Even as Sir William Jones advised the young Templar to read over law catalogues at his breakfast, that he might gain a general perception of the learning of which he desired to become the master, so I gained something like a broad view of the range of literature by my bibliographical studies. In these dealings in second-hand books, a circumstance occurred which I think had some effect in leading me to one of the most pleasant labours of my future life. I had been sent to a house at Old Windsor to make a list of books belonging to a clergyman who had received an appointment in India. When the price to be given had been settled at home, I again went to make the offer, with the money in my hand. The generous man was pleased with what he considered liberal terms, and said to me, "Young gentleman, I give you that imperfect copy of Shakspere for yourself." It was the first folio. Sadly defective it was in many places. I devised a plan for making the rare volume perfect. The fac-simile edition, then recently published, was procured. Amongst the oldest founts of type in our printing-office was one which exactly resembled that of the folio of 1623. We had abundant fly-leaves of seventeenth-century books which matched the paper on which this edition was printed. I set myself the task of composing every page that was wholly wanting, or was torn and sullied. When the book was handsomely bound I was in raptures at my handiwork. I was to have the copy for myself; but one of the Eton private-tutors, to whom my father showed the volume, and explained how it had been completed, offered a tempting price for it, and my treasure passed from me. Some real value remained. The process of setting up the types led me to understand the essential differences of the early text, as compared with modern editions with which I was familiar, especially those which had been maimed and deformed for the purposes of the stage. What would I not now give, could I obtain this testimonial that I had not been altogether uselessly employed in this morning of my life, before a definite purpose for the future had given energy and consistency to my pursuits!

My future walk in the world was gradually shaping itself into a distant view of a practicable hill-side road. It became clear to me that, as the professions seemed to be shut out from my adoption by my father's anxious desire that I should remain with him, my only way of escape from the petty cares of the trade of a country bookseller and small printer was to make literature, in some way or other, my vocation. It was not by writing commonplace essays and occasional odes and sonnets (which I had the sense to burn as fast as they were composed) that I was to carry out this purpose. If I were to accomplish anything, I must have a *locus standi.* There was my father's printing-office; he was not without capital. Windsor, with its objects of interest, was without a newspaper. Some day, not very far off, should my ambition gain me the conduct of such a journal? I felt that the vocation of a journalist—even of a provincial journalist—required thought, energy, various knowledge. I applied myself to study the history of my country and the nature of its institutions. I had De Lolme and Blackstone often at my side. Burke enchanted me. Yet I did not wholly surrender my political faith to the eloquent philosophy which had become Toryism, and which, in the dread of the French Revolution, was opposed to every change and every obvious remedy for the grossest abuses. The Hunts—John and Leigh—began to publish "The Examiner" in 1808. To my enthusiastic views, the Hunts were the true men—almost the only ones who spoke the truth—as the younger brother was the most winning of periodical writers. Then there was the "Edinburgh Review"—advocating Catholic Emancipation and many practical reforms which were held as dangerous innovations, and which, in their terror of the word "innovation," legislators were afraid to touch. But when the Reviewers were indiscriminately denouncing the conduct of the war and the imbecility of the Government—bitter in their sarcasms against administrative mistakes, depressing in their belief of the hopelessness of the contest, and ungenerous in their appreciation of the only military leader who seemed likely to stand between the living and the dead and stay the plague,—I could see, however imperfectly, the one-sidedness of political partizanship which neutralized the best efforts of the Whig Journal. Conflicting opinions sometimes distracted me. There were the alternations of joy and of gloom, of confidence and of despair, as the events of 1808-9 presented themselves to view. The insurrection of the Spanish Patriots was a beacon-light amidst the darkness. The people were shouting one day for Wellesley's triumph over Junot, and the next day cursing the Convention of Cintra. Moore had marched into Spain in November; on the 1st of January he had accomplished his disastrous retreat to Corunna, there won a victory and died a soldier's death. Never shall I forget my feelings on the bitter cold day on which this news arrived, nor the indignation with which, some months after, his Journal was perused. There came to Windsor the son of a joiner, who had left his father's house a stalwart dragoon, and returned crippled and emaciated from the Spanish campaign. He lent me his simple diary of his sufferings and privations, which told of the horrors of war far more forcibly than the newspaper reports of the wounded and fever-stricken who filled the hospitals. The public mind was inflamed by the mixed feelings of disappointment and pity. Then came the wretched inquiry into the conduct of the Duke of York. The hopes that had been revived of Germany being roused to resistance were dissipated by the battle of Wagram. The expectation of a mighty blow to be struck by England single-handed against France, by the greatest armament that had ever left our shores, came to an end in the pestilent marshes of Walcheren. Talavera failed to raise the once-sanguine national spirit. It was a long while before many people warmed into hope and confidence; months, and even years, before they could fully learn to disbelieve the prophecies of the Whigs, and refuse to throw themselves in the dust before the car of the conqueror. For myself, I had the old patriotic associations around me to prevent me wholly agreeing with the freeholders of my county in their address to the King, that, "under the government of persons apparently inadequate to avert the dangers and difficulties of the country, we see no end to our misfortunes." I was not yet prepared to write *Finis Angliæ.* With my fellow-townspeople of all ranks and ages, I went into the boundless excitement of the Jubilee of the 25th of October; was a manager of the ox-roasting in the Bachelor's Acre; marched in a procession of Bachelors, in the evening costume of blue coat, white waistcoat, knee-breeches, and silk stockings, to present slices of the ox on a silver salver to the Queen and Princesses; danced at the Jubilee Ball, at the Town Hall; and wrote satirical verses upon the genteel exclusives who attempted to separate the attorneys' wives and daughters from the grocers' wives and daughters, by stretching a silken rope across the room, thus forming two sets. I somehow recollect that the plebeian ladies were as well dressed, and rather more beautiful, than those above the rope, so that a good many of the exalted were left without partners—at least, by the younger officers of the Blues and the Stafford Militia.

Windsor was a town that had ceased, in those days, to be the residence of many persons of independent fortunes. There was mushroom gentility growing up at the Castle's foot; there was the unapproachable dignity of Canons of Windsor and Fellows of Eton; there were the pretensions of brewers and corn-dealers, who flattered themselves that they ranked far above shopkeepers. An atmosphere of proud ignorance was surrounding the whole region. I had a confident belief that I could do something, among my own class, to dissipate this fog. In 1810 I formed some dozen young men into a Reading Society. We hired a room of the corporation in connection with the Town Hall. They elected me their President. Twenty-three years afterwards Sir John Herschel was the President of a similar society at Windsor; and in a lecture which I then delivered I told my old townsmen how we had failed, and what were the changes of opinion that had made one of the greatest scientific men of the age a leader in the diffusion of intelligence, whilst ridicule awaited the earlier effort of myself and a few others. In the old box of forgotten records of my tentative progress to usefulness in my generation, I find my inaugural address. Let me copy a passage to exhibit a specimen of the good old times :—

"An opinion has been set forth with no little activity, and with a plausibility of ridicule sufficient to actuate those who ought to have united most cordially in this measure—a cry which has been raised in the haunts of the ignorant and at the tables of the educated—that it is departing from our proper sphere of action to engage in pursuits of this nature. These sagacious reasoners would imply that the common reward of ordinary occupation is sufficient to engross every faculty of the industrious part of the community. No pursuits shall fill up the hour of relaxation but those of trifling vulgarity or listless inaction. Good heavens! when I devote myself to occupations which are alike rendered necessary by my duty and my interest, am I to extinguish every honourable and praiseworthy feeling and rest satisfied with the torpid exercise of daily drudgery? When these cold-hearted bigots would thus exclude me from every gratification of intellect, why do they not demand that I should close my eyes to the appearances of universal nature, where every object excites my curiosity and my wonder? I am so sufficiently convinced of the dignity and importance of an industrious life, that I will never exchange it for the gaudy insipidity of luxurious idleness; but I will yet earnestly endeavour to raise its importance, by acquisitions that will exempt me from the oppressions of power or the arrogance of wealth."

Let me not, looking back upon these days, do

injustice to those who prevented the extension of what would now be called a "Literary and Scientific Institution." I believe we were ourselves exclusives; and that if any one of our members had proposed the admission of the most intelligent journeyman amongst us, the sons of substantial tradesmen and the lawyers' or bankers' clerks would have hooted him down. The age of mechanics' institutes, in which it is desired, if not altogether attained, that all are to meet on the common platform of knowledge, was still far off. The opinions of the great majority were against adult education altogether. The young men of the middle class were to rest satisfied with their small school acquirements. For the working class to read books was to make them dangerous members of society. Nevertheless, some did read; and their reading was not altogether of that innocent but dreary kind which those who dropped tracts in poor men's homes, about the duty of loyal obedience and reverential content, thought sufficient—the next best thing to the old safe ignorance.

A great revolution was coming over Windsor. In November, 1810, the Princess Amelia died. The youngest daughter of George III.—perhaps the most beautiful of a beautiful female family—had for some years been a sufferer from a malady which the best surgical advice had arrested but had failed to cure. One of the Frogmore fêtes was given in honour of her supposed restoration, and I remember a transparency of Hygeia, which was an emblem of gratitude for a signal blessing. After the death of the Princess, I had the task of making a catalogue of her well-selected library, in the suite of apartments which she occupied on the East side of the Castle.

It seemed like a voice from the tomb when I recently lighted upon a touching prayer, which I had copied from a blank leaf of her Prayer Book. It will not now be considered a violation of confidence if I print it:

"Gracious God, support thy unworthy servant in this time of trial. Let not the least murmur escape my lips, nor any sentiment but of the deepest resignation enter my heart; let me make the use Thou intendest of that affliction Thou hast laid upon me. It has convinced me of the vanity and emptiness of all things here; let it draw me to Thee as my support, and fill my heart with pious trust in Thee, and in the blessings of a redeeming Saviour, as the only consolations of a state of trial. Amen."

The illness of the Princess Amelia produced an effect upon the mind of the King from which he never recovered. It is scarcely necessary for me to repeat the story of the ring which she placed upon her father's finger, nor to infer the mysteries which were supposed to be involved in that solemn appeal to his affection. This interview is popularly held to have called forth, with a fatal intensity, the dormant insanity of his constitution. At the beginning of 1811 the Regency Bill passed. Then we looked upon the Queen's council—archbishops, chancellor, chief justices, master of the rolls, lord-chamberlain, master of the horse—driving through our streets, for their periodical inspection of their afflicted sovereign. The council of the 6th of April, 1811, was thus attended. Rumours soon went forth that the King was better. On Sunday night, the 20th of May, our town was in a fever of excitement, at the authorised report that the next day the physicians would allow his Majesty to appear in public. On that Monday morning it was said that his saddle-horse was ordered to be got ready. This truly was no wild rumour. We crowded to the Park and the Castle Yard. The favourite horse was there. The venerable man, blind but steady, was soon in the saddle, as I had often seen him,—a hobby-groom at his side with a leading rein. He rode through the Little Park to the Great Park. The bells rang; the troops fired a *feu de joie*. The King returned to the Castle within an hour. He was never again seen outside those walls.

The failure of my scheme of an association for mutual improvement was a blow to me. I had other mortifications which disgusted me more and more with my position, and made me fear that it would be a wild attempt to establish a journal at Windsor. I was again driven to the moody companionship of my own thoughts. For two years the dear tutor of my school-days at Ealing had resided near Windsor—occasionally doing duty at our church—once more my warm friend and instructor. Under his guidance I accomplished a distant and a wearisome travel, but with a new sense of pleasure in beholding unfamiliar scenes. With him I saw the sea for the first time. With him I made the tedious and somewhat perilous passage from London Bridge to Margate. Ye happier youths and maidens of another generation, smile not at the epithets I bestow upon this sail upon a summer-sea. None of you citizens of the 25th of Victoria can fitly understand what those had to go through in the 50th of George III., who ventured upon the deck of a Margate hoy. The quick run in the steamer from Tilbury after the comfortable early dinner, and then your shrimps and tea in your lodging-house long before the sun is down—contrast these delights with what I have to remember. A hurried breakfast at six, so as to be on board at seven; two hours of danger amidst the colliers in the Pool; a pelting storm in the river, with no luxurious cabin to fly to; Gravesend clock striking two as we drifted past the dingy town; hungry; the steward provided with no more tempting fare than a slice of hard boiled-beef and a lump of stony cheese; no drink but rum and water, for brandy was almost unknown and soda-water undiscovered; the wind rising; the waves raging; groans above and below; darkness soon after we had passed the Nore; then the hoy becalmed off Herne Bay; Margate cliffs in sight as another morning breaks; no pier to land at; a pickaback ride through the surf in a dirty fellow's grasp; a struggle between the temptations of breakfast or bed; a decision for bed; and a second day almost gone before we can find our appetite or our legs.

Circumstances too soon removed the friend of my boyhood to a distant part of the country. I was alone. I pined for the conversation of educated men. No one took heed of me. I writhed under neglect; but I lost little in not being familiar with those above me in station. There was a coarseness of manners, not only amongst half-pay officers and retired tradesmen, but amongst persons of independent means and good families—aye, even amongst courtiers—which revolted me. I have heard at our mayor's feast toasts proposed by men whose rank gave them a claim to the seats of honour, which the lowest and the most ignorant would now be ashamed to utter. Notwithstanding my strong local attachment, I grew to be thoroughly disgusted with my position at Windsor. About this time I became possessed of a small entailed estate at Iver, which I fancied would give me the means of emancipation from a life that had become distasteful to me. I entreated my father to enter me as a student at one of the Inns of Court. He at last gave a reluctant consent, and went to London, to make the necessary arrangements, as I believed. We neither of us knew much about the probationary condition of a barrister's life, and it was necessary to obtain some accurate information. His friend, the Editor of a daily paper (of whom I shall have more particularly to speak), dissuaded my father from encouraging my ambition. My father returned with such a dismal picture of the life which I had courted, that I somewhat doggedly resumed my easy and inglorious occupation; not without a belief that

> "There's a Divinity that shapes our ends,
> Rough-hew them how we will."

I stand upon the threshold of "A Working Life during Half a Century." I had a few months of experiment before the final choice of a career; but those months brought with them new responsibilities, which were essentially work. My trade apprenticeship was ended.

PASSAGES OF A WORKING LIFE:

The First Epoch.

PASSAGES OF A WORKING LIFE.

CHAPTER I.

OCCASIONAL glimpses of London had been allowed to me in my boyish days. In February, 1812, I was to be a resident therein for some weeks; to hear the pulsations of the mighty heart; to be face to face with great public things. My father's friend, Mr. George Lane, was the editor of a morning paper, the "British Press," and of an evening paper, the "Globe." The office of these papers was in the Strand, on the premises where the "Globe" is still published. Under his general guidance I was to have a brief apprenticeship as an honorary member of the staff of reporters belonging to his establishment. I might make myself useful if I could; but I was under no serious responsibility. I had, however, so much eagerness to behold the novel and exciting matters which such a position offered to me—if possible to render them an important part of my education—that my willingness to work soon obtained me work to do. I was placed under the care of my friend's stepson, upon whom devolved the duty of arranging the division of labour amongst the reporters, but taking no share himself in their actual work. He was a kind-hearted Irishman, somewhat duller than most of his literary countrymen; not very zealous in the enforcement of discipline amongst the troop of which he was the lieutenant; more frequently to be found in the neighbouring coffee-houses than in the Gallery; but, nevertheless, useful in picking up the *on dits* of the Lobby. I walked with him to the House on the second day of my new town-life.

To gratify the curiosity of the youth from the country, we go through Westminster Hall. The little shops of the seventeenth century and much later have been cleared away. Soane's ugly and inconvenient Courts between the buttresses have not yet been built. Within the hall, near the entrance in Palace Yard, are two trumpery wooden buildings, the Court of Common Pleas, and the Court of Exchequer. At the upper end of the hall are two similar erections, the Court of King's Bench, and the Court of Chancery. We pass below these through a small door in the corner, and are quickly in the Exchequer Coffee-house. There, apart from other company, are half a dozen gentlemen very merry over their wine. I am introduced to one or two of these gentlemen, and am invited to take a glass with them. Though somewhat prodigal amongst themselves of what we now call "chaff," they spared the shy stripling who suddenly found himself in the midst of men of talent, who, whether attached to the "Chronicle," the "Post," or the "Times," appeared to regard all political questions with the sublimest indifference. One I especially remember as looking upon the laughing side of human affairs, and never unmindful of the enjoyment of the passing hour, even amidst the monotonous performance of his duty in the reporter's function. Age could not wither, nor custom stale, the infinite sociality of William Jerdan, as I knew him in years when the third and fourth Georges had passed away. I saw that, in this pleasant party, he was not alone in his conviction that when one of the orators who could quickly empty the House was up, he might linger awhile before he took his turn, and pick up something of what the bore had said from those who had had the misfortune to note his platitudes.

We are at last in the lobby of the House of Commons—not a grand vestibule, but a shabby room with a low ceiling. We enter by a swing door—members and strangers indiscriminately—and move to the left side of the gangway by which members pass to the sacred door of the house. We stand by the fireplace. My companion has some information to obtain from an Irish member of his acquaintance—perhaps he has only to ask for a frank—and he waits his opportunity. I am somewhat tired of this delay, and long to be looking upon the stirring scene within. For ever and anon, as the door opens, I hear a loud voice, and catch a peep of a member gesticulating amidst cheers and laughter, and the Speaker crying "Order! order!" At length we ascend the narrow stairs to the Strangers' Gallery. I am allowed to pass as a reporter. It is the sole privilege accorded to those without whom Parliament would become a voice shut up in a cavern. The gallery is crowded with members' constituents, who have come with orders, much to the annoyance of the guardian of the toll-bar on the stairs. He would rather see his customary half-crown, which others have paid. We put our heads in; and I observe on the back bench—which by its elevation commands a view of the body of the House—half-a-dozen reporters busily employed with their note-books. This back bench is theirs by custom, but not by right. If the gallery should be cleared for a division, the staff of the Journals will take care to keep as close to the door as possible, that they may regain their places after the division. It was later, if I remember rightly, that they had a separate door of admission to this especial seat. It was fourteen years later that a Reporters' Room was assigned them at one extremity of the gallery passage.

It is enough for me, on this my first night, to look upon the general aspect of the House. In a week or two, by persevering attendance, I become familiar with the personal appearance of the leaders on either side. To the right of the Speaker, on the ministerial bench there sit, Spencer Perceval, Chancellor of the Exchequer; Vicary Gibbs, Attorney-General; Ryder, Home Secretary; George Rose; Palmerston; Croker. Castlereagh is sitting high up above the Treasury bench. Canning is on the cross bench below. To the left of the Speaker are Ponsonby, Brougham, Burdett, Grattan, Horner, Romilly, Sheridan, Tierney, Whitbread. All of these are gone but two, to whom it has been permitted to vindicate the belief that it is the privilege of genius never to grow old. I practise myself in reporting for my own amusement and instruction. In not writing short-hand, I have no inferiority to the experienced men around me; for I observe that very few have acquired, or at any rate employ, that useful art. The debates of 1812 were not expected to be reported so fully as in more recent times. Often members complained that their sayings were misrepresented. Such complaints were generally met by a disposition on the part of the House to punish the offender. It was very daring in Mr. Brougham to hint, on such an occasion in 1812, that "Gentlemen should consider the disadvantages under which reports of their debates were taken." With a mock solemnity the Speaker called "Order!" and the cry of "Order!" echoed through the House. To recognise the presence at its debates of the obscure strangers who sat on the back bench of the gallery would have been to compromise the privileges of Parliament. This hypocrisy was a queer relic of those times when the repression of public opinion was held to be the security of the State.

Thursday, the 27th of February, is to be a great field-day in the Commons. I must be there at noon, to secure a seat in the gallery. There I sit, looking upon the empty House till the Speaker comes in. The prayers are read, and some uninteresting orders of the day are disposed of. Strangers are crowding in, and we hold our places as well as we can against the rush. There are apparently two or three seats vacant on the front bench. A wicked gentleman of the press suggests to a despairing provincial that there he may be accommodated. He strides and pushes to the desired haven, amidst a suppressed titter, and is horror-struck to find that there he can neither see nor hear. The back of the great clock is his obstructing enemy. This is the standing joke nightly repeated. It was as successful in producing a titter as the *Timeo Danaos* below, when it was the fashion for young and even old members to air their musty Latin in bald quotations, as some lady novelists interlard their feeble English with boarding-school French. The routine business is over. The battle is about to begin. Sir Thomas Turton is to bring on a motion on the state of the nation. He was a true professor of the Whig creed—that the contest against the French Emperor was hopeless—that the Spanish war would last as long as the Peloponnesian, with little probability of success. He touched upon the Orders in Council; but was told by the clever ministerial supporter, Mr. Robinson, that such discussion had better be reserved for the forthcoming debate, upon the motion of which notice had been given "by a learned gentleman of great talents and extensive information." In two years from the time when he had made his maiden speech, Mr. Brougham had thus become an authority in the House. The debate of the 27th of February was spirited. It appeared likely to close at an early hour, for the gallery was being cleared for a division. But Mr. Whitbread rose, and called upon Lord Castlereagh to give some explanation of his views, especially upon the Catholic question, now that he was likely to become a member of the Administration. The Marquis Wellesley had resigned the seals of the Foreign Office a week before. The most important declarations of the session were thus called forth. Mr. Perceval and Lord Castlereagh declared that they and the Ministry were unanimous against granting the Catholic claims now. The debate was dragging on till two o'clock. The reporters had expected that, after the speech of the Prime Minister, the House would divide. I was left by the staff of the "British Press" to make a short note if anything should occur. Up rose Mr. Canning. Somewhat alarmed I began to write. I gained confidence. His graceful sentences had no involved construction to render them difficult to follow. His impressive elocution fixed his words in my memory. Some matters I necessarily passed over; but the great point of his speech, that he was for speedily granting the Catholic claims with due safeguards, was an important one for the journal which I was suddenly called upon to represent, and I caught the spirit, if not the full words, of the declaration in which he stood opposed to the Minister, and to his own ancient rival. I ran to the office (for young legs were faster than hackney-coaches), wrote my report, to the astonishment of the regular staff of reporters, and went happy to bed at five o'clock. I doubt whether any literary success of my after-life gave me as much pleasure as this feat.

The accomplished wife of my friend the editor held a sort of levée every morning in her drawing-room. Whilst he was labouring upon his evening papers, Mrs. Lane was picking up the gossip of the town from members of Parliament who dropped in—from authors, players, and artists. On the morning of the 28th, Lord Byron was the great theme in his capacity of politician, when we were anxiously expecting a poem whose excellence was bruited abroad. The night before, he had delivered his maiden speech in the House of Lords, against the Bill for making the destruction or injury of stocking or lace frames a capital offence. It was a set speech—declamatory rather than reasoning. He believed that it was a great speech, and had a right so to believe from the compliments that were paid him in the House. A week after this appeared "Childe Harold." He says in one of his journals, "Nobody ever thought of my prose afterwards, nor indeed did I." It was then that he awoke one morning and found himself famous. It is difficult, after the lapse of half a century, to describe, without the appearance of exaggeration, the effect which Lord Byron's poetry produced, year after year, upon the younger minds of that time. Its tone was in harmony with the great vicissitudes of the world. Its passionate exhibition of deep and often morbid feelings was akin with the emotions that were engendered by the tremendous struggle in which England was engaged—its alternations of rapture and depression, its courage and its despair. What we now call "sensation" dramas and "sensation" novels are the lineal descendants of the verse romances in which, under every variety of clime and costume, Byron was pouring forth his own feelings—indifferent to the possible injury to others of that contempt for the conventionalities of society which made him parade his misanthropy and his scepticism, his loves and his hatreds, before all mankind. The corruption thus engendered was more the corruption of taste than of morals. Our Castalian spring became insipid without a dash of alcohol. Scott paled in this strong light. The Lake poets underwent an eclipse. This could not have been accomplished without high genius; but it may be doubted whether the sensual egotism of Byron would have ever allowed him to take a higher place than he now takes amongst the English immortals.

My life during these two months in London was a round of excitement. The theatre was open to me—the one theatre, Covent Garden, where I could see John Kemble and Charles Young, and the best comic actors—where once, and once only, I saw Mrs. Siddons, before she left the stage in June of that year.

Drury Lane was being rebuilt. There was no other theatre in London, except "the little theatre in the Haymarket" for summer performances. The theatrical monopoly was vigorously contended for by what was deemed the liberal party in Parliament. A Bill had been brought in for establishing a new theatre for dramatic entertainments within the cities of London and Westminster. It was opposed, because, said some Liberals who had become shareholders in Drury Lane, it went to supersede the royal prerogative for granting licences for dramatic exhibition. It was in vain urged that the monopolists had built playhouses in which a great many could see and no one could hear, and thus we had dogs, elephants, and horses introduced on the stage. Mr. Whitbread, who had taken an active part in the rebuilding of Drury Lane upon the same principle of sacrificing sense to show, contended that the taste of the people must be followed as well as guided. With these notions, Mr. Whitbread was to become a caterer for the public taste, as one of the committee of management for the theatre upon whose portico Shakspere was set to shiver outside, little regarded till the greatest of modern actors should bring him once more into fashion.

Of the many intellectual excitements—not without accompanying temptations to which I was exposed,—the most attractive was the Club of the Eccentrics. Mr. Peter Cunningham, in his admirable "Hand-book of London," tells us that in May's Buildings, St. Martin's Lane, the Sutherland Arms "was the favourite place of meeting of 'the Eccentrics,' a club of privileged wits so called." The wits had certainly not here any exclusive possession of the privileges of such a club; for without a considerable infusion of dulness they would have missed many an opportunity for the exercise of their time-honoured art,—"to cut blocks with a razor." On ordinary nights the company at the Sutherland Arms had as little pretensions to the character of wits as the members of Goldsmith's "Muzzy Club." They ate their kidneys; they smoked their pipes; they read the newspaper; and they made profound reflections upon the war and the ministry. But upon Saturday nights the calm is invaded by a rush of reporters. On such a night I am admitted, upon payment of the fee of half-a-crown; am duly harangued by the chairman chosen for the occasion, who descants upon the glories of a society which numbered the greatest of the age; sign my name in the big book, which really contains some records of the illustrious, and am glad to have made my reply, and have gone to a table to eat my supper. Then it is moved that the chair should be taken by Mr. Jones, to hear "a charge." For three hours I listen to gleams of wit and flashes of eloquence—intermingled with the occasional ventures of a rash ambition which provoke laughter, and with small attempts at fun which call forth groans—so that midnight arrives and I have no disposition for rest. A name or two of those to whom I have rapturously listened have not altogether perished out of the ken of a new generation. Richard Lalor Sheil belongs to history. Once or twice I was witness to the profound admiration, entertained by men who were not incompetent judges, of the wondrous eloquence of a reporter named Brownley. Some of the elders of the company told me that he came nearer to the excellences of

Burke than any living man. He was not a Burke; for the orgies of the night clouded the intellect of the morning. Undoubtedly his powers were very wonderful. He poured forth a torrent of words; but far more regulated by a correct taste than the flowery metaphors of Sheil. Brownley had a lofty figure and a grand massive head. Sheil presented a singular contrast to him in person and in his rapid utterance and violent gestures. Sheil was then little known; and when he had finished his oration, Mr. Quin, the editor of a daily paper, rushed forward with, "Sir, I honour ye—dine with me to-morrow." Less aspiring in his declamation than Brownley was William Mudford, the editor of the "Courier," but singularly neat in his logical precision and his mild sarcasm. J. P. Davis (Pope Davis, as he was called, from a great picture which he painted at Rome—the Presentation of Lord Shrewsbury's Family to the Pope) did not belong to the Reporting tribe. We have missed him lately, in a green old age, doing violence to the natural kindness of his heart by an intense hatred of the Royal Academy, in which he persevered to the last, and in which he was ever associated with his friend Haydon.

It is time to close these rambling Reminiscences of the London of 1812. I went back to Windsor with some enlargement of my intellectual vision. The realities of life had cured me of many day-dreams. In the House of Commons I had looked night after night upon the grand spectacle of an assembly that, without any of the outward semblances of power, filled the world with a mysterious influence which kept alive the sacred fire of liberty amongst the nations.

It was an assembly imbued with party spirit, but that spirit was raised into virtue by the common love of country. Not in that House—nor in that other seat of legislation, in which the principle of honour was mainly derived from long lines of ancestry—would any one who "spake the tongue which Shakspere spake," ever think of succumbing to the gigantic ambition which was threatening to sweep away all thrones and dominations. One land should never "lie at the proud foot of a conqueror." There, was my patriotism stimulated, even whilst political rivalries appeared to forbid that union which alone could save. But what courtesy did I behold tempering the strongest denunciations and the bitterest sarcasm! What self-command—what restraints upon passion—what bursts of generosity—what candour amidst the most obstinate prejudices—marked these Commoners of the realm as essentially the gentlemen of England! From this example, the humblest aspirant to the character of public instructor might learn to be tolerant of all honest opinions—to be moderate in the expression of his own. In looking upon the great political gladiators he would perceive what talent and knowledge were required to raise a man to eminence, but especially he would learn that honesty alone could keep the high place which ability and unremitting industry might win. This lesson was for the lowly as well as for the exalted. I saw this grand Parliament of England at a grand time. Hope was beginning to spring up out of a long season of misfortune and mismanagement. I had heard it said in the House of Commons on the 27th February, with a mixed tone of reproach and despondency, "Badajoz, Gerona, Tortosa, Valencia, and almost every place of strength in Spain are in the hands of the French." On the 23rd of April the horns were blowing in every thoroughfare, and men were bawling "News—News—Great News!" Wellington had taken Badajoz. The crisis of the European conflict appeared to be at hand. Napoleon was evidently preparing for an offensive war against Alexander of Russia. If my cherished project of a newspaper could now be carried out, the mighty events of the time would give it an interest which would compensate for my editorial inexperience. I might do some good, socially and intellectually, with such an instrument, humble as it might be by comparison with the power of the London press. This was a very moderate ambition; but I was then contented with it.

I was heartily disposed to go about the work that was before me in a sanguine spirit—in a spirit which perhaps too little regarded the chances of commercial success. The field was altogether too narrow. To one who was to stand by my side through the battle of life I wrote at this transition period of its course:— "It shall go hard if I do not reform many things in this neighbourhood, and give the inhabitants a character that they never possessed. If fair argument can do it, they shall think liberally. I will set out as the temperate advocate of everything that thinking men will support—Toleration, Education of the Poor, Diffusion of Religious Knowledge, Public Economy. I shall adopt the opinions of no set of men in Church or State; but think for myself on all points. I belong to no party, for I would uphold the Roman Catholics' moderate claims as the first step to public safety, and continue the war in Spain as the last resource of national honour. This country is full of bigotry. Some are afraid to educate the poor, some are afraid of distributing Bibles, and the greater part are afraid of Popery. I hear many people who call themselves reasoners talk of the Protestant massacres in France as arguments that all Catholics are blood-thirsty. The fire-brand of religion will soon be burnt out. The very miseries of the present generation will become the means of establishing the happiness of the next." In transcribing this from a mirror of the past which lies before me, I cannot avoid what must appear as a parade of the conceit of imperfect education. But it may be a satisfaction to some other solitary and obscure young man to know, that self-instruction is not always the worst preparation for arriving at a due sense of the serious moral responsibility of a literary career which, even in its humblest attempts, must be an instrument for good or for evil. And thus—with a considerable amount of multifarious reading, with slight knowledge of the world, with aspirations very much out of proportion to any chance of their being realised—the 1st of August, 1812, saw me established as proprietor with my father in the "Windsor and Eton Express," and entrusted with its responsible editorship. That day, having passed my twenty-first year a few months before, saw me bound upon that wheel of periodical writing and publishing which was to revolve with me for fifty years. It was not to be the torturing wheel of Ixion, but one whose revolutions, wearisome as they sometimes might be, were often to become sources of pleasurable excitement.

CHAPTER II.

HE first number of the "Windsor and Eton Express" lies before me. It looks to my mind like some relic of a past era of journalism, in which I have no especial interest, any more than I have in a fac-simile of a "Times" of the days of Nelson which has been recently published. I am told that some of the middle-aged inhabitants of my native town preserve this first newspaper ever issued there, as a curiosity of the time of their fathers—a piece of dim antiquity like a guinea of George III. I look anxiously at my "Political Inquirer," and I do not blush at my earliest attempts in the vocation of "best public instructor."

Why do I not blush at some of these crude efforts of inexperience? Because, although the things which I then wrote may be something different from my maturer convictions, they were written under a strong sense of the serious nature of the vocation of a public writer. I dare say that, in my want of knowledge of the world, I wore my

"Foolscap uniform turn'd up with ink"

somewhat too grandly. "Anxious" I was, if not "fine and jealous." But this sense of my moral responsibility has saved me from a feeling of shame, as I now look back upon the feeble utterances of the time thus brought before me, something like a dream. These utterances were those of an impulsive young man ; but of one who felt the duty of controlling his inclination to express himself passionately. I wrote with a motto from Locke always at the head of my political essay,—"This is a question only of inquirers, not disputers, who neither affirm, nor deny, but examine." This motto often held my hand. I had a notion that rapid composition was a test of ability. I used to task myself to write a leading article in a given time. The habit has been of value to me in after life ; it is of infinite importance to the journalist. But it is of more importance that what he writes should not at some future day rise up in judgment against him, "trumpet-tongued," and convict him—not of the *suppressio veri*, for that is incidental to his profession, as it is to the barrister's—but of the assertion of opinions which were the exact contrary of his own convictions. Let me not, however, be held to imply that what is called political consistency is a virtue in the man of advanced age—that the rash judgments of his youth are to be preserved in his maturity. The mind that is not open to the teachings of time, and that chooses to stand upon its own "ancient way," and not look around to see "which is the right and true way," is worth little as a guide for the formation of opinion.

Amongst the startling contrasts that are presented between the England of 1812 and the England of half a century later, there is perhaps no contrast more remarkable than that which offers itself to my mind in the difficulties of setting on foot a newspaper at Windsor, such as I had projected as an easy and profitable employment for my literary ambition. These rush upon my memory as I look upon my old "folio of four pages," and think of this my first venture upon a dangerous sea.

The newspaper stamp was then fourpence. The advertisement duty was three shillings, subsequently raised to three shillings and sixpence. The blank paper was to be stamped at Somerset House, the payment being in cash, with a discount. It will be seen at once how these taxes pressed upon the capital to be devoted to such an undertaking. No article of consumption, with the exception of salt, was so highly taxed as the Newspaper. The circulation of a country journal was not a simple operation like that of a London journal, which was, and is, a wholesale transaction between the newspaper proprietor and the newsmen. The established custom was this: the country proprietor had agencies in the larger towns, who had their own retail customers; but the greater number of the papers were delivered, by newsmen specially employed, to the subscribers, whether in the place of publication or in scattered country districts. These had quarterly accounts, which often grew into half-yearly or yearly settlements. Thus the return of the capital was very slow.

The demand for the newspaper, and the number of advertisers, being thus narrowed by the high price consequent upon the tax, the cost of production was to be met by a comparatively small number of supporters. A cheap newspaper was an impossibility. But there were expenses at that time which have altogether vanished under a different state of social organization. The Windsor paper was to be published on a Saturday evening, in time to be despatched by post to the more distant places. It was essential that it should contain the latest news from the metropolis. The "London Gazette" was then published on a Saturday afternoon. How was the "Gazette" to be obtained, and also the late editions of the evening papers? For this object the long-established "Salisbury Journal" had an express direct from London to that city. By an arrangement with the London agent of that journal, its express was to bring our despatch to Staines, from which place we should have a branch express to Windsor. It would arrive about three quarters of an hour before our post departed. Then there was to ensue a scurry of editor, compositors, pressmen, to complete enough papers to fill two bags, which we were allowed to send to the receiving post-offices at Staines and Maidenhead by the mail-carts from our town. All this could not be accomplished without the most strenuous exertions and the most perfect division of labour. It was to be calculated that in the beginning of the undertaking the machinery would be often out of gear.

This laborious and costly organization was the only method of fighting with space and time before the days of railway conveyance and the electric telegraph. The London daily papers, which furnished the staple of news, had the same difficulties, though much greater in degree, to contend against. The more considerable, especially the "Times," had not only their special expresses from the outports, but occasionally had a private packet-boat to pick up news from homeward-bound ships before they came into port. The sudden arrival of foreign intelligence, and the lateness of the sittings of Parliament, occasioned the morning papers sometimes to be delayed in publication till almost noon. If this occurred on a Saturday, the "Times," or the "Post," or the "Chronicle," or the "British Press," not reaching Windsor till six in the evening, another leader would then have to be written. Sometimes the "Times," upon which most reliance could be placed for the latest news, did not come at all. During the excitement of the great war-time the demand outran the supply, for it was not till the end of 1814 that the "Times" was printed by steam machinery.

Our journal being once safely at press, there would come the arrangements for its distribution through the rural districts, in addition to the small number which had been sent off by post. The hamlets and scattered farm-houses and gentlemen's seats could not be reached by the post, at a time when not one village in twenty had a post-office—when letters and newspapers remained with the postmaster of the market-town till they were called for by the inhabitants of the surrounding district. Many a populous parish was thus left to chance for the receipt of its private or its public intelligence. Our new paper would have to meet this difficulty by our own express-carts, which were to travel long distances, and by pedestrians, who would have many a weary mile to trudge over unfrequented roads. These deliverers would seldom receive payment from the subscribers. The debts would accumulate, requiring to be collected at periodical visits. Remittances in many cases could not easily be made; in some cases they would be impossible, for the system of postal money-orders was a quarter of a century later.

The price of a country newspaper was, in almost

every case, sevenpence. The wages of mechanical labour were high, keeping pace with the price of wheat, which in 1812 was 150*s.* a quarter. Paper was extremely dear, the duty being threepence a pound, and the cheapening by the paper machine, now so efficient, being then one of the visions of the projector. In the absence, besides, of all the modern appliances of civilization such as I have recited—which have so lessened the cost of a provincial journal, and have increased the demand in a far greater ratio than the doubling of the population—the number of country newspapers was comparatively small. Throughout England there were less than a hundred. There were not a great many of them which ventured upon original writing; but the leading article had become a feature with those of the higher class, such as the "Leeds Mercury," after the beginning of the century. To express strong opinions upon gross abuses was, however, a service of danger which most editors avoided in the days of *ex officio* informations.

It was a perilous time for the newspaper press, for the people were discontented, and the authorities were sensitive. They were especially sensitive in this war-time as to any strictures which were supposed to have a tendency to weaken the allegiance of the army, or render soldiers less satisfied under the severe discipline by which alone obedience was held to be capable of enforcement. Military flogging was one of the forbidden subjects for editorial comment. In the year 1812, William Cobbett was in Newgate, having been sentenced in 1810 to two years' imprisonment and a fine of a thousand pounds for a virulent effusion upon a punishment which had taken place in the local militia of Ely. In the "Stamford News," a paper most ably conducted by Mr. John Scott (afterwards editor of the "Champion"), an article appeared at the same period, in which flogging was described as "a species of torture at least as exquisite as any that was ever devised by the infernal ingenuity of the Inquisition." This article was copied into the "Examiner," and Sir Vicary Gibbs, the Attorney-General, filed informations against both papers. The trial of John and Leigh Hunt came on the first, before Lord Ellenborough, who laboured hard for a conviction. They were defended by Mr. Brougham, and the Middlesex jury acquitted them. The subsequent trial of Mr. Drakard, the proprietor of the "Stamford News," resulted in his conviction, although the same advocate defended him. He was sentenced to eighteen months' imprisonment. Such a notable example of the uncertainty of trial by jury in matters of political libel could give a public writer no great confidence that incautious words, without evil intentions, might not be visited with punishment such as is earned by atrocious crimes. There was another subject upon which the law-officers of the Crown were equally determined to war against public opinion. In proportion as the Prince Regent was becoming unpopular, the Attorney-General resented any reflections upon his coxcombry and his frivolous tastes. Moore ran great risks when he dubbed the Prince "the Mæcenas of Tailors." But it was "most tolerable and not to be endured" by the Dogberries who guarded the honour of Carlton House, when a newspaper writer, who was not a pet of fashion, dared to say of his Royal Highness—in ridicule of a fulsome article in the "Morning Post" in which he was called "an Adonis in loveliness"—that this Adonis was "a corpulent gentleman of fifty." The *ex-officio* information against John and Leigh Hunt, for a libel in the "Examiner" of March 24th, 1812, resulted in a fine of a thousand pounds and the imprisonment of each for two years in separate prisons. Mr. Brougham had again defended the brothers, and had the satisfaction to be told by Lord Ellenborough that he had imbibed the spirit of his client, and seemed to have inoculated himself with all the poison and mischief which this libel was calculated to effect. It was undoubtedly strong language for the "Examiner" to designate the Prince as "a violator of his word, a libertine over head and ears in debt and disgrace, a despiser of domestic ties, the companion of gamblers and demi-reps, a man who has just closed half a century without one single claim on the gratitude of his country or the respect of posterity." Posterity has not given such an answer as would put to shame this daring appeal to its judgment. But the dispassionate lookers-on of that period could not think it seemly that such harsh truths should be told of him who stood in the place of a king—who, as chief magistrate, ought to claim from the people all respect and reverence.

But it was not only the dread of indictment for political libel that hung over the head of the newspaper proprietor in 1812. Any statement of fact, or any comment upon occurrences that might be supposed to affect private character, were constantly made the subject of actions, got up by rapacious attorneys, speculating upon that love of litigation which was then especially characteristic of the English. It was not till thirty years after 1812 that Lord Campbell's Act gave to the journalist the power to plead, in any action for libel, "that such libel was inserted in such newspaper without actual malice, and without gross negligence; and that before the commencement of the action, or at the earliest opportunity afterwards, he inserted in such newspaper a full apology for such libel." Imagine, at the present day, the Lord Chief Justice of the Court of Queen's Bench trying an action for libel,—with two leaders, such as Mr. Denman for the prosecution, and Mr. Scarlett for the defence,—the alleged libel being the report in a country newspaper of a flagrant case of cruelty which was a notorious subject of local indignation. The libel consisted in terming that "a brutal assault," upon which the assailants were held to bail. Imagine that the persons whose characters were thus defamed were a pig-keeper and his wife, who let lodgings to poor people; and having a dispute with a family of which the mother had only been confined a week, threatened to pull the bed from under her, and turn her into the street. Imagine a London jury finding a verdict for the plaintiff, with 50*l.* damages. Imagine a second action for the same libel being brought by the wife. Imagine ten several actions against ten London papers, for reporting the trial in the King's Bench with a few words of just comment upon the scandal of such litigation, when there was no "private malice" or "gross negligence." Imagine a hungry attorney, prowling for prey, at the bottom of all these actions, who had no object to attain but the heavy costs which he pocketed. These verdicts cost me 500*l.* in 1825. Is not the newspaper press in a better condition than it was in, forty years ago?

The perils of the Libel Law did not much affect my confident belief in 1812 that I could navigate my little bark in safety. But I did feel, perhaps too acutely, the difficulties of my position as a journalist under the shadow of the Castle at Windsor. It was a time in which the patriotism which had upheld the nation through the fierce struggle of twenty years required, at this great crisis of our history, when the fate of England was trembling in the balance, the prop of a sincere and spontaneous loyalty. I deeply felt, as one about to become a public writer, that upon the head of the Government I could only bestow

> "mouth-honour, breath
> Which the poor heart would fain deny but dare not."

I look back upon the public feeling of the first twenty years of my working life, and compare it with the quarter of a century which was blessed with a female Sovereign. Oh, could the generation which, during the reign of Victoria, has entered upon the duties of mature age, know the full value of their privilege in being able to cherish the loyalty of the subject, not as an abstract principle, but as a holy sentiment, often rising into the warmest devotion, they would pity the youth of a less happy time, who had a struggle to maintain even his love of country amidst the "curses not loud but deep" which attended its sensual and frivolous ruler! We should have been perhaps plunged into a profounder abyss of royal degradation, had not the long-established habit of decency still kept the public Court circle free from ladies whose "misfortune" (as Lord Ellenborough termed the fashionable sin upon the trial of the Hunts) met with no pity in the eyes of the rigid Queen Charlotte.

The political atmosphere was not very bright on the 1st of August, 1812, when the Windsor newspaper struggled into life. The 29th of July was a day of gloom, for the intelligence arrived that the United States of America had declared war against Great Britain. Wellington had advanced into Spain in June. His position was a very difficult one. The English army and the French army were on opposite banks of the Douro in the early part of July. Marmont was expecting a large accession of strength in the junction of King Joseph's army from Madrid. Wellington was disappointed of the arrival of reinforcements under Lord William Bentinck. There was a wide-spread conviction that the Government at home was feebly supporting the one great captain whose genius appeared likely to retrieve the disasters of a long series of "warriors" *not* "for the working-day." Parliament was prorogued on the 29th of July. The speech of the Prince Regent was in no degree a jubilant prophecy of a glorious future. It consisted of little more than tamely expressed sentiments.

It was Sunday night the 16th of August. The evening promenade in the Long Walk, which had succeeded to the regal promenade on the Terrace, had been interrupted by the sudden withdrawal of the band of the 29th Regiment, who were summoned to their barracks. The sun had gone down behind the hills of the forest, as I sat lonely in a cottage belonging to my father, which then stood apart from any other houses, fronting the Long Walk. I was meditating upon the unofficial news, which had arrived on the Saturday night, of a victory in Spain —shaping my thoughts into exulting verse as the death-song of a Guerilla who lay bleeding on that battle-field. Suddenly, from the not distant barracks, rose the burst of "God save the King," and the cheers of a multitude. I rushed to the town. The 29th Regiment was marching out of Park Street along the Frogmore Road to the inspiriting tune which revolutionary Frenchmen called "çà ira," but which loyal Englishmen translated into "The Downfall of Paris." The Extraordinary Gazette, containing Wellington's despatches relating to the great victory of Salamanca, had been published on that Sunday morning, and had arrived at Windsor, to demand from the enthusiasm of the moment this hasty night-march. I followed the measured tramp of the soldiery, in common with the great mass of our population, unknowing what was to be done, and yet filled with the passionate desire of the hundreds around me to give expression to the belief that the tide had turned—that England might shout for a mighty victory by land, as she had shouted for the Nile and for Trafalgar. The joyous troops marched into a field adjoining Frogmore Gardens, and there, formed into line, fired three volleys, and gave three cheers. Such was the British war-cry which they had given three years before, when they met the French at Talavera, and contributed their part to the great battle which, says the strategist Jomini, "recovered the glory of the successors of Marlborough, which for a century had declined, and showed that the English infantry could contend with the best in Europe." If Talavera was the hardest-fought battle of modern times, as Sir Arthur Wellesley described it, Salamanca was the most fruitful in its results. This victory of Wellington over Marmont gave confidence to Russia, and awakened the hopes of Germany that a new era was approaching. My "Dying Guerilla" was not a false prophet when he exclaimed—

> "I see embattled Europe's wrath sublime
> Rush to the field and blacken all the clime;
> Insulted nations spurn their blood-stain'd lord,
> And Vengeance draw the soul-redeeming sword." *

The first duty of a Provincial Journalist is to present always a faithful, and if possible a full, account of the occurrences of his district. But how little of all this is worth a more permanent record! I was unfortunate in having few noteable things to relate beyond the ordinary routine of the life of the Castle, and the monotonous proceedings of vestries and borough magistrates. Quarter-Sessions offered little of abiding interest. Assizes sometimes furnished something characteristic of the age, which looked like materials for the Annual Chronicler. But the most exciting of such matters are apt to become as motes in the historical sunbeam. I glance over my old newspapers, and almost wonder how many local trifles came to be printed.

The staple of my newspaper was Politics. I am not about to offer any narrative of the great events of the greatest era of modern history, but I cannot wholly pass them over. When I look back upon the autumn and winter of 1812, and call to mind the ever-varied excitement attending the wars in Spain, in Russia, in America, I feel that such a concentration of points of immense public interest scarcely ever

* Windsor Express, August 22, 1812.

before demanded the vigilant and faithful attention of the journalist. The victory of Salamanca was followed by the entrance of Wellington into Madrid, and then came the unwelcome intelligence of the raising of the siege of Burgos, and the retreat of the British army. I was the echo of the loud voice of public complaint, that in the barracks and arsenals of Great Britain should have slumbered that force which, two months before, would have put the Peninsular war beyond the reverses of fortune. I denounced the policy which still regarded the contest as a war of experiment—the policy of a weak government, ready again for the course of repairing errors by an expenditure of means which far outran the limits of their original necessity. "Demosthenes," I said, "reproached the Athenians that they were like rustics in a fencing-school, who, after a blow, guard the part that was hit, and not before." Yet the gloom produced by the retreat to Portugal, after the triumph of Salamanca, was scarcely so intense, because it was unmixed with a feeling of national disgrace, as when in that autumn three British ships, in three distinct engagements, struck the once invincible flag to the American stars and stripes. In October it was known that the French were in Moscow, and that the Emperor was lodged in the Kremlin. The fluctuating fortunes of those times might well teach the public writer the great duty contained in the sermon of six words—"in adversity hope, in prosperity consider." Even whilst the French, after a perilous occupation of the great city, marched forth from the burning ruins of Moscow, there was hope, but not certainty, that the European struggle was coming to an end. But on Christmas Day, the French papers, announcing the return of Bonaparte to Paris, and containing the famous twenty-ninth bulletin which could not conceal the almost total annihilation of the French army, rendered that joyous festival one of unusual solemnity.

The spring of 1813 brought with it a lull in the hurricane of foreign politics. Windsor was excited by a grand royal funeral—that of the Duchess of Brunswick, on the 31st of March. But there was a stronger excitement in some mysterious circumstances which followed that funeral. It was known that, previous to the interment, while workmen were employed in making a subterraneous passage from the middle of the choir of St. George's Chapel to the new Royal Mausoleum under the building called Wolsey's Tomb-House, they had accidentally broken away a part of the vault of Henry the Eighth, but which was not then opened. On the morning after the funeral the Prince Regent was seen to enter the Chapel, attended by Sir Henry Halford. A master-mason and a master-plumber had been previously sent for, who were to do some work with their own hands which could not be entrusted to common mechanics, and about which they were to preserve the most profound secresy. The Chapel was again closed; the Prince Regent returned to the Castle; the mason and plumber, burdened with some tremendous mystery, were afraid to speak to their curious neighbours; and yet the mystery did ooze out. Solemn whisperings went from the Castle to the town; from the town to the villages; and wild rumours soon found their way to London. The most various and contradictory narratives now had their due place in the daily papers. For myself, I deemed it prudent to remain silent, rather than become a propagator of erroneous details and absurd fictions. I was enabled at last to present an authentic account of the investigations which took place in the vault of Henry the Eighth. This differed very slightly from the narrative published a fortnight afterwards by Sir Henry Halford. The intimation of Clarendon, that after the Restoration the body of Charles the First could not be found after the most diligent search, was disproved by the discovery of the 1st of April, 1813. When the plumber had cut open the upper part of the leaden coffin, and the cerecloth in which the body had been wrapped was removed, there was the long oval face with the pointed beard, which reminded those present of the portraits of Vandyke. The head was loose, although it had been carefully adjusted to the shoulders, and it was taken up without difficulty, and held to view. The narrative of the court physician has no false delicacy in attempting to conceal the results of this remarkable examination.

My business and my inclination often led me now to the capital. There I was enabled to gather some flavour for my insipid dish of Windsor ideas, in the full flow of London talk. There I got away from the Court atmosphere, and the College atmosphere, and the Corporation atmosphere, to think boldly and speak freely with friends who were fighting their way amidst a crowd of aspirants in Law, in Literature, and in the Arts. Politics, however, were the absorbing topics of every society. The people of Germany had risen as one man to do battle against the conqueror, humbled but not overthrown, at whose feet the sovereigns had crouched. The adherents of the Bourbons in London were full of revived and long-suspended energies. I was introduced to one who had played an important part before the meeting of the States-General—the Marquis of Chambonas. I passed some pleasant and instructive evenings with the former lord of a great château near Montpelier, in—the Fleet Prison. Here, for some mysterious reason, he had lived, securely and contentedly, with his niece, for some years; never going beyond the walls, untouched by the squalid misery of the place, having no companionship with other prisoners, but holding audience in a large and well-furnished apartment, where men of note, even such men as George Canning, would come to visit him. His ostensible occupation was that of a teacher of the French language. On certain nights of the week he held a *soirée*, at which he would read a French author, interspersing a running commentary of spirited and tasteful criticism. I regretted that before his return to France at the peace of 1814, I had not availed myself of his proposition that I should correspond with him for my improvement in a French style. There was something more than met the eye in that proposal. I came to learn that the old Marquis had been so long secluded from the outer world, that he might be a safe and unsuspected recipient of the secrets of the Royalists on the other side of the channel. It was not to obtain a correct accent, to hear Racine and Molière read with unaccustomed elegance, that writers and statesmen went to that second floor of the Fleet Prison, where the Marquis sat through all the changes of seasons, not deficient in any of the means of procuring abundant comforts and luxuries.

CHAPTER III.

I FIND from old letters that at the end of 1813 I occupied my leisure in writing a play, which was intended to have some parallel with the uprising of the German population. My subject was the deliverance of the German nation from the Roman yoke by Arminius. It is one of the usual mistakes of young writers to believe that some temporary outburst of popular enthusiasm would ensure success to a poem, and especially to a drama, which, in the very nature of its subject, must be little more than a vehicle for rhetorical display. This is easier than to deal with the great elements of terror and pity, which must largely enter into the composition of a tragedy as a real work of art. My play was sent to Drury Lane, then managed by a Committee, of which Mr. Whitbread was a leading member. My attempt was treated with all respect; it had a fair consideration, and its rejection was accompanied with a note sufficiently complimentary:—"There is much spirited and easy writing in this tragedy. Its greatest fault appears to be a want of incident and contrivance; it is too declamatory; and I apprehend the want of interest and situation would not be compensated by the neatness and fire of the dialogue." I had sense enough to know that the objections thus stated were perfectly just; but I had not then learnt the lesson which a critical acquaintance with Shakspere, and with other great dramatists, afterwards impressed upon me,—that a play unfit for the stage is incapable of imparting true poetical pleasure in the closet. In such a drama the unity of object is wanting. The action halts. The descriptive passages are elaborated till the realities of character vanish. I printed my "Arminius." The book had some success, and caused me to be enrolled amongst the poets of England in a Catalogue of Living Authors, and more permanently in Watt's "Bibliotheca Britannica." But what is the value of such fame? One living rival of Magliabecchi,—whose knowledge of books is as universal as profound, whilst, unlike Magliabecchi, he is able profitably to use his knowledge,—tells me that there is not a copy of my play in the British Museum. My vanity is soothed a little by remembering that one of the scenes is to be found in a school-book of elocution, side by side with extracts from Addison's "Cato," and Brooke's "Gustavus Vasa." It is not a great fame.

The third week of the new year witnessed that most unusual occurrence—the stoppage of communication on some of the most frequented roads of England and Scotland. There never had been such a fall of snow in the memory of man, and there has certainly been nothing like it since. Had railways been in existence, the obstacles to all travelling and all commercial transit would have been precisely the same. It is under such unusual circumstances of interruption to the business of a busy people that we best understand the value of roads, and of all the concurrent means of communication which have grown up during a long period of civilized society. I well remember the consternation and difficulty, when, on a certain Thursday, our morning coaches set out for London and were obliged to return; when we learnt that the only mails which had reached the General Post Office on the Friday were three from Brighton, Rye, and Portsmouth; when we knew, from the report of horsemen and pedestrians, who had contrived to struggle up from Bath, that the West of England was completely impassable for carriages; that the shops in Exeter were shut up, and the doors and windows of private houses barricaded, by the drifts of snow. At Oxford no letters or papers arrived for four days, and there was a blockade far more effectual than when Cromwell's army was hemming it around. I made my way on horseback to the Bath road, and proceeded well enough from Slough to a mile or so beyond Salthill, through a lane cut through the snow. which rose on either side like the outer walls of a mediæval castle. This narrow passage had been accomplished by the exertions of many labourers, and the same process was going forward throughout the northern and western roads. On the 21st of January a notice was issued from the General Post Office to all post masters, directing them to apply to the overseers of parishes to employ all the means in their power to get the country cleared for the passage of the mails. A more stringent command was issued from the Home Office to the Lords-Lieutenants of counties, for restoring the accustomed means of communication between London and the interior. The fall of snow was succeeded by an intense frost. Between Blackfriars Bridge and London Bridge there was a sort of fair on the ice, which has been best preserved from oblivion in one of the designs of George Cruikshank, in Hone's "Every Day Book."

The milder days of February gave us back again the ordinary means of communication from Cornwall to Lanarkshire. From out of a "House of Glass" Rumour now came flying all abroad, and the land was alive with the anticipation of great events. The Allies marched on from the Rhine. Then came the fruitless struggle which manifested the military genius of Napoleon as much as any one of his great victories. From one point to another he rushed to meet his enemies wherever they appeared; sometimes victorious, sometimes defeated, but always contriving to make the great issue still doubtful. Aberdeen the peaceful was for making terms with him ; other statesmen, English and foreign, were for pushing him to extremities. The risings of Bordeaux, the second city of the Empire, in favour of the Bourbons, appeared to indicate that the popular feeling of France was changing, as regarded him who had done everything for its glory and nothing for its happiness. The negociations for peace were broken off. Whilst Wellington was fighting his final battle with Soult on the 10th of April, Paris had capitulated, and the Emperor of Russia and the King of Prussia had entered the capital which had appropriated the spoils of a hundred cities. On the 4th of April, Napoleon had abdicated, and soon after was on his road to Elba. For three nights London was in a tumult of exultation, amidst illuminations of unprecedented brilliancy. On the 3rd of May, Louis the Eighteenth was in the Tuileries. In England the beauty of the spring weather was such as had scarcely ever been remembered. Poets seized upon it as an omen of future happiness. Leigh Hunt—who had endured enough to render him cold to a cause which was that of the ruling powers at home and of royalty in general—looked at this crisis as somewhat like a final triumph over war and oppression, and in his new-born zeal wrote a Mask, "The Descent of Liberty," to which the glories of the spring lent their most poetical associations. We had our especial turn of patriotic excitement at Windsor. The great festivities in London when the Emperor of Russia and the King of Prussia arrived; when they were invested with the Order of the Garter at Carlton House; when the Prince Regent and the two sovereigns dined with the Corporation of London at the Mansion House;—these were of little importance to us compared with that of the visit to Windsor of the Emperor of Russia with his famous Platoff, and of the King of Prussia with his no less famous Blücher. In the "Poetical Remains" of William Sidney Walker, with whom I was associated in after life, there is a letter from him when a boy at Eton, dated the 6th of July, 1814, in which he says, "I have shaken hands with the King of Prussia and Platoff, and have touched the flap of Blücher's coat. I shall have it engraven on my tombstone." I cannot desire so solemn a record, that, having arrived early at the Ascot Race-ground, I saw the King of Prussia—who had ridden thither before the rest of the royal party—buying a penny roll and a slice of cheese at one of the common booths, and marching up and down, cutting his humble luncheon with a pocket-knife which I supposed he had carried through many a troublous campaign.

Of course I took a more exalted view of the historical grandeur of this season of rejoicing and felicitation when the Duke of Wellington was to arrive at Windsor, for the purpose of reviewing his regiment of the Horse Guards Blue, and I was requested by the Corporation to write an Address to be presented to his Grace by the Town Clerk. I very much fear that its stilted paragraphs were a humble imitation of that Address of the Speaker of the House of Commons, when he said, "This nation well knows that it is largely your debtor." The Duke, on the 6th of August, received the Corporation in the hall of the Castle Inn, somewhat weary, I suppose, of the manner in which, as he said, "he had been received in different parts of the kingdom." I crept into that narrow hall, between the red gowns and the blue gowns, some of whom stood in the street; and I was not very proud of my fine paragraphs when I looked upon that impassive face, and thinking of what welded iron that conqueror of Bonaparte was made, fancied how little the men of action appreciated the sounding periods of the men of words. I did not then know with what success this great soldier would vindicate his own claim to be ranked amongst the best writers.

My newspaper of the 3rd of December contained a paragraph which I had copied from "The Times" of November the 29th, 1814, not interesting, perhaps, to the majority of my provincial readers, but which strongly excited my wonder and curiosity, and led me into obscure speculations of what might be the probable consequences of what "The Times" described as "the greatest improvement connected with printing since the discovery of the art itself." Well knowing the great bodily exertion which up to that time was required of two men working at the common press, to produce two hundred and fifty impressions of one side of a newspaper in an hour, I might well be surprised when I read as follows:—"The reader of this paragraph now holds in his hand one of the many thousand impressions of 'The Times' newspaper which were taken off last night, by a mechanical apparatus. A system of machinery almost organic has been devised and arranged, which, while it relieves the human frame of its most laborious efforts in printing, far exceeds all human powers in rapidity and dispatch." The process is then briefly described; and it is added, "the whole of these complicated acts is performed with such a velocity and simultaneousness of movement, that no less than eleven hundred sheets are impressed in one hour." The invention is termed in this announcement "The Printing Machine." The inventor's name was Kœnig.

For ten years Mr. Walter, the proprietor of "The Times," had been vainly endeavouring, at a heavy cost, to perfect some machinery by which he could send forth a greater number than the four thousand copies of his journal which he was able to produce by the utmost exertion of manual labour. The machine of Kœnig was, however, a most complicated affair; expensive, liable to derangement, and not capable, therefore, of being applied to the general purposes of printing. In 1823 I read in Scott's novel of "Quentin Durward" the prophetic words of Martivalle, "Can I look forward without wonder and astonishment to the lot of a succeeding generation, on whom knowledge shall descend like the first and second rain, uninterrupted, unabated, unbounded." The Printing Press had produced the first rain; the Printing Machine was the "little cloud no bigger than a man's hand" which promised the second rain. There was now some chance that the steam-engine would accomplish for printing what it was accomplishing for navigation. In June, 1824, I attended a trial in the Common Pleas, in which the Duke of Northumberland was plaintiff, and my friend, Mr. Clowes, the defendant. The printer, who carried on his business in Northumberland Court, had erected a steam-press in his cellar, the wall of which abutted on the Duke's princely mansion at Charing Cross. Ludicrous it was to hear the extravagant terms in which the counsel for the plaintiff and his witnesses described the alleged nuisance—the noise made by this engine, quite horrid, sometimes resembling thunder, at other times like a threshing-machine, and then again like the rumbling of carts and waggons. With surpassing ability was the cause of the defendant conducted by the Attorney-General (Copley). The course of the trial is beside my present purpose. Mr. Donkin, the celebrated engineer, deposed that there were not less than twenty engines erected for printing in London. Simplifications of the original invention had rendered the Printing Machine applicable to the production of books as well as newspapers. The second rain was beginning to descend. In 1814 I was very far from a conception of the extent in which the invention of the Printing Machine would affect a future stage in my working life. But in the boundless fertility of that second rain I anticipated a wider scope for my professional labours. I had incurred new responsibilities, and had gained new motives for exertion, in marrying. The Christmas of that year saw my once solitary home lighted up with love and cheerfulness.

In February, 1815, a Bill was hurried through Parliament which absolutely closed the ports against the introduction of foreign corn till the price of wheat should rise to eighty shillings a quarter. I rejoice to see that I was fearless of the indignation which the Windsor paper, circulating chiefly in an agricultural district, would produce, when I wrote—"It is hardly fair that the landowner and cultivator should enter Parliament with such a formidable power as the united voice of the people will scarcely be able to put down, and there demand that the price of wheat should now be fixed at the average rate of a time of war. There are many noble lords and right honourable gentlemen who have doubled their rentals since the year 1794, and there are many very thrifty agriculturists who have purchased the estates which their fathers only tilled, and have adjourned, with unsoiled hands, from the oak-chair in the chimney-corner to the velvet sofa in the drawing-room. Doubtless all this is very agreeable to the parties themselves, and worldly wisdom will blame no man for preferring 20,000*l.* to 10,000*l.*, or a hunter and madeira to a market-cart and ale. But then it is rather galling to be told that all this is essentially necessary to *our* existence and prosperity, and to hear it very gravely asserted that we shall be all the happier and better for being shortly allowed to get two loaves with the money for which we now purchase three."

The "hunter and madeira" as contrasted with the "market-cart and ale" of the old times, was not ungenerously applied to the generation of Southern farmers, who had sprung up in the days of protection and paper currency.

The marriage of the Princess Charlotte with Prince Leopold, on the 2nd of May, 1816, was an event in which I took exceeding interest. It set me poetizing; for I was somewhat too apt to be moved into writing verse on passing subjects, forgetting that poetry ought to be almost exclusively conversant with the permanent and universal. My Mask, "The Bridal of the Isles," whatever might have been its defects, was not written in the spirit of a courtier; for in the Second Canto, in which I called up the shades of the great British rulers of old, I put these lines in the mouth of Alfred addressing the Genius of England:—

"O, I have watch'd thy monarchs as they pass'd,—
Now leaping upward to my tempting throne,
Now toppling down in hateful civil strife,
Or sliding to the slumbers of the tomb;
But never saw I one who fill'd that seat
In rightful ministration, who might say,
'This is my couch of ease, my chair of joy,
This sceptre is a pleasure-charming rod
To call up all fresh luxuries around me.'
The lofty soul, with reverend eye and meek,
Would look upon the trappings of its state
As emblems of a fearful trust, that ask'd
The smile of Heaven on self-denying virtue.
Yes! I will hover round those youthful hearts,
Unblighted yet by power—and with a voice
Borne on the ear by every morning breeze,
Cry—'Live not for yourselves.'"

I had a very pleasant, because a very characteristic, letter from Leigh Hunt about this Mask. He complimented me by saying, "It is very crisp and luxuriant, and shows that you possess in a great degree my favourite part of the poetical spirit—that of enjoyment." Yes. It was that spirit of enjoyment which gave Hunt his perennial youth, amidst worldly troubles as great as most men have endured; which, carried somewhat to excess, made him almost indifferent to adversity in its stern realities. "But," he continued, "I would rather talk with you about these matters than write about them; for when I get upon poetry I feel my wings on, and do not like to wait the zig-zag travelling of the pen." Happy nature! I did not cultivate his acquaintance as I ought to have done in this fresh time of hope. I knew him in later years when I was sobered; but when I had not lost the power of enjoyment in his delightful conversation, so charming—especially to one who was also battling with the world—in its constant looking at the sunny side of human affairs.

The transition from joy at the auspicious marriage of the Princess Charlotte, to the universal mourning for her death, was not sudden in point of time, but it nevertheless came upon the nation as an unexpected blow, suspending all lesser interests of domestic politics. The interval between May, 1816, and November, 1817, was one of very serious aspects. The Government and the People were not in accord; suffering and sedition went hand in hand; demagogues flourished; spies were more than tolerated. Of this unhappy period I shall have to speak in another chapter. Let me at present advert to some personal experiences at the funeral of the Princess Charlotte, on Wednesday evening, the 19th of November, which I thus related in a Supplementary Number of "The Windsor Express," published on the following morning. In this narrative I laid aside the usual editorial style, and signed my name as to facts which I was prepared individually to substantiate:—

"On the morning of Tuesday I received from one of the Canons of the College of Windsor a ticket of admission to the organ-loft of St. George's Chapel, to witness the ceremonial of the late Princess Charlotte's interment. This, I was given to understand, was presented to me by the particular direction of the Dean and Chapter, to allow me to make a faithful report of the solemnities, and as a compliment to the office of chief magistrate which my father holds in the borough. At seven o'clock this evening I claimed an entrance at the outer gate of the lower ward of the Castle, which was kept by two subalterns of the Foot Guards, and a numerous body of rank and file. Constables of the borough were also posted here, but they were evidently considered as intruders upon these unconstitutional guardians of the peace. I was roughly thrust back against the wheels of the carriages which were passing behind me, and told, in common with many others who, like myself, had tickets, that no more would be admitted. For an hour I was buffeted about, with my unfortunate companions, who comprised some of the most respectable inhabitants of Windsor; sometimes collared by the soldiers, sometimes jammed against the castle wall, and at all times insulted by dogmatical assertions or sneering indifference. We at last retired in despair, having risked our lives till danger was no longer endurable. Ten minutes before the procession entered the gate, I procured access to one of the officers, under the escort of a sentinel; and having represented the peculiar circumstances under which I had obtained my ticket, and the duty which I owed to the public to enforce my claim for admission, requested that the order of exclusion might be withdrawn. I was haughtily repulsed. At this instant, two military men, *not on duty*, with four ladies, were passed through the gate without any other authority than the *dictum* of the officer I was addressing. I complained of the unjust partiality in a respectful manner. For that presumption I was instantly handed over to the next corporal, with orders 'to take back that man.' Collared like a felon, I was forced along the line of foot-guards, and on reaching the last soldier was thrust against a carriage like an intrusive hound."

Never shall I forget the feelings of that evening. After my long detention in the vain endeavour to assert my right of passing the outer gate, I waited to look upon the street procession. When I came back to my home, exhausted, boiling over with indignation, I found my wife in a situation of extreme danger. For some days she had been seriously ill. The funeral procession had passed under our windows. The lurid glare of the torches; the roll of carriages; the tramp of horses, amidst the universal silence of the crowd;—these, almost unendurable for any invalid, who could hear all but who could not look out upon a scene so solemn and so exciting, produced the most alarming effects upon one who was at the extreme point of weakness. By God's Providence, our medical friend, a surgeon of the first eminence in Windsor, returned with me to my house, having been himself subjected to the outrages of the military. He was thus the means of bestowing such immediate attentions upon his patient as probably saved her in the dangerous crisis of that melancholy November night. The one great and enduring happiness of my life was to be preserved to me.

At this Royal Funeral, when a whole nation was present in heart and mind, these military outrages were not the sole disorders and indecencies. The undertaker's men were unmistakeably drunk, as they reeled up the steep Castle street. Within St. George's Chapel there were struggles and murmurs, as in an overcrowded pit at the theatre; for three or four hundred rank and file of the Guards were placed from the western entrance to the extremity of the nave, so as to prevent nine-tenths of the assemblage —admitted by tickets—from seeing more of the solemnity than they could have seen had the outer walls of the Chapel been the barrier to their desires. Just before the procession arrived, there was a noisy conflict at the door of the Choir, which had ulterior consequences. One of the Canons refused to admit a confidential page of the Regent, who had been commanded to notice and report to his royal master how the ceremony was conducted. "It is our freehold," said the Church Dignitary. "It is the Chapel of the Order of the Garter," replied the offended Ruler; "and until the clerical ministers of the Order can behave better, they shall come down from their accustomed seats in the stalls of the Knights."

In my newspaper of the Saturday which followed the Supplement of the 20th of November, I wrote an article entitled "Excessive Employment of Soldiery in a Religious Solemnity, and Abuses in Military Power." My animadversion on "Abuses in Military Power" was bitter enough in its general invective; but there was nothing that the epauletted puppies who talked of horsewhipping the newspaper-fellow could have produced in a court of justice as a justification of a new outrage. I have detailed this occurrence at somewhat greater length than it probably deserved; but it presents a striking contrast not only to the altered temper of the military in these happier times, but to the manner in which the conductors of the Press are now respected in the discharge of their useful functions as the accredited representatives of the people.

CHAPTER IV.

HATEVER might have been the monotony of the life of the editor of a provincial journal in the mere discharge of his office duties, I could always find an ever-changing interest in the necessity for seeing many things with my own eyes; in making personal inquiries in distant places as to the correctness of reputed occurrences—in fact, in being my own reporter. Much of my time was spent on horseback. My ordinary costume was knee-breeches and top-boots. My varied out-door life was as healthful as it was instructive. In these local operations the brain was not heavily taxed. Education was going on. Some exercise of the intellect was essential to report the speeches at a public meeting. The facts exhibited at a coroner's inquest might be best dispatched in that brief style which was once considered sufficient for the London newspaper, but which is now displaced by the most wonderful accumulation of "horror on horror's head." Sometimes, however, the country newspaper might attempt to be graphic when it had to record occurrences of an unusual nature; and yet the absolute limitation of space would often compel me to throw away the kernel of the picturesque to give my readers the hard shell of the literal.

On the 4th of July, 1816, I rode out to Maidenhead Thicket to behold a remarkable proof of the alleged want of employment in the mining and manufacturing districts. On the road from Henley there was the halt of a cavalcade—not such as the poet and the novelist have so often described as the halt of jovial pilgrims taking their morning meal in the beechen shade; but of a party of grim colliers clustered round a waggon laden with coals, which they had drawn for many miles, and whose further progress was interrupted at the mandate of a Bow-street magistrate. From Bilston Moor—where the furnaces of many iron-works no longer darkened the air with their smoke, and the windlass of many a pit was now idle—forty-one men, having a leader on horseback, had the day before passed through Oxford, dragging the waggon in solemn silence, asking no alms, but bearing a placard, on which was inscribed, "Willing to work, but none of us will beg." Their intention, as well as that of another party marching on the St. Alban's Road, was to proceed to London, in the belief that the Prince Regent could order them employment. At Maidenhead the military were prepared for some dire conflict with want and desperation. But Sir Richard Birnie very wisely went forward with two police-officers, finally persuading these men to let their coals be taken into Maidenhead, and to receive a handsome present which would enable them to return to their homes. They were punctilious in refusing to sell their coals. The march of the blanketeers of Manchester in the next year was not so quietly prevented.

There never was a problem more difficult of solution, even by the soundest political economists of the time, than that of the condition of the labouring classes in 1816 and 1817. When I look back on what I wrote on this overwhelming subject in the last four years of the reign of George the Third, I behold a succession of fallacies and half-truths propounded with a sincere belief and with a benevolent earnestness. I was groping my way, in common with most public writers, in the thick darkness by which we were surrounded. The text upon which I commonly preached was from Southey—not the Southey denounced by the "Anti-Jacobin" of 1797, but the Southey of 1817, who denounced Byron and the "Satanic School." The text was not in any great degree an exaggerated description of the condition of England. "We are arrived at that state in which the extremes of inequality are become intolerable." The fallacies and half-truths of the usual comment upon this doctrine sprang from a narrow and one-sided view of the causes of these extremes.

I maintained, not without reason, that the existence of some radical disease in the condition of the labouring classes had been long indicated by the progressive increase of the Poor Rates. I held that the prodigious increase in the demands of pauperism, from the million and a half sterling in 1776, to the eight millions in 1815, was the consequence of some system which, as it had multiplied the temporary sources of profitable labour, had a natural tendency to multiply population, without providing for the regular support of the human beings which it called forth. I averred that the mechanical improvements of the forty years constituted that system. The war, which produced a comparative monopoly of commerce, gave birth to a new machinery to supply that monopoly. The manufacturing system made no provision for that inevitable period when the trading intercourse of the world would return to its accustomed channels, and mankind would be free to use the same instruments of commercial advantage that we had employed. The system had called into action half a million of human beings whom it had now unavoidably abandoned. The State must therefore supply the means of life, which the ordinary modes of employment could no longer give.

I had never seen the practical working of the manufacturing system, and thus I talked, as it was the fashion to talk when Southey wrote, "The nation that builds upon manufactures sleeps upon gunpowder." But I was perfectly familiar with the condition of the agricultural districts. I held, truly, that the organization of society in Great Britian had been completely changed by the system of inclosures and agricultural improvements. These were forced on by the increased demand for corn, originating in the extraordinary consumption and waste of war, and in the increased wants of an increased manufacturing population. I wept over the diminution of the labour which was once required by imperfect modes of cultivation. I grieved over the extinguishing of those indirect means of support which supplied the primitive wants of the ancient peasantry. I missed the old commons on which I used to ramble in my boyhood. I saw no longer the half-starved cow of the cottager tethered before the broken-down hedge of his slovenly garden, and the pig lying on the dunghill that blocked up the dirty approach to his ruinous hovel. The additional patch of garden-ground that was allotted to him seemed to me but a poor compensation for the heath where he once might freely cut the turf for his fire. I grieved the grief of ignorance when I quoted the population returns of 1811, to prove that while two or three millions of additional mouths had been maintained *from* the land, some thousands less had been maintained *upon* the land. The interests of the consumers appeared to me small in comparison with those of the producers. Had I looked more deeply into the matter, I might have mourned over a greater evil than the destruction of the semi-barbarous independence of the squatters who had regarded the heaths and commons as their proper and peculiar inheritance. I might have reasonably mourned that the Agricultural Labourers were slaves to the Poor Laws—brought into the world as paupers by the improvident encouragement to early marriages under the allowance-system; kept through life as paupers by receiving as alms what they had fairly earned as wages; deprived of profitable employment, and hunted from parish to parish, by the laws of Settlement; punished with the most unrelenting severity if they should knock down a rabbit. I might at that time have protested against the bulk of the population being kept in the most degrading ignorance, by the dread which then very generally prevailed in rural districts, that to educate the labourer was to unfit him for the duties (they might have said the degradations) of "that state of life into which it had pleased God to call him"—the formula of consolation always addressed to the poor for the repression of any impious desire to better their condition.

The experience of all men, whether in the South or the North, was sufficient to show that a superfluous population was now pressing upon the capital devoted to the maintenance of labour. But, in that time of bold and impudent assertion, there were believers even in Cobbett when he said "I am quite convinced that the population, upon the whole, has not increased, in England, one single soul since I was born." Still less would many doubt the truth of his description of the Labourers' Paradise in the days "before they were stripped of the commons, of their kettles, their bedding, their beer-barrels."

Whatever might be my heresies as to the best modes of bettering the condition of the Poor, I never had any doubt of the advantages of educating them. It was not often that I came into contact with men who were capable of uniting strong benevolent impulses with the broad view of the consequences of making the pauper more comfortable than the independent labourer. A sort of instinctive horror of the Malthusian doctrine was at the bottom of the thoughts of many sensible persons, who, in spite of their own convictions, were for the most liberal parish allowances according to the number of children in a family, and for the best dietary within the Workhouse walls. Such were, to some extent, the convictions of one of the shrewdest and most warm-hearted of self-taught men with whom it was ever my happiness to become acquainted. Mr. Ingalton had a flourishing business as a shoemaker at Eton. His son, a young artist of great promise, was for some years the most intimate companion of my leisure; and he is one of the few whom time has spared to show me how justly I esteemed him. In his painting-room I have had many a friendly argument with his intelligent father. There was another occasional visitor of that painting-room, who was ready to discuss controverted subjects of social economy, with a perfect theoretical knowledge, but with the practical earnestness of a Christian love for his fellow-creatures. Often have I listened with real delight to an instructive dialogue between the refined scholar and the thoughtful tradesman, who was not wanting in book-knowledge but was stronger in his mother-wit. I see his stately figure in his working garb—fresh from the "cutting out" of his back-shop—standing side by side with the tall and thin clergyman before his son's easel, and discoursing, with no ordinary knowledge of the principles of Art, upon the composition of the "Cottage Interior" or the "Village Concert." The characters of the English scenes which his son painted, in the days of Wilkie, were studies from life; and thus the transition of talk was natural enough from the picture to the reality. The accomplished divine, who was not unfamiliar with many an abode of poverty, was a patient listener to every plea for tenderness to the improvident, and of compassion for the ignorant followers of things evil. But he believed in more enduring helps than casual charity. A few years before, he had proclaimed the great principle, that "the only true secret of assisting the poor is to make them agents in bettering their own condition, and to supply them, not with a temporary stimulus, but with a permanent energy . . . . . Many avenues to an improved condition are open to one whose faculties are enlarged and exercised; he sees his own interest more clearly, he pursues it more steadily, and he does not study immediate gratification at the expense of bitter and late repentance, or mortgage the labour of his future life without an adequate return." * A year or two later, I had a more intimate knowledge of this admirable expositor of principles which have even-

* "Records of Creation," 1816.

tually triumphed over the fears of the rich and the doubts of the learned. But in yielding up some prejudices to the gentle persuasiveness of the Fellow of Eton—who, by his recent sermons in the College Chapel had produced a marked effect in the moral conduct of five hundred youths—I could scarcely then have believed that I was receiving lessons of practical wisdom from a future Archbishop of Canterbury, when I was an earnest listener to John Bird Sumner.

At the Lady Day of 1818 I was placed in a position to acquire a somewhat enlarged experience of the working of the Poor Laws. My father, as Chief Magistrate, nominated me one of the Overseers of the Parish of Windsor. He wished me to become familiar with public business; and although the appointment was not much to my taste I soon came to acknowledge that he was right. I could scarcely have foreseen the benefit that such experience, however limited, would be to me in my future professional pursuits. As there is no man from whom something may not be learnt, even in standing with him under a gateway in a shower of rain, so there is no public office, however little elevated above that of the Constable, and far below the grandeur of the Justice of the Peace, from which he who sets about the performance of its duties in a right spirit may not acquire some practical wisdom to fit him for a higher sphere of action.

CHAPTER V.

T this period, when I was working energetically at parish affairs in addition to my ordinary business, I was equally busied with literary schemes. The practical and the ideal had possession of my mind at one and the same time, and had no contention for superiority. I may truly say—and I say it for the encouragement of any young man who is sighing over the fetters of his daily labour, and pining for weeks and months of uninterrupted study—that I have found through life that the acquisition of knowledge, and a regular course of literary employment, are far from being incompatible with commercial pursuits. I doubt whether, if I had been all author or all publisher, I should have succeeded better in either capacity. It is true that these my occupations were homogeneous; but I question whether that condition is necessary in any case—in a lawyer's, for example—where there is sufficient elasticity of mind to turn readily out of the main line to the loop-line (how could I have expressed this in the days before Stephenson?), and sufficient steadiness of purpose to return to it. In my time of humble journalism at Windsor, I was constantly devising some magnificent scheme of books that I thought the world wanted; in which opinion, it is most probable, I should have found no encourager in the cautious experience of "The Row" or

in the venturous liberality of Albemarle Street. One small project I carried out myself without commercial aid.

Keats has described his acquaintance with our grand old poets:

> "Oft had I travell'd in the realms of gold."

Now and then I came across a volume which I could take up again and again, even whilst Byron was stimulating me with his "Corsair" and his "Giaour," and whilst Wordsworth was awakening a more profound sense of the higher objects of poetry. Such a volume was Shakspere's "Sonnets," rarely published with the Plays, and known only to a few enthusiasts who did not believe, with Steevens, that they were sentimental rubbish. Such was "England's Parnassus," which I borrowed, and longed to appropriate. No publisher had then thought it worth while to reprint Drayton, or Wither, or Herrick, or Herbert. The delight which Keats expressed in his noble Sonnet upon the discovery of Chapman's "Homer" was mine, when I first lighted upon Fairfax's "Tasso." I had entered a new realm of gold. To me that small folio—the first edition, revised by Fairfax himself—was a precious treasure. There had been no edition of the book for seventy years. Resolved that I would achieve the honour of reprinting it, I issued an Advertisement, in October, 1817, in which I said, "Dr. Johnson, with somewhat of his characteristic temerity, ventured to predict that the 'Tasso' of Fairfax would never be reprinted. If the national taste in poetry had not mended since the days of that critic, his prophetic flattery of Hoole would not yet have been disproved." The production of two small volumes at our Windsor Press of the exquisite translation that had been forgotten since Collins had rejoiced to hear Tasso's harp "by English Fairfax strung," was received by a few critics as creditable to the taste of a country printer. The editing of this volume was a pleasant occupation to me. I prefixed to it a Life of Tasso, and a Life of Fairfax. In that of Fairfax I inserted an Eclogue which was first printed in Mrs. Cooper's "Muses' Library"—a volume which had become scarce, and which I found at the London Institution. Mr. Upcott was then the librarian in the new building, which, in its handsome elevation and its judicious interior arrangements, did credit to the architect, then a young man—Mr. William Brooks, the father of Mr. Shirley Brooks. My reprint appeared a little before that of Mr. Singer; or probably I might have shrunk from the competition.

Every now and then, however, my newspaper opened subjects of a new and interesting character, which engaged my attention for a time. Such was the question of inquiry into the Endowed Charities of the country, which in 1818 had assumed a national importance. By the strenuous exertions of Mr. Brougham a Commission was appointed—first to inquire into charities connected with Education, and then into all charities. Pending the results of this investigation, a volume was published by a member of the Bar, Mr. Francis Charles Parry, on the Charities of Berkshire. Such an account as this gentleman collected, somewhat too full of vague charges of abuses, determined me to undertake a really useful labour—that of carefully searching all the documents relating to the charities of Windsor, and of publishing them in the most complete form in my newspaper. It was an honour to my native town that no information was withheld from me; and that I could discover no misappropriation of bequests, and no violation of "the will of the founder." Nor was there any example of that species of legal construction of "the will of the founder" which has built up the magnificence of many of the London Companies. Vast are their rent-rolls. In days when houses and lands were not worth a twentieth part of their present nominal value, these magnates became the inheritors of many a fertile acre and many an improveable tenement, in trust that they should pay, for defined charitable purposes, a particular amount of pounds sterling, annually and for ever—probably the then rent of those lands and houses leaving something for needful charges. The rents of the fourteenth, or fifteenth, or sixteenth centuries—the defined sums—are justly paid. The surplus of the rents of the nineteenth century, increased twenty-fold or even fifty-fold, are partially employed for useful purposes; but they go very far towards the cost of the turtle and loving-cups upon which so much of the public welfare depends. Though Windsor had no flagrant abuses, a few of our charities furnished an example of the necessity of giving large powers to Charity Commissioners, if not for authorizing the Government, to deal with some benevolent provisions of ancient times in a way better adapted to the wants of modern society. But the greater number were not wholly for past generations in their usefulness. There was a Free School, with a considerable permanent income, where fifty boys and girls were educated and clothed.

It did not belong to the then much abused class of Grammar Schools—of which there were several specimens within my knowledge—where the clergyman, who was also the schoolmaster, put the funds into his pocket because the farmers' and labourers' sons did not want to learn Latin. The poor children of our borough were taught those humble accomplishments which Sir William Curtis eulogised as the three Rs—Reading, Riting, and Rithmetic. With the aid of supplementary endowments for Apprenticing Poor Boys and Rewarding Diligent Apprentices, many of these lads became thriving tradesmen. I could point to one man whom I am proud to call my friend, who came to my father to be apprenticed with his blue livery on his back; received the reward upon the faithful completion of his indentures; pursued the trade on his own account in which he had been a valuable assistant; is now not unknown to the world, as having, before the days of railroads, organised a newspaper-system which fought against space and time to give the earliest intelligence to the Liverpool Exchange; and has become himself a newspaper proprietor, and one of the chief mediums for the journalistic communication between England and her Colonies as well as with North and South America. Honoured be the memory of Archbishop Laud, who by his will thus made provision not only for the apprenticeship of "children of honest poor people;" but laid the foundations of their future prosperity. Many a young woman, through his provident care, has kept her position in "the faithful service of the antique world," and has not rushed into premature wedlock, sustained by the hope of receiving a marriage-portion on the condition of having served the same master or mistress for three years. Let us cherish the memory of Laud for the sake of his Berkshire Charities. What matters it to us that we have outgrown his politics and his polemics! May we never, in dreams of universal philanthropy, believe that we are growing in true philosophy when we attempt to exclude individual sympathies for the lowly by larger aspirations for the human race. Above all, let us not presume to obliterate the Past, by turning aside from those who have helped, each according to his lights, to build up a wider Present—erring men—short-sighted—enemies to progress in the abstract, but nevertheless, in their practical benevolence, working for the "one increasing purpose" of human improvement.

Social Science in 1818 had a very small attendance of disciples in her schools. For an inquiring few, she had her Primers and her Junior Class Books; and in her inner courts for the initiated, Bentham was preaching in a language the farthest removed from popular comprehension. Romilly, in the House of Commons, had been labouring for ten years to amend the Criminal Laws. His valuable life was closed prematurely before he had achieved any marked victory over the system under which the death penalty was capriciously enforced, to inspire "a vague terror" amongst the whole criminal population. The prisons were nurseries of crime. The detective police were amongst crime's chief encouragers. Forgery flourished above all other crimes, for the Government offered the temptation whilst they unsparingly hanged the tempted. The Game Laws raised up pilfering peasants into gangs of brigands. Smuggling was nurtured into the dignity of commercial enterprise, by protective duties so absurdly high that a wall of brass could not have kept out the brandies and lace and silk that the Continent was ready to pour in. The great bulk of the population was wholly ignorant and partly brutal. The Church had not awakened from its long sleep. If the schoolmaster was abroad, he was rather seeking for work than doing it. Looking as a journalist upon our social condition, I was sometimes unhappy and desponding. My dissatisfaction found a vent in letters from an imaginary correspondent:—

"The prevailing feeling which a newspaper excites in my breast, without the indulgence of any sickly sensibility, is that of melancholy. It presents a gloomy portrait of our species. It is a living herald of the bad passions of individuals and the mistakes of society. It discovers little of the better part of mankind, for the most elevated virtue is the most unobtrusive. The atmosphere of vice is a broad and visible darkness overspreading the land, through which the gaunt spectres of crime glare fearfully upon us. The newspaper applies its microscopic eyes to these miserable objects; like Tam O'Shanter, it looks upon their secret revels—it notes every movement of the infuriated dance; it traces the progress of evil from its mazy beginning to its horrible close; it anatomizes the deformities of the heart, and encases them for public exhibition. Should these spectacles be withheld from the general eye? Unquestionably not. They administer, indeed, to that love of strong excitement which characterizes the human mind in every state, but which operates most powerfully upon a highly refined community—and so far they are mischievous. But still they have a voice of edification. They summon us all to the labour of opposing that flood of iniquity which threatens to break down the dykes and mounds of our social institutions; they call us to eradicate the canker which interrupts the natural spring of moral health. The evil is in the root. The institutions for the prevention and punishment of crime are founded upon a wrong view of human nature; they have a direct tendency to confirm and multiply the effects of depraved ignorance.

"Your weekly 'map of busy life' reaches me in the solitude of the most beautiful and the least visited part of Windsor Forest. This morning I rose ere the sun had lighted the autumnal foliage with a brighter yellow and a richer brown. My walk was in the silent woods. All around me was cheerfulness. The birds of song were pouring forth their instinctive gratitude for returning day—the noisy rooks had a spirit of gladness in their whirling flights—the graceful deer glided before me with fearless nimbleness. My heart expanded at the enjoyments of these humble beings. Surely, I exclaimed, every creature that lives in conformity to its nature is happy. I returned to my home. Your journal was on my breakfast-table. The calendar of the 'Old Bailey' met my view. I read of the condemnation of thirty-five persons to the penalty of death, and of nearly two hundred to lesser degrees of punishment. I considered that these scenes are repeated every six weeks!* The impressions of my morning walk had a redoubled force. I felt assured that man was not destined to crime and misery.

* The Central Criminal Court was not established till 1834. The Sessions of the Old Bailey, previous to that change, were held eight times a year for the trial of offences committed in Middlesex.

Are, then, these penal modes of counteracting the corruptions of society suggested by reason and benevolence?"

I believe that at this period I got into a morbid state of mind, by thinking too much of

> "the heavy and the weary weight
> Of all this unintelligible world."

I had no large and definite object of ambition. My occupations were not engrossing enough to carry me away from dreamy speculations. I pored over the Platonic writers, Proclus and Plotinus, in Taylor's translations; and accepted the philosophy of which Coleridge was the modern expositor, as far nobler than the doctrine of ideas derived from sensation. I sometimes thought that the great mysteries of human life were clearing up; and then again I relapsed into bewilderment. May I venture to dig out from its recesses a sonnet which represents my state of mind at this crisis, when the blessing of the primal curse was not sufficiently laid upon me?—

> "Unquiet thoughts, ye wind about my heart
> In many-tangled webs. My daily toil,
> The obstinate cares of life, the vain turmoil
> Of getting dross and spending, bear their part
> In this entanglement; and if my mind
> Shake off its chains, and, free as mountain-wind,
> Repose on Nature's pure maternal breast,
> Interpreting her fresh and innocent looks
> Discoursing truth and love clearer than books,
> Thoughts are still weaving webs of my unrest.
> O grant me, Wisdom, to behold thee near,
> Deep, clear, reveal'd as one all-perfect whole;
> Or give me back the sleep to worldlings dear—
> Thy glimmerings disturb my heated soul."

Turning from metaphysics to hard realities, and looking upon the apparently interminable warfare between Ignorance and Power, I could perceive very few reconciling principles of social policy, or influential mediators between the lawless and the governing classes.

As early as 1814 I had the notion of becoming a Popular Educator. I have a letter before me, written on the 24th of January of that year to the more than friend to whom I laid open all my feelings and plans, in which I said—"I want to consult you about a cheap work we think of publishing in weekly numbers, for the use of the industrious part of the community, who have neither money to buy, nor leisure to read, bulky and expensive books. It will consist of plain Essays on points of duty; the Evidences of Christianity; Selections from the works of the most approved English Divines; Abstracts of the Laws and Constitution of Great Britain; History; Information on useful Arts and Sciences; and Select Pieces of Entertainment." The scheme was constantly in my mind; and it was often present in day-dreams of a more extended area of employment than I then occupied, especially after I had acquired a little familiarity with the general ignorance of the working classes, knew something practical of their habits, saw in some few a desire for knowledge, and felt how ill their intellectual wants could be supplied. Now and then, on our market-day, in strange juxtaposition with the brown earthenware and the coarse brushes of the itinerant dealers, would be placed upon a stall the old dog's-eared volume, and the new flimsy numbers of the book-hawker. I have seen with pity some aspiring artisan spend his sixpence upon an antiquated manual of history or geography, to which he would devote his brief and hard-earned hours of leisure, gaining thus the "two grains of wheat hid in two bushels of chaff." Or I have beheld some careful matron tempted to buy the first number of the "Pilgrim's Progress" or the "Book of Martyrs"—perhaps one less discreet bestowing her attention upon the "History of Witchcraft" or the "Lives of the Highwaymen"—each arranging with the Canvasser for a monthly delivery till the works should be completed, when they would find themselves in possession of the dearest books that came from the press, even in the palmy days of expensive luxuries. For the young, such stalls would offer the worst sort of temptations in sixpenny Novels with a coloured frontispiece; whose very titles would invite to a familiarity with the details of crime—of murders and adulteries, of violence and fraud, of licentiousness revelling in London, and innocence betrayed in the country—something much more harmful than the old-world stories, the dreams and divinations, of the ancient chap-books. Would the book-hawker of that time, with his costly, meagre, useless, and worse than useless, wares, be able to satisfy the intellectual cravings of any young man sincerely desirous profitably to exercise his newly-acquired ability to read?

I shall have to relate, in the next chapter, how, nearly six years after the idea of a Cheap Miscellany had been gradually shaping itself in my habitual thoughts, but still without any notion of an immediate practical result, I suddenly made my first excursion into the almost untrodden field of cheap and wholesome Literature for the People. The necessity for some educational efforts to counteract the influence of dangerous teachers had become more and more apparent. The Government was watchful. It had the power of repressing tumult by the military arm, and of suspending the public liberty for the discovery of conspirators. But it did nothing, and encouraged nothing, that indicated a paternal Government. There were crafty men in most towns, who stimulated discontent into outrage, and for a sufficient motive would betray their associates. Such a man was living at Eton. Upon the trial of the wretched participators in the Cato-Street Conspiracy, Arthur Thistlewood denounced this man, as "the contriver, the instigator, the entrapper." We are told, from unquestionable authority, in the "Life of Lord Sidmouth," that the principal informant of the Home-Office "was a modeller and itinerant vendor of images, named Edwards, who first opened himself at Windsor, as early as the month of November, to Sir Herbert Taylor, then occupying an important official situation in the establishment of George III." This Edwards was not an *itinerant* vendor of images. I have spoken with him in his small shop in the High Street of Eton—perhaps at the very time when he was plotting and betraying. He had some ingenuity as a modeller; and produced a very tolerable statuette of Dr. Keate, in his cocked hat. His sale of this little model was considerable amongst the junior boys of Eton College—not exactly out of reverence for their head-master but as a mark to be pelted at. Does any copy exist of this historical Portrait? The subject of the little bust and its modeller are both historical. They each belong to a state of society of which we have, happily, got rid. The schoolmaster, albeit a ripe scholar and a gentleman, belonged to the past times, when Education, like Government, was conducted upon that system of terror which was the easiest system for the administrators. "The greatest happiness for the greatest number," whether of boys or men, had to be discovered. In the scholastic, or political, exaltation of the aristocratic system, there was ample scope for the few clever and aspiring. To these the patrician and the pedagogue graciously afforded encouragement and substantial patronage. But the mass of the dull, the unambitious, and the reckless, were left to their own capacity for drifting into evil. If the misdoers came under the imperfect cognizance of the authorities, they were heavily punished as a salutary terror to others. The flogging-block was the first step to personal degradation in the school; the prison, in the State. If these did not answer, the school was ready with expulsion; the State with the gallows. One essential difference there was in the two systems. The honour of the Etonian was proof against spydom and treachery as regarded his fellows. In the terror-stricken politics of that time there was verge enough for the instigator and entrapper. I have written that Sir Herbert Taylor, whose honour was unimpeachable, was utterly incapable of suggesting to the spy that he should incite the wretched associates in the conspiracy to the pursuance of their frantic designs. ("Popular History of England," vol. viii. p. 160.) Yet, if I remember rightly the face of George Edwards, Sir Herbert Taylor might have seen that he was a rogue by nature. This diminutive animal, with downcast look and stealthy face, did not calculate badly when he approached one who, although bred in court-habits, had a solid foundation of honesty which made him unsuspicious. Sir Herbert was a man not versed in the common affairs of the outer world.

He had been the depository of many a political secret which he could confide to no friend. Shy, painfully cautious, I have heard him break down in the most simple address to the electors when he first stood for Windsor; and yet a man of real ability. Imagine a crafty mechanic procuring access to him at the Castle as the starving man of taste—a plaster cast of his workmanship carefully produced—the guinea about to be proffered—and then a whisper of some terrible Secret which he could disclose at the peril of his life—all the outer evidences of contrition, and the resolve to make a clean breast. Imagine this repeated day by day—with the plot-haunted Lord Sidmouth eagerly calling for more evidence, and urging Sir Herbert Taylor to palter with this devil, and not hand him over to the Privy Council, who might have crushed the cockatrice before the egg was hatched. We may imagine all this; and yet acquit Sir Herbert Taylor of a participation in the guilt which too often attaches to those, in all ages, who have fostered treason in waiting for overt acts.

Before the outbreak of the Conspiracy, an event occurred, which, although not unexpected, nor fraught with consequences unforeseen, opened a further certain prospect of political disquiet. The death of George the Third took place on the evening of Saturday, the 29th of January, 1820. The Duke of Kent, his fourth son, had died only six days before. The Regent became King; the Duke of York was the Presumptive Heir to the Throne; the Duke of Clarence the next in succession. The infant daughter of the Duke of Kent would succeed, if the three elder brothers of her father should die without issue. The position of George the Fourth and Queen Caroline might again open that miserable "Book" which the public welfare required to be for ever shut.

The Funeral of George the Third appeared to me like the close of a long series of reminiscences. Windsor had to me been associated with the loud talk and the good-natured laugh of a portly gentleman with a star on his breast, whom I sometimes ran against in my childhood; with a venerable personage, blind, but cheerful, who sat erect on a led horse, as I had seen him in my youth; with the dim idea of my manhood, that in rooms of the Castle which no curiosity could penetrate, there sat an old man with a long beard, bereft of every attribute of rank, who occasionally talked wildly or threw himself about frantically, and sometimes awoke recollections of happier days by striking a few chords on his piano. Then came the final pageant. It was a Poem rather than a show. The Lying-in-State was something higher than undertaker's art. As I passed through St. George's Hall, I thought of the last display of regal pomp in that room—the Installation of 1805—when at the banquet the Sovereign stood up and pledged his knights, and the knights, in full cups of gold, invoked health and happiness on the Sovereign. The throne on which George the Third then sat was now covered with funeral draperies. I went on into the King's Guard-Chamber. The room was darkened—there was no light but that of the flickering wood-fires which burnt on an ancient hearth on each side. On the ground lay the beds on which the Yeomen of the Guard had slept during the night. They stood in their grand old dresses of state, with broad scarves of crape across their breasts, and crape on their halberds. As the red light of the burning brands gleamed on their rough faces, and glanced ever and anon upon the polished mail of the Black Prince, on the bruised armour of the soldiers of the Plantagenets, and on the matchlocks and bandoleers of the early days of modern warfare, some of the reality of the Present passed into visions of the Past. I thought of Edward of Windsor, the great builder of the Castle, deserted in his last moments. I thought of other "sad stories of the deaths of kings." I came back to the immediate interest of the scene before me, by remembering that not one of the long line of English sovereigns before George the Third had died at Windsor. I passed on into the chamber of death. All here was comparatively modern. The hangings of purple cloth which hid West's gaudy pictures of the Institution of the Order of the Garter; the wax-lights on silver sconces; the pages standing by the side of the coffin; the Lord of the Bedchamber sitting at its head; much of this was upholstery work, and did not affect the imagination, except in connexion with the solemn silence,—a stillness unbroken, even when rustic feet, unused to tread on carpets, passed by the bier, awe-struck.

One such Royal Funeral as I had previously seen was not essentially different from another. The out-door ceremonial at the interment of George the Third was not readily to be forgotten. It was a walking procession. The night was dark and misty. Vast crowds were assembled in the Lower Ward of the Castle, hushed and expectant. A platform had been erected from the Grand Entrance of the Castle to the Western Entrance of St. George's Chapel. It was lined on each side by a single file of the Guards. A signal-rocket is fired. Every soldier lights a torch, and the massive towers and the delicate pinnacles stand out in the red glare. Minute guns are now heard in the distance. Will those startling voices never cease? Expectation is at its height. A flourish of trumpets is heard, and then the roll of muffled drums. A solemn dirge comes upon the ear, nearer and nearer. The funeral-car glides slowly along the platform without any perceptible aid from human or mechanical power. The dirge ceases for a little while; and then again the trumpets and the muffled drums sound alternately. Again the dirge—softly breathing flutes and clarionets mingling their notes with "the mellow horn"—and then a dead silence; for the final resting-place is reached. Heralds and banners and escutcheons touch not the heart. But the Music! That is something grander than the picturesque.

CHAPTER VI.

I MAY trace my first venture, as an Editor and Publisher, into the dimly-descried region of Popular Literature, to a paper which I wrote in the Windsor Express of December 11, 1819, headed "Cheap Publications." In this article I set forth, as one of the most remarkable, and in some degree most fearful "signs of the times," the excessive spread of cheap publications almost exclusively directed to the united object of inspiring hatred of the Government and contempt of the Religious Institutions of the country. I noticed the singleness of purpose, in connexion with the commercial rivalry, with which this object had been pursued. With Cobbett's "Twopenny Register" a race was run in London by Wooller's "Black Dwarf," "The Republican," "The Medusa's Head," "The Cap of Liberty," and many more of the same stamp; whilst every large manufacturing town had its own peculiar vehicle of seditious and infidel opinions. I had mentioned in a previous article that a Manchester paper was advertising a catalogue of books, occupying one column, nearly the whole of which, aiming at the overthrow of Christianity, "are all published in numbers," at a price accessible even to the unhappy mechanics who labour sixteen hours a-day for less than a shilling. I continued my essay on "Cheap Publications" by adverting to the rapid advances that had been made during the previous twenty years in the Education of the Poor, upon systems of instruction under which a considerable proportion of young men moving in the working classes had grown up. It was amongst these persons, possessing a talent unknown to their fathers—perhaps a little ardent and presumptuous, and certainly craving after information with a passionate desire that might become either a blessing or a curse—that cheap publications had been most widely diffused. The anarchists of that day were a subtle and acute race. They had watched the progress of knowledge amongst the people. Their publications teemed with allusions to the increased intelligence of the working classes. "There is a *new power* in society, and they have combined to give that power a direction. The work must be taken out of their hands."

After the lapse of more than forty years, I feel that a desire to exhibit some characteristics of the tentative process by which useful knowledge was then to be diffused will excuse me for giving a longer extract from this essay.

"We have already said, and it is perhaps necessary to repeat it, that there is a *new power* entrusted to the great mass of the working people, and that it is daily becoming of wider extent and greater importance. It has been most wisely and providently agreed to give that power one principal direction by interweaving it with religious knowledge and feelings, that they might thus blend with the whole current of mature thought, and sanctify the possession of the keys of learning to useful and innocent ends. We are yet disposed to think that this is not all which the creation of such a new and extraordinary power demands. Knowledge must have its worldly as well as its spiritual range; it looks towards Heaven, but it treads upon the earth. The mass of useful books are not accessible to the poor; newspapers, with their admixture of good and evil, seldom find their way into the domestic circle of the labourer or artizan; the tracts which pious persons distribute are exclusively religious, and the tone of these is often either fanatical or puerile. The 'twopenny trash,' as it is called, has seen farther, with the quick perception of avarice or ambition, into the intellectual wants of the working-classes. It was just because there was no healthful food for their newly-created appetite, that sedition and infidelity have been so widely disseminated. The writers employed in this work, and their leader and prototype, Cobbett, in particular, show us pretty accurately the sort of talent which is required to provide this healthful food. '*Fas est ab hoste doceri.*' They state an argument with great clearness and precision; they divest knowledge of all its pedantic incumbrances; they make powerful appeals to the deepest passions of the human heart. Let a man of genius set out upon these principles, in the task of building up a more popular literature than we possess; and let him add, what the seditious and infidel writers have thrown away, the power of directing the affections to what is reverend and beautiful in national manners and institutions—tender and subduing in pure and domestic associations—sacred and glowing in what belongs to the high and mysterious destiny of the human mind—satisfying and consoling in the divine revelations of that destiny,—and then, were such a system embodied in one grand benevolent design supplementary to the Instruction of the Poor, National Education, we sincerely think, would go on diffusing its blessings over every portion of the land, and calling up a truly English spirit wherever it penetrated. Neglect this provision, and we fear that no penal laws will prevent the craving after knowledge from being improperly gratified, and then —but the evidence of the danger is before us."

The publication of this article led to an intimacy between Mr. Locker and myself, which I count amongst the most gratifying recollections of my life. Within twenty-four hours of its appearance he called upon me; and we very soon agreed to be joint editors of a Monthly Serial work, intended, in some degree, to supply the want I had pointed out. Within a fortnight our plans were matured; and in the "Express" of Christmas-day it was announced, that on the 1st of February, 1820, would appear No. I. of "The Plain Englishman."

When I first had the happiness of acquiring the friendship of Mr. Locker he was in his forty-second year. His life, before he came to reside at Windsor, had been one of large and varied experience. The names of Edward Hawke were given to him in honour of the illustrious officer under whom his father had served in the middle of the last century. In his charming memoir of Admiral Locker, in "The Plain Englishman," he dwells with just pride upon the attachment of our great naval hero to his father. "Horatio Nelson, to the last hour of his life, regarded him with the affection of a son and with the respect of a pupil." After the battle of the Nile he did not forget his old commander amidst the flatteries and seductions which followed his victory.

"I have been your scholar," he wrote; " it is you who taught me to board a French man-of-war, by your conduct in the *Experiment*. It is you who always said, 'Lay a Frenchman close, and you will beat him.'" The private life of such a man, as glanced at by his son, is very interesting.

My friend had the advantage of an Eton education; but he was destined for an active rather than a learned life. He was in a government-office till he was twenty-three, and then became Private Secretary to Sir Edward Pellew. When his admiral was commander-in-chief in the Mediterranean, Mr. Locker discharged the arduous duties of Secretary to the Fleet. He had a printing-press on board the flag-ship which materially assisted his labours. In his official capacity he visited Napoleon at Elba, a few days after the fallen Emperor had taken possession of his narrow territory. His narrative of their conversations is exceedingly interesting. ("Plain Englishman," vol. iii. p. 475.) After the peace, Mr. Locker married, and came to reside at Windsor. From the period when our intimate acquaintance commenced, I enjoyed his friendship for a quarter of a century. He was to me an example of a true gentleman—intelligent, well-read, energetic, charitable, religious, tolerant—such as I had scarcely met in the limited society in which I lived when I first knew him. He soon removed from Windsor, to become the Secretary of Greenwich Hospital, and afterwards the Resident Civil Commissioner. His hospitable home was always open to me; his active friendship was never withheld; his judicious advice was my stay in many a doubt and difficulty.

For three years Mr. Locker and I worked together,

with a cordiality never disturbed, in conducting "The Plain Englishman." Our views were set forth in an Introduction, which I wrote. Much of this composition had necessarily regard to the peculiar danger of that period—the irreligion and disloyalty that were associated, or seemed to be associated, with the spread of education. We were prepared to meet this danger in an honest spirit: "We think highly of the understandings of the people of our country. We shall address them, therefore, not as children, but as men and women. If we combat Infidelity, we shall look for our arguments in those volumes which have made the deepest impression on the wise and learned. If we would disprove the falsehoods which designing persons have propagated against our Government, we shall republish those reasons for a reverence of its forms and institutions which have convinced the ablest minds, and shown them its practical excellence. If we would awaken all the noble feelings which belong to the real patriot, we shall go back into the chronicles of old for a history of those deeds which rouse the spirit 'as with a trumpet.' We shall not conceal anything or distort anything. We shall enable all who seek for knowledge to judge for themselves."

This plain avowal did not receive the approbation of the constituted authorities for making the people wiser and better. The Christian Knowledge Society was, at that period, the representative of what was supine, timid, and time-serving in the Church. That venerable corporation had not yet roused itself into activity, to meet the new wants created by the growing ability to read. It had a depository of books, in which were to be found antiquated works on the Evidences, such as that of the learned and amiable Bishop

Wilson, entitled "Instructions for the Indians,"—so low was the intellectual power of his countrymen rated by the good prelate. Many new compilations had they in their store, through which they hoped to meet the evils of the time, by talking to working people as if they were as innocent of all knowledge, both of good and evil, as in the days when their painstaking mothers committed them to the edifying instruction of the village schoolmistress, to be taught to sit still and hold their tongues, forty in a close room, for three hours together, at the moderate price of twopence each per week. They meddled not with dangerous Science or more dangerous History. Poetry and all works of Imagination they eschewed. Over their collection of dry bones the orthodox publishers, Messrs. Rivington, presided. My brother-editor believed that this time-honoured Society would willingly lend a helping hand to our well-meant endeavour. Their booksellers agreed to be our London publishers. But High-Church frowned; and we were driven to the Low-Church rivals of the shop that had long had "the Bible and Crown" over its door. We had fallen into the common error of the infancy of Popular Knowledge, in believing that any scheme for its diffusion could be successful which was not immediately addressed to the people themselves, without in any degree depending upon the patronage of gratuitous, and therefore suspicious, distribution, by the superiors of those for whose perusal works of a popular character are devised. It was well for us that we got out of the shackles of this Society, which was then wholly ignorant of the intellectual wants and capabilities of the working population; and would have insisted upon maintaining the habit of talking to thinking beings, and for the most part to very acute thinking beings, in the language of the nursery — the besetting weakness of the learned and aristocratic, from the very first moment that they began to prattle about bestowing the blessings of education. If we were tolerated in the adoption of a higher tone, we must still have assumed the attitude of writers who had come down from their natural elevation to impart a small portion of their wisdom to persons of very inferior understanding. "The Schoolmaster was abroad,"—and so was Cobbett. As Scarlett always won a verdict by getting close to the confiding twelve as if he were a thirteenth juryman, so Cobbett forced his "Register" into every workshop and every cottage, not only by using the plainest English, but by identifying himself with the every-day thoughts—the passions, the prejudices—of those whom he addressed. It was very long before any of us who aspired to be popular instructors learnt the secret of his influence, and could exhibit the "vigour of the bow" without "the venom of the shaft."

The title-page of "The Plain Englishman" some what too prominently described the work as "comprehending Original Compositions, and Selections from the best Writers, under the heads of The Christian Monitor; The British Patriot; The Fireside Companion." I look back upon this division of subjects as a mistake. In 1832, at the commencement of my editorship of "The Penny Magazine," Dr. Arnold wrote to Mr. W. Tooke, the Treasurer of the Useful Knowledge Society, to speak in terms of somewhat extravagant commendation of a short article on Mirabeau which I had written; and to express his opinion that the infusion of religious feeling into the treatment of secular subjects was far more valuable for popular instruction than any direct exhortations.* In "The Plain Englishman" it was perhaps essential to our objects to have separate papers on religious matters; but I am inclined to think that they lost much of their usefulness by standing separate from those of "The British Patriot" and "The Fireside Companion." In the same way the historical and constitutional articles of the second section would have had a much better chance of being read if they had been mixed up with the third miscellaneous division. At any rate, as we soon became aware, our Serial stood very little chance of an extensive natural sale amongst the young and newly half-educated. A Weekly Penny or Twopenny Sheet, such as I had proposed in 1812, might have had a better chance of success, but still a very small chance. I could not have rendered it attractive by pictures, in the then condition of wood-engraving, without a greater cost than the probable circulation of such a work would have justified. The good engravers were few, and the Art had been almost lost since the death of Bewick. For ordinary purposes of book-illustration it was scarcely used. "The Mirror," established about that time, was slightly but very indifferently illustrated. Its laudable endeavours to furnish information and amusement, without stirring up the passions of the people, were not crowned with any signal success. The great artist of half a century, whose etchings and whose designs for wood present that rare union of truth and fancy which has made Hogarth im-

* Life of Dr. Arnold.

mortal, was at that time enlisted in the work of political caricature, in which he was the creative spirit whilst another gave the rough idea. When William Hone and George Cruikshank met in 1820, to devise "The Political House that Jack built," there was a veracious man present who has described to me one of the amusing scenes of which he was a witness. The obscure publisher of "Parodies" in 1817,—who, with his bag of books spread on the table of the King's Bench, had done battle against the ablest and boldest judge of the time, and had driven him from the field,—was now a public character. Whatever little stinging pamphlets he issued were sure to find their way over the land. But assurance of success was made doubly sure when he had enlisted Cruikshank in the cause which to them appeared resistance to oppression and vindication of innocence. Three friends—fellow conspirators, if you like—are snugly ensconced in a private room of a well-accustomed tavern. Hone produces his scheme for " The House that Jack built." He reads some of his doggerel lines. The author wants a design for an idea that is clear enough in words, but is beyond the range of pictorial representation. The artist pooh-poohs. The bland publisher is pertinacious, but not dictatorial. My friend, Alfred Fry, the most earnest, straightforward, and argumentative of men, is no greater judge of the limits of Art than the man who had the best of the discussion with Lord Ellenborough but cannot vanquish or convince George Cruikshank. "Wait a moment," says the artist. The wine—perhaps the grog—is on the table. He dips his finger in his glass. He rapidly traces wet lines on the mahogany. A single figure starts into life.

Two or three smaller figures come out around the first head and trunk—a likeness in its grotesqueness. The publisher cries "Hoorah." The looker-on is silent after this rapid manifestation of a great power. A pen-and-ink sketch is completed on the spot. The bottle circulates briskly or the rummers are replenished. Politics are the theme, whether of agreement or disputation. Alfred Fry quotes Greek, which neither of his auditors understand, but that is no matter. There is one upon whom his learning will not be thrown away. He gets admission to the House of Lords during the Queen's trial, and passes on to Mr. Denman a slip of paper which contains a sentence from Athenæus. The apt quotation appears in the official Minutes of the Proceedings. This recollection of Cruikshank and his friends may seem out of place; but it is not wholly without relation to the slow progress of my "Plain Englishman." The violent politics of that unhappy time were all-absorbing. The newspapers furnished the most stimulating reading. Even Cobbett, with his denunciations of boroughmongers and bank-directors, was little heeded. The pamphlet-buyers rushed to Hone. "The House that Jack built" ran through forty-seven editions; "The Queen's Matrimonial Ladder," forty-four; "Non mi ricordo," thirty one. London, and indeed all the kingdom, had gone mad. It would be very long before the people would listen to the small voice of popular knowledge, which possessed no ephemeral influence, and which was utterly drowned in the howlings of that storm.

In such a heaving up of the crust of society by the volcanic fires below, it was not very likely that the benevolent optimism of our Monthly Serial would produce much influence upon the peasant and the mechanic, each designated by us as "The Plain Englishman of the Working Classes." Looking at the "burning fiery furnace" that we have all walked through since that period, it seems to me something like hypocrisy when I wrote, in 1820, of the Plain Englishman who felt, if he could not describe, the foundations of his respectability. But it was not hypocrisy. I believed what I wrote when I talked of "the happiness peculiar to the course of peaceful labour;" of "the security which rendered him master of his own possessions, however small;" of "the kind look or the benevolent visit from his wealthier neighbour, which cheered him in his humble station." It certainly was not true,—as regarded the majority of those who earned their bread by the sweat of their brow,—that the Plain Englishman "viewed the difference of ranks without envy, convinced that, as subjects of the same laws, sharers in the same infirmities, and heirs of the same salvation, the rich and the poor of England were all equal." * I followed in the wake of men most anxious for the welfare of the lower classes, but who were at that time convinced that the first and greatest object of all popular exhortation was to preach from the text of St. James, "Study to be quiet." There never was a more sound political economist than Dr. John Bird Sumner—never one who took a more enlarged view of the necessity of looking at economical questions over a wider area than that which was bounded by the material "wealth of nations." He was amongst our first contributors. His "Conversations with an Un-

* "Plain Englishman," vol. i. Introduction.

believer," or "Dialogues between Eusebius and Alciphron" may be regarded as elegant cooling mixtures such as a timid physician might prescribe to a patient in a burning fever. He made no attempt to grapple stoutly with the arguments of the "Unbeliever," as he would probably have done with the opinions of the "Communist." He meets the Unbeliever in the mild persuasive spirit which was the index of his own character—no assumption of superiority, no anathemas. This tone was perhaps scarcely suited to the time; but, after all, the lessons of the Christian teacher must win before they can convince. The heart must be touched before the reason can be subjected. Even the style that borders upon the poetical may allure, and then hold captive, those, especially the young, whom a severer logic might repel. Taylor has probably made more converts than Barrow. Nothing can be prettier than the following opening of a "Conversation," as he was returning from his parish church on Christmas-day, and fell in with an acquaintance whom he knew to entertain what he called *free thoughts* on the subject of Revelation: "I always pity you, Alciphron, and particularly at the present season. The air of cheerfulness which so generally prevails, and makes even winter smile, must fill you with melancholy when it reminds you of the errors of your fellow-creatures. The village steeple, which from time immemorial has been accustomed to proclaim the message of glad tidings, must appear to you to usher in the reign of superstition; since bells repeat what the hearers think. No sight is more welcome to my eye than that of those knots of country people, as they wind among the hills which intercept the spire from our view, returning in family groups from the church where their fathers and forefathers have been long used to celebrate the assurance of God's good-will towards men. It brings a thousand delightful associations to my mind. You, the meanwhile, must be inwardly lamenting such idle commemoration of the origin of their bondage and their error. To-day, too, the sun re-appearing after a season of unusual gloominess and severity assorts with the impressions on my mind. The clouds and darkness which had long shrouded the throne of God seem suddenly dispersed; the scene is lighted up and brightens; but yet it is the sunshine of winter still. For you, and such as you, who close your eyes against the light—and many others who hate the light because their deeds are evil,—spread a gloom over the distance, and, like the patches of snow which lie unmelted on the hills, remind us that it is a wintry world after all." Alciphron argues that Revelation is an imposture, and that "an army of well-paid priests is leagued together to keep up the deceit." Eusebius answers him thus: "So you have really been persuaded by Paine and his disciples to imagine that a Christian minister, for the sake of lucre, imposes on the credulity of his hearers a system of Religion which he knows to be without foundation! I little expected an insinuation like this from any adversary less ignorant than Carlile, or less vulgar than Paine. But, to meet you here also, you forget that the benefices which engage your *well-paid army* to practise this baseness, do not average a hundred pounds per annum; you forget how many follow their profession to their grave, without ever obtaining one of the lowest of its prizes. Would not the same education and the same talents, exerted in any other profession, ensure a much higher reward? Depend upon it, if the clergy had no other than a temporal inducement to maintain the Christian faith, it would not continue twenty years." Before our excellent contributor had finished his career of piety and active goodness as archbishop, he would have had a perfect experience that the Alciphrons never point their attacks upon *the well-paid* army by the example of the under-paid curate of a hundred a year. In that great lottery the prizes are sufficient to keep even the worldly aspirants stedfast, as Sydney Smith wisely and wittily argued. And yet such a man as the late Archbishop of Canterbury might win the highest prize, and still be as spiritually-minded as he was when thus writing in his pretty parish of Mapledurham. The mildness with which the commonplace objection is met might have the effect of leading some, step by step, to go deeper into the great question, glad to have their surface doubts cleared away with a tender hand.

The "Lectures on the Bible and Liturgy" contributed to "The Plain Englishman" by Mr. Locker, were the substance of a course of familiar Addresses delivered by him to his shipmates on board the *Caledonia,* when he was Secretary of the Mediterranean Fleet. They have been published in a separate volume, and well deserve to hold a place in an elementary library of Christian instruction; for they are realities. They were addressed to sailors who required no subtle arguments of doctrine to induce them to be religious. They were plain, earnest, affectionate. They must have touched the heart of "Poor Jack," like Dibdin's transfusion into nautical language of Hamlet's "there's a special Providence in the fall of a sparrow." They have passed into oblivion. Our theology, like our novels, has become sensational.

Amongst our intimate and constant contributors was a scholar whose memory I regard with sincere respect — the Rev. J. M. Turner, who succeeded Daniel Wilson as bishop of Calcutta. His papers on the "Naval Victories" are capital summaries of those great triumphs which kept England safe in the midst of dangers that looked overwhelming. When I knew him he was private tutor at Eton to the sons of Lord Londonderry. In religion, tolerant; in politics, almost liberal. I often met him at Mr. Locker's table at Greenwich; and never left him without feeling that he was a friend to make one wiser and better. We passed into different spheres of exertion. His last letter to me was one of encouragement to go on with a bolder attempt at Popular Instruction than our "Plain Englishman." To our "British Patriot" we had a valuable contributor in a personal friend—John Steer, who was diligently studying as a pupil of Mr. Chitty. His mastery of the principles of jurisprudence and the practice of the courts was evidenced in his excellent papers on "Popular Law." His valuable life was cut short before he reached that eminence at the Bar which seemed fairly within his power to attain.

For myself, I worked with hearty good will at our Miscellany. It took me out of the region of political controversy, for which I had no great love at any time, and especially in times when it was very difficult to be impartial and sincere. A journalist in my position was between the Scylla of bad government, and the Charybdis of no government. In "The Plain Englishman" it was impossible to allude to the necessity of any Parliamentary Reform; for the Radical Reformers were sending their foxes all over the country, with lighted brands at their tails, to burn the standing corn and the vineyards and olives. We were friends of Catholic Emancipation, and yet we dared not advocate so vital a change without a dread that the Church of England would lose its anchorage. The scandalous abuses of the Irish Church could not be spoken of; although I have heard one of the ablest of our reverend associates devoutly wish that the rope could be cut by which the gallant ship towed the overladen and rotten hulk through a perilous sea. I had to write a "Monthly Retrospect of Public Affairs," in which the first necessity was caution. For a year or more all "Public Affairs" were seething in a witch's cauldron, with the scum uppermost. I had to write, here and elsewhere, about the Queen's trial. I said truly, "We have restrained ourselves from the expression, almost from the admission, of any decided conviction in this matter." But not the less did I feel that Caroline of Brunswick was an injured wife, although I could not doubt that she was a depraved woman. Why, I asked of my brother-editor, was Lord Exmouth, unused to take part in politics, so marked in his manifestation of a hostile feeling towards the Queen? "We saw and heard too much in the *Caledonia* of what was passing on the Italian shores. The lady came one day on board, and was received with all the honours due to her rank. She dined at the Admiral's table, and left an impression that will never be forgotten. Her talk was of such a nature that Lord Exmouth ordered the midshipman to leave the cabin."

If much of the wide domain of domestic politics was tabooed to us, there was a region where we could "expatiate free," in advocating certain social improvements of whose efficacy no one now doubts. The doubters and the adversaries of reforms which the people might effect themselves were then a majority. An excellent friend of my youth, who had established an extensive practice as a surgeon in London —John Cole—wrote several papers of this nature. An admirable article on "Cleanliness and Ventilation" suggests how little had been accomplished twenty years before the days of Arnott, and Kay, and Southwood Smith, and Chadwick. My friend told a great moral truth when he said, "If men are once so far overtaken by sloth or poverty as to submit unresistingly to the utter destitution of comfort that attends excessive dirtiness, all sense of shame will soon be lost, and with it all disposition to exertion." But London then, and most other great towns, had a very insufficient supply of water for the preservation of cleanliness. He spoke of the most expensive of luxuries when he talked of the advantages of a tepid bath once a week. The young men and women of the present day may incline to believe that a medical practitioner was giving very unnecessary advice, suited only to the darkest ages, when he wrote, "Those who can be brought to venture on *so unheard of a thing* as to wash the whole of their bodies, will generally be induced to repeat the experiment from the comfort it affords." The household sages of the last years of George III. had heard that there was "Death in the Pot;" and they were perfectly satisfied that there was Death in the Bath, as a domestic institution. It is related by Miss Martineau that an ancient dame, who was taken suddenly ill, having been recommended to put her feet in warm water, exclaimed, "I've not wet my feet for thretty years! I once had a daughter who was persuaded to wash her feet, and who died afterwards. Nobody can prove that she would have died if she had not washed her feet." When Mr. Cole was treating of Ventilation and Cleanliness, he was setting forth some of the then neglected "modern instances" of scientific discovery which have come to be popular "wise saws." Yet it is still necessary to preach from this text: "In the construction of houses for the poor, the great object of ventilation has too generally been overlooked." I had myself seen some of the miseries of badly-situated dwellings. There was a memorable flood at Eton, and the lower parts of Windsor, in the December of 1821; Eton was traversed in boats. Provisions were taken in at the windows by the unfortunate persons in the upper rooms of many a house. Looking from the North Terrace, "the expanse below of mead and grove" was one vast lake. In "Hints to the Cottager on the Choice of a Dwelling," I wrote, "There are many dangerous fevers which are produced by the vicinity of stagnant waters; and houses which, from their site, are constantly damp, expose those who inhabit them to rheumatism, croup, ague, and other painful disorders. The same effects are produced by dwelling-houses which are subject to occasional inundations of rivers. We have lately seen the misery which is produced by such a circumstance; and are quite sure that none would be subject to the visits of a flood if they could possibly avoid it. To be driven in cold weather from the accustomed fireside; to shiver in bed-rooms which have probably no grate; to have two or three feet of water running through the lower part of the house, destroying many things and injuring more; and at last, when the inundation ceases, to find the whole dwelling damp and miserable for several weeks;—this is a visitation which no one would willingly seek."

I have now been separated for nearly forty years from the home of my youth and my early manhood. When I trace in various faithful records the evidence of my intense local atachment to Windsor, I wonder how I ever endured this separation. In "The Plain Englishman" I wrote a series of simple Tales. It is long since I looked at them; but now I am struck with the local colour which nearly all of them exhibit. There are personal recollections of a deeper character associated with "The Plain Englishman." During the summer and autumn of its first year I occupied a cottage on the bank of the Thames. In the winter I was settled in a house to me most interesting in its connexion with the dim antiquity of the Castle. Its entrance was in the smaller cloisters to the north of St. George's Chapel, but its principal rooms were over the great Cloister on the east of the Chapel. I wrote here in the most charming of studies. The organ swell, the choral harmonies, more solemn in their indistinctness, often made me pause at my work and throw down my pen, to surrender my thoughts to the spiritual charm. The ceiling of this antique room was of the most exquisite carving—so beautiful that George Cattermole, then a young man doing task-work for John Britton, was my guest for a day or two, that he might preserve it in one of his charming architectural drawings. There is no fear now of its destruction, for this suite of rooms forms part of the Chapter-House of the College of Windsor. In 1821, I rented this unique dwelling of the Dean and Canons. Beautiful it was, but the want of free air made it unfit for healthful existence. Here we had a daughter born; here we lost a son. My dear friend Matthew Davenport Hill here passed some happy hours with us at Christmas. Before Easter I had to record "My First Grief." I was then, as I am now, as little disposed as Coriolanus was, to show my wounds in the market-place; but my feelings overflowed into a paper which I printed in "The Plain Englishman." Two sentences will be sufficient to mark this passage in my life. "Until I had reached my thirtieth year I had known nothing of what I can properly term sorrow. The evils of mortality had not begun to come home to me. The wings of the destroying angel had rested upon the dwellings of my neighbours; but death had never yet crossed my threshold, and sickness seldom. I had heard the voice of misery like the mutterings of a distant storm; but the thunder had not yet burst over my head—I had not covered my eyes from the passing lightning." . . . . "I now knew, for the first time, what it is to have death about our hearths. The excitement of hope and fear in a moment passes away; and the contest between feeling and reason begins, with its alternation of passion and listlessness. It is some time before the image of death gets possession of the mind. We sleep, perchance, amidst a feverish dream of gloomy and indistinct remembrances. The object of our grief, it may be, has seemed to us present, in health and animation. We wake in a struggle between the shadowy and the real world; and we require an effort of the intellect to believe that the earthly part of the being we have loved is no more than a clod of the valley."

"The Plain Englishman" was closed, upon the completion of the third volume, in December, 1822. I may incidentally mention, as a curious fact, that the title of one of our articles of that year anticipated the identical name of the Society which, in 1827, was enabled to accomplish much that I had dreamt of (and a great deal more), in my beginnings of Popular Literature. That paper was headed, "DIFFUSION OF USEFUL KNOWLEDGE."*

* Plain Englishman, vol. iii., p. 277.

CHAPTER VII.

N the 13th of June, 1820, I received an offer, conveyed to me in confidence by my zealous friend Mr. Locker, to become the Editor and part Proprietor of a London Weekly Paper, "The Guardian." The tone of my political opinions had been collected from the "Retrospect of Public Affairs" in "The Plain Englishman." The violence of political agitation appeared to be fast subsiding. Some of the physical-force Reformers were in prison. The miscreants who had contemplated assassination as a cure for political evils were hanged. There was only one chance of a convulsion. The Queen, contrary to all reasonable expectation, had landed at Dover, and on the 6th of June had entered London amidst the shouts of thousands. On that evening a Message from the King was presented to the Lords and Commons, and a green bag was laid on the table of each House, containing papers respecting the conduct of Her Majesty when abroad, which the King had thought fit to communicate to Parliament. When I entered upon my new editorial duties at the end of the month, the hope was at an end which wise men of all parties had entertained, that a compromise would avert the scandal and danger of a public inquiry. Through July, after the Secret Committee of the House of Lords had made its Report, and a Bill of Pains and Penalties was read

a first time, the mob excitement of London was such as few had before witnessed. When the Queen took up her residence at Brandenburgh House on the 3rd of August, there began a series of processions, from the extreme East to the extreme West, that manifested at once the energy and the folly of democracy in its wildest hour of excitement. Often riding to Windsor have I been detained by the impossibility of passing through an army of working men, with bands, and banners, and placards, headed by deputations of their several committees with wands of office—all terribly in earnest—all perfectly convinced of the Queen's immaculate purity—all resolved that oppression should not triumph—a peaceful multitude, but one that in any other country would have seemed the herald, if not the manifestation, of Revolution. In the fierce battle of journalism which was then fought throughout the year, I was not called upon for a declaration of extreme opinions. If such a course had been insisted upon I should have resigned my charge. I wrote to my co-proprietor, when it was suggested that a stronger tone ought to be adopted with regard to the Queen, "I can only say that I feel confident that the language of moderation ought to be most aimed at, as the likeliest to prevent the existing ferment increasing into a state of perpetual division and anarchy." This was written at the end of November; when, although the Government had terminated this unhappy contest, the political animosities that had grown up with it were raging in a flood of personality such as had never before disgraced the Press of England. The "Guardian" had not flourished under the gross mismanagement of its early career, nor under my too conscientious interpretation of the duties of a journalist. I became its sole proprietor upon easy terms. Gladly did I leave the rough work of party to *John Bull*, which, established in December, 1820, soon obtained an influence which was earned by something more than its cleverness. A year after, in both the papers which I then conducted, I expressed my opinion of the danger and disgrace of the prevailing tone of the "public instructors." This opinion is perhaps worth transcribing, as affording a contrast between the London newspapers of 1821—with a fourpenny stamp, paying a duty of 3*s.* 6*d.* on every advertisement, printed on heavily-taxed paper, hemmed round by all imaginable safeguards against libel—and the newspapers of 1863, with no stamp whatever and no advertisement-duty, paying no tax upon paper, fettered by no securities; between the London newspapers whose aggregate circulation in one week was about a quarter of a million, and the newspapers that upon a moderate estimate may be held to circulate five millions weekly. In the country newspapers the contrast is perhaps still greater. Much as I believed in the regenerating power of the Press, I could scarcely have imagined that some distant age of cheapness would have been an age when the impure, seditious, violent, intolerant, and libellous writer would have become a rare exception amongst journalists. Nevertheless, I rightly considered that out of the increase of knowledge amongst the people would arise a better spirit of journalism; which, in its turn, would become one of the most efficient instruments of education.

Thus I wrote in 1821: "A general view of the influence of the Press would lead us to judge that very much of that influence is injurious to the safety of the Government; opposed to the happiness of the people; and destructive of that real freedom of thought and writing upon which the glory and prosperity of England have been built. But we believe that a great deal of the evil will cure itself. It is the half-knowledge of the people that has created the host of ephemeral writers who address themselves to the popular passions. If the firmness of the Government, and, what is better, the good sense of the upper and middle classes who have property at stake, can succeed for a few years in preserving tranquillity, the ignorant disseminators of sedition and discontent will be beaten out of the field by opponents of better principles, who will direct the secret of popular writing to a useful and a righteous purpose. But this change in the temper of the multitude is not to be effected by borrowing the dirty weapons of those who are engaged in stimulating them to acts of atrocity. It is not to be effected by raking up scandalous stories against the demagogues of a faction—by penetrating into the recesses of private life to drag forth the evidence of a forgotten fault or an expiated folly—by pouring forth the coarsest abuse against the principles and practice of eminent men of adverse opinions, with a blind and levelling fury. There is a revolutionary temper in such ultra-publications which degrades the cause it affects to support, and furnishes an example to the dangerous doctrines it pretends to resist. *The Black Dwarf* and *John Bull* are scions from the same stock. The dictates of interest only have made the one a pander to the passions of the little vulgar; the other, a hunter of scandal for the vulgar great."

It was time to speak out when a Society had started up to do the work of a Censorship, in the blindest fashion of ultra-loyal partisanship. In March, 1821, the "Constitutional Association" was formed, for the purpose of prosecuting printers and publishers who went beyond what they deemed the proper bounds of political discussion. This despicable Association—despicable, however supported by rank and wealth—saw no mischief in the gross libels of one set of writers who professed to be the friends of the Government, but instituted the most reckless prosecutions against "liberal" newspapers. The term "liberal" had then begun to mark a certain set of opinions which had outgrown their former title of "jacobinical." This Association acquired the name of "The Bridge Street Gang." After three or four months of a hateful existence—denounced in Parliament—execrated by every man who had inherited a spark of Milton's zeal for "the Liberty of Unlicensed Printing" — this Association was prosecuted for oppression and extortion. The grand jury found a true bill against its members. They were acquitted upon their trial; but practices were disclosed which showed how dangerous it was for a crafty attorney and a knot of fanatical politicians to play at attorney-generalship. The true public of this country was getting as sick of outrageous Loyalty as of desperate Radicalism.

Looking around me at the Newspaper Press of London, I saw very few papers that attempted to combine the literary and the political character. John Hunt was still the editor of "The Examiner;" but his brother Leigh, who had raised the critical department of the paper to the highest eminence might well be tired of newspaper occupation, and was meditating the unfortunate union with Byron in "The Liberal." John Hunt, in May, 1821, was prosecuted for a libel on the House of Commons, and was sentenced to two years' imprisonment. "The Champion," "The News," and one or two others, had literary pretensions, but they made their criticism little more than a vehicle for their politics. I fancied there was an opening for a paper that, giving a temperate support to the Government, might deal with Literature in a spirit of impartiality. I panted for a region of pure air and clear skies, lifted out of the heat and fever of the plains, where public writers lost all natural freedom and vigour in a constant round of controversial dram-drinking.

I have the merit, humble as it may be, of having created a new department of Newspaper Literature. On the 3rd of March, 1821, "The Guardian" had the first of a series of articles, regularly continued month by month, entitled "Magazine-Day." This paper opens with a glimpse of "The Row," forty-two years since. What changes have come over the then narrow world of Magazines! Periodical writing had then a few able workmen, and some, rather more numerous, of the "Ned Purdon" school. But now! Let me copy from this paper a few sentences of what then struck me as one of the remarkable indications of a new "Reading Age," upon which age Coleridge made some lumbering jokes:—"There is no bustle, to our minds, half so agreeable as the bustle of Paternoster Row on the last day of the month. This is Magazine Day—the most important division in the life of a bookseller's collector; as important as settling day to the stock-broker, or quarter-day to the annuitant. We delight, on these memorable mornings, to lounge through the narrow approaches of Ave-Maria or Warwick Lanes, and then to make a dead stop in the Paradise of Publishers—to hear the hum of the great hive of literature—to see its bees going forth in search of, or returning with, their spoils. As the dusky porter, catching the rapid step of the periodical lore which he bears, brushes past us, we delight to speculate upon the component parts of his burden—to estimate the relative proportions of *Blackwoods* and *Baldwins*, of *Monthlies* (*Old* and *New*), of *Gentleman's* and *Ladies'*, of *Belle Assemblées* and *Evangelicals*. It is a special pleasure to us to dive into some of the celebrated *penetralia* of the Row, and there learn to estimate the merits of these monthly candidates for applause, not by the beauty of their styles, but by the bulk of their heaps." I then described how, by these walks, I obtained possession of half a dozen periodicals, and was able to taste the fruit, not before it was ripe, but before it was brought into the market. I had long thought, I said, of turning this passion to account; and at length resolved to give my readers some of the chit-chat of Magazine Day. "With a fearless hand we will twitch your mantles, blue, or drab, or green, ye

'Abstract and brief chronicles of the time.'

Your days of dulness are overpast. Ye are no longer the reversionary property of the pastrycook and the trunk-maker. Ye are well worth a regular monthly notice; aye, and much better worth than many a lumbering quarto." This article made a stir in "The Trade," and before next Magazine Day, these "squires of the moon's body" trooped into my office without giving me the trouble of a journey to Paternoster Row.

The new era of Magazines may be said to have commenced in 1817. In that year "Blackwood's Edinburgh Magazine" startled the London publishers into a conviction that for a new generation of readers more attractive fare might be provided than at some of the old established *restaurateurs*, whose dishes were neither light, nor elegant, nor altogether wholesome. When Blackwood was started—apparently without any very correct knowledge that something was wanted in periodical literature beyond political bitterness—the old magazines and their new rivals had gone on without much deviation from the hackneyed paths in which they had first walked. The possibility was then scarcely conceived that they could afford to pay handsomely for contributions; and thus their chief dependence was upon their gratuitous correspondence. They were the vehicles for the communication to the world of all sorts of opinions, theological, moral, political, and antiquarian. They were the tablets upon which the retired scholar or the active citizen might equally inscribe their theories or their observations, in a familiar and unpretending style; and they at once kept alive the intelligence of their own generation, and formed valuable records for succeeding eras. In one magazine, "The Gentleman's," which had lived the most respectable of existences for nine decades, the antiquarians stoutly held their own. In its volumes from 1731 there is more valuable "tombstone information" to be found than in any other work in our language; and this, to speak truly, is not knowledge to be despised. The honest printer of St. John's

Gate, of whom Johnson said that he scarcely ever looked out of the window without a view to the improvement of his magazine, had seen the births and the deaths of many rivals. There was a "London" to enter the lists against him when the booksellers had discovered the value of this new lode in the mine of literature. There was a "Monthly." There was a "Ladies'." The old names were supposed to retain their old influences; and so at the time of my "Magazine Day" there was a "Monthly," and there was a "New Monthly;" there was a "London," and there was a "Ladies'." Mr. Phillips, afterwards Sir Richard, had revived the "Monthly" in 1796, pretty much upon the ancient "correspondence" principle. The "New Monthly Magazine and Universal Register" had scarcely more ambitious pretensions, when set up in 1814. The "London," of all the metropolitan magazines, was the most distinguished for its literary excellence. It had been re-established in 1820 by Mr. Robert Baldwin, and was as often called "Baldwin," as the Edinburgh Magazine was called "Blackwood." A controversy between the two leading Miscellanies, conducted with that bitterness on both sides which was an evil characteristic of the periodical literature of those days,—when writers of all grades readily plunged into the waters of strife and there wallowed like the heroes of "The Dunciad" in Fleet Ditch—led to the fatal catastrophe of the death in a duel of Mr. John Scott, the amiable and accomplished editor of the "London." I knew not Mr. Scott; but in common with all who felt that the pistol was the worst arbiter of differences, literary or political, I deeply grieved for such an end of his career, in which he had in various ways shed a lustre upon journalism.

In my first article of "Magazine Day," I said, "Looking at the melancholy circumstances under which the present "London" has been brought out, we are surprised that there is so much excellent matter in it; and argue thence that the fatal termination of a foolish affair will not greatly impair the future gratification of the public in this very agreeable miscellany."

The "Blackwood" of this period had attained a reputation which made all successful rivalry very difficult. "Nothing," says Mrs. Gordon, "was left undone to spread the fame and fear of Blackwood." The indefatigable publisher, who, as we now learn, was its real editor, was as careful to propitiate a favourable opinion of his "Maga" amongst periodical writers who admired its talent, as its great supporters, Wilson and Lockhart, were ever ready for a warfare in which no quarter was given or expected. It was a surprise to me when I received from the dreaded William Blackwood a letter of thanks for "your kind and early notices of my magazine." Still more was I surprised when he wrote, "Permit me to return you the author's and my own best thanks for your splendid critique upon 'Valerius.' Your opinion (which was the first given upon the work) seems to be fully confirmed by the public voice." Was this the style, I thought, in which it was necessary for a publisher to administer small doses of flattery to periodical critics, however humble, for what ought only to be considered an act of justice? In after years, occasionally coming across the cold and proud author of "Valerius," when he had become Editor of the "Quarterly Review," I have thought of "the author's best thanks," &c.; and have suspected that the ultra-courteous phrase was a mere *façon de parler* of the skilful charioteer who could show such a high-mettled racer in his team. Of Professor Wilson I could readily have believed that any cordial acknowledgment of a supposed courtesy would be in accordance with his genial nature. In later years, he and I may be judged to have adopted very different opinions upon public questions, but his hand of kindness was always held out to me; and in his social hour, when I first knew him, and in those days when sorrow and sadness had impaired but not subdued the elasticity of his nature, I had a confirmation of my belief, established in many instances before and since, that a political partisan and satirist may have the warmest heart and be capable of the truest friendship.

In "Blackwood" at this time was finished "The Ayrshire Legatees," in which Galt first opened his rich vein of observation and humour. Had that publishing economy of the present day been then fully established, which consists in making a work of fiction do double service, originally as a series of magazine papers and then as a complete work, Galt would have spread his next venture over a dozen numbers of the closely printed pages that had rendered Buchanan's head so familiar to the Southern public, and then have made his more dignified appearance. The canny publisher seems to have had some doubts of our metropolitan tastes, for he writes to the editor of 'The Guardian:"—"With this you will receive a very singular book, which I shall publish in a few days, 'Annals of the Parish.' How it may be liked in England I cannot exactly say; but I am sure it will be highly relished by all

Scotsmen, because the sketches of Scottish country life are so true to nature." Do any of the younger readers of the present day care to look into a book whose chief merit is that it is "so true to nature?" Do they care to turn to that storehouse of quiet humour, "Sir Andrew Wylie, of that ilk," which came in rapid succession? Perhaps some of my Georgian-era contemporaries who are sick of sensation novels, may turn again to what afforded them delight forty years ago. Proud as he was of the men of genius that he had gathered around him, Mr. Blackwood could not forego his political antipathies; and, somewhat too confidently, fancied that the "able editor" whom he flattered would partake them. He wrote, "As the magazine has been so much attacked and misrepresented by the Whig and Radical press, I would be particularly obliged to you if you could notice the article on 'The Personalities of the Whigs.'" I did notice it in these words: "The letter on 'The Personalities of the Whigs' is forcible, and convincing enough—to a partizan. The object of the writer is to prove that the Whigs commenced this species of warfare, and that those opposed to their principles have a right to bring the same weapons into the field which their enemies have so long been exclusively permitted to employ. For our own parts, we had rather that political contests were conducted according to the usual rules of honourable warfare; but if one party use catamarans and infernal machines, it would be hard to restrict the other to simple steel and gunpowder."

The new facilities of communication were beginning to tell upon the commerce of Literature as upon all other commerce. Railroads were yet ten years off in an undreamt-of future. But in 1821 the potent agency of steam-packets was breaking down the difference between Paternoster Row and Princes Street. On the 28th of September I was reading "Blackwood," when the magazines of our metropolis were just getting on their outer garments; while their northern brethren were quietly reposing, in well arranged heaps, in our southern warehouses, perfectly sleek and dry, after a happy voyage of sixty hours. This new condition upon which competition was to be carried on made the London publishers more solicitous for the excellence, rather than the cheap cost, of their periodical offerings to a public that had begun to be clamorous for novelties, and somewhat more critical than a previous generation. Unmoved amidst the general rivalry was that staid and sober brown-coated companion of our forefathers, who scorned the fluctuations of fashion, and was still the *Gentleman* of the days of Pulteney and Walpole. His costume was preserved as unchangeably as that of the statue of George the Second in Leicester Square. He still gloried in being one of the staunchest cocked hats of the Society of Antiquaries; knew nothing of Wellington boots or Cossack trousers; dined at one o'clock; and if he could have been persuaded to go to the play, would have been at the pit-door at five, as in his spring-time. It would have puzzled the dandyism of the days of George the Fourth and Brummell to have found Mr. Urban an endurable companion; but he was eminently respectable; and no magazine critic could honestly pass over this excellent hermit of modern literature. One of his old companions, "The European," was smartening up. Mr. Colburn, not to be left behind in the periodical race, had, in 1821, engaged Campbell to be the avowed editor of "The New Monthly Magazine and Literary Journal." Campbell's own lectures on poetry were elegant and dull. His contributors had not caught the spirit of liveliness by which even the old stock of ideas could be successfully reproduced. The poet made, as we then thought, a mistake in proclaiming his acceptance of the editorial office. There is a good deal to be argued for and against anonymous editorship and anonymous contributorship. We then said, and we are not quite sure that we were wrong —"His power of selection from the contributions of his assistants must be fettered, and the freedom and boldness of his own opinions encumbered, by a thousand personal considerations, which ought not to weigh, and would not have weighed, a feather in the scale, had he preserved that best of all forms of government in periodical literature—a secret despotism."

After the unhappy death of John Scott, the "London" had passed from Mr. Baldwin into the hands of Messrs. Taylor and Hessey. These were its palmy days—the days of Lamb and De Quincey; of John Hamilton Reynolds; of Thomas Hood, whose first introduction to the literary world was that of its sub-editor. I wrote, in September, 1821: "We never read anything more deeply interesting than the 'Confessions of an English Opium-Eater.' We can put implicit faith in them. They have all the circumstantial sincerity of Defoe. They are written in a fine flowing style, in which the author is perfectly forgotten." After the publication of two articles on the Pleasures and Pains of Opium, the majority of their readers doubted the reality of these Confessions. The author, in a letter to the editor of the magazine, declared that the narrative contained a faithful statement of his own experience as an Opium-Eater, drawn up with entire simplicity, except in some trifling deviations of dates and suppression of names which circumstances had rendered it expedient should not be published. I had ample opportunities, a few years after, of knowing how unexaggerated were Mr. De Quincey's statements of his extraordinary power of taking opium, injurious indeed to his health, but without any perceptible deterioration of his wonderful intellect. Of "Elia" I was almost extravagant in my admiration. I sometimes ventured upon verse in my "Magazine Day," and thus I wrote, in 1822, after speaking dispraisingly of some articles:

"But Elia, Elia, he is half divine,
Fragrant as woodbines in the evening sun,
Fresh as the jasmines round his porch that twine,
Happy as school-boy when his task is done,
And simple as the village-maid that sings
Her bubbling song of old forgotten things."

I can scarcely understand De Quincey when he says of Charles Lamb, and particularly of his delightful prose essays under the signature of Elia, that "he ranks amongst writers whose works are destined to be for ever unpopular, and yet for ever interesting; interesting, moreover, by means of those very qualities which guarantee their non-popularity" (De Quincey's *Works*, 1st edit., Leaders in Literature, p. 109). If De Quincey be right, is popularity worth having?

My life, during the period of my London editorship was one of very pleasurable excitement. My solitary musings, my morbid fancies, had reached their term. I had ample occupation—perhaps too much for tranquil thought. We had a branch-office of our newspaper at Aylesbury, where the last page of "The Bucks Gazette" was printed, whilst three pages were supplied by the printed sheets of "The Windsor Express." To despatch these sheets by a special conveyance thirty miles, so as to be in time for the due appearance of the secondary paper, required careful organization. This I had to accomplish on a Saturday morning, leaving my Windsor paper in a state fit for publication. To ride up to London, or to mount one of the long coaches in the afternoon, so as to be at the "Guardian" office for new work, was my next exertion. The day had perhaps brought forth fresh aspects of political affairs. Often, before writing my leader, have I discussed the great topics of the hour with two valued friends, whose opinions were not entirely in accordance with my own. Mounted upon stools at my editorial desk, have Matthew Davenport Hill and John Steer (who was my sub-editor), argued with me about the delinquencies and short-comings of the Government, the necessity of Parliamentary Reform, the degradation of England in all matters of foreign policy. My work done, we have gladly foregone all disputation, to place ourselves under the genial presidency of the worthy immortalized by Tennyson—"the waiter at the Cock." In the lapse of time we gradually grew nearer in our opinions. The world was changing. The miserable convulsion on the subject of the Queen was terminated by her death. Lord Castlereagh was no more, carrying with him a good deal of undeserved obloquy. Canning was come back to power. He was to inaugurate a new era of liberty for the nations. I had access to one who was at that time Canning's political adherent upon the subject of Catholic Emancipation, and that of the pretensions of a Congress to decide upon the destinies of Europe. Mr. John Wilson Croker was always ready to give me his opinions, as I believed, honestly. They were to a great extent liberal, as liberalism was then understood by those opposed to extreme views. He was always glad to gossip upon subjects of literature, and he earnestly counselled me to settle in London as a publisher. I am bound to say, advisedly, that I think his character has been misrepresented ; and that the "Rigby" of "Coningsby" is an ebullition of personal spite.

My occupation as the editor of a literary paper necessarily made me somewhat familiar with the aspects of the Publishing Trade of London. I gradually looked at the great establishments and the small, somewhat more closely, through my vague desire to find a place amongst them. There was a new world all before me "where to choose," not my "place of rest," but my sphere of action. Let me glance back at my rough survey of this *terra incognita*.

Paternoster Row, and the immediate neighbourhood of St. Paul's Churchyard and Ave-Maria Lane, were the principal seats of the wholesale book-trade. At the beginning of the century, according to Mr. Britton, "most of the tradesmen attended to their respective shops, and dwelt in the upper part of their houses." He had lived to see "the heads of many of the large establishments visit their counting-houses only for a few hours in the day, and leave the working part to junior partners, clerks, and apprentices." The greater number of city booksellers did not carry on the business of publisher *pur et simple.* They were factors of books for the London collectors; they were the agents of the country booksellers; they almost all were shareholders of what were called Chapter Books, from the business concerning them being conducted at the Chapter Coffee House. If we open a book of fifty years ago, which had become a standard work in its frequent reprints, we find the names of twelve or twenty or even more booksellers on the title-page. The copyright had probably long expired. But these shareholders, who formed a Limited Liability Company (not registered), were considered as the only legitimate dealers, and their editions the only genuine ones. It was long before their monopoly was broken up by a few daring adventurers who defied these banded hosts, and were ready to pounce upon an expired copyright before it could be appropriated by the large and small potentates who had parcelled out the realms of print, with absolute exclusiveness, in the good times before Innovation. Trade Sales, as they were called, were frequent and general amongst the primitive race of booksellers; at which sales these share-books were sold, amongst other wares, to the best bidders. The company was not attracted by elegant banquets, such as those at which, in later times, I have assisted as a guest and as a host. There was a plain dinner of substantial beef and mutton, which the bookseller ordered at an adjacent tavern, directing what dishes should be provided to meet the number of his expected guests. I have heard an illustrative anecdote—I do not vouch for its truth—of one of the respectable firm that lived under the sign of the Bible and Crown. In the midst of family prayer he suddenly paused, and exclaimed, "John, go and tell Higgins to make another marrow-pudding."

The "legitimate" trade had its code of "protection," on which it had reposed since the days of the Tonsons and Lintots. Its system of associating many shareholders in the production and sale of an established work kept up its price. The retailers were only allowed to purchase of the wholesale houses upon certain conditions, which had the effect of making it difficult, if not impossible, for the private purchaser to obtain a book under the sum advertised. No publisher had discovered that it was to his interest that the profit of the middle-man should be small, so that a book should be vended at the cheapest rate. The very notion of cheap books stank in the nostrils, not only of the ancient magnates of the East, but of the new potentates of the West. For a new work which involved the purchase of copyright, it was the established rule that the wealthy few, to whom price was not a consideration, were alone to be depended upon for the remuneration of the author and the first profit of the publisher. The proud quarto, with a rivulet of text meandering through a wide plain of margin, was the "decus et tutamen" of the Row and of Albemarle Street.* Conduit Street now and then vied in this grandiosity; but more commonly sent forth legions of octavos, translated from the French with a rapidity that was not very careful about correctness or elegance

* The Albemarle Street of Mr. Murray is still famous. The Conduit Street of Mr. Colburn is no longer renowned.

—qualities which were not contemplated in the estimate of the literary cost. These were the books whose cheapness was deceptive, like the books issued by the Number-publishers. One of these successful tradesmen, who, although he became Lord Mayor, was once "Thomas" the porter in an old concern for the production of the dearest books in folio—such as we may still find amongst the heir-looms of a humble family in some remote village—was never solicitous to buy an author; his great object was to buy "a ground." "A ground" was like a milk-walk—there were a body of customers to be transferred to the new capitalist. He was once tempted into the employment of original authorship. When his press one day stood still for want of a sufficient supply of the commodity for which he had indiscreetly bargained, he exclaimed, "Give me dead authors!—they never keep you waiting for copy."

The publishers of classical books were not numerous. Amongst the most celebrated was Richard Priestley, who undertook many reprints of Greek and Roman authors and ponderous lexicons. His career was not a successful one. In 1830, I occupied for the summer a cottage near Hampstead. My landlord, who had become rich by a bequest, had been a sheriff's officer. "Did you know poor Dick Priestley?" he said. "He was a good fellow. I had him often under my lock. We were great friends; and after I left my calling I lent him a couple of thousand." Was a sentimental friendship ever before or since formed under circumstances so unromantic? Amongst the new class of publishers there were several whose republications of standard works were as beautiful as they were cheap. The names of Major and

Pickering are still deservedly in repute. But till Constable started his "Miscellany," in 1827, no one had thought it possible that an original work could be produced in the first instance at the price of the humblest reprint. His three-and-sixpenny volumes, and his grand talk of "a million of buyers," made the publishing world of London believe that the mighty autocrat of Edinburgh literature had gone "daft." And so the Row sneered, and persevered in its old system of fourteen-shilling octavos and two-guinea quartos. The Circulating Library was scarcely then an institution to be depended upon for the purchase of a large impression, even of the most popular Novels. Travels and Memoirs rarely then found a place on the shelves of which fiction had long claimed the exclusive occupation. There were Book-Clubs, whose members aspired to be patrons of a more solid literature; but they were far from universal. All circumstances considered, it was extremely difficult for one like myself, very imperfectly acquainted with the Trade, to form a correct estimate of what number of a new book he might venture to print. Caution and common-sense might save inexperience from ridiculous ventures, such as had ruined many who fancied there were no blanks in that tempting lottery. I had known an unhappy man, who had come into the possession of a considerable fortune, rush into the wildest dealings with literary schemers, who regarded him as a whale cast upon the shore, to be cut up as speedily as possible. Poor fellow! he was always ready to buy—he would even buy a title-page, the more absurd the more attractive. "Mumbo Jumbo," in the egg, was held by him cheap at a few hundreds. I looked upon his fate as a warning. But yet I could not resist the temptation to enter upon a career of usefulness, in which there was reputation, and possible wealth, to be won by diligence and integrity. Not to be embarrassed with conflicting occupations, I sold my pet "Guardian" at the end of 1822, and in the season of 1823 I had taken my position in Pall Mall East.

CHAPTER VIII.

THE Etonians of 1819 had set on foot a "College Magazine," which was circulated in manuscript amongst a favoured circle of schoolfellows. At the office of "The Windsor and Eton Express" we printed for them a selection from their contributions, which was entitled "The Poetry of the College Magazine." As this pamphlet came under my view in its course through the press, I was much struck by the exceeding beauty of some of these compositions—striking in themselves, but more remarkable as the productions of young men, who seemed to have escaped from the classical trammels of the "Musæ Etonenses" to wear a modern English garb with grace and freedom. Amongst the most remarkable of these poems were "The Hall of my Fathers" and "My Brother's Grave." These were reprinted in the more ambitious work which grew out of the manuscript periodical.

In the latter half of September, 1820, the Eton vacation was at an end. The proceedings against the Queen had been suspended till the 3rd of October. The evidence to support the Bill of Pains and Penalties had been concluded. Gladly did I hail the prospect of some pleasant occupation—some relief from the routine of the filthy journalism of that time—when, arriving from London, I found two youths waiting for me at my cottage by the side of the Thames, who proposed to me to print and publish an Eton Miscellany. The one was Walter Blunt, the other Winthrop Mackworth Praed. There was nothing to discuss beyond the estimate for printing; for if the magazine did not pay its expenses the deficiency was to be met by a subscription. It was not to be a weekly essay, such as "The Microcosm," but a magazine of considerable size, that might aspire to take its place amongst the best of the monthly periodicals. On the 1st of November appeared "The Etonian," No. I.

The remembrance of my intercourse with the two youthful editors, and with a few of their contributors, takes me back to a delightful passage of my working life. I have before me the bright, earnest, happy face of Mr. Blunt, who took a manifest delight in doing the editorial drudgery. The worst proofs (for in the haste unavoidable in periodical literature he would sometimes catch hold of a proof *unread*) never disturbed the serenity of his temper. To him it seemed a real happiness to stand at a desk in the composing-room, and laugh over the blunders which others more experienced in the editorial craft would have raved at as stupidity unbearable. In our printing-office there was a most intelligent overseer and reader, who soon grew into favour with the editors, one of whom did not forget, after forty years had passed, the man who delighted to anticipate their wishes. The Rev. Mr. Blunt, in a letter full of his wonted kindliness, invited me, in 1859, to his house, and thus recalled the old days: "The fact of my writing this from a sofa, with gout in both legs, bespeaks the lapse of time since I used to skurry up to Windsor to M'Kechnie, with the proofs of 'The Etonian.'" Mr. Praed came to the printing-office less frequently. But during the ten months of the life of this Miscellany—which his own productions were chiefly instrumental in raising to an eminence never before attained by schoolboy genius similarly exerted—I was more and more astonished by the unbounded fertility of his mind and the readiness of his resources. He wrote under the signature of "Peregrine Courtenay," the President of "The King of Clubs," by whose members the magazine was assumed to be conducted. The character of Peregrine Courtenay, given in "An Account of the Proceedings which led to the Publication of the 'Etonian,'" furnishes no satisfactory idea of the youthful Winthrop Mackworth Praed, when he is described as one "possessed of sound good sense, rather than of brilliance of genius." His "general acquirements and universal information" are fitly recorded, as well as his acquaintance with "the world at large." But the kindness that lurks under sarcasm; the wisdom that wears the mask of fun; the half-melancholy that is veiled by levity;—these qualities very soon struck me as far out of the ordinary indications of precocious talent.

It is not easy to separate my recollections of the Praed of Eton from those of the Praed of Cambridge. The Etonian of 1820 was natural and unaffected in his ordinary talk; neither shy nor presuming; proud, without a tinge of vanity; somewhat reserved, but ever courteous; giving few indications of the susceptibility of the poet, but ample evidence of the laughing satirist; a pale and slight youth, who had looked upon the aspects of society with the keen perception of a clever manhood; one who had, moreover, seen in human life something more than follies to be ridiculed by the gay jest or scouted by the sarcastic sneer. I had many opportunities of studying his complex character. His writings then, especially his poems, occasionally exhibited that remarkable union of pathos with wit and humour which attested the originality of his genius, as it was subsequently developed in maturer efforts. In these blended qualities a superficial inquirer might conclude that he was an imitator of Hood. But Hood had written nothing that indicated his future greatness, when Praed was pouring forth verse beneath whose gaiety and quaintness might be traced the characteristics which his friend Mr. Moultrie describes as the peculiar attributes of his nature—

> "drawing off intrusive eyes
> From that intensity of human love
> And that most deep and tender sympathy
> Close guarded in the chambers of his heart."
>
> *The Dream of Life.*

I soon had many opportunities of observing the Praed of Eton in other relations than those of our business intercourse. Whilst the first number of "The Etonian" was growing into shape, I often breakfasted with the two young editors in Mr. Blunt's room out of the College bounds; it being then the practice, as all familiar with Eton know, for the scholars of the foundation to get a breakfast as they best could from their own means, or go without. There were sometimes three or four at this social meal. I had perhaps been in the House of Lords, attending the Queen's trial on the previous afternoon; and could tell them something of the withering eloquence of Brougham and the searching subtlety of Copley. Praed took far more than a schoolboy's interest in the questions of the day, and his sly or sharp commentary would show how well he understood them. To me it was a rare pleasure to have an occasional companionship with these fresh young men, so fearless in the expression of their opinions; so frank in the display of their sympathies or antipathies; full of the best associations of ancient learning without a particle of pedantry; quizzing each other with the most perfect good temper; passing rapidly from an occasional argument of mock solemnity to talk of their theatre in Datchet Lane, and "the best bat in the school"—these blithe spirits, some of whom, in after years, might be wrangling at Nisi Prius, or struggling in the muddy waters of party politics. Upon these Eton days Praed looked lovingly back in verses which he wrote for me when he had taken his place in the great world :—

"I wish that I could run away
  From house, and court, and levee,
Where bearded men appear to-day
  Just Eton-boys grown heavy ;
That I could bask in childhood's sun,
  And dance o'er childhood's roses ;
And find huge wealth in one pound one,
  Vast wit in broken noses ;
And play Sir Giles at Datchet Lane,
  And call the milk-maids houris ;—
That I could be a boy again,
  A happy boy at Drury's."

London Magazine, 1829.

A boy such as Praed, who possessed his genius, and was not possessed by it (as I once heard the great Coleridge say in comparing the peculiarities of two young men), was sure to be happy at Eton. He was in every respect the opposite, in certain qualities which may be called physical rather than intellectual, to another contributor to "The Etonian." William Sidney Walker was in 1820 a Fellow of Trinity College. I had no acquaintance with him till the end of 1822, but I saw a great deal of him in after years, both at Cambridge and in my family circle. I may say that I never beheld in any man, even of the lowest ability, such a striking example of the every-day want of "decision of character"—that most valuable quality, which is the subject of one of Foster's interesting "Essays." Irresolute, even in the most trivial actions of life; hesitating in the utterance of the commonest colloquial forms; utterly incapable of sustaining a share in conversation even amongst his familiar friends—Sidney Walker was inferior to very few in some of the higher qualities of genius—second to none in a marvellous power of memory—and, having won his Fellowship by his brilliant scholarship, might have left an imperishable reputation, if his will had been sufficiently strong to counteract the morbid tendencies of his feelings. As an Eton boy, there was no one in the school who had given such an early promise of poetical ability, apart from his school studies. At seventeen, his epic poem of "Gustavus Vasa" was published by subscription. And yet this wonderful boy was the subject of the direst persecution by the common herd of his schoolfellows. Mr. Moultrie, who was his junior by four years, has, in a beautiful Memoir prefixed to Walker's "Poetical Remains," described him at Eton as flying for refuge from his tormentors, even into the private apartments of the assistant-masters. Another friend, Mr.

Derwent Coleridge, alludes to this victim of school-boy-tyranny, as "one of the very largest natural capacity, whose whole moral and intellectual nature had been dwarfed and distorted by the treatment he received at school." Mr. Walker had a profound admiration for female loveliness, and yet he induced no sentiment but pity in his grotesque approaches to ladies, and his extraordinary modes of testifying his devotion. When one of the most beautiful, as well as the most gifted, women of her time appeared at a public ball at Cambridge, he peered into her face, and clapped his hands in an ecstasy of delight. "It was the joy of the savage," said Macaulay, "when he first sees a tenpenny nail." His admiration was too deep for words. I once, however, witnessed a demonstration at a social meeting of his friends at Trinity, which took every one by surprise. The wine was passing round, when he suddenly jumped upon a chair, and flourishing his glass, exclaimed, "The Greeks!" The introduction of the toast by the most brilliant harangue of Macaulay, who was present, could not have produced a more profound sensation. Incapable as he was of expressing it, there was a tenderness in Walker's appreciation of the pure and beautiful in Women, as there was of loftiness in his estimate of the heroic in Nations. If the author of "The Lover's Song," in "The Etonian," could have spoken as he wrote, his terror of a life of perpetual celibacy as the Fellow of a College might have been happily ended, in spite of his slovenly dress, his pirouetting walk, his want of the outward attributes of manliness. When "the toils of day are past and done," and he invokes the image of his "lost, remember'd Emily," few passages of the best amatory lyrics may compare with four lines of this exquisite little poem :—

> " Too solemn for day, too sweet for night,
> Come not in darkness, come not in light;
> But come in some twilight interim
> When the gloom is soft and the light is dim."

Mr. Praed and Mr. Moultrie were the life-long friends of this unhappy man. Praed made the most noble exertions to clear off his debts, and to place him above actual want, when he had lost his Fellowship from his honest scruples as to taking Orders, bewildered as he ever was by his habitual scepticism on all subjects. Moultrie cherished him living, and he has done justice to his memory when dead—touching lightly upon his foibles—lamenting over the " shapeless wreck " of a lost mind—

> " by what mysterious bane
> Of physical or mental malady
> Disorder'd, none can tell."
>
> *Dream of Life.*

Let me turn to Mr. Moultrie himself, as a contributor to "The Etonian."

In the collected edition of " Poems by John Moultrie," amongst the "Poems composed between the years 1818 and 1828," there are found those most touching and graphic lines which first gave assurance to the world of his rare qualities as a poet. " My Brother's Grave " is one of those outpourings of the heart that never fail to command human sympathy. The two longer poems in " The Etonian," of "Godiva" and " Maimoune," are not reprinted in this collection. When, in 1837, Mr. Moultrie was looking back upon the productions of 1820, he might probably have considered that the occasional levities of the young student of nineteen might scarcely be deemed fit for republication by the clergyman of six-and-thirty. Yet it is to be regretted that these poems should not have been preserved, other than as a portion of a Miscellany now scarce and little known. The same minute and careful excisions which have been bestowed upon the long poem of "Sir Launfal" (the "La Belle Tryamour" of "Knight's Quarterly Magazine") might have given these two productions a wider celebrity. The two or three fragments which are republished offer no adequate idea of the more than cleverness of these early poems. In the stanzas which tell the well-known story of the gentle lady of Coventry, there are passages of rare beauty, which may justly compete with the "Godiva" of Tennyson, written ten years afterwards. "Maimoune" is more unequal; and there are occasional licences in it which now would call up frowns from some, which might have been smiles forty years ago. But the author may justly claim never to have written a verse that was really corrupting, even in the unpruned luxuriance of his spring-time. Looking back upon his Eton experiences he describes his chief poetical characteristics:—

"If my song
Hath ever found its way to gentle hearts,
'Twas by the nurture and development
Of dormant powers, then first and only found,
That its wild notes were fashioned to express
A *natural tenderness.*"

Dream of Life.

Henry Nelson Coleridge was in 1820 a scholar of King's College, Cambridge. At the time when he was a contributor to "The Etonian" he had given evidence of his great abilities and scholarship, by winning two of Sir William Brown's medals—one for the Greek ode and one for the Latin ode. His poetical faculty, although not of a common order, was less remarkable than his literary taste. The nephew of Samuel Taylor Coleridge, his admiration of those who were then sneered at as "the Lake School" was only natural. But it required some courage in the young critic to stand up to defend Wordsworth and Coleridge from that never-ceasing ridicule of the Edinburgh Reviewers, which, it appears, was in some favour at Eton. He did more than this. He endeavoured to explain and illustrate Wordsworth as a very singular and peculiar poet, quite set apart from the troop of every-day metrists, and living and breathing in a world of his own. When Wordsworth was then spoken of as a great poet, the ordinary question was, "Why is he not more popular?" The process through which public opinion gradually turns from an ephemeral popularity, permanently to repose upon works of imagination that are not extravagant stimulants, is admirably illustrated by his own experience:—"I remember distinctly, when 'Lalla Rookh' first came out, I read it through at one sitting. To say I was delighted with it is a poor word for my feelings; I was transported out of myself—entranced, or what you will. The men did not appear to me half fierce and beautiful enough, and the women had nothing in their eyes at all like those of the gazelle; —not to mention that the flowers were very meagre, and the wind cold, and the chapel-organ out of tune, and 'the blessed Sun himself' but a poor substitute for the god of the Guebres. This seems extravagant, and yet I believe that many a young heart has felt nearly the same, if those feelings were uttered. Well—after a few days it occurred to me as something very odd that I had no patience now with old Homer, or Virgil, or even Milton, and scarcely with Shakspere;—they were not transporting enough. This made me reflect upon the causes which could work such a revolution in me; for I used to think the aforesaid poets the very first in their lines, and lo! now a greater than they had swept them out of my favour! After the cooling interval of three weeks I sat down to read this book again—but oh! '*quantum mutatus ab illo Hectore!*' I cannot describe my feelings, but suffice it to say, the potent charm had vanished; but still I was bewitched in a minor degree by the glare and dazzle of the scenery and the music of the versification. Will you believe me, that a whole year afterwards I read this same book a third time; and then I felt and knew, as all will feel and know who will take the trouble of making the experiment, that the only parts of the work that are worth a farthing are precisely those which are the simplest, the most plain, and free from the beauties of the author, and which, on that very account, I, on my first acquaintance with him, disliked or neglected."

Henry Coleridge, by his republication of "The Friend," and other materials for a proper estimation of his illustrious uncle's labours, testified in his maturer years a profound admiration of his character as a philosopher and a critic. But the Cambridge scholar, while regarding him as the greatest poetical genius of that day, does not hesitate to ask, "Where are we to find in Mr. Coleridge's philosophy that solid, sensible ground upon which we may venture to build up an abiding-place for our doubts and our desires?" Such are the changes which years produce in every mind in which the process of educating itself is always going on.

There were altogether fifteen contributors to "The Etonian." I have mentioned the more prominent. But there was no one who, in the extent and variety of his articles, approached Mr. Praed. They occupy more than a fourth of the whole Miscellany. His prose contributions are far less striking than his poetical. His verse bore a remarkable resemblance to his handwriting. It was the most perfect caligraphy I ever beheld. No printer could mistake a word or letter. It was not what is called a running-hand, and yet it was written with rapidity, as I have often witnessed. Such, too, was the flow and finish of his compositions. In the poems which earliest appeared in "The Etonian" we scarcely trace that peculiar vein which peeps out in his later verse in the same work. And yet these first of a numerous series are essentially different from the common run of classical imitations or juvenile sentimentalities. "The Eve of Battle" is an example. Eighteen hundred and twenty was sufficiently nigh the year of Waterloo to have suggested recollections of many an Etonian who there fell. For those who closed their career in the Crimea there is a memorial-window at Eton. Praed's poem is most probably a memorial, in some particulars, of real persons who had left memories of their happy boyhood. Yet how strikingly has he varied their characters! There, is "the beau of battle;" there, is the would-be poet, who "on the fray that is to be" is writing "a Dirge or Elegy;" there, is "the merriest soul that ever loved the circling bowl;" there, is "Etona's wild and wayward son" who will "break Frenchmen's heads, instead of Priscian's;" there, is "Sir Matthew Chase," in whose dreams "blood and blood-horses smoke by turns." How unlike the thoughts of eighteen is the description of a youth who was "all by turns, and nothing long:"—

"A friend by turns to saints and sinners,
Attending lectures, plays, and dinners,
The Commons' House, and Common Halls,
Chapels of ease,—and Tattersall's;
Skilful in fencing and in fist,
Blood—critic—jockey—methodist;
Causeless alike in joy—or sorrow,
Tory to-day and Whig to-morrow,
All habits and all shapes he wore,
And lov'd, and laugh'd, and pray'd, and swore."

In the eighth Number of "The Etonian," Praed found out his forte of poetical narrative, in which the legendary stories of the old Romances are told with touches of wit and humour, far more effective than the coarse burlesque of such forgotten modernizations as "The Dragon of Wantley." As an example of his clever management of antithetical images take these lines of "Gog:"

"Oh! Arthur's days were blessed days,
When all was wit, and worth, and praise;
And planting thrusts and planting oaks,
And cracking nuts and cracking jokes,
And turning out the toes and tiltings,
And jousts, and journeyings, and jiltings.
Lord! what a stern and stunning rout
As tall Adventure strode about,
Rang through the land; for there were duëls
For love of dames and love of jewels;
And steeds that carried knight and prince
As never steeds have carried since;

And heavy lords and heavy lances;
And strange unfashionable dances;
And endless bustle and turmoil,
In vain disputes for fame and spoil.
Manners and roads were very rough;
Armour and beeves were very tough;
And then—then brightest figures far
In din or dinner, peace or war—
Dwarfs sang to ladies in their teens,
And giants grew as thick as beans!"

Mr. Praed left Eton for Trinity College at the summer vacation of 1821. In his parting poem of "Surly Hall" he thus apostrophizes Eton:

"A few short hours, and I am borne
Far from the fetters I have worn;
A few short hours, and I am free!
And yet I shrink from liberty;
And look, and long to give my soul
Back to thy cherishing control.
Control! ah, no! thy chain was meant
Far less for bond than ornament;
And though its links be firmly set,
I never found them gall me yet.
Oh! still, through many chequer'd years,
'Mid anxious toils, and hopes, and fears,
Still I have doted on thy fame,
And only gloried in thy name."

In Mr. Moultrie's "Maimoune," of the same concluding Number of "The Etonian," he half seriously alludes to the approaching privation of that vehicle for his poetical effusions which had grown out of the manuscript "College Magazine" which he conducted. "Sweet Muse," he says,

"'Tis a sad bore to have thy fancies pent
Within my brain—all joys of printing flown—
No praise my dear anonymous state to sweeten,
And all because some folks are leaving Eton."

In the concluding Number of "The Etonian" the list of fifteen Contributors is signed, as Editors, by "Walter Blunt, Winthrop Mackworth Praed." In a parting address, Peregrine Courtenay thus gracefully records his obligations to his editorial coadjutor: "Most of all, I have to speak my feelings to him, who, at my earnest solicitations, undertook to bear an equal portion of my fatigues and my responsibility,—to him, who has performed so diligently the labours which he entered upon so reluctantly,—to him, who has been the constant companion of my hopes and fears, my good and ill fortune,—to him, who, by the assiduity of his own attention, and the genius of the contributors whose good offices he secured, has ensured the success of 'The Etonian.'"

Deeply did I regret my separation from two or three with whom an intimacy had grown up, which, in spite of the differences of ages and pursuits, was something higher than the cold intercourse of business. Some months had passed away. Mr. Praed was now a Brown's medallist for the Greek ode and for Epigrams. In December, 1822, I received from him a letter which materially influenced my determination to enter upon a new career: "I shall labour in no periodical vocation until you publish one in which I can be of service to you; and divers other Etonians long to hear of your happy establishment in town." I spent a week most pleasantly at Cambridge. I was welcomed by a knot of young men who belonged, as one of them has described, to

"a generation nobler far
Than that which went before it—more athirst
For knowledge—more intent on loftiest schemes

And purposes of good—and if more prone
To daring speculation—apt to tread
More venturous paths—yet purer from the stain
Of gross and sensual vice."

The Dream of Life.

In addition to those I had previously known in connexion with "The Etonian," I was introduced to Mr. Derwent Coleridge, Mr. Malden, and Mr. Macaulay. It was a cold and wet season, but I was well pleased to wander with such intelligent guides amongst those venerable buildings, which had then lost little of their antique character; to look into libraries and museums; to see something of the observances of College life, in prayers at Chapel and dinners in Hall; to ride to Ely along slushy causeways, which were in parts flooded by the waters of the fens, with baby-windmills striving to keep them down. In the mornings there were pleasant breakfasts and luncheons; in the evenings cheerful wine-parties,—and sometimes the famous milk-punch of Trinity and of King's. But there was no excess. Amongst my enjoyments the general plan of "Knight's Quarterly Magazine" was settled.

CHAPTER IX.

THE title of our projected work had not been decided when contributions reached me, sufficient in number and quality to indicate that my Cambridge friends were thoroughly in earnest. The "English Magazine" was rather a favourite name with us. I scarcely recollect how "Knight's Quarterly Magazine" was adopted; but there appears to have been no doubt upon the point when Mr. Praed sent me his opening article, called "Castle Vernon." A very singular paper it was, quite removed from the ordinary tone of what Leigh Hunt has somewhere designated as the most amiable but least interesting part of a book. The only prospectus which I issued was an extract from this eccentric Introduction:

"To the Lady Mary Vernon, the Mistress of all Harmony, the Queen of all Wits, the Brightest of all Belles, we, the undersigned, send greeting:

"We, the undersigned, are a knot of young men, of various forms and features—of more various talents and inclinations; agreeing in nothing, save in two essential points—a warm liking for one another, and a very profound devotion for your Ladyship.

"Some of us have no occupation.

"Some of us have no money.

"Some of us are desperately in love.

"Some of us are desperately in debt.

"Many of us are very clever, and wish to convince the Public of the fact.

"Several of us have never written a line.

"Several of us have written a great many, and wish to write more.

"For all these reasons, we intend to write a Book.

"We will not compile a lumbering quarto of Travels, to be bound in Russia, and skimmed in the Quarterly, and bought by the country book-clubs;—nor a biting Political Pamphlet, to be praised by everybody on one side, and abused by everybody on the other, and read by nobody at all;—nor a Philosophical Essay, to be marvelled at by the few, and shuddered at by the many, and prosecuted by His Majesty's Attorney-General;—nor a little Epic Poem in twenty-four books, to be loved by the milliners, and lauded in the 'Literary Gazette,' and burnt by your Ladyship.

"But a Book of some sort we are resolved to write. We will go forth to the world once a quarter, in high spirits and handsome type, and a modest dress of drab, with verse and prose, criticism and witticism, fond love and loud laughter; everything that is light and warm, and fantastic, and beautiful, shall be the offering we will bear; while we will leave the Nation to the care of the Parliament, and the Church to the Bishop of Peterborough. And to this end we will give up to colder lips and duller souls their gross and terrestrial food; we will not interfere with the saddle or the sirloin, the brandy-bottle or the punch-bowl;—our food shall be of the spicy curry and the glistening champagne; our inspiration shall be the thanks of pleasant voices, and the smiles of sparkling eyes. We grasp at no renown—we pray for no immortality; but we trust, that in the voyage it shall be our destiny to run, we shall waken many glowing feelings, and revive many agreeable recollections; we shall make many jokes and many friends; we shall enliven ourselves and the public together; and when we meet around some merry hearth to discuss the past and the future, our projects, and our success, we shall give a zest to our bottle and our debate by drinking a health to all who read us, and three healths to all who praise."

Twenty-five signatures followed this address to "the idol before whom they were to prostrate their hearts and their papers." Some eight or ten of these *noms de guerre* clung to the real men during their connexion with the Magazine. Take as the more distinguished examples:—

PEREGRINE COURTENAY VYVYAN JOYEUSE . .	WINTHROP MACKWORTH PRAED.
GERARD MONTGOMERY.	JOHN MOULTRIE.
DAVENANT CECIL . .	DERWENT COLERIDGE.
TRISTRAM MERTON . .	THOMAS BABINGTON MACAULAY.
EDWARD HASELFOOT .	WILLIAM SIDNEY WALKER.
HAMILTON MURRAY .	HENRY MALDEN.
JOSEPH HALLER. . .	HENRY NELSON COLERIDGE.

Peregrine Courtenay was the signature of Praed in "The Etonian." Vyvyan Joyeuse was the one he adopted for his gay and laughing moods in the "Quarterly Magazine." The name was in accordance with the description of him who bore it, when he was called up to explain to Lady Mary and her coterie the meaning of the address which had been presented to her: "'You shall call nobody but me,' cried a shrill voice; 'you shall call nobody but me, Vyvyan Joyeuse!' And immediately a whimsical apparition leaped with an opera step into the front of the battalia; a tall thin youth, with long sallow features; thick brown hair curled attentively, and small gray eyes. He threw a quick shifting glance upon his auditors, and then, dangling the ribbon of his glass with both hands, stood prepared for his interrogator." Christopher North introduced Vyvyan Joyeuse into his "Noctes," when he described the Magazine as "a gentlemanly Miscellany, got together by a clan of young scholars, who look upon the world with a cheerful eye, and all its on-goings with a spirit of hopeful kindness." There is another portrait drawn by Praed, in which, as in many sketches approaching to caricature—such as those of H. B. forty years ago—we may trace the best likenesses of eminent men who lived on into another generation:

"'Tristram Merton, come into court.' There came up a short manly figure, marvellously upright, with a bad neckcloth, and one hand in his waistcoat-pocket. Of regular beauty he had little to boast; but in faces where there is an expression of great power, or of great good humour, or of both, you do not regret its absence.

"'They were glorious days,' he said, with a bend, and a look of chivalrous gallantry to the circle around him, 'they were glorious days for old Athens when all she held of witty and of wise, of brave and of beautiful, was collected in the drawing-room of Aspasia. In those, the brightest and the noblest times of Greece, there was no feeling so strong as the devotion of youth, no talisman of such virtue as the smile of beauty. Aspasia was the arbitress of peace and war, the queen of arts and arms, the Pallas of the spear and the pen: we have looked back to those golden hours with transport and with longing. Here our classical dreams shall in some sort wear a dress of reality. He who has not the piety of a Socrates, may at least fall down before as lovely a divinity; he who has not the power of a Pericles may at least kneel before as beautiful an Aspasia.'

"His tone had just so much earnest that what he said was felt as a compliment, and just so much banter that it was felt to be nothing more. As he concluded he dropped on one knee, and paused.

"'Tristram,' said the Attorney-General, 'we really are sorry to cramp a culprit in his line of defence; but the time of the court must not be taken up. If you can speak ten words to the purpose——'

"'Prythee, Frederic,' retorted the other, 'leave me to manage my own course. I have an arduous journey to run; and, in such a circle, like the poor prince in the Arabian Tales, I must be frozen into stone before I can finish my task without turning to the right or the left.'

"'For the love you bear us, a truce to your similes: they shall be felony without benefit of clergy; and silence for an hour shall be the penalty.'

"'A penalty for similes! horrible! Paul of Russia prohibited round hats, and Chihu of China denounced white teeth; but this is atrocious!'

"'I beseech you, Tristram, if you can for a moment forget your omniscience, let us——'

"'I will endeavour. It is related of Zoroaster, that——'"

Others of the "knot of young men—of various forms and features, of more various habits and inclinations," were called before "the Mistress of all Harmony." There was Cecil, of whose character no idea could be conveyed in the compass of a few lines, "except that which will be naturally associated with a highly-flushed cheek, and a magnificent forehead, and thick black hair." There were others whose names figured in the address who were not called at all. Mr. Peregrine Courtenay "having said a few words in kind remembrance of his *quondam* passages with Mr. C. Knight," it was resolved that "the most entertaining publication of the day be immediately set on foot, under the title of 'Knight's Quarterly Magazine.'" But there was no chance of coming to a conclusion upon the question, "who was to edite the work?" The publisher drifted into the editorship, much against his will; but if his anomalous power had its pains, it had also its pleasures.

There is perhaps no happiness of the editorial life equal to that of first reading the manuscript of a contributor in which original genius is so manifest that none but a blockhead would venture upon an alteration. I have, however, seen a little of such blockheads in my day—real live editors, obtuse and prosaic as the mysterious Mr. Perkins of the Shakspere folio. Very early amongst the contributions came "La Belle Tryamour," which Mr. Moultrie described as "the threatened Beppo," which, if I thought it too long, or had better matter to supply its place, I was to pack off without ceremony. I did not avail myself of the permission. One contribution of no common order was at least secured. In a week or two followed a prose contribution. Those who do not possess, or cannot obtain—even at such cost as that of works figuring in old catalogues as *rare*—the "Quarterly Magazine," which the intelligent public of forty years ago did not exactly appreciate, may find the noble "Fragments of a Roman Tale" preserved from oblivion in the "Miscellaneous Writings of Lord Macaulay." They may also find there an article on "The Royal Society of Literature." If they should not care to trace how the scheme of patronage for the incubation of great authors was mauled by one who was to take the foremost rank amongst those who have but one patron, the public, he may be struck with the apologue that clenches the argument. "About four hundred years after the deluge, when King Gomer Chephoraod reigned in Babylon,—and was so popular that the clay of all the plains round the Euphrates could scarcely furnish brick-kilns enough for his eulogists, at a time when all authors inscribed their compositions on massive bricks—this beneficent Prince was petitioned that he should take order that his people should only drink good wine. A decree was passed that great rewards should be bestowed upon the man who should make ten measures of the best wine. The examiners, assembled to judge the wine, decided that all sent in was little better than poison. There had been a singularly good season, but the only bad wine was that tasted by the judges. Who can explain this? said the King. An old philosopher then came forward, and spoke thus:

"'Gomer Chephoraod, live for ever! Marvel not at that which has happened. It was no miracle, but a natural event. How could it be otherwise? It is true that much good wine has been made this year; but who would send it in for thy rewards? Thou knowest Ascobaruch, who hath the great vineyards in the north, and Cohahiroth, who sendeth wine every year from the south over the Persian Gulf. Their wines are so delicious that ten measures thereof are sold for an hundred talents of silver. Thinkest thou that they will exchange them for thy slaves and thine asses? What would thy prize profit any who have vineyards in rich soils?'

"'Who, then,' said one of the judges, 'are the wretches who sent us this poison?'

"'Blame them not,' said the sage, 'seeing that you have been the authors of the evil. They are men whose lands are poor, and have never yielded them any returns equal to the prizes which the King proposed. Wherefore, knowing that the lords of the fruitful vineyards would not enter into competition with them, they planted vines, some on rocks, and some in light sandy soil, and some in deep clay. Hence their wines are bad. For no culture or reward will make barren land bear good vines. Know, therefore, assuredly, that your prizes have increased the quantity of bad but not of good wine.'

"There was a long silence. At length the King spoke. 'Give him the purple robe and the chain of gold. Throw the wine into the Euphrates; and proclaim the Royal Society of Wines is dissolved.'"

There was another prose article by Mr. Macaulay in the first number of the Magazine which has not been reprinted. The evil which was there combated with unusual energy was remedied when the young writer, who had been bred up in the doctrines of the school of Wilberforce to which his father belonged, had become a legislator. It was before the days of his political responsibility that he thus introduced the article on "West Indian Slavery":—"We espouse no party. Zadig himself did not listen to the memorable controversy about Zoroaster and his griffins with more composure and impartiality than we hope to display on most of the subjects which interest politicians. We are neutrals." To write against Slavery seemed likely to have interested "the Clapham sect" in the "Quarterly Magazine"—perhaps to have induced them to tolerate even its occasional levity. Painful must have been the struggle when Macaulay felt himself compelled to secede after the publication of the first number. But how honourable to his memory is the letter which he addressed to me, and which this conviction would alone induce me to publish:—

"Rothley Temple, Leicestershire,
June 20, 1823.

"My dear Sir,—As I fear that it will be impossible for me to contribute to your Magazine for the future, I think it due to you and to myself to acquaint you, without reserve, of the circumstances which have influenced me.

"You are probably aware that there are among my family connections several persons of rigidly religious sentiments. My father, in particular, is, I believe, generally known to entertain in their utmost extent what are denominated evangelical opinions. Several articles in our first number, one or two of my own in particular, appeared to give him great uneasiness. I need not say that I do not in the slightest degree partake of his scruples. Nor have I at all dissembled the complete discrepancy which exists between his opinions and mine. At the same time, gratitude, duty, and prudence, alike compel me to respect prejudices which I do not in the slightest degree share.

And, for the present, I must desist from taking any part in the 'Quarterly Magazine.'

"The sacrifice gives me considerable pain. The Magazine formed a connecting tie between me and some very dear friends, from whom I am now separated, probably for a very long time; and I should feel still more concerned if I could imagine that any inconvenience could result from my conduct.

"I shall probably be in London in about a month. I will then explain my motives to you more fully. In the meantime, I can only say that all that has passed between us increases my regrets for the termination of our connection, and my wishes that it may be renewed under more favourable circumstances.

"Let me beg that you will communicate what I have said to nobody excepting Coleridge, Moultrie, Praed, and Malden; and to them under the injunction of secrecy.

"Believe me, my dear Sir, yours sincerely,

"T. B. Macaulay."

Derwent Coleridge, who has been addressed by his bosom friend as

"A poet's child, thyself a poet born,"

contributed "Beauty, a Lyrical Poem." Henry Nelson Coleridge sent a paper full of deep thought eloquently expressed, "Scibile,"—a paper which De Quincey, writing to me some months after its publication, regarded as truly admirable. Henry Malden furnished a graceful Italian tale, "Agostino della Monterosa," in which the romantic superstitions of the Middle Ages are reproduced with the completeness of a full knowledge. He describes an enthusiast whose mind was subdued by the arts of a false friend to believe in "the secrets of the Rosy Cross, and of those spirits of the elements who pervade all that we hear and see and touch, although we hear them not, and see them not, and feel them not,"—(a nobler form of credulity, it seems to me, than a belief in spirits whose presence is indicated by rapping and table-lifting)—to believe in tales of unhappy spirits lingering over graves and charnel-houses, of unquiet tenants of the tomb; of mighty magicians. "He pored over ancient chronicles, and read of the black Boy who was the attendant of Julius Cæsar, and who, though he lived many years, grew never the older;—of the strange knight, who came, sore spent with travel, on a huge-boned mulberry-coloured horse, to the court of Charlemagne; and no one knew his name or lineage, or whence he came, yet he was ever with the Emperor, who did nothing that he did without his counsel, save when he went down to the great battle of Roncesvalles; and the strange knight went into the battle, and came not out of it, yet was not his body found among the slaughtered Paladins;—and of the deaf and dumb dwarf with the yellow beard, who had the secret ear of the Soldan Saladin, and went with him wherever he went, save into the holy city of Jerusalem. On tales as wild as these he suffered his mind to dwell with a blind and visionary faith, and he was filled with a vague and anxious longing for such supernatural converse." The power displayed in this tale might almost lead one to lament that such qualities of genius should have merged into a life of unambitious usefulness, did we not know that in such a life—that of the trainer of the young to sound learning, that of a teacher commanding obedience through love—the truest happiness and honour are to be found.

The smaller poetical contributions of the Magazine were to be grouped in a concluding paper, entitled, "What you will." In the first number we have some exquisite Sonnets by Moultrie, which have been reprinted in his collected Poems. We have one of Praed's charming Enigmas. We have, what no one would expect to find, amatory verses by Tristram Merton, who might perhaps have rivalled "Tom Moore," had he not been born for higher things. It is almost needless to say that there is no reprint in "Lord Macaulay's Miscellaneous Works" of the ballad of which we give two stanzas :—

"Oh Rosamond! how sweet it were, on some fine summer dawn,
With thee to wander, hand in hand, upon the dewy lawn,
When flowers and heaps of new-mown grass perfume the morning breeze,
And round the straw-built hive resounds the murmur of the bees;
To see the distant mountain-tops empurpled by the ray,
And look along the spreading vale to the ocean far away;
O'er russet heaths, and glancing rills, and massy forests green,
And curling smoke of cottages, and dark grey spires between.

"And oh! how passing sweet it were, through the long sunny day,
To gaze upon thy lovely face, to gaze myself away,
While thou beneath a mountain-ash, upon a mossy seat,
Shouldst sing a low wild song to me, reclining at thy feet!
And oh! to see thee, in some mood of playful toil, entwine
Round the green trellice of our bower the rose and eglantine,
Still laying on my soul and sense a new and mystic charm
At every turn of thy fairy shape and of thy snowy arm!"

The secession of Macaulay was felt by all of us as an almost irreparable loss. There was one of our band whose energies were ever called forth with new vigour under pressure and difficulty. Praed had that confidence in his own powers which is at the root of all greatness, and which is far removed from the vanity of mediocrity. Amidst the disappointments which had arisen, he wrote to me to entreat that I would not think of postponing the appearance of the second number. "For myself, I will give night and day to the Magazine, rather than see it so assassinated." He amply redeemed his pledge. He produced for that number more than a fourth of the whole—the first canto of his Poem "The Troubadour," and five prose articles. My other Cambridge allies seconded his endeavours. But I had also looked around me amongst my own old familiar friends. Such a friend was Matthew Hill. We had often planned literary enterprises in concert, in the days when the young barrister was struggling, as most lawyers have to struggle, when the collar presses hard upon the weak but willing horse if he be permitted to work, and when hope deferred presses still harder when no profitable work falls in his way. Of those times my friend had vivid recollections, and he gave utterance to them in "My Maiden Brief"—that paper to which an eminent judge alluded from the bench, and nodded kindly to the stuff gown in the back rows. Hill contributed also a very striking picture of the Staffordshire Collieries — of that dreary country through which I walked some thirty years afterwards with Charles Dickens, and saw whence he had derived one of the most telling scenes of the wanderings of "Little Nell." But Mr. Hill's vocation was to describe the people of this region. He thus concludes his paper:—"I wished to preserve some sketch, while the original is yet in existence, of a race which refinement, that fell destroyer of character, has hitherto spared. Soon will these be tales of other times. The primitive simplicity even of the collieries is threatened. Already have the eyes of Bell and Lancaster searched out this spot of innocent seclusion; and the voice of education will ere long be heard above the wild untutored sounds which have so long charmed the ears of the traveller." I am not sure that "the voice of education" is yet very powerful in the land where the dwellers had "no similarity either in speech or features with the peasantry of the neighbouring districts." If my friend could spare a day or two from other departments of "Social Science," it might be worth while for him to go over the ground once more, to compare 1823 with 1863.

In this second number of the Magazine I wrote a paper, upon which I may not improperly say a little, as it in some measure related real incidents of my Working Life. "An unpublished Episode of Vathek" is reprinted in my volumes of "Once upon a Time." Mr. Rutter, an enterprising bookseller of Shaftesbury, had proposed to me to publish a splendidly illustrated work, which he was preparing, on Fonthill, soon after the period when the wondrous building, of which every one had some marvel to relate but which no one had ever seen, was thrown open to those who chose to travel over Salisbury Plain, and pay a guinea for the long-coveted sight. Bekfudi, says my tale, the superb merchant, had gone on for many moons building and embellishing his mosque, and living in a round of selfish enjoyment. But gradually Bekfudi found there was a limit to his extravagance. Bekfudi was in debt.

"He resolved to invite all Samarah to see his mosque, and purchase his curiosities. For three moons all Samarah went mad. Away ran the idle and the busy to scramble up Bekfudi's tower,—to wander about his long galleries upon carpets from Cairo, —to touch his gold censers, or to pore upon his curious pictures. As to his books, Bekfudi carefully locked them up. He was a great commentator, and his relish for theological speculations led him to fear that his performances might introduce him to too close an acquaintance with the mufti and the cadi." I was amongst the curious, and had an agreeable holiday. But some months later I went to Fonthill to assist the worthy quaker bookseller of Shaftesbury in getting up his quarto. Fonthill had then passed into the possession of Mr. Farquhar, in the negotiation for which purchase Mr. Phillips, the famous auctioneer of Bond Street, was the agent. He stipulated for the purchase of Fonthill and everything which it contained: "'I will purchase thy lands and thy mosques, and thy silken draperies, and thy woven carpets, and thy golden vessels, and thy jewels, and thy books, and thy pictures, and all that thy palace contains; and here, without, I have twenty dromedaries laden with four hundred thousand sequins, which shall be thine.' Bekfudi was in a rage, but the eloquence of the dromedaries prevailed; and that night the little Jew locked up the mosque with the airs of a master." At this juncture I went to Fonthill. Artists were there making drawings. Journalists were there writing elaborate paragraphs, with a slight tendency to puff. My friend Stedman Whitwell was with me, and we rambled freely over the American gardens, and partook of the choice fruit of the hothouses, and had a sumptuous table every day. To me the ostensible lord of the place, the clever auctioneer, was particularly civil. The first night I was led by him through a long corridor apart from the saloons and galleries of this architectural marvel, and was installed in a chamber of state, where the hangings of the bed were of velvet, and the chairs were of ebony reputed to have belonged to Wolsey. I sat in a reverie, moralizing upon the probable dispersion of these splendid things, when I heard a whirr—my wax candle was suddenly extinguished—the bat that had dwelt in the gorgeous draperies was hovering about me. I was glad to creep into the downy bed. But I could not sleep. "Why rather, sleep, liest thou in smoky cribs?" There were others to whom sleep was that night more difficult to be secured than to myself. Two or three adventurous artists—I think George Cattermole was of the number—elected to lodge in the dormitories of the great tower, some hundred and fifty feet above the floor from which it sprang. The wind rose; the storm grew louder and louder; the frail structure rocked, as Gulliver's cage rocked in the eagle's beak. The terrified guests rushed down the broad stairs, and sat drearily in the dark saloon till the daybreak gave them assurance of safety. But I am rambling from my Episode of Vathek. "Within a week the superb merchant began to indulge a wish for the possession of some of his former most splendid baubles; he bethought him that his free habit of expressing his thoughts in the broad margins of his beautiful manuscripts might one day cause some awkward inquiries." I was taken by my host to the Library. "You are free," he said, "to make any transcript you please of marginal notes on these books. I have sent an invitation to Hazlitt to come also ; but I hear that he has not got beyond Winterslow Hut." Something was whispered about a new book, to be called "Fly Leaves from Fonthill." My curiosity was roused, though I shrank from making profit by book or article out of my notes. In truth, as far as I could trace, there was little in these volumes to alarm their annotator or interest the public. I need not have tested my conscience. When the Library had been glanced at by profane eyes the object was accomplished. "The articles," says the Episode, "were selected, but the little Jew had yet to name the price. Bekfudi raved and tore his hair when a fourth of his four hundred thousand sequins were demanded for what had cost even him not a tenth of the sum."

The second number of the Magazine was getting into shape in the middle of the September of 1823, although its publication was a month behind its due time. With me this was a pleasant autumn. Mr. Moultrie had come to reside at Eton. We had friendly walks together. He was writing the second Canto of "La Belle Tryamour," and as we sat on the lawn of a little village inn he was rapidly jotting down his verses. In a piece of nonsense which I also wrote as we laughed and lounged, I said, "I have seen, as I watched Gerard's impassioned countenance, the infancy of a thought struggling into energy in its perilous contest with the fetters of a rhyme, and at last triumph in the maturity of a stanza." Mr. Derwent Coleridge came to visit Mr. Moultrie. He was also to write for the forthcoming number. I dare say he forgave me when I ventured to say, that before he went to work "Davenant had first to be delivered of a theory on the supernatural creations of Shakspere, and this carried us to Racine and Voltaire, Aristotle and Confucius ; a slight dissertation on the merits of the Italian Platonists led us to Germany ; and we ended, as the candles were brought, with Kant and Jacob Behmen."

In that autumn of 1823, looking back through four decades, I see a youth of twenty-two, and a man ten years his senior—one who had given "hostages to fortune"—anxiously engaged in discussing all the circumstances which had led to a challenge to fight a duel, in which the younger was to be one of the principals. My wife and I were at breakfast, when Mr. Praed came in, looking pale and anxious. He begged me to walk out with him. It was nearly the end of the term, and most of his intimates had left Cambridge. He had come to town by the early coach, having arranged for a hostile meeting, in London, with a gentleman with whom he had quarrelled the night before. The subject of difference had been the date of the battle of Bunker's Hill. The heat of argument had been so great, that the three unforgiveable words which, spoken in Parliament, always sent honourable members to their hats, had been uttered by him. We went from house to house, and from chamber to chamber, to find a *friend*. No one was to be found. No one could be found. Would I be his *friend?* I at once consented, for I was determined that, if possible, there should be no duel. The place of rendezvous was the Swan with two Necks in Lad Lane. After a little suspense, a young man came in, who was deputed by his brother, the challenger, to make the needful arrangements with Mr. Praed's *friend.* He and I retired. My course was clear. I was instructed not to tender an apology, but the way, I saw, was open for a compromise. Rustication, expulsion, all the possible dangers of a meeting, were nothing to the horrors of a younger brother standing by to see his elder brother shot at; or to imagine the possibility of both of them appearing in the dock of the Old Bailey on their trial as murderers. I conquered at last. We signed a paper that was satisfactory, and it was sent under cover to Mr. Macaulay. Mr. Praed returned to Cambridge by the afternoon coach. A few hours after Mr. William Henry Ord, then a Fellow Commoner of Trinity, arrived at my house in great agitation. He was soon made happy. He had come up to London in all haste with the Tutor of Trinity, Mr. Whewell. To Dick's Coffee House we immediately went, to relieve the apprehensions of this eminent scholar and man of science, then rising into general reputation. We spent a happy evening together, and nothing more was heard of the matter. Mr. Hill, in a very admirable paper "On Duelling," in our first number, had said—"In the present state of society, the total abolition of duels cannot, as experience abundantly shows, be effected." God be praised, the "state of society" has so changed, that the change has carried with it not a few great moral as well as political reforms. The Duel has become as much a thing of the past as the Wager of Battle.

CHAPTER X.

T was with no common pleasure that I opened a letter from Mr. Macaulay—a few lines to say that he was ready to resume his contributions to "The Quarterly Magazine." He enclosed two Manuscripts. These scarcely filled two sheets of paper, but they were as precious as fine gold. Well do I remember the delight with which I read with a friend in London, and afterwards heard read by Mr. Moultrie at Windsor in a way in which few could read, the "Songs of the Huguenots." These are almost as well known as Campbell's "Mariners of England" and "The Battle of the Baltic." The "Montcontour" is reprinted in Macaulay's "Miscellaneous Works"—the "Ivry" was republished by himself with "Lays of Ancient Rome." But they ought never to have been separated. There is a dramatic unity in the two poems which makes each more valuable. The song of lamentation should be read before the song of triumph.

In a few months came another pair of lyrics, which no change in the fashion of literature can ever consign to oblivion—"Songs of the Civil War." These, again, ought to be read together. "The Cavaliers' March to London" has not been reprinted by the author, nor in his "Miscellaneous Works."

The return of Macaulay was the herald of "the most high and palmy state" of the Magazine, when its first fruits were succeeded by a rich harvest. Macaulay was now unquestionably its leading spirit. In the third number, in addition to his "Songs of the Huguenots," we have "Scenes from Athenian Revels" and "Dante." In the fourth number we have, as well as "Songs of the Civil War," the criticism on "Petrarch," and the "Great Law-Suit between the Parishes of St. Dennis and St. George in the Water." This is something more than an imitation of Swift. Those who venerate, and most justly, the memory of Burke, will not be displeased to see him in a caricature portrait as effective as that of Gilray:

"There was an honest Irishman, a great favourite among them [the Vestry of St. George in the Water], who used to entertain them with raree-shows, and to exhibit a magic-lantern to children on winter evenings. He had gone quite mad upon this subject [the refractory conduct of the tenants of Sir Lewis, the Lord of the Manor of St. Dennis]. Sometimes he would call out in the middle of the street—'Take care of that corner, neighbours: for the love of Heaven, keep clear of that post; there is a patent steel-trap concealed thereabouts.' Sometimes he would be disturbed by frightful dreams; then he would get up at dead of night, open his window, and cry 'fire,' till the parish was roused, and the engines sent for. The pulpit of the parish of St. George seemed likely to fall; I believe that the only reason was, that the parson had grown too fat and heavy; but nothing would persuade this honest man but that it was a scheme of the people of St.

Dennis's, and that they had sawed through the pillars in order to break the rector's neck. Once he went about with a knife in his pocket, and told all the persons whom he met, that it had been sharpened by the knife-grinder of the next parish to cut their throats. These extravagances had a great effect on the people, and the more so because they were espoused by the Squire Guelf's steward, who was the most influential person in the parish. He was a very fair-spoken man, very attentive to the main chance, and the idol of the old women, because he never played at skittles or danced with the girls; and indeed never took any recreation but that of drinking on Saturday nights with his friend Harry, the Scotch pedlar. His supporters called him Sweet William; his enemies the Bottomless Pit."

The fifth number gave us "The Athenian Orators;" and a paper which, to my mind, if it wants something of the force of the great article on Milton in the "Edinburgh Review," has a quiet beauty which is even superior. The "Gentleman of the Middle Temple," who relates a "Conversation between Mr. Abraham Cowley and Mr. John Milton, touching the great Civil War," tells us how, in the warm and beautiful spring of 1665, "two men of pregnant parts and great reputation" dined with him at his lodging in the Temple.

Macaulay, in the height of his fame, looked back upon the Conversation between Cowley and Milton with a just pride. And yet it would seem that he could scarcely have felt, when he thus concluded his article on "The Athenian Orators," that there was something in these Magazine papers of a Cambridge under-graduate which "the world would not willingly let die."

After the return of Mr. Macaulay, the Quarterly

Magazine went on flourishingly to the completion of the fifth number. The "Troubadour" of Mr. Praed vied with the "Tryamour" of Mr. Moultrie. Mr. Henry Coleridge produced admirable historical articles on "Mirabeau" and the "Long Parliament." Mr. Malden wrote papers as entertaining as they were learned on "Lucian's True History," and the "Literary History of the Provençals." In the fourth number appeared "The Bœotian Order of Architecture"—an article upon which I must somewhat dilate, for the purpose of referring to a most extraordinary attempt to restrain the liberty of opinion in matters of taste. The case of "Soane *versus* Knight," recorded in the King's Bench Term Reports, remains as a warning to over-sensitive artists not to sally forth with the heavy ordnance of Law to do battle against the "light artillery" of Criticism.

"The Bœotian, or Sixth Order," professed to be an analytical account of a work on the principles of Architecture, almost unknown in this country. This production of the great Vander von Bluggen set forth canons of Art which had not been lost upon a few modern architects, and which were illustrated in their practice. Mr. Soane, although his name was not mentioned in the article, thought fit, in 1827, to bring an action against me for the libellous matter contained in the publication of 1824. The cause was tried in the Court of King's Bench on the 12th of June, 1827. The array of counsel for the plaintiff was most formidable—Mr. Gurney, Mr. Brougham, and two juniors. The defendant was fortunate in having retained Mr. Scarlett and Mr. Hill. When Mr. Gurney solemnly read some of the axioms of Vander von Bluggen, contending that they were doubtless intended to apply to Mr. Soane, there was a titter throughout the court. I was sitting near Mr. Brougham (to whom I had been introduced in the previous November), and looking at me with a face of imperturbable gravity, he whispered, "Oh! you wicked fellow." I had taken some pains in getting up what may be termed the literature of such actions. The sort of essay which was embodied in the brief of "The Defendant's Case" is before me. I scarcely need say that Mr. Scarlett interpreted the matter to the jury in a very different form, though much of the substance of his speech was the same as my brief. There was not the least hesitation in the verdict being for the defendant.

In the fifth number of the "Quarterly Magazine" there appeared a miscellaneous paper entitled "The Anniversary." It was a vehicle for the introduction of a considerable variety of stray contributions. My article had little of originality in its conception; for Blackwood had published something similar, occupying a whole number of his Miscellany. I could scarcely have dreamt that, eight and twenty years afterwards, this piece of merriment would have been received *au pied de la lettre;* that in a Memoir of Macaulay—"with some account of his early and unknown writings"—so charming a simplicity would have been manifested by this "shilling" biographer, as to demand from him an elaborate abridgment of the narrative of what he terms "a jollification amongst the young contributors" to "Knight's Quarterly Magazine." He has, however, a saving clause which may cover a little of his greenery—"The whole affair may have been heightened by the pen of the reporter."

When the fifth number of the Magazine was

published in July, 1824, I had become acquainted with Mr. De Quincey; and he had contributed a paper translated, as he purported, from the German of Laun, called "The Incognito." It was a very lively and pleasant paper; but as to the strict fidelity of the translation I might have had considerable doubts. He could not go about this sort of work without improving all he touched. In November he was engaged upon a translation of "Walladmor," which some Curll of Germany advertised as the translation of a suppressed work of Sir Walter Scott. Messrs. Taylor and Hessey put the German hoax into the hands of De Quincey to be re-translated. I saw him groaning over his uncongenial labour, by which he eventually got very little. It was projected to appear in three volumes. He despairingly wrote to me, "after weeding out the forests of rubbish, I believe it will make only one decent volume." At that time he was direly beset with visitations more terrible than the normal poverty of authors. A little before I knew him he had come one morning to my friend Hill, wet and shivering, having slept under a hayrick in the Hampstead fields. I have a letter from him of this period, in which he says, "anxiety, long-continued with me—of late years in consequence of my opium-shattering —seizes on some frail part about the stomach, and produces a specific complaint, which very soon abolishes all power of thinking at all." In "The Anniversary" I thus introduced De Quincey: "A short spare figure, with an expression in his eye that at once indicated the strength of the man of genius and the weakness of the valetudinarian, advanced with a slow pace of diffidence towards us, and thus addressed us:—'I fear, sir, that I am an intruder both upon your interesting conversation and your purposed enjoyments. I was looking round, sir, for my worthy friend, Mr. Paterson Aymer. By his cordial invitation I have been tempted from my solitude, to join a company that I cannot but feel desirous of knowing, though I fear much the weight, the heavy and unutterable weight, of depression that bears me down, will render me an unfit partaker of your intellectual pleasures. Oh, sir, even now do I feel the gnawings of that poison with which I have drugged my veins. Fly the cursed spell, if you would continue to know peace of mind and body. But you will excuse me talking of myself.' We all looked at each other with surprise. 'Can it be!' was on every tongue. 'May I venture to ask, sir, whom I have the honour of seeing amongst us? Though Mr. Paterson Aymer be not yet arrived, his friends are ours.' 'My name, sir, is——; but you have heard of me as a too-celebrated Opium-Eater.' We all involuntarily bowed; and in two minutes Haller and our illustrious friend were deep in a discussion on political economy, while Murray and Tristram appealed to him, in the intervals of the debate, upon their contrary views of the knowledge of Greek in Europe at the time of Dante."

The Macaulay biographer receives this as a curious anecdote of De Quincey, which "indicates that he was fast changing into that little dried-up, parchment-hided man that he became years afterwards." This it is, to make a book without the least knowledge of the men and things of which it treats. "Dried-up! parchment-hided!" "Oh, for one hour of Dundee!" One hour of De Quincey—better, three hours from nine till midnight—for a rapt listener to be "under the wand of a magician"—spell-bound by his wonderful affluence of talk, such as that of the fairy whose lips dropped rubies and diamonds. Many a night have I, with my wife by my side, sat listening to the equable flow of his discourse, both of us utterly forgetting the usual regularity of our habits, and hearing the drowsy watchman's "past one o'clock" (for the old watchman then walked his round) before we parted. There was another newly acquired intimate of that time—Barry St. Leger—who also had contributed to the "Quarterly Magazine." Our friendship was of the warmest nature during the remainder of his too short life. The wit-combats between him and De Quincey were most amusing. Never were two men greater contrasts in their intellectual characters. The one passionately rhetorical—the other calmly logical,—the one making a fierce onslaught upon his apparently unwatchful opponent,—the other with a slight turn of his wrist striking the sword out of his adversary's hand, leaving him defenceless. In the ordinary intercourse of society, St. Leger was self-possessed, perfectly at his ease, ready for every emergency, a man of the world, yet with a heart for friendship as warm as that of a schoolboy. De Quincey, vast as were his acquirements, intuitive as was his appreciation of character and the motives of human actions, unembarrassed as was his demeanour, pleasant and even mirthful his table-talk, was as helpless in every position of responsibility, as when he nightly paced "stony-hearted Oxford Street" looking for the lost one. He was constantly beset by idle fears and vain imaginings. His sensitiveness was so extreme, in combination with the almost ultra-courtesy of a gentleman, that he hesitated to trouble a servant with any personal requests without a long prefatory apology. My family were in the country in the summer of 1825, when he was staying at my house in Pall Mall East. A friend or two had met him at dinner, and I had walked part of the way home with one of them. When I returned, I tapped at his chamber-door to bid him good night. He was sitting at the open window, habited as a prize-fighter when he enters the ring. "You will take cold," I exclaimed. "Where is your shirt?" "I have not a shirt—my shirts are unwashed." "But why not tell the servant to send them to the laundress?" "Ah! how could I presume to do that in Mrs. Knight's absence?"

One more illustration of the eccentricity of De Quincey. I had been to Windsor. On my return I was told that Mr. De Quincey had taken his box away, leaving word that he was gone home. I knew that he was waiting for a remittance from his mother, which would satisfy some clamorous creditors and enable him to rejoin his family at Grasmere. Two or three days after, I heard that he was still in town. I obtained a clue to his hiding-place, and found him in a miserable lodging on the Surrey side of Waterloo bridge. He had received a large draft on a London banker at twenty-one days' sight. He summoned courage to go to Lombard Street, and was astonished to learn that he could not obtain the amount till the draft became due. A man of less sensitive feelings would have returned to Pall Mall East, and have there waited securely and comfortably till I came. How to frame his apology to our trusty domestic was the difficulty that sent him into the den where I found him. He produced the draft to me from out of his Bible, which he thought was the best hiding-place. "Come to me to-morrow morning, and I will give you the cash." "What? how? Can such a thing be possible? Can the amount be got before the draft is due?" "Never fear—come you—and then get home as fast as you can." * * *

At the beginning of October I went to Cambridge with Mr. Hill. We arrived on a day of jubilation, for Mr. Macaulay and Mr. Malden had each gained a Trinity fellowship. There was a happy dinner in Mr. Malden's rooms. But a cloud had come over the bright prospects of the "Quarterly Magazine." Two of its first supporters were holding back their contributions. "Some trick not worth an egg"—some misunderstanding about the future editorship—had produced a coldness in those with whom I had been most intimate. I was weary and heartsick. I was worn out with anxiety at the dangerous illness of my father. Cares of business were pressing upon me heavily. I had engaged in large undertakings which demanded my constant attention in London, and I had a divided duty at Windsor. The Magazine was a loss and a trouble. With the sixth number I determined to announce that its career was ended.

I had spent a night at my father's bed-side. The crisis was fast approaching. My wife had been too ill, in Pall Mall East, to take her willing part in this sad office—but, at all risks, she came in time for the end. As the November sun was rising brightly above the trees of the Long Walk, I poured out to her my thoughts in a long letter.

The future of my London life loomed dark and

dangerous. My mind rested upon the contented past that had not known many fears.

> Nel mezzo del cammin di nostra vita
> Mi ritrovai per una selva oscura
> Che la diritta via era smarrita."
>
> DANTE—*Inferno.*

> " In the midway of this our mortal life
> I found me in a gloomy wood, astray,
> Gone from the path direct."
>
> CARY.

Reserving for the next epoch of my "Working Life" the recital of some of its passages in my vocation of a London publisher from 1823 to 1826, I have here to complete my notice of the close of "The Quarterly Magazine." A glance at the short life of a second series, and at a small experiment upon the public taste which was attempted by me, in conjunction with Mr. Praed and Mr. St. Leger, will be briefly given in the present volume.

The "advertisement" in the concluding Number, wherein I announced the discontinuance of a work which, "as it proceeded, had acquired a considerable distinction amongst the discerning and the intelligent," was certain to give offence. I was unwilling to offend; but I was sorely wounded. I wrote—"The publisher has lately had to choose between surrendering that responsibility which his duties to society have compelled him to retain, and which has in many cases prevented this work offending those whose esteem is most to be desired, or losing much of the assistance which has given to the 'Quarterly Magazine' a peculiar and original character. He could not hesitate in his choice. He would not commit his own opinions to an inexperienced and incautious dictation; and he prefers the discontinuance of the work to conducting it with diminished talent."

This led to a controversy. An article appeared in "The Cambridge Chronicle," written by Mr. Praed. It was more temperate than I had anticipated. He described the Magazine as having been intended originally to assume something of a more classical tone than its periodical contemporaries. He spoke of the publisher as an honest and liberal man, but expressed a somewhat disparaging opinion of his competence to retain the direction of the Magazine permanently and exclusively. I replied in the same newspaper. There was a correspondence between Mr. Praed and myself,—formal and reserved on either side. Willingly would I forget the whole affair, did I not feel it my duty and pleasure to record that, within two months, Mr. Praed spontaneously called upon me, held out once more the hand of friendship, and never afterwards lost an opportunity of testifying his goodwill towards me. He took no part in the continuation of the "Quarterly Magazine." In the editorship of its one number, published in the autumn of 1825, Mr. Malden assisted. In its general tone it was much more sober—and of course less interesting—than its predecessor. It might have made its way; for one of the great wholesale houses in Paternoster Row proposed to take a share in it, after its first appearance. The Panic came, and disposed of this and of many other schemes.

Mr. Derwent Coleridge had returned to assist in rearing our callow Phœnix. His paper on "The Chevalier Bayard" is curious, as showing how the romantic may gradually slide into the practical.

De Quincey had written to me in December, 1824, in the belief that, as he expressed it, "many of your friends will rally about you, and urge you to some new undertaking of the same kind. If that should happen I beg to say, that you may count upon me, as one of your men, for any extent of labour, to the best of my power, which you may choose to command." He wrote a translation of "The Love Charm" of Tieck, with a notice of the author. This is not reprinted in his collected works, though perhaps it is the most interesting of his translations from the German. In this spring and summer of 1825, De Quincey and I were in intimate companionship. It was a pleasant time of intellectual intercourse for me. My father, a little before his last illness, had far advanced in building a cottage, by the side of his own, for my family to occupy. That hope of his heart to have us near him was not fulfilled. But in that summer we spent much of our time there. Mr. Praed and Mr. Moultrie were living at Eton as private tutors. They had taken a great liking to my friend Mr. Tarver, and were most assiduous in promoting his interests, as French master at the college. In his society, after he came to reside at Windsor when the war was at an end, I had found a clever and accomplished companion, who had the peculiar advantage of knowing intimately both the French and English languages, and was familiar with the literature of both countries. He was born and bred up in France,—but was of English parents. Mr. Malden came to visit me for a week or two. There was a re-union in which all unpleasantnesses were forgotten. When I went to London, I was associated with Hill, and St. Leger, and De Quincey, who each thoroughly relished the conversation of the others. De Quincey, as I have incidentally mentioned, went away home in the summer of 1825. We were all truly sorry to part with this valued friend, whose eccentricities made him even more dear to us—whose helplessness under the direst pressure of want of means, brought no feeling of contempt, for his abilities and learning commanded our reverence. We scarcely knew then what he had to endure during his London sojourn. We may now judge of his miseries from a letter which he wrote to Professor Wilson in February, 1825:—

"At this time calamity presses upon me with a heavy hand. . . . . At this moment I have not a place to hide my head in." (Mrs. Gordon's 'Christopher North,' vol. ii. p. 79.) He left London in the summer, exulting in the prospect of freedom from debt, and from the necessity that had pressed upon him "to maintain the war with the wretched business of hack author, with all its degradations." (*Ibid.*) I occasionally had a warm-hearted letter from him; but our correspondence, after a year or two, had ceased. I was delighted at its renewal in July 1829, when he wrote me the most pressing invitation from Mrs. De Quincey and himself, to come, with my wife and children, to visit them. He had quitted his home at the Lakes in 1827, to remain in Edinburgh for two years, writing, but separated for the greater part of the time from his family. Wonderfully characteristic are some passages of this letter: "Well, by good management and better luck, I contrived early in this present year to silence *mes Anglois* (as the French do, or did, use to entitle creditors). This odious race of people were silenced, I say, or nearly so: no insolent dun has raised his disgusting voice against me since Candlemas 1829; they now speak softly, and as if butter would not melt in their mouths; and I have so well planted my fire-engines, for extinguishing this horrid description of nuisance, that if by chance any one should smoulder a little too much (flame out, none durst for shame), him I shall souse and drench forthwith into quietness." Whilst "this great operation" was in progress he had been negotiating for the purchase of a "rich farm-house, flowing with milk and honey, with mighty barns and spacious pastures," in the vicinity of his cottage at Grasmere. "'Purchasing,' you say, 'what the devil?' Don't swear, my dear friend; you know there is such a thing as buying a thing and yet not paying for it, or, at least, paying only the annual interest. Well, that is what *I* do, can do, and will do. For hear, finally, that the thing is done." To this farm of Rydal Hay, from which he had written to me, were we to be welcomed. Mighty was the temptation, but mightier the difficulty in the days before railways. "And now, my friend, think what a glorious El Dorado of milk and butter and cream cheeses, and all other dairy products, supposing that you like those things, I can offer you morning, noon, and night. You may absolutely bathe in new milk, or even in cream; and you *shall* bathe, if you like it. I know that you care not much about luxuries for the dinner table; else, though our luxuries are few and simple, I could offer you some temptations: mountain lamb equal to Welsh; char famous to the antipodes; trout and pike from the very lake within twenty-five feet of our door; bread, such as you have never presumed to dream of, made of our own wheat, not doctored and separated by the usual miller's process into fine insipid flour, and coarse, that is, merely dirty-looking white, but all ground down together—which is the sole receipt (experto crede) for having rich, lustrous, red-brown, ambrosial bread; new potatoes, of celestial earthiness and raciness, which, with us, last to October; and, finally, milk, milk, milk—cream, cream, cream (hear it, thou benighted Londoner!) in which you must and shall bathe."

In the spring of 1826, St. Leger and I,—at a time when there was little prospect of publishing books with any success,—thought that a smart weekly sheet might have some hold upon the London public, who were sick of all money questions, and wanted something like fun in that gloomy season of commercial ruin. We went to Eton to consult Praed. He entered most warmly and kindly into the project. We settled that "The Brazen Head" should be its title; and that "The Friar" and "The Head" should discourse upon human affairs, chiefly under the management of our brilliant associate. For ourselves, we had a supplementary machinery, that of "Harlequin," whose laughing face had been too long hidden by a wretched black mask, and who had been too long doomed to perpetual silence,—a woeful contrast to the overflowing wit of his dear Italian days. We had four weeks of this pleasantry; and, what was not an advantage, we had nearly all the amusement to ourselves; for the number of our purchasers was not "Legion." Yet in the "Brazen Head" there are poems of Praed—(unknown, from the scarcity of these sixty-four pages, to the Americans who have printed three editions of his poems)—which are every way worthy of that genius which his countrymen will be soon permitted more fairly to appreciate in an edition of all his poetical pieces, issued by an English publisher. There is one poem purporting to be a chaunt of The Head while the Friar falls asleep, which exhibits the remarkable power of blending earnestness with levity, philosophy with jest, so peculiarly characteristic of Praed's happiest vein:

"I think, whatever mortals crave,
With impotent endeavour,
A wreath,—a rank,—a throne,—a grave,—
The world goes round for ever;
I think that life is not too long,
And therefore I determine
That many people read a song,
Who will not read a sermon.

"I think you've look'd through many hearts,
And mused on many actions,
And studied man's cómponent parts,
And nature's compound fractions;
I think you've picked up truth by bits
From foreigner and neighbour,
I think the world has lost its wits,
And you have lost your labour.

"I think the studies of the wise,
The hero's noisy quarrel,
The majesty of woman's eyes,
The poet's cherish'd laurel;
And all that makes us lean or fat,
And all that charms or troubles,—
This bubble is more bright than that,
But still they all are bubbles.

"I think the thing you call Renown,
The unsubstantial vapour
For which the soldier burns a town,
The sonnetteer a taper,

Is like the mist which, as he flies,
  The horseman leaves behind him;
He cannot mark its wreaths arise,
  Or, if he does, they blind him.

"I think one nod of mistress Chance
  Makes creditors of debtors,
And shifts the funeral for the dance,
  The sceptre for the fetters;
I think that Fortune's favour'd guest
  May live to gnaw the platters;
And he that wears the purple vest
  May wear the rags and tatters.

"I think the Tories love to buy
  'Your Lordships' and 'Your Graces,'
By loathing common honesty,
  And lauding common-places;
I think that some are very wise,
  And some are very funny,
And some grow rich by telling lies,
  And some by telling money.

"I think the Whigs are wicked knaves,
  And very like the Tories,
Who doubt that Britain rules the waves,
  And ask the price of glories;
I think that many fret and fume
  At what their friends are planning,
And Mr. Hume hates Mr. Brougham
  As much as Mr. Canning.

"I think that friars and their hoods,
  Their doctrines and their maggots,
Have lighted up too many feuds,
  And far too many faggots;
I think while zealots fast and frown,
  And fight for two or seven,
That there are fifty roads to town,
  And rather more to Heaven.

"I think that, thanks to Paget's lance,
  And thanks to Chester's learning,
The hearts that burned for fame in France,
  At home are safe from burning;

I think the Pope is on his back,
  And, though 'tis fun to shake him,
I think the Devil not so black
  As many people make him.

"I think that Love is like a play
  Where tears and smiles are blended,
Or like a faithless April day,
  Whose shine with shower is ended;
Like Colnbrook pavement, rather rough,
  Like trade exposed to losses,
And like a Highland plaid, all stuff,
  And very full of crosses.

"I think the world, though dark it be,
  Has aye one rapturous pleasure,
Conceal'd in life's monotony,
  For those who seek the treasure;
One planet in a starless night,—
  One blossom on a briar,—
One friend not quite a hypocrite,—
  One woman not a liar!

"I think poor beggars court St. Giles,
  Rich beggars court St. Stephen;
And Death looks down with nods and smiles,
  And makes the odds all even;
I think some die upon the field,
  And some upon the billow,
And some are laid beneath a shield,
  And some beneath a willow.

"I think that very few have sigh'd,
  When Fate at last has found them,
Though bitter foes were by their side,
  And barren moss around them;
I think that some have died of drought,
  And some have died of drinking;—
I think that nought is worth a thought,
  And I'm a fool for thinking!"

"I think" my readers will not complain of the length of this reprint. I could not select stanzas without injury to the unity of thought. The poem, after having been published six-and-thirty years, is far less known than was Macaulay's famous "Election Ballad" of 1827, before the "Quarterly Review" disentombed it from the columns of "The Times."

I must hold my hand. I must look forward to my proper work of sober narrative in the next stage of life's journey—to trace the progress of education—the growth of popular literature. The following lines from the "Arlechino Parlante" of "The Brazen Head"—the Harlequin "who everything changes"—verses which St. Leger and I produced in happy association, are suggestive of the opening, in a new condition of society, for labours that might be useful to my fellow-men:

"I have whistled up sprites to bestow my new lights
On all that is ancient, exclusive, and dark;—
I have spread around knowledge—I build London College—
I have steam on the Thames, I have gas in the Park.
No longer a minister frowns and looks sinister,
When philosophy mingles with maxims of state;
Economical squires deride their grand-sires,
And reasoning citizens lead the debate."

PASSAGES OF A WORKING LIFE.

The Second Epoch.

CHAPTER XI.

N 1824, I am settled as a Publisher in a newly-built house in Pall Mall East, the next house to the College of Physicians. I had occupied for a year a much smaller place of business on the opposite side of the way. This was altogether a new neighbourhood. On the west side of what is now called Trafalgar Square, houses had grown up, which were terminated towards Charing Cross by the Union Club. But there was as yet no Nelson's column; no fountains in the centre, to be ridiculed as dumb-waiters.

During the first years of my residence in Pall Mall East, Saint James's Park was getting rid of its old squalidness. The road after nightfall had ceased to be a place of danger and licentiousness. "There is gas in the Park." At the time of the Stuarts the Mall had been the lounging place of the highest—the favourite ground of assignation of the Comedies in which Wit and Profligacy long maintained a flourishing co-partnership. Forty years ago the fashionable idlers had given place to happy children and smart nursery-maids. Mechanics out of work, and street vagabonds, always formed a crowd to see the relief of the Guard. Gapers from the country stood wonderingly upon the Parade, watching the working of the Telegraph at the top of the Admiralty. The old machine, which told its story by the opening and closing of shutters, was superseded by a greater wonder, the Semaphore, which threw out an arm, first on one side and then on another, and at varying heights. Very tedious was the transmission of the message, even by this improved instrument; sometimes impossible from the state of the atmosphere. About 1824 I was summoned as a witness upon a trial in which Mr. Croker was also required to give his testimony. I walked with him for an hour or more up and down Westminster Hall. So full of anecdote was his talk, that I could scarcely agree with him when he said, "The French are right in calling the vestibule to their Palace of Justice *la salle des pas perdus*." My steps with him were neither lost nor wearisome. At last, looking at his watch, he exclaimed, "Go I must. There is a frigate waiting at Portsmouth for orders to sail, and it will be dark before I can set the Telegraph in motion if I stay longer." The Secretary of the Admiralty writes a few words now, regardless of dark or light, and the faithful wire conveys his orders from port to port, and from sea to sea, far quicker than the flight of Ariel.

The neighbourhood in which I am seated is not as yet a very busy or a very lively one. It is gradually growing into a region dedicated to the Fine Arts. The Society of Painters in Water Colours have fixed their Gallery opposite me. The Society of British Artists have their Exhibition close at hand in Suffolk Street. My next-door neighbour is Mr. Colnaghi, the printseller. From him, and from his excellent son Dominick, I had some lessons in taste, as they would occasionally show me a few of their choice importations.

It is forty years ago since the Londoners began seriously to think that their traffic was becoming too large for their streets. The broad-wheeled waggon generally crept in and out at nightfall, as it had crept since the days of Fielding and Hogarth. The hackney-coach, never in a hurry, went on "melancholy, slow," patient under every stoppage. No meddling policeman yet presumed to regulate the movements of the driver with a dozen capes, who pulled up when he pleased, unheeding his silk-stockinged fare who was too late for dinner, and sat in the damp straw, shouting and cursing. The omnibus appeared not in our streets till 1831, and when it came, the genteel remained faithful to the foul hackney-coach, mounting its exclusive iron steps with true English satisfaction at not being in mixed company. There were schemes of sub-ways, but they met no encouragement. Colonel Trench obtained an audience at the Mansion House, to listen to his proposal of a terrace, eighty feet wide, from London Bridge to Westminster Bridge. Some thought the scheme a good one, but far too grand. Most sneered at such projects of Laputa. The sneerers and doubters kept their ground through a generation; and now we are thinking in reality about such an obvious improvement.

In the semi-thoroughfare of Pall Mall East we had few passing sights. But on the 12th of July, 1824 I stand with my family on our balcony, looking out for a grand funeral procession that is to come from

Great George Street, Westminster, and to pass from Charing Cross up the Haymarket. On the 19th of April Lord Byron had died at Missolonghi. The hearse which was moving up the Haymarket, to end its journey at Newstead Abbey, was followed by a few who loved him, and by many who reverenced his genius. Poets were there—Moore, Campbell, Rogers; statesmen—Grey, Lansdowne, Holland; Greek Deputies, who thought he was to have been the saviour of their country; and English guardians of his fair fame, who had honoured his memory by burning his autobiography. His sudden death—in the land where he was attempting to express by heroic deeds that sympathy with the "Cause of the Greeks" which other eminent men were content to associate with their speeches and their writings—had moved all (excepting a few who refused his body sepulture in our temple of the illustrious dead) to forget how he had latterly abused his great powers, and to remember only how ineffaceably he had inscribed his name amongst the immortals of literature. The pageant is over. Forty years have passed away, and Byron is now judged with the impartiality of posterity. He is not held to be the greatest poet that modern England has produced; he is not execrated as amongst the most immoral. There was much to pity and forgive in his frailties. The mellowing influence of a few more years might have lifted his words and his deeds out of the slough in which he sometimes seemed unwilling to strive for a firmer footing.

At the time of Lord Byron's funeral I was involved in a matter of public interest connected with the career of the deceased poet. I was enduring a disappointment, such as I had scarcely contemplated as a possible incident of my publishing career. I will relate, as briefly as I can, the story of a Chancery Injunction to restrain me from publishing certain Letters of Lord Byron, which was served upon me five days before the funeral procession which I witnessed on the 12th of July.

Robert Charles Dallas was connected by marriage with the family of the poet. Captain George Anson Byron, the uncle of Lord Byron, married the sister of Mr. Dallas. In 1824, through the intervention of my kind friend, the Rev. Charles Richard Sumner, then residing at Windsor as Domestic Chaplain to George IV., I was offered the publication of a book to be entitled "Correspondence of Lord Byron." Upon receiving intelligence of the death at Missolonghi of the eminent man of whom he had some interesting memorials, Mr. Dallas came from Paris to England to arrange for the publication of some work in which should be exhibited his "Recollections of the Life of Lord Byron from 1808 to the end of 1814." I saw him at the house of his son Alexander, who, having been formerly in the army, had taken orders, and was in 1824 in the ministerial charge of the village of Wooburn, near Beaconsfield. The elder Dallas was then in his seventieth year—a handsome old man, of refined manners, of varied and extensive information; manifesting an affectionate attachment to the memory of the poet, but with a strong religious feeling as to his moral aberrations since the period of their intimate acquaintance, which in some respects might have been called friendship. That intimacy ceased after 1814. Mr. Dallas had many times heard Lord Byron read portions of a book in which he inserted his opinion of the persons with whom he mixed, which book, he said, he intended for publication after his death. This, I conceive, was the Memoir upon which Mr. Murray advanced two thousand guineas to Thomas Moore; and which was torn and burned, under advice, in the presence of Moore, the advance being repaid to Mr. Murray. Such is Mr. Moore's account of this mysterious transaction.* From hearing some of Lord Byron's opinions of his contemporaries, Mr. Dallas took the hint of writing a volume to be published after his own death and that of Lord Byron, which should present a faithful delineation of the poet's character as he had known him. The judicious advice of the elder author—for Dallas had been a not unsuccessful historian and novelist—was useful to Byron in his tentative walk to fame; and the obligation was amply repaid by the present of the copyright of the first two cantos of "Childe Harold," which, strange to say, Byron was unwilling to publish till encouraged by the judgment of his experienced friend. Byron died at the age of thirty-seven; Dallas could have scarcely contemplated to have been his survivor. The world was eager to learn all it could about the man who had filled so large a space in its thoughts for fourteen years; and Mr. Dallas, not from mere sordid motives, remodelled his Memoir into "Correspondence of Lord Byron." I purchased the manuscript for a large sum; and in June it was advertised for publication. On the 30th of that month Mr. Hobhouse called on me with a friend who, as it subsequently appeared, was to be a witness to our conversation. I was not aware of the disadvantage under which the presence of a witness

* See his letter, dated May 26, in "Annual Register" for 1824.

was intended to place me, but immediately after the interview I made a full note of what took place. Mr. Hobhouse came to protest, as one of the executors of Lord Byron, against the publication of this correspondence. I stated that I had read the manuscript carefully, and that the family and the executors need feel no apprehension as to its tendency, as the work was intended to elevate Lord Byron's moral and intellectual character. Mr. Hobhouse observed, that if individuals were not spoken of with bitterness, and if opinions were not very freely expressed in these letters, they were not like Lord Byron's letters in general. The result was, that the Vice-Chancellor granted an injunction upon the affidavits of Mr. Hobhouse and Mr. Hanson, co-executors, that such contemplated publication was " a breach of private confidence, and a violation of the rights of property." There was an appeal. Our counter-affidavits affirmed that the letters were not of a confidential character. After two months of anxiety, Lord Eldon, the Chancellor, decided "that if A. writes a letter to B., B. has the property in that letter for the purpose of reading and keeping it, but no property in it to publish it." The unfortunate quarto volume, as printed to p. 168, is before me. In a few years, Mr. Moore, in his "Life of Byron," gave his testimony to the value of "a sort of Memoir of the noble Poet, published soon after his death, which, from being founded chiefly on original correspondence, is the most authentic and trustworthy of any that have yet appeared." That Memoir was published by me at the end of 1824, after the death of Mr. Dallas on the 21st of October. It was edited by his son, the Reverend Alexander Dallas, who, throughout the whole of this affair, acted in the most honourable and conscientious spirit. In the omission of passages of the original manuscript, he evinced a truly Christian temper of moderation towards those who had endeavoured to damage his father's character, by the imputation of unworthy motives in seeking to publish this Correspondence. I was never brought so near to Lord Eldon as during the hours when this case was argued in his private room. I observed with admiration the patient spirit of inquiry; the desire to uphold the authority of previous cases; but with a strong inclination not to decide against the right of publication, when no satisfactory reason could be shown but that of individual caprice or self-interest for suppressing the work. Mr. Kindersley, now a Vice-Chancellor, was our Counsel, and most ably did he perform his duty. At times I thought that the "I doubt" of the great Chancellor would have terminated in our favour. He seemed, even in pronouncing judgment, to have some hesitation about affirming the principle upon which he ultimately decided as to the property in letters, as settled by the law. "Whether that was a decision that could very well have stood *at first* or not I will not undertake to say." But for most purposes of public utility his judgment was valuable. "It is a very different thing, as it appears to me, publishing as information what these letters contain, and publishing the letters themselves." Upon this principle we acted, in regard to the volume which was published at the end of 1824, as "Recollections of Lord Byron." Mr. Moore reaped the full advantage of the suppressed Correspondence, by filling many pages, in 1829, with the letters of Dallas and

Byron that the executors had thought fit to suppress in 1824.

In the midst of these Chancery proceedings a Captain Parry was announced. "A fine rough subject"—as Byron designated this "fire-master who was to burn a whole fleet,"—came into my private room, with a leathern bag slung over his shoulder. He threw it on the table, exclaiming, "There you have the best book that any one can write about the Right Honourable George Gordon, Lord Byron." He opened the wallet; handed me some of the illiterate scrawl; vaunted again and again his friendship with the Right Honourable George Gordon, Lord Byron—always naming him by his titles at full length; and was very much astonished when I declined having anything to say to the affair. Captain Parry found some person to prepare his MS. for the press. An action of some sort arose out of the publication; and I was called as a witness to prove the nature of the contents of that leathern bag, Parry having maintained that he was the sole author of the book. The most remarkable part of this piece of literary manufacture was a ribald description of Jeremy Bentham, running up Fleet Street pursued by a notorious woman called "The City Barge." Parry had indoctrinated his scribe with his own hatred of the Utilitarians of the Greek Committee in London, who sent out printing-presses and pedagogues in more plentiful supply than Congreve-rockets. Byron writes on the 8th February, "Parry says B...... [? Bentham] is a humbug, to which I say nothing. He sorely laments the printing and civilizing expenses, and wishes that there was not a Sunday school in the world."

The business-house of a young publisher had, at the time of which I am writing, the sort of attraction for flights of authors as a *saltcat* has for pigeons. The whole commerce of Literature is, happily, so changed; the buyers of books and the vendors of books have become so numerous; the competition for the power of securing literary merit, when it first imps its wing, has so enlarged,—that the publishers have now to seek the authors—if they be worth seeking. I am not sure, even, that mediocrity is now the thing abhorred by gods, men, and booksellers. However this may be, I had, in 1824, heaps of unpublished manuscripts to look over; and, what was more troublesome, a good many indignant writers to bow out. There were strange small fishes trying to swim in the wake of the Leviathans in that "yeasty main." Some brought their wares in bulk, and some offered their samples. I honestly think that I tried to be conscientious in my refusals to deal, for I had experienced myself a little of the unknown author's difficulty of obtaining a publisher. Yet it was hard work. I had not learnt the art of refusing in terms that should be meaningless and yet effective. One eminent publisher was the most skilful practitioner of that art with whom I was acquainted. I have heard some such dialogue as this: A. "I presume, Sir, you have at length been able to peruse my novel?"—C. "H'm! chair . . . my reader . . . clever . . . . not quite adapted to public taste . . . . glut . . . . trade very dull . . . perhaps next season."—A. "Would a volume of poems?"—C. "Poems? . . . . oh! . . . . drug . . . ."—A. "But so many come out!"—C. "Yes . . . . on commission . . . . Messrs. —— will publish for you . . . . print on your own account . . . . sell five-

and-twenty . . . . not our line . . . . excuse . . . . gentleman waiting." I began at last to think that for a fashionable publisher there was a grand subject for imitation in Lord Burleigh's shake of the head. Sometimes a book would be offered me that appeared really worth a venture. A huge ungainly Scot walks in, dressed in a semi-military fashion,—a braided surtout and a huge fur cape to his cloak; spluttering forth his unalloyed dialect, and somewhat redolent of the whiskey that he could find south of the Tweed. He at length interested me. He had come to London a literary adventurer. He had been his own educator, for he was once a working weaver. Many were the schemes of books that he was ready to write—schemes that had been in the hands of most publishers, famous or obscure. He was known, I found, to one of the ablest of the staff of the "Times," —a gentleman to whom was committed the charge of the Foreign department of that Journal, which, even forty years ago, founded its success upon the marked talent and reliable knowledge of its writers. Out of the budget of Robert Mudie I selected a plan for a book on London—something in the manner of one which he had published, "The Modern Athens." It was to be called "Babylon the Great." The work was a success. I was acquainted with this singular man for some years. He would occasionally use his powers to good purpose; but his writings were too often inaccurate. He approached nearer to the idea of a hack author of the old times than any man I ever saw. He would undertake any work, however unsuited to his acquirements or his taste. Late in his career, he produced a book—forgotten now perhaps, and too much overlooked by scientific naturalists in his own day—which exhibits remarkable powers of observation and description. Before he had been condemned to a life of incessant literary toil in London—only made more heavy by sottish indulgence—he was a genuine naturalist, who had looked upon the plants, the insects, the birds, and other animal life of his own moors and mountains, with a rare perception of the curious and beautiful. "The Feathered Tribes of the British Islands" is not an every-day work of science without imagination.

I used sometimes to avail myself of the privilege of propinquity to have a gossip with the worthy old gentleman who first made the name of Colnaghi famous amongst collectors. He once gave me a piece of advice, which to some extent made me shy of pursuing an interesting study of human character. He had seen William Henry Ireland entering my door, and sometimes making a long visit. I delighted to talk with the author of the Shakspere forgeries, having no very harsh opinion of the man who, when a lad of eighteen, had hoaxed the big-wigs of his day, and had laughed in his sleeve when Dr. Parr reverently knelt and rendered thanks that he had lived to read a prayer by the divine poet, finer than anything in the Liturgy. How joyously would he now look back upon his imposture of 1795, preserved by his inordinate vanity from any compunctious visitings that might lead him to think that a fraud was not altogether to be justified by its cleverness! He was now nearly fifty years of age; doing hard work of authorship wherever he could find employment; wretchedly poor, and perhaps not altogether trustworthy. "Take you care of that Mr. Ireland," says my kind neighbour the printseller. "He used to be very fond of looking over my Rembrandt etchings and other portable rarities. But— I will say no more." I was not taken with any of poor Ireland's schemes. He had outlived his very questionable fame as the author of Shakspere's "Vortigern and Rowena." Thirty years had passed since he made his "Confessions."

When I was first planted in the West End as a Publisher of Miscellaneous Works, I adopted the honest, but somewhat impolitic, rule of never suffering myself to be denied. The natural consequence was, that half my day was spent in listening to very dull harangues upon neglected merit, from authors who were making the round of hard-hearted and mercenary dealers, who, with the hereditary effrontery of the trade, refused to embark their capital in printing books that they were satisfied would not sell. But there would often come a welcome relief in clients of a better order. Of such I may mention Captain John Dundas Cochrane, whose "Pedestrian Journey through Russia and Siberian Tartary," I published with great success. Most amusing was the conversation of this eccentric traveller, who did me the honour to introduce me to his wife, brought to England by him from the end of the Kamtchatkan peninsula—a beautiful little flaxen-haired creature, who shrank from my presence and hid behind a table. He did not persuade me to adopt the custom which had been forced upon him in default of other food—that of eating fish raw, which he retained in the heart of civilised life as a luxury far greater than any nice cookery could produce. In a varied intercourse such as that of an aspiring publisher, he must have very dull faculties to allow them to stagnate.

Give him a prosperous career and few occupations can be happier, great as may be his risks and responsibilities. Even the loungers who had no objects of business to propound kept up a pleasant excitement. The mere gossipers were not unprofitable visitors. I endured much desultory tattle in the conviction that a successful publisher must make up his mind to give many hours to what, in the crowded marts "where merchants most do congregate," would be deemed utter waste of time. Some of the pleasant friends of those mornings in Pall Mall East now "come like shadows" before me. Let me call up the memory of one to whom the words of Junius might be applied, "he is a *genus*—let him stand alone." Thomas Gent sits rollicking on the largest chair that he can find—as fat, not quite as witty, but with as sufficient an amount of "impudent sauciness," as Falstaff. I have witnessed the irresistible joke come slowly and demurely off the tongue of Hood, he perfectly grave and silent after the effusion, whilst his hearers are bursting again and again into peals of laughter. I have seen the retort, quick and blinding as lightning, flash from the lips of Jerrold, whilst he himself led the chorus of mirth at his own success, and the victim would laugh the longest and the loudest. But never saw I such effects of mere drollery, resting upon the slightest sub-soil of intellect, as my corpulent friend produced, whether he encountered an acquaintance as he slowly paced the Strand "larding the lean earth;" or gathered a crowd round him in the box-lobby to grin as they had just grinned at Liston; or, falling asleep the instant he had dined, suddenly woke up and set the table in a roar, again closing his eyes and again waking up to the same success. And yet I can recollect none of this humourist's jests or his anecdotes. Yes—one. He was a Yarmouth man, and there also was sojourning his reverend friend, Mr. Croly, and their genial associate, J. P. Davis. A hospitable alderman of that flourishing port had invited them to dinner; the three were the earliest of the guests. As usual Gent fired off some absurdity which put an end to all conventional gravity, even in the stark clergyman, and the trio began "to giggle and make giggle." The solemn host, unused to such explosions, exclaimed in an agony, "Gentlemen, gentlemen—pray be quiet—the company arn't come." Croly drew himself up to his full height, and addressing the unfortunate man with that withering haughtiness which was sometimes a mask for his good nature, said, "What, sir! are we hired?—are we hired?" I must not linger amongst the loungers of my back room, yet I cannot forget one of the pleasantest and most improving, Dr. Maginn. To him the gossip of the modern world was as familiar as the learning of the ancient. From some organic defect of utterance his speech was occasionally hesitating; yet when his words came forth they were full of meaning—always pleasant, often wise. It cannot, however, be denied he was best of a morning,—the double excitement of the table and the talk was sometimes too much for him.

CHAPTER XII.

E have no sufficiently clear record of the commerce of books in the days of Pope and Addison, to be enabled to say that there was a marked Publishing Season. The fact that there was a Long Vacation may lead us to conclude that when "Chambers in the King's Bench Walk" were deserted, Mr. Tonson was entertaining the Kit-Cat Club in his Thames-side Villa, and that Mr. Lintot had left the custody of his "rubric posts" to his shop boys. Whatever may have been the custom in the reign of the first George, undoubtedly the publisher of any note asserted his right to a Season in the reign of George IV. For the three months of autumn, the Circulating Libraries were indifferently supplied with Travel and Romance; but great were the preparations for the coming campaign. Manuscripts were in critical hands, proofs were circulating by post, negotiations were on foot, advertisements were being prepared, mysterious hints about "the Journal of a noble lady, that had been read to a select circle of fashionables," appeared in the papers. Like the mighty ones of my craft, I was glad that the Season had come to an end, in the July of 1825. With me it was closed by the publication of a work of unusual importance. Milton's Latin Treatise on Christian Doctrine, having been discovered in the State Paper Office, was placed

in the hands of the Librarian and Historiographer to George IV., for the laudable purpose of giving to the world an unpublished work of one of the greatest of English poets. That office was held in 1824 by the Rev. Charles Richard Sumner. The original, and a translation, were printed at the Cambridge University Press, and I was selected as their Publisher.* At the time of its publication the editor and translator was D.D., and a prebendary of Canterbury. In 1827 he succeeded Dr. Tomline, as bishop of Winchester. I cannot advert to the confidence which Dr. Sumner placed in me, and bear in mind the whole nature of my intercourse with him, without a feeling of affectionate gratitude to a most zealous and constant friend, whose kindness was never alloyed by any of the condescension of patronage—who, when he had arrived at almost the highest ecclesiastical dignity, preserved the same frank and amiable demeanour that he had exhibited when I first knew him at Windsor—who, a year or two later, won my heart by his public spirit, as well as by his personal kindness,—for it was he, in his diocese of Llandaff, who, in a letter of interrogatories sent round to his Clergy, asked a question which became famous—"Are there infant schools in your parish—and, if not, why not?" It is in me an act of simple justice here to record a circumstance which has been misunderstood in connection with the translation of Milton's posthumous work.

In 1824 I went with Mr. Sumner to Cambridge, to arrange for the printing of the original Latin MS. at the University Press. Marvellous to relate, there

* A reprint of the translation has been published by Mr. Bohn.

was no functionary of that printing office who was competent to see that the corrections upon the proofs as they passed out of the hands of the editor were properly attended to. I had the pleasure of introducing Mr. Sidney Walker to Mr. Sumner, and it was agreed that he should undertake this duty. The printing of the Latin edition, and of the English translation, was completed in the course of a twelvemonth. The Preface by the translator contains the following paragraph: "He cannot conclude these preliminary remarks without acknowledging his obligations to W. S. Walker, Esq., Fellow of Trinity College, Cambridge, who has not only discharged the greater part of the laborious office of correcting the press, but whose valuable suggestions during the progress of the work have contributed to remove some of its imperfections." The Rev. J. Moultrie, in his Memoir of Mr. Walker, prefixed to his "Poetical Remains," says of this incident in his friend's literary career, "The work being printed at the University Press, Walker was selected as resident on the spot, and eminently qualified for the office, to revise and correct the proof sheets. In the performance of this task he considerably overstepped the limits of his commission, reviewing not only the printer's but the translator's labour, and leaving upon the work the indelible impress of his own masterly scholarship and profound appreciation of the author's genius." Compared with this statement the acknowledgment by Dr. Sumner of his obligations to Mr. Walker may appear not only cold, but insufficient. It is my duty to state that not only had the accomplished Fellow of Trinity "considerably overstepped the limits of his commission," but had concealed the fact of having done so till the printing of the work was completed. He was fastidious to excess in his critical scholarship. His clandestine mode of proceeding was to be attributed to his utter want of decision of character. To me he at length made the tardy communication of his error. "I ought properly to address Mr. Sumner, but I cannot muster confidence to make the communication to him. The truth is, that I have been guilty of great and unwarrantable liberties with regard to the translation of Milton. I understood it to be his wish that I should make no alterations, except such as were approved of by him; and with this wish I conformed for a short time, except some minute encroachments *after the sheet was returned from Windsor;* but as I went on, so many instances occurred to me in which, so I thought, the translation might be bettered, that at last I dropped all remorse and altered without compunction. The truth was, that although the translation would in any case have been quite as good as is generally thought proper to bestow on modern works, written in foreign languages—so that the public would not have complained,—I could not be satisfied, unless it were something better." Many, he says, may think he had too rigid ideas of the duties of a translator. His justification was to be found, he maintains, in the desire he felt "that the work might be, not good in a certain stated degree, but as good as it could be made."

The days before "Murray"—the days when the tourist went groping his way through foreign towns without the friendly aid of the famous "Hand Books for Travellers"—seem to belong to an era when the majority of Britons were, in some sense, "almost separated from the whole world." Yet, in 1825, these excellent books would have been before their time. Travelling had not then become a fashion. The modes of conveyance were tedious, uncertain, and expensive. An opportunity was presented to me in the August of that year of seeing Paris under agreeable circumstances; and I persuaded myself that through a personal intercourse with French publishers I could unite business with pleasure. I joined a family, of which the mother had been the friend of my childhood—whose elder daughter was growing into the elegant and accomplished woman—whose two sons were Etonians, full of spirit and curiosity. We travelled through Picardy with a calèche and pair of horses that we had hired at Calais; accomplishing about forty miles each day, with ample opportunities of seeing the country and observing the manners of the people. The Diligence often passed us or met us. We could never want a hearty laugh whilst the postilion diverted us with his jack-boots and his pigtail. We drew up beneath the hedge-row apple-trees as he cracked his leathern whip with the noise of a little blunderbuss. We rather pitied the poor creatures, who, in the hottest of weather, were shut up in the interior of that machine. We did not even envy the uninterrupted prospect of the few who sat aloft with the conducteur in the cabriolet. So we leisurely journeyed, pleased with all we saw; enjoying the quails and partridges, which we often found at dinner or supper, although the glory of bread-sauce was reserved for our own country, according to the belief of Lord Devon; mightily relishing the wine which we always thought surprisingly cheap; and well inclined to believe that there were no bad inns upon the road which the English were wont to use in the days of leisurely travelling. They are gone,—for the tourist from Boulogne to Paris of 1864—the Diligence, the Malle poste, the colossal boots, and the queues. He cannot enjoy, as we enjoyed, the quiet dinner at Montreuil; the nice supper at Abbeville; the market day at Beauvais, amidst smiling vendors of eggs and poultry in their wondrous caps and sabots, who did not seem as if they ever toiled in the harvest time as we had seen some of their hard-worked country-women. We now rush from London to Paris in twelve hours, and fancy we have seen France.

The Paris of Charles X. was as suggestive of political and social contrasts to the Paris of the first Napoleon, as its physical aspects gave no promise of the wonders that might be effected under a sagacious despotism during the lapse of another generation. There was a constitutional Government; a vigorous opposition; an unlicensed Press. There were earnest speakers in the Chamber of Deputies; bitter satirists in prose and verse; Beranger was on all lips, and Courier might be read in castrated editions; the officers of the Crown instituted proceedings against journalists, but the tribunals refused to condemn them. There was then an open struggle between the narrowest bigotry and the broadest licence in matters of religion. The priestly and ultra-royalist parties, with the Court at their head, were despised. They were "*les infiniment petits,*" whose fall would be a Revolution. I saw the King and the Royal family walk from the Tuileries in procession to Notre Dame, on the Feast of the Ascension of the Virgin, amidst a population intent upon a holiday and in tolerable good humour. But there was no enthusiasm, and there were significant shrugs of the shoulders. While the King was marching through the streets at the head of an army of priests, the people were discussing the atrocity of the law of sacrilege which was being debated in the Chamber of Deputies, under which law the profanation of the sacred utensils was to be punished with death. Nevertheless, all was gaiety in this beauteous summer time. There were then noble trees on the Boulevards, beneath whose shade we sipped our ices, or lingered till the deep blue sky was gemmed with stars. The gardens of the Tuileries and the Champs Elysées were filled with crowds of idlers. Versailles, with its *Grandes Eaux*, was to us a place of wonder and delight. The Palace of the Grand Monarque, before Louis Philippe had dedicated its saloons to the glories of the Consulate and the Empire, presented historical memorials more interesting than picture after picture of battle fields, most of them bad and all wearisome. The streets of Paris were fertile in remembrances of a past generation of comparative uncivilisation. The stinking gutter stagnated in the middle of the causeway, which had no *trottoirs*. The rope stretched from side to side, with the lamp in the centre, made us understand the meaning of *à la lanterne*. I was awakened every morning at five o'clock by the cleaving of wood in the Rue Richelieu, for the winter supply of the Hôtel des Princes, in which I had the misfortune to be lodged in a front bed-room. In spite of some discomforts—even in a first-rate hotel—which have now vanished, we were well pleased with our fortnight of sight-seeing; were not discomposed by assisting at the representation of three farces at the Theâtre des Variétés, in which the chief humour was a burlesque of English manners. At the Theâtre Français I saw Talma in Sylla, and lost my belief that French dramatic poetry was essentially a conventional and tame affair. The great tragedian united, as I then felt, the majestic impressiveness of Kemble with the passionate energy of Kean. I am afraid that I was too much pleased and excited in Paris to attend very profitably to business. I found the publishers with whom I had negotiations very obliging and unpretentious; living plainly in their houses of business; and not affecting to be anything grander than dealers in books, who had a shrewd eye to a bargain. We travelled homeward through Normandy, where the green fields and the pretty churches reminded us of English scenes. We rested for a night at Neufchâtel, where we tasted the delicious little cheeses fresh in the place of their production—a luxury made just then somewhat famous by the mistake of a worthy alderman of London, who, having first seen the delicacy at a great man's table, said he would order a hundred of his correspondent, and was astonished by the delivery at his door of a ton or two of the hard cheeses of Switzerland, almost as big as a cart wheel. May I dare to say, that some of the leisure of the ladies of our party was employed in sewing sundry yards of French silk within the lining of my cloak. Smuggling was then deemed a venial offence. Huskisson's great measure removing the prohibition upon the importation of foreign silks was not to take effect till 1826.

When I returned in September, my family were at Windsor. I had the opportunity, in company with Dr. Sumner, of seeing the progress of the great improvements of the Castle, and of listening to the clear explanations of his plans, which Mr. Wyatville gave with the straightforward simplicity characteristic of his practical genius. In the previous summer, soon after the commencement of the works, I had gone into the old building with Mr. Britton. We had found the architect sitting alone surrounded with demolished walls at the north-east angle of the Terrace front, deeply engaged in the study of a ground plan. His idea of the beautiful octagon tower, called Brunswick, was then shaping itself into that harmonious combination of somewhat incongruous parts which he so happily effected in many portions of the fortress-palace of Edward III., by the careful preservation of old features and the happy adaptation of new. I could not long linger at Windsor in the enjoyment of a beautiful autumn, but had to be much in London, as the publishing season was approaching. Every day was then giving birth to some new project for the employment of capital, although during the Session of Parliament, which closed on the 6th of July, two hundred and eighty-six private bills had been passed for schemes of local improvement, chiefly to be effected by the agency of Joint Stock Companies. You could scarcely meet a man in the city who had not something to say about the rise or the fall in shares—shares in Canals, in Rail-roads, in Packets, in Gasworks, in Mines, in Banks, in Insurance Offices, in Fisheries, in Sugar and Indigo cultivation, in Irish Manufactures, in Newspapers. At the beginning of the Session the King had "the happiness of congratulating" his Parliament on "general and increasing prosperity;" at the end of the Session the same prosperity "continues to pervade every part of the kingdom." These sanguine views gained for the Chancellor of the Exchequer the title of "Prosperity Robinson." Turning aside from thoughts of French translations and other productions of ephemeral Literature, I had devised a large and comprehensive scheme of a "National Library"—a cheap series of books which should condense the information contained in voluminous and expensive works. I prepared a Prospectus, in which I truly said, "It is to be remarked that, with some few striking exceptions, the general Literature of our country is either addressed to men of leisure and research, and is, therefore, bulky and diffuse; or it is frittered down into meagre and spiritless outlines, adapted only for juvenile capacities." I settled the subjects of about a hundred volumes, in History, Science and Art, and Miscellaneous Literature. I submitted this Prospectus to Mr. Colburn, who expressed his desire to join me in the undertaking, in conjunction with some wholesale house. It was settled that Mr. Whittaker should be applied to, and accordingly the general terms of an agreement were soon arranged between us.

During November I applied myself assiduously to the preparation of a complete scheme to go before the public. I obtained the opinion of judicious advisers. I made overtures to writers. I received a letter from my old friend the Rev. J. M. Turner, in which he says, "I hear from Mr. Locker that you are about to undertake an extensive scheme of publication something like that which Constable is advertising so assiduously. I shall be very glad to enlist as a contributor to your stores. Constable's programme seems very imposing, but like all comprehensive sketches it is both deficient and redundant." My own plan was no doubt open to the same objection. It was more systematic than Constable's, and, therefore, perhaps less attractive. I was in high spirits at the prospect of congenial occupation in the editorship of this series, and in a probable source of profit with a limited responsibility. Mr. Whittaker was as sanguine as myself. We had contracted an intimacy as members of a Club of a peculiar character, of which there was no previous example, and which, as far as I know, has had no imitators. "The Publishers' Club" included under that comprehensive name Authors as well as Publishers *proper*. Mr. Jerdan, in his "Autobiography," describes this Club as "The Literary Club," but I never knew it under any other name than "The Publishers'." Our monthly dinner was at the Albion, in Aldersgate Street. It was an exceedingly pleasant association, even when the proceedings were not enlivened by invited guests, such as the great comedians Munden and Mathews. I remember an evening of rare enjoyment, when I sat by Munden—a man of the most exquisite humour—a great actor when asked for an exercise of his art, but returning naturally to take an intelligent share in general conversation. On ordinary occasions, Mr. Croly harangued in a style which some deemed eloquence; Mr. Jerdan made puns which some regarded as wit; and Dr. Kitchener pronounced dogmatic opinions upon cookery and wine. Hood, a few years before, had spread his fame far and wide in his "Ode to Dr. Kitchener;" but I was not quite aware of our Vice-Chairman's greatness in the world of gastronomy till I saw the rich landlord of the Albion address himself to the sage physician, whose maxim to ward off dyspepsia was "masticate, denticate, chump, and chew." As he sat, eagerly looking for the remove, with his pocket-case of sauces by his side, Mr. —— humbly requested that he would deign to taste of a certain dish which the genius of his *chef* had recently produced. The fiat of approval was given. Henceforth the luxury would be classical.

The first meeting of our Club season of 1825 was joyous. The second meeting was dismal. The commercial world was in alarm. How well I remember the anxious face of Mr. James Duncan, one of the most prudent and sagacious of publishers! Even such a man

> "Drew Priam's curtain in the dead of night,
> And would have told him, half his Troy was burnt."

Duncan would have told us, had he dared, that half the Row was shaky. Few of our Club after this meeting were in the humour for a monthly festivity. The Panic had come, passing over all our tribe like the Simoom, bringing with it general feebleness, if not individual death. Scott, in the blind confidence which he felt, even whilst he and Constable were signing "sheafs of bills," writes in his Journal of November 25th, "After all, it is hard that the vagabond stock-jobbing Jews, should, for their own purposes, make such a state of credit as now exists in London." If the "pleasant vices" of speculative men had not found work for the stock-jobbing Jews, there would have been no panic to become one of the "instruments to scourge us"—the humblest subjects, and the highest potentates, of "the realms of print." The house of Whittaker succumbed very early, and its affairs were righteously administered by Trustees, who in a few years restored it to its old position. Hurst and Robinson fell, never to rise again, and pulled down Constable and Ballantyne with them. Then began the heroic period of Walter Scott's life, when we might almost envy him his misfortunes and mistakes, in the contemplation of the grandeur of his efforts to retrieve them.

On the 6th of December I had been at Windsor. Returning to London by the afternoon coach, I learnt that the banking-house of Williams & Co. had stopped payment. They were the bankers who transacted the business of Messrs. Ramsbottom and Legh, the partners in our sole Windsor bank, and large brewers. I was upon intimate terms with both these gentlemen, and I dreaded the consequence to them of this unexpected calamity. Late at night they both arrived at my house in Pall Mall East. We spent several hours in anxious consultation; but it was at length agreed that Mr. Legh should immediately return to Windsor, to countermand an order that had been given for the closing of their bank on the morning of the 7th. It had seemed impossible upon the first receipt of the disastrous intelligence to prevent a fatal run upon them; for their resources, beyond the regulated supply of specie and banknotes to pay their own well-worn pieces of paper—the ordinary currency of the town and neighbourhood—were now locked up in the unfortunate London house. Mr. Ramsbottom was one of the members for the borough, very popular, and of unimpeached credit. He and I set out on an excursion, west and east, to seek the assistance of bankers and other capitalists, his friends. In the Albany we found the partners of one firm, that of Messrs. Everett, deliberating by lamp-light. A few words showed how unavailing was the hope of help from them: "We shall ourselves stop at nine o'clock." The dark December morning gradually grew lighter; the gas-lamps died out; but long before it was perfect day we found Lombard Street blocked up by eager crowds, each man struggling to be foremost at the bank where he kept his account if its doors should be opened. We entered several of the banks where the counters were surrounded by the presenters of cheques; and were witnesses to the calm which sustains the honest English trader in the hour of difficulty, even as it has sustained many a naval commander when the ship has struck upon a sunken rock, and his own safety is the last consideration. There was a London office of Messrs. Ramsbottom's brewery; and here we found a considerable sum that, through the prudence of the principal clerk, had not been paid in on the 6th to their banking agents in Birchin Lane. We decided upon a plan of action, the artifice of which was justified by the necessity of the case. I took my seat in a postchaise with my treasure—something less than a thousand pounds—and was whirled to Windsor in a couple of hours by four horses. As I changed horses at Hounslow, or stopped at turnpikes, I proclaimed, "funds for the Windsor Bank." The news spread down the road in that extraordinary way in which news, good or bad, is promulgated. I drove triumphantly into the yard of the Bank, amidst the hurrahs of a multitude outside, to whom I had proclaimed my mission. There was a meeting at the same time taking place at the Town Hall, at which my townsmen entered into resolutions declaring their opinion of the solvency of the firm, and the necessity of not pressing upon them in the hour of difficulty. The bank was saved. Its failure would have spread general dismay and misery; especially as several of the tradesmen largely employed in the alterations of the Castle depended upon advances for wages upon their credit accounts with Messrs. Ramsbottom. I went the next day to Dr. Sumner, and represented to him that a prompt payment of arrears from the Board of Works would be an immense relief. With a ready kindness he applied to the highest quarter. The King's intervention,—then, perhaps, more potent in overcoming obstacles of routine than in the present day—quickly accomplished this object. Williams & Co. resumed payments in a few weeks.

Lockhart, in his life of Scott, relates that in January, 1826, Constable, awakening from his dream of safety from impending ruin, had come to London with the resolution of applying to the Bank of England, "for a loan of from 100,000*l.* to 200,000*l.* on the security of the copyrights in his possession." Copyrights, in that perilous season, were a most unmarketable commodity; and the Governor and Company of the Bank of England, or indeed any other bankers, would have regarded such securities, and even the most valuable stock of a publisher, as so much waste paper. My own credit was unassailed amidst suspicions on every side. I had no engagements that had arisen out of the system of accommodation bills,—those treacherous allies who pull down the strongest in the hour of mortal conflict. Such desperate help in tiding over difficulties was fully developed in all its evils by that unsparing Panic. I had trade engagements that would have been duly met, if a paralysis of commerce had not been eventually as dangerous as its apoplexy; chronic decay as fatal as sudden extinction. The publications of 1825 would no longer sell in 1826; the new works projected, written, half printed, advertised, must wait for a more propitious time. The "tender leaves" would not endure that "killing frost." This was the reasoning of most of us—of nearly all, with the exception of Mr. Colburn, who pushed his new works with great vigour, having the market of light literature almost wholly to himself. He was perhaps more right than his fellows, in following a course which the most wonderful Common-sense, lifted into the noblest poetry by the power of Imagination, has prescribed as well for publishers as for statesmen:—

> "To have done, is to hang
> Quite out of fashion, like a rusty mail
> In monumental mockery."
>
> *Troilus and Cressida.*

For myself, I saw and heard so much of commercial misery, of fear that kills, of unmerited suspicion troubling the sleep of the most prudent, that the spring was passing into summer, and I began to look upon 1826 as a lost year of business. I could not resolve to "take the instant way"—to "keep the path." I had achieved something like a position in 1825. I could scarcely hope to regain it by following the usual course of publishing books that might live their little hour of novelty and then pass to the trunkmakers. Every day made me sick of my occupation. "The Brazen Head," of which I have spoken, dropped upon the town like a leaden lump. Credit was whispered away. Harsh judgments were pronounced upon the unlucky. In this dark season I sometimes heard the raven-croak of a man who peeped into every corner, and was nightly exhibited in his peeping attitude to laughing play-goers. The Paul Pry of Liston was a chubby, rosy-faced, good-natured, but essentially mischievous meddler, known as Tom Hill. He would lay hold of your button in the streets, and detain you by some such talk as this:—"Do you know if W— has given up his hunter? I asked one of his porters, and he wouldn't tell me . . . . . Isn't it suspicious to see —— and Co. sending a waggon load of stock from their warehouse? . . . . Do give a hint to your friend in —— Street, that his servants are very extravagant. I looked down his area and saw them having hot rolls for breakfast." I got away from this moral fog of London as soon as I could. I was shut up, moody and irresolute, at Windsor, in the summer, projectting, planning, re-arranging my "National Library" scheme, which had been stifled by the panic before its birth; adding a book here and there, or curtailing the list, already too long. I was about to return to London with no more preparation for a coming campaign than half a dozen various prospectuses of this work. It had become a fixed idea with me, to the exclusion of all minor purposes of business or literary occupation.

In the autumn of 1826 Mr. Brougham was organizing his "Society for the Diffusion of Useful

Knowledge." The Long Vacation was at an end, and in that November, the prospectus of the new society was privately circulated. It said,—"The object of the Society is strictly limited to what its title imports, namely, the imparting useful information to all classes of the community, particularly to such as are unable to avail themselves of experienced teachers, or may prefer learning by themselves." Here, then, appeared an opening for the nurture of my cherished scheme, of which I ought to avail myself. At Windsor, in November, I received a letter from Mr. M. D. Hill, wishing me to come to town immediately, as he had mentioned my plan of popular books to Mr. Brougham, and to a committee for the encouragement of such a project, and that he thought great things might be done. Of course this communication brought me instantly to London; and I was very quickly introduced by Mr. Hill to Mr. Brougham. That interview is indelibly impressed upon my memory with all its attendant circumstances. I had never come across the renowned orator in private life, or had seen him under an every-day character. There was an image in my mind of the Queen's Attorney-General, as I had often beheld him in the House of Lords, wielding a power in the proceedings on the Bill of Pains and Penalties which no other man seemed to possess—equivocating witnesses crouching beneath his withering scorn; mighty peers shrinking from his bold sarcasm; the whole assembly visibly agitated at times by the splendour of his eloquence. The Henry Brougham I had gazed upon was, in my mind's eye, a man stern and repellent; not to be approached with any attempt at familiarity; whose opinions must be received with the most respectful deference; whose mental superiority would be somewhat overwhelming. The Henry Brougham into whose chambers in Lincoln's Inn I was ushered on a November night was sitting amidst his briefs, evidently delighted to be interrupted for some thoughts more attractive. After saluting my friend with a joke, and grasping my hand with a cordial welcome, he went at once to the subject upon which I came. The rapid conception of the features of my plan; the few brief questions as to my wishes; the manifestation of a warm interest in my views without the slightest attempt to be patronizing, were most gratifying to me. The image of the great orator of 1820 altogether vanished when I listened to the unpretentious and often playful words of one of the best table-talkers of 1826,—it vanished, even as the full-bottomed wig of that time seemed to have belonged to some other head than the close-cropped one upon which I looked. The foremost advocate of popular education made no harangues about its advantages. He did not indoctrinate me, as I have been bored by many an educationist before and since, with flourishes upon a subject which he gave Mr. Hill and myself full credit for comprehending. M. Charles Dupin said to Mackintosh, after a night in the House of Commons—"I heard not one word about the blessings of Liberty."—"No, no," replied Mackintosh, "we take all that for granted." So did Henry Brougham take for granted that he and I were in accord upon the subject of the Diffusion of Knowledge. He was then within a few days of the completion of his forty-seventh year; full of health and energy—one who had been working without intermission in literature, in science, in law, in politics, for a quarter of a century, but one to whom no work seemed to bring fatigue; no tedious mornings of the King's Bench, no sleepless nights of the House of Commons, able to "stale his infinite variety." From that hour I felt more confidence in talking with perfect freedom to him who worthily filled so large a space in the world's eye, than to many a man of commonplaces, whose depths I had plumbed and had found them shallow. That first interview with Mr. Brougham was an event that had a marked influence upon many subsequent passages of my life.

It would be a fruitless and wearisome story of private affairs, were I to detail the circumstances under which my unfortunate "National Library," having been at first taken up by the Society of which Mr. Brougham was President, and negotiations having been opened with their publishers, was finally adopted by Mr. Murray, with an earnestness which was to me very assuring, after my long term of enforced idleness and dark apprehensions. The eminent West-end publisher was committed to the enterprise, by the issue of the Prospectus in his own name, which I had so carefully prepared. In my original Prospectus, which I had submitted to Mr. Murray in February, 1826, I had said, "It is our peculiar object to condense the information which is scattered through voluminous and expensive works, into the form and substance of Original Treatises." In the Prospectus issued on the 24th of December, it was set forth that "the divisions of Popular Knowledge in which the National Library is arranged, will comprehend, in distinct Treatises, the most important branches of instruction and amusement. They will present the most valuable and interesting articles of an Encyclopædia, in a form accessible to every description of purchaser." This final Prospectus is printed, *in extenso*, in Goodhugh's "English Gentleman's Library Manual,"—published in May, 1827. Differences of opinion about the editorial responsibility of the series too soon arose. *Quis custodiet* was answered by the apparition of a very solemn divine, who talked as a "Sir Oracle." Arrangements regarding my old stock and copyrights, which it was considered—I may say perfectly understood—were to be taken at a valuation, when I was about to merge my business in the great house of Albemarle Street, presented new obstacles. Thus were my prospects clouded in a few weeks of 1827. I was heartsick at last, and abandoning the whole scheme left it for the imitation of others of more independent means. The Society for the Diffusion of Useful Knowledge produced their "Treatises" in March, and Messrs. Longman their Lardner's "Cabinet Cyclopædia" a few years afterwards. Mr. Murray, I had reason to believe, had become frightened at the magnitude of my plan. He several times said to me, "where will you find the men to write these books?" In my maturer experience I came to perceive that this was the real difficulty in such undertakings.

Let me hasten to close these recollections of the spring of 1827. Scott writes of old letters, somewhere in his Diary, "they rise up as scorpions to hiss at me." So may I write of the documents by which I trace this crisis of my life. My abortive efforts to begin a new career, shaking off future responsibilities of trade, made the responsibilities which remained more onerous. My boat was stranded. Happily for me there were no wreckers at hand ready for the plunder of my damaged cargo. A private trust administered my affairs, whose only concern was to realize—to sell, to the best advantage, land, houses, newspaper, stock, copyrights. I would not be a burden. I would earn my own bread. I walked forth from my business homes in London and Windsor, after the fashion of a man represented in a wood-cut in a title-page of one of the old printers (I think it was a work of Budæus) which comes into my thoughts—a man, not bowed down by age or sorrow, moving forward, not briskly, but not unsteadily, with his stout staff, and his small wallet, and a label of four words, —"OMNIA MEA MECUM PORTO."

CHAPTER XIII.

AM living at Brompton, with my wife and four little girls. The house which we have chosen in which to begin a new and unambitious life is in a narrow road, called Cromwell Lane, through which few people pass. Our long slip of garden is bounded on one side by the high wall of Cromwell House, the reputed mansion of the Protector. We are surrounded by nursery grounds. I can no longer find the place where I dwelt for two or three years. The few unpretending houses, nestling in snug gardens, have given place to squares, and rows, and to "Great Exhibition" buildings—themselves doomed prematurely to perish. Perchance I might discover some traces of the quiet corner if the humble tavern still remains that was once known as "The Hoop and Toy." Does the "Goat in Boots" still exist?—another landmark. The daughter of a very dear friend, who afterwards occupied our house, was eager to tell us that, when she visited the Exhibition of 1862, she rejoiced to find, in a small plot of ground not yet subdued to the tyranny of brick and mortar, a single apple-tree, which she could identify as the tree under which she had sat as a child, looking wistfully up at the ripening fruit. Why do I linger about this unpretentious abiding place of 1827? Because it was to me as a city of refuge. Here I first relinquished the hope of commercial success, having surrendered to others my commercial responsibilities. I had much for which to be grateful to the All-giver. I had preserved my bodily and mental health. I had domestic confidence and peace. The "precious jewel" in the toad's head was not undiscovered. I was determined to work, and I was equally resolved to be as happy as I could be. I did not repine at the turn of Fortune's wheel. Amongst some papers of this period I find a scrap on which I had written,—If the capacity to enjoy were commensurate with the power to possess, we then, indeed, might complain of the inequality of our conditions.

Looking back upon the summer of 1827, I have no recollection of such hours of gloom as belonged to the previous year. No unkindness wounded my pride; no desertion of old friends rendered me misanthropical. I had quickly obtained an engagement as a writer in Mr. Buckingham's new paper, "The Sphinx." High-priced as it was—a shilling—it had a considerable sale. I wrote political articles and reviews. At that time I was an enthusiast in public affairs. Canning was the head of a new administration. On the 1st of May I had stood in the crowded avenues of the House of Commons, and had seen for a moment his radiant face, as he rapidly mounted the old staircase which led to the lobby, about to take the foremost place, and vindicate his policy before many detractors and some new friends. There were whispered blessings upon many lips. In that triumph of the minister who had shaken off the shackles of the great Continental Powers, and had carried England "into the camp of progress and liberty," I regarded the man as the "deliverer" described by Burke, in words almost profane in their idolatrous admiration. But I may look back upon that memorable occasion, and soberly say,—"Nor did he seem insensible to the best of all earthly rewards, the love and admiration of his fellow citizens. Hope elevated and joy brightened his crest."—[*Speech on American Taxation*, 1774.] On the 16th of August I saw him laid in his grave, in the north transept of Westminster Abbey. On the previous 20th of January, I had seen him standing for two hours of the bitterest night, upon the cold unmatted pavement of the nave of St. George's Chapel, at the funeral of the Duke of York. He did not take the precaution which he had suggested to Lord Eldon, to stand upon his cocked hat. That funeral broke up the delicate health of George Canning.

My course of journalism under Mr. James Silk Buckingham was not agreeable. Perhaps I had been too long my own master in such matters to brook control and criticism. Perhaps I formed too low an estimate of his knowledge and ability. His wonderful fluency as a platform speaker, pouring forth platitude after platitude, was calculated to catch the multitude. He has *written* scores of volumes in the same style, and I may ask "where are they?" I cared not how wearisome were his own newspaper prolusions; but I rebelled against his unparalleled conceit. He outraged me by presuming to alter, in his own obtuse fashion, some spirited lines on the death of Canning, which Praed had sent me. I at once quitted his office—where I had diligently laboured, and not without success—when he proposed an amended scale of remuneration for critiques on new books, beginning at half-a-crown and rising to a guinea, according to the length of the article. I know not whether he found journeymen at this rate. I know not whether literature was degraded then, or is now, by the pretence of giving an opinion of a book amongst what are called "short notices," at the rate of threepence a line, to be earned by men who ought to have been hewers of wood and drawers of water. Happily a more worthy course of industry was opening for me. But before I enter upon the "passages" of an employment which was spread over nearly twenty years, let me glance at a temporary labour of 1827. What were then called "The Annuals" were introduced to England by Mr. Ackermann, in his "Forget-me-not" of 1822. Alaric Watts followed with his "Literary Souvenir." Samuel Carter Hall started "The Amulet," for the especial use of "serious persons." In 1827 I was asked to edit "Friendship's Offering." It was an enterprise hastily entered upon by Messrs. Smith and Elder, late in the season, and I had to obtain pictures for engraving, secure contributors, and see the book through the press in two or three months. The pleasantest thing about the engagement was that my friends of the "Quarterly Magazine," Mr. Praed and Mr. Moultrie, with others of their following, rallied round me, and contributed the most original pages of a volume, for which, like its rivals, there would be no lack of sentimental stories, and verses somewhat mawkish with their bowers and flowers. The most disagreeable thing was, that a blockhead behind the scenes, in the confidence of the publishers, took upon himself to change the title which Praed had given to his poem, and had it printed as "The Red Fisherman" instead of "The Devil's Decoy." My friend had nearly quarrelled with me about this matter, in which I was really blameless. He had a right to be angry, for the poem was, I am inclined to think, his *chef-d'œuvre.* New Annuals started up, in the next and few following years, amongst the best of which was "The Anniversary," edited by Allan Cunningham, who had it in his power to make as good a book of this sort as could be produced, from the esteem with which he was regarded by the best writers and the best artists. There were Keepsakes, and Gems, and Bijous; but these delicate flowerets of the literary hotbed had a brief existence. They did more for the arts than for letters. They had set a great many people scribbling, who would never have dreamt of committing the sin of rhyme without such excitements, and they had compelled some of those who could write well to adopt a style anything but vigorous and original. They were perhaps right, and so were the editors and publishers. It was a period in which, except in a few rare instances, mediocrity was essentially necessary to great literary success. There was a poem entitled "The Omnipresence of the Deity," by one whose fame settled into the name of "the wrong Montgomery;" the good old champion of freedom, the *right* Montgomery, being then alive and honoured by all competent judges. It went rapidly through five or six editions. The "Excursion" had reached a second edition in ten years.

A document, which I value as a soldier who has seen long service values his first Commission, lies before me:—

"GENERAL MEETING of the Committee for the Diffusion of Useful Knowledge.—26th July, 1827.

"James Mill, Esq., in the Chair.

"Mr. Hill having informed the Committee that Mr. Charles Knight was willing to undertake the superintendence of the Society's Publications, it was

"Resolved,—

"That his services be accepted, and that it be referred to the Publication Committee to furnish him with the necessary instructions."

At that time the only publications of the Society were the Treatises of the "Library of Useful Knowledge," issued fortnightly in sixpenny numbers. The Series had been commenced in the Spring, with Mr. Brougham's "Discourse on the Objects, Advantages, and Pleasures of Science." The sale of this work had been as extraordinary as its merits were striking and almost unexampled. Some called it superficial, because it touched rapidly upon many departments of scientific knowledge; but the more just conclusion was that it was the work of "a full man," who had not laboriously elaborated this fascinating treatise out of books recently studied or hastily referred to, but had poured it forth out of the accumulated wealth of his rich treasury of knowledge. No reader to whom the subjects treated of were in any degree new could read this little book without feeling an ardent desire to know more—to know all. Such were my own feelings as I devoured this tract on the outside of an Aylesbury coach, and bitterly regretted that upon mere business considerations I had lost the chance of becoming intimate with the author of such a book, as his fellow-labourer in the work of popular enlightenment. It could scarcely be expected that many other Treatises could have the same attraction as this Preliminary Discourse. They were to be manuals for self-education—clear, accurate, but not to be mastered without diligence and perseverance. Their success made it clear that there was a great body of students—whether in Colleges or Mechanics' Institutes, in busy towns or quiet villages, to whom such guides would be welcome. My duties, in connexion with this Series, were scarcely more than ministerial. I had to read manuscripts and give an opinion upon them, although the decision did not rest with me but with the Committee. Upon the higher scientific subjects I was not competent to give an opinion as regarded their correctness, but I could judge how far they were adapted for popular use. I was thus what the Germans, I believe, call a *Vorleser*. Proofs went through my hands as they passed the Committee, and the printers were kept up to their work. I could not reasonably shrink from this drudgery, for I saw men of high station and literary eminence —statesmen, lawyers, physicians, willingly performing it. It was not necessary that I should regularly attend at the Offices of the Society in Furnival's Inn; but I had often to confer with Mr. Coates, the active and intelligent Secretary of the Society, and to attend some meetings of the general and special Committees. I gradually came to form a just estimate of the individual characters and qualifications of those with whom I was brought in contact. I found them, collectively, very different from provincial Committees of which I had once had some experience —earnest in the pursuit of a common object; not intent upon personal display or the assertion of petty self-importance; men of cultivated minds, each treating the opinions of the others with respect; the most capable amongst them the most modest; in a word, gentlemen and scholars. I felt that it depended upon myself some day to win their confidence in a position of higher responsibility than my early labours demanded.

In these pursuits, the summer of 1827 wore away. I was not without my pleasures. I delighted to walk in Kensington Gardens, sometimes on a holiday afternoon with my elder girls—more frequently in the early morning on my way to town. Glancing—in the intervals of my present task of reviving old memories,—at the work of a poet who ought to be more widely known, I find these lines:—

"Once as I stray'd a student, happiest then,
What time the summer's garniture was on,
Beneath the princely shades of Kensington,
A girl I spied, whose years might number ten,
With full round eyes, and fair soft English face."*

In such a season, when the sun was scarcely high enough to have dried up the dews of Kensington's green alleys, as I passed along the broad central walk, I saw a group on the lawn before the Palace, which, to my mind, was a vision of exquisite loveliness. The Duchess of Kent, and her daughter, whose years then numbered nine, are breakfasting in the open air—a single page attending upon them at a respectful distance—the matron looking on with eyes of love, whilst the "fair soft English face" is bright with smiles. The world of fashion is not yet astir. Clerks and mechanics, passing onward to their occupations, are few; and they exhibit nothing of

* "Lays of Middle Age;" by James Hedderwick, 1859.

that vulgar curiosity which I think is more commonly found in the class of the merely rich, than in the ranks below them in the world's estimation. What a beautiful characteristic it seemed to me of the training of this royal girl, that she should not have been taught to shrink from the public eye—that she should not have been burthened with a premature conception of her probable high destiny—that she should enjoy the freedom and simplicity of a child's nature—that she should not be restrained when she starts up from the breakfast-table and runs to gather a flower in the adjoining parterre—that her merry laugh should be as fearless as the notes of the thrush in the groves around her. I passed on and blessed her; and I thank God that I have lived to see the golden fruits of such training.

At this period the Almanacs of the Stationers' Company were published within a few days of Lord Mayor's Day, the 9th of November. Before their issue, the Master and other magnates of the Company used to go in their barge to Lambeth, to present copies of all their Almanacs to the Archbishop of Canterbury. In Erskine's famous Speech in 1779, when Lord North brought a Bill into the House of Commons for re-vesting in the Stationers' Company a monopoly which had been declared illegal by the Court of Common Pleas in 1775, he adverted to "the episcopal revision" which formerly existed, when the Universities, as well as the Stationers' Company, were alone authorised to print Almanacs. "It is notorious," said the great advocate, "that the Universities sell their right to the Stationers' Company for a fixed annual sum; and it is equally notorious, that the Stationers' Company make a scandalous job of the bargain; and to increase the sale of Almanacs amongst the vulgar, publish, under the auspices of religion and learning, the most senseless absurdities." His respect for the House, he said, prevented him from citing some sentences from the one hundred and thirteenth of the series of Poor Robin's Almanac, published under the revision of the Archbishop of Canterbury and the Bishop of London. "The worst part of Rochester is ladies' reading, compared with them." The monopoly of 1779 was destroyed. But the powerful Company bought off the competitors who rose up from time to time. They had become possessed in 1827 of an exclusive market for stamped Almanacs; and, in the absence of all competition, the absurdities and the indecencies flourished as vigorously as when Erskine denounced them half a century before. The solemn farce was still enacted once a year of laying these productions at the feet of the Primate, when "episcopal revision" for state purposes was as extinct as the Star Chamber. They were still, as Erskine described the ancient mockery, to be "sanctified by the blessings of the bishops."

I had long been conversant with the character of these productions. Upon the day of their publication for the year 1828 I bought them all, and eagerly applied myself to discover if they had become more adapted to the improving intelligence of the age. First, there was "Francis Moore, Physician," who had commenced his career of imposture in 1698. He then dated his productions "from the sign of Lilly's Head, in Crown Court, near Cupid's Bridge, in Lambeth parish;" where he advertised for sale "his famous familiar family cathartick and diuretick purging pills." Here the "author also cures all sorts of agues at once;" and he adds, in the true spirit of his almanac, "this distemper often comes by supernatural means, which is the reason it will not yield to natural means." In 1827, when the Almanac stamp was fifteen pence, the people of England, calling themselves enlightened, voluntarily taxed themselves to pay an annual sum of fifteen thousand pounds to the government, for permission to read the unchanged trash which first obtained currency and belief when every village had its witch and every churchyard its ghost—when agues were cured by charms, and stolen spoons discovered by incantation. Surely it was full time that "Francis Moore, Physician," should be boldly dealt with. No common assaults would do. He would survive ridicule, as "Partridge's Almanack" survived the wicked wit of Swift, although Bickerstaff had killed the real Almanac for a season, and frightened the seer from ever attempting to set it up again. The Stationers' Company were not to be so beaten; and they had the impudence to publish a "Partridge's Almanack" with a portrait of the discomfited astrologer, which he refused to acknowledge, obstinately persisting not to prophesy in the flesh. The Company evoked the ghost of Partridge to do the needful work, and the Almanac for 1828 bore this motto,—"*Etiam mortuus loquitur.*" Another astrological Almanac, "Season on Seasons," still existed for 1828, modelled after the fashion of the palmy days of Lilly and Gadbury. "Moore Improved," particularly adapted for farmers and country gentlemen, was as impudent in his astrology as his great ancestor. All the Almanacs of the Stationers' Company had their prophecies that on a particular day of the coming year it would rain or shine—that there would be "good weather for the hay season in July, and in August fine harvest weather about the middle of the month." In Swift's wonderful piece of solemn humour, the account of Partridge's death, he makes the old sinner confess his "impositions on the people," and say, "We have a common form for all these things: as to foretelling the weather, we never meddle with that, but leave it to the printer, who takes it out of any old almanac as he thinks fit." This, which looks like a mere joke in 1709, was easy of proof in 1827, by comparing the Almanac of the reign of Charles II. with the Almanac of George II., and both with the Almanac of George IV. The only variation in the weather prophecies was in "Poor Robin's Almanac" for 1828, when he closed his hundred and sixty-eighth year, a drivelling idiot, still clinging to his old filth. Could any reader of this day imagine that in the year when the London University was opened, and the Society for the Diffusion of Useful Knowledge was beginning its work, he could find these lines at the head of the Calendar for January?

"If it don't snow
I don't care.
But if it freezes
It may as it pleases
And then I sneezes,
And my nose blow."

Armed with such materials, I immediately went to work, to elaborate the scheme of a rational and useful

Almanac. It was completed in a few days, and I took it to my steady friend, Matthew Hill. We went together to Westminster, to consult Mr. Brougham. What an incalculable source of satisfaction to a projector, even of so apparently humble a work as an Almanac, to find a man of ardent and capacious mind, quick to comprehend, frank to approve, not deeming a difficult undertaking impossible, ready not only for counsel but for action. "It is now the middle of November," said the rapid genius of unprocrastinating labour—"can you have your Almanac out before the end of the year?" "Yes; with a little help in the scientific matters." "Then tell Mr. Coates to call a meeting of the General Committee at my chambers, at half-past eight to-morrow morning. You shall have help enough. There's Lubbock and Wrottesley and Daniel and Beaufort—you may have your choice of good men for your astronomy and meteorology, your tides and your eclipses. Go to work, and never fear." The market-gardeners of Brompton were scarcely yet astir when I started to walk to Lincoln's Inn. The morning was dismal; the road was solitary. When I reached the top of Sloane Street, I was encountered by a dense fog—so heavy that I remember feeling my way by the iron railings in front of Apsley House, and so groping through Piccadilly. I began to despair of keeping the appointment which I deemed so important. But I persevered. That fog seemed to me as a type of the difficulties that I might have to encounter in this novel attempt, and in the realization of other projects floating in my mind. In Mr. Brougham's chambers there was assembled a quorum of the Committee. The energy of the Chairman swept away every doubt. The work was committed to my charge. The aid which had been suggested to me was freely given. I remembered the sarcastic exclamation of Erskine, when he was contending against the re-establishment of the usurped monopoly of the Universities—"Is it imagined that our Almanacs are to come to us, in future, in the classical arrangement of Oxford,—fraught with the mathematics and astronomy of Cambridge?" It might be so with one Almanac *not* "printed with the correct type of the Stationers' Company." Our supporters would little care for the pretence, still kept up, that the responsibility of that Company prevented the inconveniences that might arise to the public from mistakes in the matters that Almanacs contained. A constant friend through many years, the hydrographer of the Admiralty, Captain Beaufort, found a gentleman in his office who quickly prepared the various astronomical tables. There were senior wranglers, "fraught with the mathematics and astronomy of Cambridge," whose names had been rapidly mentioned to me by Mr. Brougham, ready to look over the proofs. I arranged the business terms with the Finance Committee of the Society, upon the principle of paying a rent upon the numbers sold. "*The British Almanac*" was published before the 1st of January. Late as it was in the field, high as was its unavoidable price—half-a-crown, to cover the heavy stamp duty, and allow a profit to the retailers—ten thousand were sold in a week. I had thus encouragement to propose a col lateral scheme to the Society. In their Annual Report issued at the beginning of February, was this announcement:—"A *Companion to the Almanac* is in the press, which will treat of many important branches of knowledge." The pair have travelled on together for thirty-seven years under my direction, through many changes of times and men—through many a social revolution, bloodless and beneficent—through a wonderful era of progress in commerce, in literature, in science, in the arts—in the manifestations of the approach of all ranks to that union of interests and feelings which is the most solid foundation of public happiness, and the best defence against assaults from without. The general features of these publications have undergone very little change during this long period. The two objects which have been always kept in view in the preparation of the "Companion" were set forth in 1828:—"1st. That the subjects selected shall be generally useful, either for present information or future reference. 2ndly. That the knowledge conveyed shall be given in the most condensed and explicit manner, so as to be valuable to every class of readers."

CHAPTER XIV.

N my return to London at the end of June, 1828, after a journey through "the provinces" to aid in furthering the object of our association, the meetings of the Useful Knowledge Society were approaching their termination for the season. Parliament was prorogued. The members of our committee had mostly left town; lawyers were on circuit; members of Parliament were looking after their local interests. But I had to keep up a tolerably active correspondence with some who took an especial interest in the works upon which I was occupied—with none more unremittingly than Mr. Brougham. Whether contending in friendly rivalry for the leadership of the Northern Circuit with Mr. Pollock, or enjoying the delicious quiet of his family home in Westmoreland, his mind was ever occupied with thoughts of the society which he had founded, and which was daily growing more important. Mr. Hill writes to me from Ambleside on the 30th of August:—"I came here with Mr. Brougham, from Lancaster, to-day. Scenery glorious of course. But I fear we talked more about diffusion of knowledge than anything else. Mr. B. is delighted with all you have done." It was very pleasant to know that my preparations for the "Library of Entertaining Knowledge" were approved. I was chiefly engaged in writing "The Menageries," which was a sufficient task for my faculties; for I had to learn a good deal

of the subjects upon which I was to write. But Mr. Brougham, estimating the powers of other men by his own, would have had me engage in some by-work for both of the series—the Useful and the Entertaining. I had intimated a desire to write a Life of Alfred. With his characteristic readiness, while expressing his gratification, he suggests to me not to lose sight of one interesting part of the subject—"the ancient form of our government—there are many errors afloat in this matter." He then states that Mr. Allen, of Holland House, has, more than all lawyers and historians, studied it deeply, and he sends me a list of Mr. Allen's articles in the "Edinburgh Review," on topics connected with this question. I had also given to Mr. Brougham the introductory portion of a life of Las Casas—a subject which had deeply interested me, as a very young man, when I had read in Croft's singular volume, "Love and Madness," that, "all things considered, Bartholomew Las Casas was perhaps the greatest man that ever existed." Mr. Brougham writes—"I have lost sight of Las Casas. How near making a volume is it for the L. E. K.? If not for that, there must be at least enough for a treatise in the L. U. K." How could I let the grass grow under my feet with such an inciter to activity?

In looking back at some correspondence of September, 1828, I am enabled to form an accurate conception of the technical difficulties of producing a cheap book with excellent wood-cuts. I had arranged to have my "Menageries" illustrated with representations of animals drawn from the life. I was fortunate in securing the assistance of several rising young men, who did not disdain what some painters might have deemed ignoble employment. Two of these are now Royal Academicians. There were not many wood-engravers then in London; and this art was almost invariably applied to the production of expensive books, printed in the finest style. The legitimate purpose of wood-engraving was not then attained. It is essentially that branch of the art of design which is associated with cheap and rapid printing. In the costly books of the period a single woodcut introduced into a sheet to be worked off with the types, enhanced the cost of manual labour in a proportion which would now seem incredible. In engraving the wood-cuts for the "Menageries," some attention of the artist was necessary to give his shadows the requisite force, and his lights the desired clearness, so as to meet the uniform application of the ink, and the cylindrical pressure, in the printing-machine process. It was long before this excellence could be practically attained. Without this explanation it would appear ludicrous that Mr. Hill should write to me from Mr. Brougham's house,—"Everybody here is in raptures with the proofs of the wood-cuts; but we have misgivings about the machine." A sheet of my book was to be set up with the engravings in their due place, and a hundred or two were to be printed off by the rapid operation. "Mr. Loch is here," writes Mr. Hill. "We have held a committee. He will be in London in a fortnight, quite at leisure, and anxious to attend to our affairs. He has promised to assist at Clowes's. I hope you will succeed in assembling everybody." "Everybody" not only meant the patentee of the machine, the wood-engraver, the stationer, the ink-maker, and the ingenious overseer of the printing office, but as many of the committee as I could get together. Imagine a learned society thus employed! Imagine a hard-worked editor thus exhorted to interference with a printer's proper duty! Yet such was a part of my editorial duty at a time when the great revolution in the production of books to be accomplished by the printing machine, was almost as imperfectly realised as when Caxton first astonished England by the miracles of the printing press. We succeeded in partially overcoming the difficulties of making an illustrated volume not despicable as a work of art, and yet cheap—something very different from the lesson books with blotches called pictures, that puzzled the school-boy mind half a century ago, to distinguish what some daub was meant to delineate; "It is backed like a weasel's," says Brown—"or, like a whale," says Jones—"Very like a whale," concludes Robinson.

At this time my duties in connection with the "Library of Entertaining Knowledge" were simply those of author and editor. I had retained a proprietary interest in the Almanac and Companion, although it was published for two years by Messrs. Baldwin. But the new series was a large undertaking, from the risk of which I shrank. Again, Mr. Murray, as a publisher, was to have been associated with my labours. In November, 1828, Mr. Tooke, the treasurer of the society, informed me that Mr. Murray desired that I should send him "the form of a reduced advertisement, descriptive only of the intended volume." The "Menageries" was then sufficiently advanced for me to comply. Before the volume was ready for publication the proprietor of the "Quarterly Review" took some alarm. The Society and he parted company, but upon very friendly terms. I was urged to take "at the flood" this opportunity of the "tide in the affairs of man." I found a capitalist ready to bear his part in my new venture. I made terms with the Society, which secured to them a rent upon the copies sold of the "Library of Entertaining Knowledge." I was again a publisher in Pall Mall East, before Midsummer, 1829, when the first volume of the "Menageries" was published. At the same period Mr. Murray issued the first volume of his "Family Library."

The sub-committees of the Society are once more in active work when the long vacation had come to an end. The monthly meetings now regularly take place. At these periodical gatherings there is a dinner at five o'clock—a plain English dinner, at a moderate fixed charge, to which each present contributes. There is a subscription for wine. On these occasions the organisation of the Society is fully developed. The sub-committees report their proceedings; the general committee confirm them. Questions are asked; suggestions are made. The chairman conducts the proceedings with the least possible parade of words. The members express their opinions in the same quiet conversational tone. I never heard but one oration in that assembly of which so many eloquent statesmen and lawyers formed a part. That display came from a president of the Royal Academy, whose rhetoric is as forgotten a thing as his "Rhymes on Art." Let me look back upon those pleasant meetings, at which I had generally the happiness to be present during more than fifteen years. Let me, without confining myself to a particular session of my early years in connection with the Society, look round that social table, to call up the shadows of some whose reputations only survive, and to renew, as it were, the friendships which I have still the happiness of possessing.

The dinner is over in an hour. There has been pleasant gossip and occasional fun. A few cordial greetings have passed in the old form of the wine-pledge, which we of a past generation regret to find almost obsolete. The cloth is cleared. Mr. Coates, the secretary, moves to the side of the chairman, and there are then two hours of solid business. Subjects of science, of art, of literature, having to be discussed, the talk is sure to be improving, and occasionally amusing. The chair is generally filled by Mr. Brougham, and, in his rare absence, more frequently by the treasurer, Mr. William Tooke, than by Lord John Russell, the vice-chairman. Other members, however, are occasionally called to take the chair. Mr. Tooke was one of the founders of the Society, and was for some years an active member. He was somewhat ambitious of literary distinction, priding himself upon being one of "the family of Tooke," his father having been known as the author of some valuable works on Russia; his brother Thomas being the eminent political economist, the historian of "Prices." Our treasurer had somewhat harsh treatment from the critics as the biographer of Churchill. I always regarded him as a kind-hearted man of moderate abilities—somewhat fussy, not altogether disinclined to a job, and always disposed to be patronizing.

Where shall I begin with those who did not fill the offices of the Society amongst the sixty members of its committee? I cannot classify them according to their professional pursuits; for in this gathering, statesmen, lawyers, physicians, professors, not only clubbed their technical knowledge, but their various acquirements in science, in history, in art, in ancient scholarship, in modern literature. I must take the individuals somewhat at random, as they crowd upon my memory in connection with my own experience.

James Mill. I see the historian of British India, sitting near Mr. Brougham, listening to his opinions with marked attention. It always appeared to me a signal tribute to the intellectual eminence of the great orator, that the writer who, of all others, aimed most at terseness and perspicuity, should exhibit such deference to one whose reputation was built upon broader foundations than logical profundity or metaphysical subtlety. Yet so it was. Their minds were not certainly cast in the same mould; yet there must have been deep sympathies between them—as is perhaps often the case when two men of apparently opposite temperaments, and pursuing very different paths to eminence, are brought into friendly contact for a common object. Mr. Mill was too soon removed from us. To me he rendered valuable aid in the early numbers of the "Companion to the Almanac."

Henry Hallam was one of the original promoters of the Society, of which, during many years, he was an active member. That the historian of the "Middle Ages," was an authority in the committee cannot be doubted. He was a sedulous attendant upon sub-committees. He read proofs diligently. In his general manner rather cold and dry, he would occasionally deliver an energetic opinion, pregnant with good sense and refined taste. I used at first to feel some shrinking from his critical faculty, but no one could be more tolerant or encouraging; and if he made objections it was generally without harshness. He was in the full possession of his high faculties when I first had the opportunity of benefiting, in a small degree, by the quiet exhibition of his varied acquirements. The great sorrow of his life had not then chilled his energy. He lived to recover, outwardly, the loss which gave occasion to the noblest elegiac poetry in our language.

I turn to a man eminent in a pursuit not less useful than that of the historian—to Francis Beaufort, the hydrographer to the Admiralty, under whose especial superintendence the Atlas of the Society attained a perfection never before realised in this country. His design of producing the most trustworthy maps at the cheapest rate, would have conferred an honourable distinction upon this Association, if it had accomplished nothing else. But Captain Beaufort (afterwards Admiral Sir Francis) did not confine himself to the duties of this great undertaking. I could always rely upon his sound judgment in discussing any project that I offered, or in the correction of proofs. No member of the committee wrote purer English. Of his unremitting kindness I had ample experience. The frankness, almost bluntness, of the sailor was never offensive, for it had the true ring of the sterling metal of an honest mind, and the unvarnished courtesy of a gentleman. Shall I place by the side of this worthy plain dealer and plain speaker one of whom it has been said he often tried to make himself disagreeable, but never succeeded? There was no man with whom I less perfectly sympathized when I first joined the Society than Henry Bellenden Ker; gradually I learnt to understand him. I have the happiness still to enjoy an intimacy that has endured since those early days of our intercourse—proof against banter on one side, and pettishness on the other. He was the most fertile in projects of any member of the committee. Apart from the Society, he had ever some new scheme to suggest to me as a publishing enterprise. His plans were not always practicable; but they always indicated the fertility of his mind, and the refinement of his taste. He did me incalculable good in his rough-riding when I was learning my paces in this intellectual manége. It was like the discipline which a young barrister receives on his first circuit. Not to wince under a joke; to see the kind heart and the earnest good will, ill-concealed by the levity of tongue; to find indifference growing into cordiality, and then ripening into friendship—this was my experience of a man whose ready talent, whose social aptitude, rarely failed to secure the friendship of the young and of the aged—one who was a warm politician without the bitterness of a partisan; whose companionable qualities gave pleasure to the declining vigour of Lyndhurst, and who continues, as he had begun, to be the cherished friend of Brougham.

In the present instance, as in others that will constantly occur, I find it exceedingly difficult to speak with the same freedom of the living as of the dead. Yet, looking back for more than a generation upon the eminent persons with whom I had become acquainted, they all assume with me an aspect approaching to the historical. I run over the list of the committee prefixed to the "British Almanac" for 1830. Of forty-five members, whose essential services in the diffusion of knowledge live in my remembrance, twenty-five are gone where "all hidden things shall be made manifest." Yet to speak impartially, I must not pass over those who remain with us, believing that the "*nil nisi verum*" is a better principle to act upon either for the living or the dead than the "*nil nisi bonum.*"

I have already, several times, mentioned Matthew Davenport Hill as a member of the committee; and it is therefore unnecessary that I should here dwell upon the energy of his character as a diffuser of knowledge. He was one of the earliest members of the Society. His brother Rowland was elected when it was fully in action. Of modest demeanour; courteous but independent; expressing his opinions with a prudent brevity,—few could have given him credit for that unwearied industry in following out all the ramifications of a complicated question; for that power of marshalling all the possible details of a great theory which in practice resolved itself into the most complete organisation. The inventor of the Penny Postage made no eager rush to the display of an imperfect project. He felt every step of his way, and when he had ceased to have any doubt of the certainty of his convictions, he put them forth with the confidence of genius, and was ready to do battle for them with the courage which is the best pledge of victory. The young schoolmaster of Hazelwood became one of the greatest of public benefactors.

Amongst the founders of the society, Dr. Roget was, from his accepted high reputation, the most eminent of its men of science. He wrote its treatises on Electricity and on Magnetism. He was a diligent attendant on its committees; a vigilant corrector of its proofs. Of most winning manners, he was as beloved as he was respected. I met him in 1863, at an evening party, and had much talk with him about our old intercourse. Full of animation,—with undimned intelligence—his age was "as a lusty winter, frosty but kindly." In his beaming face there could scarcely be found the traces of that hard work—made up of professional practice, of scientific writing, of secretaryship of the Royal Society, of lecturer at the Royal Institution,—which he had gone through since he graduated in medicine at Edinburgh in 1798. Upon all questions of Physiology, Peter Mark Roget and Charles Bell are the great authorities in the Useful Knowledge Society. No higher service could have been rendered to the association in its early stages than Mr. Bell's contribution to its treatises. His "Animal Mechanics" is a model of popular writing upon subjects which demand high scientific knowledge. This charming production was published in 1828. At that time there was another member of the medical profession —one, however, unconnected with our Society—who also contributed most effectually to disperse the belief that science could only be taught in the use of technical language;—that the uninitiated in the technicalities had better not attempt to comprehend the mysteries of that temple where there was scant room for the worship of the multitude. Dr. Neil Arnott, in 1827, published the first portion of his

"Elements of Physics; or Natural Philosophy, General and Medical, explained in plain or non-technical language." Never was book more popular; never was the completion of any undertaking more anxiously looked for. The first volume of the "Sixth and Completed Edition" reaches me while I write this chapter. It is a presentation copy from one who for five-and-thirty years has won the love and gratitude of me and mine, as the wise physician and the hearty friend. I could not forego this digression from the matters more immediately before me.

The Useful Knowledge committees, as I have looked upon these monthly assemblages, present the aspect of something higher than toleration—a cordial union of men of very different persuasions in religion, who have met upon a common platform for the advancement of knowledge, to which religion can never be opposed. Let me group three representatives of opinions that appear as far removed as possible from amalgamation. Dr. Maltby, a great classical scholar, the preacher at Lincoln's Inn, the future bishop, first of Chichester, and then of Durham, is a dignified representative of the Church of England. He is zealous for the welfare of the Useful Knowledge Society, of which he was one of the earliest members. He will do its work assiduously and carefully. He will not insist upon religious topics being thrust in amongst secular. He will not stickle for the due honour of the Established Church. How can he do either? By his side, it may be, sits Mr. Isaac Lyon Goldsmid, the wealthy Jew, whose ambition, as that of the Rothschilds and of other men of large property and unimpeachable loyalty, is to have a voice in the British Parliament.

Mr. Goldsmid is a man of something more than business talent; good tempered; not obtruding the pride of riches; hospitable. Mr. William Allen, the Quaker, may form the third in this group. I have often called on him at his old place of business in Plough Court, where, a practical chemist, he had been a thriving tradesman, and at the same time a Fellow of the Royal Society and a valuable contributor to its transactions. He well merited the honour of his countrymen for other qualities than his scientific acquirements. He was a liberal promoter of every public scheme of benevolence. He established upon his estate at Lindfield, in Sussex, after he withdrew from the cares of a commercial life, schools for boys, girls, and infants,—real schools of industry, where agriculture was taught, as well as many useful arts. Whilst the children had every opportunity for acquiring health in recreation, and improvement in a good library, he built cottages for the labourers of his village, such as ought to have shamed many a landowner out of his neglect. The memory of this good man is to me fresh and fragrant.

There was perhaps no society in England, with the exception of the Royal Society, which could present such a knot of young men of high promise as were assembled at our committees in the earliest stages of their organisation. Mr. John William Lubbock, the only child of the eminent city banker, assiduously followed his father's calling, whilst he was attaining the highest reputation as a mathematician. In 1825 he had graduated as M.A. at Cambridge. In 1828 he was rendering me the most important assistance in the preparation of the "British Almanac." For several years he worked with the heartiest zeal at this apparently humble contribution to the objects of the Society. But the occupation was not a humble one, for he was practically developing his investigations upon the Tides, which subject formed several papers in the Philosophical Transactions. Devoting himself with the same readiness to superintend the astronomical portion of the British Almanac, I was also brought into intercourse with Mr. John Wrottesley, afterwards Lord Wrottesley, and President of the Royal Society. He was a member of the bar. Mr. Benjamin Malkin—afterwards Sir Benjamin, when he accepted a high judicial appointment in India, and there too soon closed his valuable life—devoted his great talents and acquirements with indefatigable industry to the business of our committee. His forte was mathematics. His brother Arthur was elected to the committee a few years after, and in several departments rendered essential service as a writer and editor. Mr. T. F. Ellis, the friend and executor of Macaulay, had many opportunities, in the revision of the Society's works, to exercise his acute critical faculty. Mr. Lefevre (now Sir John) was also one of the distinguished Cambridge graduates who gave to the Useful Knowledge Society the prestige of their academical honours.

The University of London (as the College was then called) numbered amongst its Professors some of the ablest members of our committee. Amongst the first of those who joined the Society was Mr. George Long. In subsequent "Passages," I shall have so frequently to mention his name, as one of the most important of my associates, that it will be scarcely necessary for me here to do more than allude to his unequalled industry, his rich scholarship, his sound judgment, which very soon gave him his right position amongst the eminent persons by whom he was surrounded. Mr. De Morgan became a member somewhat later. I first saw him in 1830. The occasion will arise for mentioning the eminent services he rendered to the works in which I have been engaged. Mr. Key, and Mr. Malden, about the same period commenced their distinguished career as teachers of youth, and very soon also devoted their unprofessional services to the general diffusion of knowledge.

Mr. Leonard Horner was the Warden of the London University, when he became a member of the Useful Knowledge committee. In their early stages the new preparatory institution "for affording to young men adequate opportunities for obtaining literary and scientific education at a moderate expense;" and the new society for "imparting useful information to all classes of the community," were considered by many to be engaged in a co-partnership for the political and theological corruption of youths and adults. In some arrangements prescribed by a rigid economy in the finances of each, they did appear to carry on their operations in concert. Thus, when I first attended in Percy Street to read manuscripts and proofs, I had to thread my way up a staircase, on the walls of which Dr. Lardner was hanging models for the illustration of his approaching Lectures on Mechanics. As a necessary consequence, the council of the University, and the committee of the Society, had several members in common. Mr. Horner was not only surrounded with the reflection of his eminent brother's fame, but had that brother's testimony, in his published letters, to the interest which young Leonard, as early as 1811, took in the education of the people. How well he was qualified for popular instruction was shown by an admirable series of articles on "The Mineral Kingdom" which he contributed to the "Penny Magazine." How ardently and unremittingly he strove to elevate the condition, and provide for the health of the Working Classes, has been manifested by his labours as a Factory Commissioner.

I am still hovering round the remembrance of the earlier members of the Society, whose literary or scientific qualifications gave the assurance that no publication would go forth, deformed by the inaccuracies of superficial information. In a volume written by me ten years ago, I have expressed my opinion upon the system pursued in our committees:—"From the time when the Society commenced a real 'superintendence' of works for the people—when it assisted, by diligent revision and friendly inquiry, the services of its editors—the old vague generalities of popular knowledge were exploded; and the scissors-and-paste school of authorship had to seek for other occupations than Paternoster Row could once furnish. Accuracy was forced upon elementary books as the rule and not the exception. Books professedly 'entertaining' were to be founded upon exact information, and their authorities invariably indicated. No doubt this superintendence in some degree interfered with the free course of original composition, and imparted somewhat of the utilitarian character to everything produced. But it was the only course by which a new aspect could be given to cheap literature, by showing that the great principles of excellence were common to all books, whether for the learned or the uninformed."* To accomplish such real superintendence there were the services at hand, in the department that may be broadly characterised as Natural History, of Mr. Daniel, in Meteorology; of Mr. De La Beche, in Geology; of Mr. Vigors, in Zoology; and of Dr. Anthony Todd Thomson, in Botany and Vegetable Physiology. With each of these gentlemen I was, in various labours, brought into pleasant and profitable intercourse. I was in more direct and constant intimacy with Mr. William Coulson, the translator of Blumenbach's "Comparative Anatomy." In the composition of my little book on "Menageries," I could always apply, in cases of doubt, to his technical information, and to the wide range of the scientific knowledge of Mr. Vigors. The aid which Dr. Conolly rendered to the diffusion of knowledge was not special or professional. In those departments of what we now call "social science," which include the public health in its largest sense, his experience was always working in companionship with his benevolence. In 1831 we were united in the production of a series which was directly addressed to the working classes. Dr. Conolly brought to this useful labour—of which I shall have to make more particular mention—a lucid style, and an accurate conception of the true mode of reaching the uneducated. "Be thou familiar, but by no means vulgar," is as good a maxim for a popular writer, as for a young courtier going forth into the world, to deal with all sorts and conditions of men.

* "The Old Printer and the Modern Press." Murray. 1854.

We had many lawyers on the committee. I have mentioned several who were distinguished for their remarkable scientific qualifications. Others of the bar were accomplished scholars. But no one displayed a more elegant taste than John Herman Merivale. His translations from the Greek Anthology, and from the minor poems of Schiller, have not been condemned to that oblivion which attends the greater number of poetical attempts. The purity and elegance of the whole mind of Mr. Merivale is reflected in his poems. Courteous and sympathizing, I look back upon my occasional intercourse with him with respect almost bordering upon affection. Mr. George Cornewall Lewis brought his various high qualifications to the service of the Society at a later period, when he became a contributor to its publications. I mention him among the lawyers, for before he joined the Useful Knowledge committee he had been called to the bar. Of the elder lawyers, no one was more valuable to the society than Mr. James Manning—perhaps the most profound of the historical and antiquarian lawyers of his time. His accurate information upon many abstruse legal matters was amply displayed when he became one of the most important contributors to the "Penny Cyclopædia." Mr. David Jardine was also a most useful contributor to the legal department of the Cyclopædia, and was the author of "Criminal Trials," published in the Library of Entertaining Knowledge—a valuable contribution to our constitutional history. Let me not omit to mention the youngest of the lawyers amongst us—Mr. Thomas Falconer, who was called to the bar in 1830. He inherited literary tastes, and was an acute as well as a modest critic upon the unpublished volumes and articles that were submitted for his revision.

I have finally to turn to a knot of men, eminent in the political annals of our country. They might at first view be regarded as the Corinthian capitals of our edifice. But this would only be a half-truth. Lord John Russell, Lord Auckland, Lord Althorp, Mr. Denman, Mr. Spring Rice, Sir Henry Parnell, were always ready to work as members of our committee, even after they had been called to the highest offices of the State. After the Reform era I have sat at the monthly dinner with five Cabinet Ministers, to whom it appeared that their duty was to carry forward that advancing intelligence of the people which had conducted them to power, and which would afford the best security that liberal opinions and democratic violence should not be in concert, as the "one increasing purpose" was working out the inevitable changes of society and government. The first poet of the generation that was immediately to follow them has probably shadowed out the convictions that made Ministers of State zealous educationists:

> "Yet I doubt not through the ages one increasing purpose runs,
> And the thoughts of men are widened with the process of the suns."
> *Locksley Hall.*

It was not only in the meetings of our committees that I had the advantage, for my editorial guidance, of the opinions of men of accurate minds and sound information; but I was frequently also in correspondence with those who took a more than common interest in particular works. Such a work was that well-known contribution to the "Library of Entertaining Knowledge," which first established the reputation of Mr. George Lillie Craik as a sound thinker and an accomplished writer. To myself, individually, the recollection of that autumn of 1828 is especially dear, for it saw the commencement of an intimacy which ripened into the unbroken friendship of six-and-thirty years. In the preliminary stages of discussion on the objects and mode of treatment of a book such as this, which was to embrace a vast number of illustrative anecdotes of the love of knowledge overcoming the opposition of circumstances, there were necessarily different estimates of the value of scientific and literary studies, whether "for use," or "for delight," or "for ornament." The great distinction between the love of knowledge for its own sake, and the love of knowledge as the means of worldly advancement, may be traced very distinctly in the two popular volumes of Mr. Craik, and the equally popular "Self Help" of Mr. Smiles.

Mr. Craik had written a preliminary dissertation in the sound views of which Mr. Brougham expressed himself to me as generally coinciding. But in a portion of a letter, dated from Westmoreland in September, 1828, Mr. Brougham takes a different view of the range of such a work as that proposed:

"His (Mr. Craik's) idea of the line to be drawn as to self-educated men in modern times, is also quite correct; but we must, nevertheless, confine the examples to cases which are quite plainly those of men who have greatly altered their situation by force of merit. As Watt, Arkwright, Franklin, Burns, Bloomfield, Mendelssohn—making the ground of division or classification *self-exaltation* rather than self-education, though they often will coincide. This field is quite large enough for one book; but the work might be followed by another comprehending the rest of it, and including all self-taught Genius in the larger sense. To give an example—I should certainly exclude Newton, though, like Pascal, he taught himself mathematics; also Granville Sharpe, though he raised himself by his merit to great fame; but he was grandson of the Archbishop of York, and could not be said to alter his station in life. I look forward to Mr. Craik's labours as of the greatest use to the Society, and to the good cause; having the greatest confidence in his sound principles, and a very high opinion of his talents."

This interesting discussion was continued between Mr. Brougham, Mr. Hill, Mr. Craik, and myself, till it was seen how the opposite views could be resolved into a general agreement. I have before me Mr. Brougham's *proof* of Mr. Craik's first volume. To Mr. Brougham is to be assigned the merit of giving to the book in this proof the title which has come to be one of the commonest forms of speech:

"THE PURSUIT OF KNOWLEDGE UNDER DIFFICULTIES."

The title originally stood,—

"THE LOVE OF KNOWLEDGE OVERCOMING DIFFICULTIES IN ITS PURSUIT."

CHAPTER XV.

EVERAL years had passed, crowded with political events. The amended Reform Bill was passing through Committee in the House of Commons in February, 1832. There seemed to be little doubt that a Ministerial majority would be too strong in the Lower House to allow any re-actionary measure in the House of Lords to be successful. The new Government officials were settling themselves to the discharge of their administrative duties as if a long and quiet possession of place had been won. On the 13th of February, I received a note from Lord Auckland, the President of the Board of Trade, expressing his desire for a few minutes' conversation with me in the course of the afternoon. The interview was a very brief one, but its importance to me was not to be measured by its duration. The Cabinet Minister offered me a new office, which it was proposed to create at the Board of Trade, for digesting and arranging Parliamentary and other official documents for the information of members of the Government, and possibly for publication. This duty would have involved a regular attendance at Whitehall; the salary proposed was not a tempting one; but the offer seemed to open the way for a more ambitious career than that of a publisher. I requested time for deliberation. Having consulted a distinguished friend, he advised me to decline the

proposal, however flattering. Lord Auckland was surprised but not displeased at my rejection of his kind overture. He asked me to recommend some gentleman fitted for the post. There was one with whom I had recently formed an acquaintance, Mr. George Richardson Porter. He had written a paper on Life Assurance for the "Companion to the Almanac," and he was the author of a volume on the Silk Manufacture, published in Lardner's "Cyclopædia." Mr. Porter received the appointment. The experiment was perfectly successful, and much of its success may be attributed to the ability and industry of him whom, so fortunately for the public good, I had recommended. Mr. Porter became the head of the statistical department of the Board of Trade, and in 1841 he was promoted to be one of the joint-secretaries of that board. Till the time of his lamented death in 1852, we were mutually attached friends, and he was one of the most valuable contributors to several of my publications.

Had I accepted the appointment of the Board of Trade in that February, it is probable that the whole course of my future life would have been changed. It was upon the cards that either I should have been sitting in an office at Whitehall from ten till four, cramming Ministers and Members of Parliament with statistical facts, or become identified with the most successful experiment in popular literature that England had seen. On March 31st, 1832, appeared the first number of "The Penny Magazine of the Society for the Diffusion of Useful Knowledge."

In a debate in the House of Commons on the 22nd of May, 1834, on a motion for the Repeal of the

Stamp Duty on Newspapers, Mr. M. D. Hill, then member for Hull, in reply to Mr. Bulwer who moved the Repeal, thus described the origin of that work: "The Honourable Gentleman was pleased to characterize 'The Penny Magazine,' as affording a trumpery education to the people, because he says it deals in accounts of birds and insects, and such matters. I certainly was a little astonished to find my Honourable Friend scout an insight into the wonders of creation, as a trumpery affair. I should be sorry if his designation of that little work were correct, because the blame of its existence rests with myself, it being a project of my own; neither am I innocent of the course it has pursued; which from first to last has had, and still has, my hearty concurrence." The circumstances connected with this "project" were these. The town in that time of political excitement abounded with unstamped weekly publications, which in some degree came under the character of contraband newspapers, and were nearly all dangerous in principle and coarse in language. Mr. Hill and I were neighbours on Hampstead Heath, and as we walked to town on a morning of the second week in March, our talk was of these cheap and offensive publications. "Let us," he exclaimed, "see what something cheap and good can accomplish! Let us have a Penny Magazine!" "And what shall be its title?" said I. "THE PENNY MAGAZINE." We went at once to the Lord Chancellor. He cordially entered into the project. A committee of the Society was called, and such a publication was decided upon after some hesitation. There was a feeling amongst a few that a penny weekly sheet would be below the dignity of the

Society. One gentleman of the old Whig school, who had not originally belonged to the Committee, said again and again, "It is very awkward." Lord Brougham, however, was not accustomed to let awkward things stand much in his way. "The Penny Magazine" was decided upon. I undertook the risk of the publication, and was appointed to be its editor. The task was not a very easy one in the onset, for it was impossible to say, before the issue of a few numbers, whether the periodical sale would be twenty thousand or a hundred thousand, and whether a large demand would be a permanent one. It was therefore necessary to have a due regard to economy; and thus the attraction of expensive woodcuts could scarcely be ventured upon in the early days of the experiment. It was imperative also to proceed very cautiously in treading near the ill-defined line that separated the essayist from the newspaper writer. I have a letter before me from the Solicitor of Stamps, in which he says he has perused the specimen numbers (1 and 2) of the Magazine intended to be published by the Society, and that he sees nothing in these numbers that will render the publication liable to stamp duty. So I went confidently to my work. Perhaps no circumstance gave me greater encouragement than a letter from Francis Place, who knew more about the working classes, and had probably more influence with them, than any man in London. He describes his pleasure at seeing the prospectus. He begs me to let him have a quantity, which he would cause "to be usefully dispersed in the houses of call for journeymen, in workshops, and factories." Mr. Place united to his business of master-tailor, at Charing Cross, an intense devotion to all the leading questions of politics that had been agitating the world since the time of the French Revolution. His collection of contemporary pamphlets was as extensive and complete as any man could have formed. I believe it was dispersed at his death, but it ought to have gone to the British Museum.

The excellent Dr. Arnold, some months after the "Penny Magazine" had appeared, described it as "all ramble-scramble." It was meant to be so—to touch rapidly and lightly upon many subjects. In the introductory article of the first number, I wrote: "Whatever tends to enlarge the range of observation, to add to the store of facts, to awaken the reason, and to lead the imagination into agreeable and innocent trains of thought, may assist in the establishment of a sincere and ardent desire for information; and in this point of view our little miscellany may prepare the way for the reception of more elaborate and precise knowledge, and be as the small optic-glass called *the finder*, which is placed by the side of a large telescope, to enable the observer to discover the star which is afterwards to be carefully examined by the more perfect instrument." I certainly never received any more striking testimony to the usefulness of the "ramble-scramble" in supplying a want to those who were striving to gain knowledge, but who were too poor to buy books, than the following passage in the "Autobiography of an Artisan," published in 1847. Christopher Thomson, the author of this interesting book, had settled as a house-painter at Edwinstowe, a village in Nottinghamshire:—"Squatting down here penniless, without a table or three-legged stool to furnish a cottage with, it may easily be imagined that I had tough work of it. My great want was books; I was too poor to purchase expensive ones, and the 'cheap literature' was not then, as now, to be found in every out-o'-the-way nooking. However, Knight had unfurled his paper banners of free trade in letters. The 'Penny Magazine' was published—I borrowed the first volume, and determined to make an effort to possess myself with the second; accordingly, with January, 1833, I determined to discontinue the use of sugar in my tea, hoping that my family would not then feel the sacrifice necessary to buy the book. Since that period, I have expended large sums in books, some of them very costly ones, but I never had one so truly valuable as was the second volume of the 'Penny Magazine;' and I looked as anxiously for the issue of the monthly part as I did for the means of getting a living." This then was the service which the "Penny Magazine" was rendering, at the beginning of 1832, to the general cause of letters. I must associate with it "Chambers' Edinburgh Journal," a publication which was established a few weeks before mine. They were making readers. They were raising up a new class, and a much larger class than previously existed, to be the purchasers of books. They were planting the commerce of books upon broader foundations than those upon which it had been previously built. They were relegating the hole-and-corner literature of the days of exclusiveness to the rewards which the few could furnish; preparing the way for writers and booksellers to reap the abundant harvest when the "second rain" of knowledge should be descending "uninterrupted, unabated, unbounded; fertilizing some grounds and overflowing others; changing the whole form of social life." *

The success of the "Penny Magazine" was an astonishment to most persons; I honestly confess it was a surprise to myself. It was not till the autumn that an attempt was made by the means of woodcuts to familiarise the people with great works of art. Then were presented to them engravings of a costly character, of such subjects as the Laocoon, the Apollo Belvedere, the Cartoons, and the great Cathedrals, British and Foreign. At the end of 1832, the "Penny Magazine" had reached a sale of 200,000 in weekly numbers and monthly parts. In the preface to the first volume, under the date of December the 18th, I thus wrote:—"It was considered by Edmund Burke, about forty years ago, that there were 80,000 *readers* in this country. In the present year it has been shown, by the sale of the 'Penny Magazine,' that there are 200,000 *purchasers* of one periodical work. It may be fairly calculated that the number of readers of that single work amounts to a million. If this incontestable evidence of the spread of the ability to read be most satisfactory, it is still more satisfactory to consider the species of reading which has had such an extensive and increasing popularity. In this work there has never been a single sentence that could inflame a vicious appetite; and not a paragraph that could minister to prejudices and superstitions which a few years since were common. There have been no excitements for the lovers of the marvellous—no tattle or abuse for the gratification of a diseased taste for personality, and, above all, no party politics."

* Scott. "Quentin Durward."

Although the "Penny Magazine" has a peculiar interest as a subject of literary history, it would be tedious if I were to attempt any minute notice of its contributors; but I may mention a few whose names occur to me as I turn over its early pages. There were members of the Committee who had a very just conception of what writing for the people meant. An article by Mr. Long, in the seventh number, on the value of a penny, is as clear and impressive as any statement from the pen of Cobbett. Mr. De Morgan wrote mathematical papers, in which the rationale of Fractions was exhibited, and the fallacy of such notions as squaring the circle was pointed out. Mr. Craik could be depended upon for enlightened as well as familiar expositions of the value of standard works, under the head of "The Library." Mr. Charles Macfarlane, of whom I shall have subsequently to speak, wrote most amusing accounts of his travelling experiences. There were authors not regularly engaged as contributors, who furnished valuable papers of marked ability. I had been in the habit of familiar intercourse with Allan Cunningham, even before the time when he wrote a paper in the "Quarterly Magazine." For the "Penny Magazine" he furnished a series of articles on "The Old English Ballads." I must not omit to mention the interesting relations of his South African experience, contributed by Thomas Pringle, one of the most amiable of men, with whom I had cultivated something higher than mere intimacy, when our friendly relations were cut short by his death in 1834. His biography of Sir Walter Scott, was called forth by the great novelist's lamented death on the 21st of September, 1832. It occupied an entire number of the "Penny Magazine," and contains some valuable facts regarding Mr. Pringle's personal intimacy with Scott in 1819.

It may not be without an interest of no transient nature that I proceed to notice the beginnings of my intercourse with a man who left his mark upon his time, but who, when I first knew him, was not only under the check of "poverty's unconquerable bar," but was suffering under a great physical privation which appeared likely to disqualify him for any prosperous career in life. On the 18th of July, 1833, a short stout man, of about thirty years of age, presented himself to me at my place of business in Ludgate Street, to which premises, nearer the great hive of "*the* Trade" I had found it indispensable to remove. He tendered me a note from Mr. Coates, at the same time uttering some strange sounds, which could scarcely be called articulate. The few lines of introduction said that the bearer, Mr. Kitto, laboured under the misfortune of nearly absolute deafness, and that I must therefore communicate with him in writing. Mr. Coates enclosed me a letter from Mr. Woollcombe, the chairman of our local committee at Plymouth. That letter is now before me, dated the 10th of July. This gentleman—who appears to have been peculiarly fitted, by his compassion for misfortune and his sympathy with talent, to rescue a pauper boy from the misery and degradation of a parish workhouse—pleaded the claims of the unknown John Kitto for literary employment in a way so interesting that I cannot hesitate to transcribe his words: "He is a native of this town, and became known to us by his misfortunes, as a lad of extraordinary capacity, though reduced by the vices of his father to the condition of an inhabitant of our workhouse, and by an accident to an almost entire loss of the sense of hearing. He has subsequently been employed as a printer at Malta, by a religious society. But he is now just returned from a residence of some years at Bagdad; having embarked from England for Petersburg, and descended from thence through Russia to Moscow and other towns, entering Persia by the Desert; of that country he has acquired considerable information, which he is ready to communicate through your publications. He returned to England in June last. * * * His appearance is not prepossessing; his deafness is somewhat embarrassing; his talents are considerable, memory retentive, observation quick, and undivided as other men's are. His life is a series of extraordinary incidents, such as one is unwilling to acknowledge as being natural. I laugh and tell him the world is to be now indebted to two Devonshire men for the information it is to receive of distant countries. The one a blind man (Lieut. Holman), who is to publish what he has *seen* in his progress round the world. And (John Kitto) a deaf man, of what he has *heard* in Persia!"

I may have had something like an anticipation of this poor man's future eminence, judging from the unusual care with which I appear to have preserved some memoranda of our intercourse. I find a paper dated July the 21st, headed "Conversation with Mr. Kitto," of which the following is the substance of half a dozen pages of my notes. I asked him what European languages he knew. He said Italian, French perfectly, not German. He had proposed a new project, into which I thought the Society would not at present enter; but, I should be glad to endeavour to arrange for his employment in the "Penny Magazine" and "Penny Cyclopædia." I asked if he could undertake to give a personal narrative of his travels in Persia. That would show what he could do, and he might be afterwards engaged on geographical articles for the "Cyclopædia," requiring more precise and systematic information. I then arranged with him to furnish a few articles of the nature I had mentioned, to be paid for at the rate of a guinea and a half a page. And so John Kitto, the future Biblical critic and commentator, went away perfectly happy, to produce the first number of "The Deaf Traveller," which appeared in "The Penny Magazine" of the 10th of August. A month of experiment had passed, and I then engaged Kitto at a regular salary, to work in my own room in Fleet Street. I could thus assist him whenever he had any question to propose, and to me he was no interruption, for our golden silence was rarely broken. He writes to a friend on the 18th of August, after he had been regularly employed for a week:—"I have little doubt that, through Mr. Knight's indulgence, I shall be able to keep this situation; the rather, as whatever spare time 'The Penny Magazine' does not require, is spent in perfecting my knowledge of French and Italian, and in acquiring the German. I do thank God for this relief from a state of great anxiety, in which I had begun to entertain the most melancholy view of the things before me, and saw possible consequences that I could not bear steadily to contemplate." Sitting, as he describes, "in Mr. Knight's room, with plenty of books about me, and more below," authors, printers, country agents, and other men of business come and go to impart something to my private ear. They addressed me in whispers, when they saw a somewhat dwarfish man of sallow complexion, bright eyes, and lofty forehead, sitting close to my table at a separate desk, writing incessantly. To some he might have looked as a very suspicious person, who was placed there to note down their conversation. They soon became accustomed to this companionship, and learnt that he would be the most faithful depository of their spoken secrets, whether they were to roar as loud as Bully Bottom when he desired to play the lion, or spake "in a monstrous little voice," as when the same actor of all-work would have played "Thisby dear."

It appears from the correspondence of Dr. Arnold, that in the early stages of "The Penny Magazine" he felt a strong desire to see something of the religious spirit imparted to the works of the Useful Knowledge Society. His views upon the subject were so just and reasonable, that it is to me a matter of the deepest regret that I was never brought into direct communication with him in my editorial capacity. He says: "It does seem to me as forced and unnatural in us now to dismiss the principles of the Gospel and its great motives from our conversation,—as is done habitually, for example, in Miss Edgeworth's books,—as it is to fill our pages with Hebraisms, and to write and speak in the words and style of the Bible. The slightest touches of Christian principle and Christian hope in the Society's biographical and historical articles would be a sort of living salt to the whole; and would exhibit that union which I never will consent to think unattainable, between goodness and wisdom; between everything that is manly, sensible, and free, and everything that is pure and self-denying, and humble, and heavenly." * Dr. Arnold's strong desire was that of being able to co-operate with a body which he "believed might, with God's blessing, do more good of all kinds, political, intellectual, and spiritual, than any other society in existence." † He was anxious, he wrote, "to furnish them regularly with articles of the kind that I desire." For myself I can distinctly state that no expression of such a desire ever reached me; nor do I know that any communication to such an effect was ever formally put before the sub-committee for "The Penny Magazine." Dr. Arnold's nephew, Mr. John Ward, a solicitor in Bedford Row, to whom he writes in 1832, about "your Useful Knowledge Society Committee," was a member of that committee, and he contributed some very useful but rather dry "Statistical Notes" to "The Penny Magazine." These certainly were not calculated to carry out Dr. Arnold's views. But he himself has borne the most cordial testimony to one circumstance in the conduct of "The Penny Magazine," which shows that there was no settled purpose to exclude from that work "the slightest touches of Christian principle." I have said with reference to the religious articles of the "Plain Englishman," that Dr. Arnold wrote "in terms of somewhat extravagant commendation of a short article on Mirabeau which I had written." ‡ The letter was to Mr. Tooke, the treasurer of the

* "Life and Correspondence," vol. i. p. **274.**

† *Ibid.*, p. 275.

‡ "Passages," vol. i. p. **243.**

Society, and for the sake of clearing up this important question of principle, I must quote the passage to which I referred. "I cannot tell you how much I was delighted by the conclusion of an article on Mirabeau, in 'The Penny Magazine' of May 12. That article is exactly a specimen of what I wished to see, but done far better than I could do it. I never wanted articles on religious subjects half so much as articles on common subjects written with a decidedly Christian tone. History and Biography are far better vehicles of good, I think, than any direct comments on Scripture, or essays on Evidences." * The conclusion of the article to which Dr. Arnold refers, is as follows:—"The career of Mirabeau offers a few consolatory remarks to those who are gifted with no extraordinary faculties, either for good or for evil. Mirabeau swayed the destinies of millions, but he was never happy; Mirabeau had almost reached the pinnacle of human power, and yet he fell a victim to the same evil passions which degrade and ruin the lowest of mankind. He could never be really great, because he was never freed from the bondage of his own evil desires. The man who steadily pursues a consistent course of duty, which has for its object to do good to himself and to all around him, will be followed to the grave by a few humble and sincere mourners, and no record will remain except in the hearts of those who loved him, to tell of his earthly career. But that man may gladly leave to such as Mirabeau the music, the torches, and the cannon, by which a nation proclaimed its loss; for assuredly he has felt that

* "Life and Correspondence," vol. i. p. 299.

inward consolation, and that sustaining hope throughout his life, which only the good can feel; he has fully enjoyed, in all its purity, the holy influence of 'the peace of God, which passeth all understanding.'"

I think that I may confidently say, that without attempting to impart to the "Penny Magazine" a distinctly religious character, I did not interpret in a too literal signification the original rule of the Society with reference to religion—that is, to abstain from publishing on that subject, "convinced that the numerous institutions already existing for the diffusion of religious knowledge in every shape will best advance that momentous end." * That I might have been encouraged to do more in the incidental manner advocated by Dr. Arnold I cannot doubt, had his approval of what he had read been communicated to me. When I first saw the opinion of this good and great man in his "Life," by the Rev. Arthur Stanley, published after his decease, I felt it was an injustice to myself on the part of the treasurer of the Society that this letter had been withheld from me.

I cannot conclude this notice of the early history of the "Penny Magazine" without adverting to one who first gave me the benefit of his assistance, in the office generally known as that of a sub-editor, soon after I became connected with the Useful Knowledge Society. Alexander Ramsay has been for five-and-thirty years my friend and fellow-labourer. He has worked with me in every undertaking in which I

* First Annual Report of the Society, 1828.

have been engaged, from the second volume of the "British Almanac and Companion" for 1830, to the last for 1864. He has brought to this long course of duty not only the ministerial services which belong to a reader of manuscripts and a corrector of the press, but taste, and knowledge, and readiness of resource, well adapted for original composition, in the accustomed progress and occasional exigencies of periodical works. I think it is creditable to both of us that in a long struggle by societies and individuals for the establishment of cheap and wholesome literature, we have been labouring side by side—that

> "In this glorious and well-foughten field,
> We kept together in our chivalry!"

CHAPTER XVI.

"THE success of the 'Penny Magazine' has induced the Committee to undertake the publication of a 'Penny Cyclopædia,' in Numbers and Monthly Parts. A work of such magnitude and novelty requires all the assistance which can be afforded it by the Members of the Society, both in London and in the Country, in order to give it publicity and circulation." Such was the announcement of their greatest undertaking in the annual address of the Useful Knowledge Society, dated June 30, 1832. A specimen of the projected "Penny Cyclopædia" had been printed by Mr. Clowes on the previous 2nd of June. This fact was certified by him after a surreptitious "Penny Cyclopædia" had been advertised in the daily papers of the 16th of August "as now ready." This had been met on the 17th by an advertisement from the Committee, cautioning the public against an attempt to impose upon them. The career of this pretender was terminated before the issue of the first number of the real "Penny Cyclopædia," on the 2nd of January, 1833.

In characterizing their undertaking as "a work of such magnitude and novelty," the Committee appear to have looked at its magnitude, rather with reference to the universal range of the proposed information, than to the contemplated limits in point of size. I have stated that the "Penny Cyclopædia" was projected by me "to form a moderate-sized book of eight volumes."* The novelty was not to consist in producing a Cyclopædia under one alphabetical arrangement, but in its issue in weekly sheets, each of which was to be sold at a penny. But there was another novelty which would very soon be discovered by the educated portion of the public, upon a comparison of this work with existing Cyclopædias. It was not an affair of scissors and paste. It was not a hash from German and French sources. Its writers had not "been at a great feast of languages and stolen the scraps." Every article was to be original; to be furnished by various men, each the best that could be found in special departments of knowledge. The essential difficulty of making the contributions at once brief and complete was discovered when the experiment came to be tried for a few months. It was impossible, moreover, to offer an adequate remuneration to a competent scholar or man of science, when it was said to him—You must give us the very cream of your knowledge; you must pour out the fullest information in the most condensed form of words; your articles must nevertheless be readable and perfectly intelligible to the popular mind; and yet, under these difficult conditions, you must be paid at a certain rate per page. This "solatium," not low as compared with reviews and magazine articles in reference to the mere number of words, was very low if the merit of the Cyclopædia was to consist in extreme compression, whilst the Review and the Magazine conductors would allow of

* Companion to the Almanac, 1858.

any amount of expansion not altogether extravagant. The plan would never work. It would pay the gardener to grow dwarf pear trees and peach trees, but it would not pay the writer to produce dwarfed articles that, like the rarities of the hot-house and conservatory, should be perfect in form, if not in size, bear good fruit, and not die very prematurely. A very clever and accomplished author, Mr. Samuel Phillips, thus described the issue of this experiment: "When the Cyclopædia was started, the public were invited to pay their penny a week, and to seize the opportunity of securing, not only a valuable, but also an incomparably *cheap* publication. 'Useful knowledge' was to be 'diffused' by a society appointed for the express purpose, but it was not to be 'diffusive.' It was to be poured abroad, but in such a form as should instruct, not weary or perplex the recipient. If we remember rightly, eight good compact volumes were to contain the substantial food for which the working mind was pining. Before one volume, however, was completed, the Committee thought it expedient to hint that it must 'be observed that the plan of the *Cyclopædia* had been rather enlarged.' After a year the plan had enlarged so much that the rate of issue was doubled. It was no longer a penny a week, but twopence. After three years it was quadrupled—fourpence a-week instead of twopence. Had the original plan of a penny weekly issue been persevered in, it would have taken exactly thirty-seven years to complete the business." *

The extension of the quantity of the Cyclopædia

* "Times," Oct. 12, 1854.

was no doubt unavoidable under the superintendence of the Society, but it destroyed its commercial value. Had it been a careful compilation, instead of an original work furnished by nearly two hundred contributors, it would have been to me a fortune. In that case, its preparation being confined to a few persons, its proposed limits could have been steadily adhered to. I have recorded,—without inferring that any blame was in the least degree to be attached to those who were responsible for its conduct—what was the commercial result of this enterprise. "The Committee had the honour of the work, in its extended form, but without incurring any of the risk, or contributing one shilling to the cost, the literary expenditure alone having reached nearly 40,000*l*. Upon the completion of the Cyclopædia, the balance upon the outlay above the receipts was 30,788*l*." * The regular decrease in the sale was very marked. While it continued to be published upon its original plan of one number weekly, the sale was 75,000. The instant there was an issue of two numbers a week it fell to 55,000, and at the end of its second year it had fallen to 44,000. When the twopence a week became fourpence, the rate of diminution became still more rapid. The sale of the first year was double that of the fourth year. The sale of the fourth year doubled that of the eighth year. It then found its level, and became steady to the end—the 55,000 of the latter months of 1833 having been reduced to 20,000 at the close of 1843. The Committee of the Society, when the original project had been departed from, and they saw that the under-

* Companion to the Almanac, 1858.

taking had become to me a burden and a loss, passed a resolution that no rent be paid upon the first 110,000 copies of each number of the "Penny Cyclopædia." Rent was then to commence; and to continue till the work had reached a sale of 200,000, when the Society would no longer ask for a remuneration for its superintendence. No doubt I was grateful for this sanguine anticipation of a good time coming, but it is scarcely prudent or satisfactory for a commercial man to postpone his profits *ad Calendas Graecas.* The chronic loss for eleven years, which was induced by the Cyclopædia, and which fell wholly upon me, absorbed every other source of profit in my extensive business, leaving me little beyond a bare maintenance, without the hope of laying by for the future.

There was a very serious interruption to the sale of the Cyclopædia after it had existed about six months; which may be worth recording, as exhibiting the evils of unrepealed laws passed in former states of society and under different circumstances. I find this record in the Minutes of the Committee of the 12th of June, 1833: "Mr. Knight laid on the table a letter from Mr. Drake, of Birmingham, dated the 10th instant, which stated, that informations had been filed, and convictions obtained, under the 27th clause of the 39th George III., chap. 79, against booksellers in that town, for selling a publication whereof the printer's name did not appear on the first and last pages; and that in consequence many booksellers were fearful of selling the 'Penny Magazine' and 'Cyclopædia.'" Copies of these and other letters received on this subject were transmitted to Mr. Spring Rice, with whom I had an interview. The result was that, although a law might eventually be passed to remedy the oppression of these *qui tam* informations, the statute of the 39th George III. could not at once be repealed. I had no remedy but to call in the whole of the stock in the hands of many wholesale agents scattered through the country, who had to go through the same process with those they had supplied. The law was subsequently altered in its effect by the Government deciding that it should be left to the discretion of the Attorney-General to prosecute publishers in all cases where the statute was not strictly adhered to.

Mr. Phillips has said in his article on the "Penny Cyclopædia"—"Mr. Knight, the publisher and prime mover of the undertaking, proudly congratulated himself at its close upon having achieved a great literary triumph; he had also, as was usual in his pæans, to mingle in his song the melancholy note of one suffering under the consciousness of great commercial loss." The melancholy note which was out of harmony with my pæans was almost invariably connected with the pressure of the paper duty upon all works of large circulation and low price. With the high duty of threepence in the pound, it required a steadfast resolution on my part not to be beaten by excessive taxation, and an equal hope that the duty might be abolished or reduced, to prevent me throwing up the Cyclopædia in despair. In 1836 the duty was reduced to three halfpence in the pound. This was a relief; but it was not commensurate with the constant falling sale to which I have adverted. I gladly suspend "the melancholy note" and turn to a much more interesting subject—the reminiscence of some of the most valued contributors to the Cyclopædia, whose services conferred upon it a reputation which has survived during all the varied changes of literature and science that we have seen, and which is capable of a constant renewal of its pristine vigour, such as has been accomplished in "The English Cyclopædia."

The author of "The Rehearsal" has made merry with the notion of "two kings of Brentford sitting on one throne, smelling to one nosegay." If Mr. Long and myself had persevered for more than a few months in the attempt to divide the editorial duties connected with the "Penny Cyclopædia" we might possibly have been presented to the world in this ludicrous attitude. As it was, I very soon most gladly resigned the reins into the hands of one who managed his team with consummate skill during many years. For such a work as the Cyclopædia a thoroughly competent Editor was indispensable. He must combine the moral qualities of unwearied industry and undeviating punctuality, with the firmness which is best supported by courtesy and kindness. I have heard that a man of letters who was rather raw, laid down as a maxim for his editorial guidance that he must be polite to his contributors, but by no means familiar. Mr. Long's contributors gathered round him as friends. On his intellectual qualities it is unnecessary for me to dilate. Lord Brougham, in his Address to the Association for the Promotion of Social Science in 1857, referred to the operations of the Committees of the Useful Knowledge Society as an example of "the beneficial effects of united action." In the "Companion to the Almanac" for 1858, I noticed, as I felt it my duty to do, the somewhat exaggerated estimate which the Chairman of the Society had formed of the results of this *united* action, without making the slightest reference to *individual* actions. Speaking more especially of Mr. Long's labours as Editor of the Cyclopædia, and incidentally alluding to my own in connection with the "Penny Magazine" and other works, I said—"That the Society presented many advantages as a base of operations is unquestionable. It had the prestige of great names connected with it. Its members were of high intelligence and various learning; they were industrious; and, what was of equal importance, they confided in their editors. Had this confidence not existed, the periodical works could not have gone on a single month. They would have broken down under a divided responsibility, and have been suffocated in the red-tapeism of what Lord Brougham described as 'a vigilant superintendence over the style, so that errors in composition and offences against correct, and even severe, taste were sure to be corrected,'—always provided that the editors had any reliance upon the correct, and even severe, taste of the correctors. That 'the great number of our members' produced even these minor results is a figure of speech. There were a few working members, as there are in every association, who were valuable referees; but that the Society, as a body, was the moving power which enabled it to publish for twenty years 'with unbroken regularity,' we humbly beg to say is a continuance of a delusion which was not entertained by those members who were content to aid in doing what they thought a work of public utility, without attempting to shut their eyes to what had been accomplished, during many years, by editorial responsibility."

In the sixth chapter, I have incidentally mentioned several of the earlier members of the Useful Knowledge Committee as contributors to the Cyclopædia. Upon looking over the general list of the contributors to this work during the many years of its publication, I cannot but regard it as most fortunate that a rule, which was attempted to be established in the first stages of the Society, soon came to be held as perfectly impracticable. This rule, to which Lord Brougham gave the name of the Self-denying Ordinance, was in effect that no member of the Committee should be paid for his writings. It was perhaps desirable that such a rule should have existed at the origin of the Society, when it was considered that public subscriptions would be necessary for its maintenance. But when it was found that during five years this source of revenue had only yielded to the Society a clear annual sum of 125*l.*, and that its publications might be carried on upon the commercial principle alone, and afford a profit partly to the Society and partly to its publishers, it would have been the extreme of false delicacy to deny to the Editor of the Cyclopædia, especially, the services of some of the best contributors he could anywhere find. The time was past when the highest in rank, as well as the most eminent in literature or science, would think it a degradation to be paid for their writings. And thus, whether members of our Committee or otherwise, every writer in the Cyclopædia was paid at a fixed rate, whose aggregate at the end of the work had amounted to the large sum I have previously stated. Standing, therefore, upon the same principle as regulated the pecuniary arrangements with other contributors—the only principle upon which the relations of author and publisher can be harmoniously maintained—I shall not attempt to separate the two classes in referring with necessary brevity to the chief supporters of this undertaking in the character of writers.

First in importance of the great departments of the "Cyclopædia," may be reckoned that of mathematical and physical science. Upon Professor De Morgan rested its heaviest labours. It was essential that one mind should have the almost undivided charge of Mathematics, considering that, the order of the articles being alphabetical, the relation of one portion of a subject to the other had constantly to be regarded so as to render the whole series of articles complete and harmonious. Thus this collection of mathematical papers, when duly arranged by their author according to his own views, have been constantly referred to in his classes at University College. Astronomy necessarily formed a portion of this division, and to Professor De Morgan are due the accuracy and completeness of the general articles on this subject. There were special papers on this branch of science by other contributors. In speaking of the series on astronomical instruments, by the Rev. Richard Sheepshanks (who became a member of the committee soon after the first publication of the Cyclopædia), I cannot forbear to express the admiration I always felt for this distinguished man. There was a breadth in his understanding which carried him beyond the range of the minute and laborious scientific operations to which he devoted the greater part of his time. He was a liberal thinker in political matters, although never publicly meddling with the great questions whose triumphs he rejoiced to behold. His conversation on matters of history and literature always presented the evidence of sound thought and rich learning. He was ready to assist in any well-considered project of utility with a self-devotion quite untainted by any desire of profit or distinction. The same generous spirit seems to have been a family inheritance, for it was his brother John, who, in 1856, presented to the nation his noble collection of pictures by British artists.

Lord Brougham used to point with a just pride to the one contribution of the Astronomer-Royal to the "Penny Cyclopædia," as a notable example of the value of popular literature in the eyes of one of the most eminent scientific men of his day. Mr. Airy's paper on Gravitation is indeed a masterpiece of lucid exposition without the employment of mathematical formulæ.

I turn to the applications of science to the arts. First in importance in the past and in the present state of civilisation is Agriculture. I have a note before me, dated February 25th, 1833, from the Rev. William Lewis Rham, whom I had slightly known during my Windsor experience as the Vicar of Winkfield, in Berkshire. He therein proposes, upon the suggestion of his friend, Mr. Jardine, to write for the "Penny Cyclopædia," "as affording a considerable variety of subjects, and especially those connected with agriculture, to which I have paid some attention, and in which I have some practical experience." This proposition was gladly closed with; for it was not easy then to find one of "practical experience" in agriculture who had the power of expressing his ideas in a style which should unite brevity with clearness, and by its popular qualities turn aside the country gentleman and the cultivator from their ordinary contempt of "book-farming." Mr. Rham immediately commenced that series of papers in the "Penny Cyclopædia," which were subsequently collected in a volume entitled "The Dictionary of the Farm." He wrote the first of these articles at the beginning of 1833. He wrote the last of the series, "Yorkshire Husbandry," in 1843, only a few weeks before his death.

CHAPTER XVII.

TO attempt the most general view of the condition of manufactures and machinery during the progress of the "Penny Cyclopædia,"—especially bearing in mind the vast changes that would grow out of the removal of the fiscal burthens upon industry, and the gradual development of Free Trade—would be far beyond the scope of these incidental glances at a brighter future. I have touched very lightly upon the subject in the fourth and fifth chapters of this volume. Of the contributors to this department of the "Cyclopædia," I may mention an old friend who has worked with me during many years upon matters of a cognate character, Mr. George Dodd. His careful observation and his punctual industry made him then, as he still continues to be, one of the most useful contributors to serial works. Furnishing not so much in quantity, but what he did always being of signal value, was Mr. Edward Cowper. As an inventor, Mr. Cowper was to me peculiarly interesting, as being connected with those simplifications of the printing machine which brought it into common use. He felt that it was his great pride to have rendered what was originally a complicated instrument, one capable of adaptation to the purposes of rapid and cheap book-printing, and of producing such illustrated works as the "Penny Magazine" and the "Penny Cyclopædia." In an examination before a Committee of the House of Commons, he said: "The ease with which the principles and illustrations of Art might be diffused, I think is so obvious that it is hardly necessary to say a word about it. Here you may see it exemplified in the 'Penny Magazine.' Such works as this could not have existed without the printing-machine." Amongst the leading questions or observations by the Committee was this: "In fact the mechanic and the peasant in the most remote districts of the country, have now an opportunity of seeing tolerably correct outlines of form which they never could behold before?" His answer was, "Exactly; and literally at the price they used to give for a song." When asked "Is there not, therefore, a greater chance of calling genius into activity?" he answered, "Yes; not merely by these books creating an artist here and there, but by the general elevation of the taste of the public." Beyond what Mr. Cowper so justly stated with regard to our own country, I may add, that at this period, 1836, the "Penny Magazine" was producing a revolution in popular Art throughout the world. Stereotype casts of its best cuts were supplied by me for the illustration of publications of a similar character, which appeared in eleven different languages and countries. Many interesting considerations are involved in the mere recital of the names of these countries: Germany—France—Holland—Livonia (in Russian and German)—Bohemia (Sclavonic)—Italy—Ionian Islands (modern Greek)—Sweden—Norway—Spanish America—the Brazils.

The entire work was also reprinted in the United States from plates sent from this country. I was not only bound to be grateful to Mr. Cowper for his evidence, but I had long entertained the highest respect for the wide range of his information, and the simplicity of his character. In his latter years he became Professor of Mechanics and Manufacturing Arts at King's College. His mode of teaching was singularly lucid, never trusting to mere descriptions of machinery, so difficult to understand, but illustrating what he had to say by models constructed with a most minute ingenuity. He did not consider it beneath the dignity of a Professor to superintend daily, and actually to work without assistance, a machine of his invention, at the blacking manufactory of Messrs. Day and Martin, for secretly printing the labels of their bottles in a manner which would preclude imitation. It was long before the Arts that had been effectually used for preventing the forgery of blacking labels, were allowed to interfere with the flourishing manufacture of forged bank notes.

Dr. Andrew Ure was a contributor to this department of the "Cyclopædia." In 1835, I published his very interesting volume on "The Philosophy of Manufactures;" and in 1836, his larger work on "The Cotton Manufacture of Great Britain compared with other Countries." He was then analytical chemist to the Board of Customs. There were many special articles on Manufactures and Machinery, by men conversant with particular branches. Amongst various names, there is one which stands out prominent, although processes and mechanical principles were not exactly in his line. Edwin Norris has won his distinguished position and his high reputation by his labours as a philological and ethnological writer. In the "Companion to the Almanac" for 1830, he furnished a striking example of the range and accuracy of his peculiar knowledge, in a most complete explanation of "The Eras of Ancient and Modern Times, and of various Countries." He still renders me the kindness of supplying to the "British Almanac" the brief notices under each month of the Hebrew Calendar and the Mohammedan Calendar. I knew him with some degree of intimacy, upon which I look back with pleasure, in the years before his great knowledge of languages gave him the high appointment of Secretary to the Royal Asiatic Society, and the onerous responsibility of translator to the Foreign Office. In our earliest intercourse, he not only won my regard by his intellectual and moral qualities, but to me he was especially interesting as the son of a newspaper proprietor at Taunton. He had acquired the practical knowledge of a printer; but, passionately fond of travelling, and devoted to studies whose usefulness was not exactly to be manifested in provincial journalism, he went to the continent as a private tutor, and remained abroad several years. In his pedestrian tours from city to city his remittances from home sometimes failed to reach him. He had resources in himself which were ever ready to secure his independence as a citizen of the world. Arriving at a certain town, he found himself almost penniless. Applying to the principal printer, he solicits employment as a compositor. He states his knowledge of foreign languages. Work is slack, and the young linguist is about to look further. "Stop!" says the typographical successor of the Stephenses (for I believe the town was Geneva). "Stop! I have been printing a Hebrew Bible, of which a little is done; but I can find nobody here to finish it. Can you undertake the job and go through with it?" The job was undertaken, and it was completed. I need give no better illustration of that force of character which, in the instance of Mr. Norris, was one of many manifestations of that power which we are accustomed to call Genius.

In the department of the Fine Arts, Mr. Eastlake (now Sir Charles) contributed a few valuable papers —such as Basso Rilievo. Sir Edmund Head also wrote on painting, as did my old friend J. P. Davis. Mr. R. N. Wornum (now Keeper of the National Gallery) gave to the Cyclopædia the advantage of his almost unequalled knowledge of the general history and character of Schools of Art, and of the lives of the great painters. And here I may take occasion to mention—not only with reference to the biographies of artists, but of those of the eminent in Science, in Literature, in Statesmanship, in Theology, in Law—that the plan of the "Penny Cyclopædia" being such as to forbid the introduction of any living person, was necessarily limited and imperfect. Under the superintendence of the Useful Knowledge Society, it would have been very difficult, if not impossible, to have widened the biographical circle, so as to include many of those who were daily coming into contact with members of its committee in the friendships or the rivalries of Politics or letters. When the superintendence of the Society had ceased, the "English Cyclopædia" was free to take a wider range. It was with considerable reluctance that, as the conductor of the enlarged work,

I decided upon the introduction of the names of living persons, British and Foreign. There are, doubtless, grave objections to such a course; but the advantages, looking at them strictly in the literary point of view, are very manifest. A Cyclopædia that deals only with those of whom it may speak with the absolute freedom of the "honest chronicler" who is to keep the honour of the dead from corruption, must be, if not half a century, at least three or four decades behind the wants of the existing generation. This is an era in no respects more remarkable than for the long lives of many eminent men. Lord Lyndhurst, for example, died in 1863, at the age of ninety-one. Because his place was not in the necrology of the century till that year, is the historical student to learn nothing from a biographical dictionary of the John Singleton Copley, who was counsel for Watson and Thistlewood in 1817? William Mulready died in 1863, at the age of seventy-eight. The young Irishman was a student of the Royal Academy in 1801. He was a Royal Academician in 1816. Was the most successful rival of Wilkie not to be noticed in a popular biography whilst his works were still the theme of admiration, and the old man could still look critically, but generously, upon the productions of celebrated artists who were unborn, or were mere boys, when he was in the zenith of his fame? Difficulties in such an undertaking there unquestionably were; but these were to be overcome by obtaining, wherever possible, from living persons themselves authentic materials; and above all, by avoiding rash inferences and hypothetical explanations.

Photography, in spite of the protests of landscape painters and portrait painters, has taken rank amongst the Fine Arts. Its imperfect beginnings only could have been noticed in the "Penny Cyclopædia." When Arago, in 1839, communicated to the French Academy of Sciences that Daguerre had discovered a process by which objects could be faithfully represented by other agencies than the hand of man, the world was at first incredulous, as if an attempt had been made to revive the middle-age miracles. Englishmen came home from Paris with dim representations of buildings, and hideous copies of their own features, sun-painted on metal. Such were the first Daguerreotypes. Mr. Fox Talbot, who had been working out this discovery at the same period as Daguerre, soon produced his Talbotypes on paper, and, in 1841, described his process to the Society of Arts. But, as yet, photographic portraits and landscapes were regarded as mere curiosities. In twenty years photography was to bestow an amount of pleasure upon every class of society which had never been attained in any age by the imitative arts. It may not be too much to regard it as one of the special blessings of a beneficent Providence, that, at a period when steam navigation has dispersed the European races over the most distant regions of the habitable globe, there should have sprung up an invention which brings into the dwelling of the colonizer, whether a mansion or a cabin, the very scenes of the *home* he has left, and the images of the loved ones from whom he is separated.

This leads me briefly to advert to the Geographical department of the "Penny Cyclopædia." This section also stopped short in 1843, in tracing that march of English adventure which had made new nations in the days of Elizabeth, but which had not yet accomplished the wonderful development of the Australian colonies during the reign of Victoria. There was a great deal to be done by the encyclopædist of the next twenty years. But what was done by us, especially in the department of Physical Geography, was of a character very different from the matter that had previously occupied the most elaborate geographical works. The chief contributor was Mr. William Wittich, who became Teacher of German at University College. I have heard Mr. Long declare, that he considered Mr. Wittich as the father of descriptive geography in this country. Of many other contributors to the geographical department, I must be content to mention the names of Sir Francis Beaufort, Sir J. F. Davis, Colonel Jackson, Mr. Smith, Secretary of King's College, and Mr. Means. Karl Ritter, the celebrated professor at Berlin, wrote the important article "Asia." Of André Vieusseux and of William Weir, whose contributions were extensive, I shall have subsequently to speak.

In the Natural History division of the Cyclopædia, I must especially mention Mr. William John Broderip, who contributed nearly all the Zoological articles of the entire work. No more remarkable example could have been presented of a man zealously discharging responsible official duties, and finding his best recreation in scientific pursuits, than Mr. Broderip. He was for thirty-four years one of the most industrious and upright Police Magistrates of the Metropolis. In writing a brief memoir of this learned and at the same time entertaining naturalist, I have said: "His articles in the 'Cyclopædia' are models of scientific exactness and popular attraction; and whilst they have instructed and delighted thousands of readers, have won the suffrages of the most fastidious, even amongst those who are slow to believe that the solid and the amusing have no necessary antagonism." In the section of Geology, Mr. John Phillips, Professor of that science in King's College, was a most valuable contributor. In that of Botany, Dr. Lindley wrote all the articles up to the letter R. Dr. Edwin Lankester, who had studied under Dr. Lindley at University College, gave also his valuable assistance to the original work, and subsequently edited the Natural History Division of its successor.

In Law and Jurisprudence, the "Penny Cyclopædia" was a most complete repository of information, historical and practical. The constitution of the Useful Knowledge Society, of which many eminent lawyers were members, gave an authority to its legal articles even before the names of its contributors were given to the world. As there were also eminent physicians and surgeons, the same prestige attached to its articles on Medical Science. A mere catalogue of the names of these professional men would scarcely be interesting, unless I were to trace the career of some who were only slightly known at the period of their early contributions, but who have subsequently risen into high reputation. Such, amongst the medical contributors, was the late Dr. Baley, whose useful life was so grievously cut short by a railway accident; such was Mr. J. Paget, the distinguished surgeon; such, Mr. John Simon, who, as the medical officer of the General Board of Health, has accomplished so much for sanitary reform. Dr. Robert Dickson, whose benevolence is as conspicuous as his knowledge, contributed all the articles on Materia Medica. Nor must I omit Dr. Southwood Smith, who supplied many of the articles on Anatomy, Medicine, and Physiology. I was his publisher also of that interesting popular work, "The Philosophy of Health." Now that his most useful life has closed, I may mention a circumstance which I should have hesitated previously to print. Dr. Smith's book, "The Use of the Dead to the Living," chiefly led to the passing of the Anatomy Act, by which an end was put to the necessity of the hateful tribe of Resurrection Men, and to such atrocities as those which had been committed in Edinburgh and London, where adults and children had been systematically murdered by the vampires of modern times, who sold their bodies to the anatomical schools. Dr. Southwood Smith had been the intimate friend of Jeremy Bentham. It was the wish of the venerable philosopher that his body should be dissected, and for that purpose he left it to the enlightened physician who had been his attendant at the time of his death. Having called upon Dr. Smith at his house in the city, as I was going away he said, in his quiet manner, "Would you like to see Bentham?" I could not quite comprehend him; but leading the way into his hall, he unlocked, with a small key that hung to his watch-chain, a mahogany case, something like the sedan chair of a past generation. Behind an inner covering of plate-glass sat the figure of the old jurist in the identical clothes which he had worn living; a waxen face, round which was clustering the white hair, was covered with his well-known broad-brimmed hat, and he leant on the trusty stick with which he had so often paced the Green Park. I long stood absorbed in many thoughts of the great man's career. Dr. Smith withdrew the glass, opened the few buttons of the waistcoat, and then showed the skeleton, which preached the same lesson to the pride of human wisdom as the skull of "poor Yorick" did to the gibes that were wont "to set the table in a roar."

Collected for the purpose of separate publication in the remodelled "English Cyclopædia," it was found that the biographical articles of the original work constituted its largest division. It may, therefore, be concluded that in this place I can only notice the leading features of that division, and a few only of its contributors. Those who wrote the articles on history and literature, ancient and modern, furnished, for the most part, the series of biographies. It may be sufficient to point to articles by Thomas Hewitt Key, George Cornewall Lewis, George Long, Leonard Schmitz, Dr. Donaldson, Philip Smith, and William Smith, to show how completely these Lives were calculated to supersede the inaccurate sciolisms of Lemprière and similar manufacturers of Classical Dictionaries. Nor is it necessary that I should particularly specify those who brought their historical and literary knowledge to build up the compact, but yet full, Biographia Britannica, which our work presents, even without the subsequent addition of living names. The writers of these articles are generally well known in their more extended reputations as authors of separate works. But there was a class of writers whom Mr. Long had the good fortune to collect around him, who had previously added little to the stores of English learning. I allude to the eminent foreigners who wrote in the "Cyclopædia," some in our language, others in their own. The editorial care either corrected the foreign idioms—sometimes peeping out of their English compositions—or procured accurate translations of the French, Italian, German, Spanish, and Portuguese, in which some wrote. One foreigner whose English required little correction, if any, was André Vieusseux. I had been intimate with this most amiable and accomplished man from the time when he wrote in the "Quarterly Magazine." I had published, in 1824, his delightful work, "Italy and the Italians." My pleasant and improving intercourse with him was renewed when he became one of the most industrious contributors to the "Cyclopædia." His life had been a varied and eventful one. As a youth he had seen the bloody course of revolution in Naples, when it was doubtful which was most to be hated—monarchical oppression or democratic fury. He had fought in the Peninsular War, as an officer in one of the foreign legions. After the peace, he had settled in England upon a small independence, to which he was enabled to add by literary labour. His conscientious devotion to the right performance of whatever he undertook, his large experience, and his correct taste, made him one of our most valuable coadjutors. In German literature, Dr. Leonard Schmitz was as useful as in classical. Pascual de Gayangos, who had married an English lady, also wrote fluently in our language during his residence amongst us. His perfect acquaintance with Arabic gave him a mastery over the general and literary history of Spain during the mediæval period, which few of his countrymen have attained. His biographies in the "Cyclopædia"—Spanish and Oriental—are, therefore, particularly valuable. Another great Oriental scholar, Frederick Augustus Rosen, was the Sanskrit Professor in University College. In the "Penny Cyclopædia" he wrote all the articles on Oriental literature from "Abbasides" to "Ethiopian Language." His labours were terminated by his sudden death in 1837, at the age of thirty-two. This distinguished native of Hanover acquired in England a host of friends, whose admiration he had won by his high intellectual attainments, and whose love was commanded by his gentle manners and kind heart. Count Krasinski was one of the Polish exiles in England to whom literature had become the only means of support. He came here on a diplomatic mission, in 1830, from the revolutionary government, of which Prince Czartoryski was president. In 1831, when the hope of Polish independence was again crushed, he dwelt among us a penniless fugitive, until his death in 1855. His contributions to the "Penny Cyclopædia" were on the Sclavonian history and literature.

I have passed over Music, in referring to the department of Fine Arts, that I may more particularly notice the amount of musical taste and knowledge amongst us twenty years ago. Mr. William Ayrton could scarcely, during the time I knew him, be called a Professor of Music, although some few years previous the opera had been under his management. A man of education, he moved in the best society; whilst his ability as a writer, combined with his extensive musical knowledge, fitted him to contribute the whole series of musical biographies to the "Penny Cyclopædia." He had previously edited for me a work which, I may flatter myself, contributed something to that great change which has made the

English of the reign of Queen Victoria as musical a people as their ancestors of Queen Elizabeth's time. The moveable types used in the "Musical Library" furnished the means of producing vocal and instrumental music from the best masters, in weekly sheets of eight pages, sold at about a quarter of the price of the ordinary sheet of the music shops. The period was then only beginning when an idea penetrated the English mind, that in music, as in the other Fine Arts, anything but the common-place and vulgar could have any charms for the bulk of the people. Profound philosophers believed that nothing else could please, theatrical managers affirmed that nothing else would draw. The great and fashionable firmly relied upon the unchangeableness of the opinion—though a hundred and twenty years old—of Isaac Bickerstaff, who says: "In Italy, nothing is more frequent than to hear a cobbler working to an opera tune; but, on the contrary, our honest countrymen have so little an inclination to music, that they seldom begin to sing till they are drunk." In the "Penny Magazine" for 1834, it was said: "The theatres and other public places have administered to bad taste: little or nothing except trash has been open to the people; and they have been deemed barbarians because they took what fell in their way, and showed no love for what they never had an opportunity of knowing. We trust, however, that, for the future, good music, like good literature, may be made accessible to all; and that, as a mode of enlarging the cheap enjoyments of a poor man's life, even every village school in the kingdom may possess the means of teaching (as they are taught at similar establishments in several districts of Germany, in

Bohemia, and even in the snow-covered, poverty-stricken island of Iceland) the art of reading musical notation and the first rudiments of music."

I have traced the greatest work of the Useful Knowledge Society to its completion at the end of eleven years. Let me revert to its opening period, when the friends of Popular Education had not only to build up the walls of their citadel, but to work with weapons at their side. When the "Penny Magazine," during two years' existence, had reached a sale quite unprecedented in Popular Literature, and after the first year's publication, with marked success, of the "Penny Cyclopædia," a series of attacks, as unceasing as they were virulent, were directed against the Society for the Diffusion of Useful Knowledge, and against me, especially, as their chief instrument in the fearful revolution which was threatening to destroy the legitimate thrones and dominations of the empire of books. The Society was a monopoly; the "Penny Magazine" was "a glorious humbug upon the reading portion of the operatives," for it was nothing more than a bookseller's speculation, which "brings in Knight some thousands per annum;" the idea of the "Penny Cyclopædia" was stolen from a respectable man, who was struggling to maintain a young family, "by a trader, who, because he has the name of the Society painted on his sign-board, seems to think himself entitled to throw off all the ordinary restraints to which fair rivalry in trade is subject;" the writers in these works were literary drudges—obscure literary drudges, without a single idea in their heads, save what they filch from the British Museum.

Such was the temper in which the "New Monthly Magazine" poured out the vials of its wrath on my devoted head. It was necessary to publish a few facts, with very little comment, to show the falsehoods and absurdities of the daily, weekly, and monthly assaults of this complexion. That was done, with the sanction of the Society, in the "Companion to the Almanac," in December, 1833. On the 15th of February, 1834, I published No. I. of "The Printing Machine, a Review for the Many;" and therein, in an article entitled "The Literary Newspapers," I uttered, perhaps with more spirit than prudence, some unpalatable remonstrances against the systematic hostility of the two journals which I described as "the advanced guard of the army of letters, who carry small baggage on their march." The attacks soon became more personal.

Towards the end of that February, I was proposed as a member of the "Garrick Club." In the second week of March a very dear friend, my solicitor, Mr. Thomas Clarke, came to me to say that the Committee of that Club were hesitating about my election, as I had been excluded from a Club which had been formed out of members of the "Literary Union," such exclusion involving some serious imputation upon my character and conduct. I had been a member of the "Literary Union" for three or four years. Several gentlemen immediately undertook to ascertain the nature of the charges against me; and I was in a few days authorised by two of these friends to rest the vindication of my character upon the ground that the imputation made in the Committee of the "Literary Union Club," appointed for the formation of a New Club, was, that I had formerly failed in business—and dishonourably failed—that I "had made a bad bankruptcy." In twenty-four hours I had possessed myself of the means of my vindication. The publication of an indignant letter addressed by me to the Committee, accompanied by the documents which they had refused to look at, was my only course. That paper was circulated by me to a limited extent. It consisted of letters from my three trustees, a London printer, a London stationer, and a banker of Windsor, and one also from the solicitor to the trustees. They were to the effect that my suspension of payments was not to be attributed in the slightest degree to any misconduct, or even imprudence, on my part; but was an unavoidable result of the Panic of 1825, which so materially diminished the value of all bookselling property; that the final resolution to place my affairs under the management of trustees was come to by my creditors with the greatest reluctance to interfere with my own administration of my estate; that the anxious and self-denying care with which I abstained from receiving a single shilling of its proceeds after that resolution had been come to, was a striking instance of firmness and integrity; that I had been unvarying in my determination not to consider the release from my engagements as at all binding, except in a legal point of view, and had unweariedly laboured to discharge every debt in full, just as if no such acquittance had taken place, going far beyond what they thought a duty to my own family.

It is not from any motive of self-exaltation that I revive this matter, never to touch it again. My own deep feeling of gratitude to the eminent men with whom I was associated in the Useful Knowledge

Society is called forth now, when I glance at the many warm letters from them which this occurrence produced. Nor do I feel less grateful to Mr. Coates, their secretary, for his letters to me at this juncture. My friends were anxious that the stigma of my exclusion from this so-called Literary Club should be effectually wiped off by my election to the most distinguished Club in London. Lord Lansdowne, in a letter addressed to the Lord Chancellor, full of the most hearty kindness towards me, declared his opinion upon the wishes that my friends had expressed on my behalf: "There is no man in England better entitled than Knight to come into the Athenæum," and he subsequently agreed to propose me as a member. This Lord Lansdowne did, with a full knowledge of the circumstances. The Bishop of Winchester, whose conduct to me since 1827 had been marked by unvarying kindness and generosity, wished to support my nomination. Many other leading members of that Club—and I was glad to have Mr. Murray amongst the number—volunteered their aid. But party feeling then ran high, and I was unwilling to risk a contest, which might renew what was very disagreeable to me as a subject of public discussion. The "Garrick Club Committee" elected me after a brief interval. I became also one of the early members of the "Reform Club."

The hostility against the Society for the Diffusion of Useful Knowledge, which had been manifested by a small section of the periodical press, gradually died out. Public opinion was louder than the cuckoo cry of "monopoly" that was shouted by fashionable publishers and echoed by a clique of the regular professors of "*la littérature facile.*" Those who wrote for the Society had been called in derision "compilers." The "men of genius" who despised industry as dulness had their little day of sarcasm against "literary drudges," but in the end the public many was too strong for the exclusive few. The bookselling trade —publishers as well as retailers—had also discovered that, in the manifest extension of readers, a reliance might be placed upon the principle of increased numbers co-operating to purchase cheap books, and that enlarged returns would make up for diminished profits upon dear books. They had discovered that the trade of books would not be destroyed by cheap weekly sheets. If they had not arrived, through a process of reasoning, at the belief that the more people read the more they will read, they had the evidence of their own ledgers to inform them that the literary returns of the United Kingdom had nearly doubled since the terrible era of cheapness which commenced in 1827. Books, which at the beginning of the century had been a luxury, had now become a necessity. Still the objection was urged that, however extended was the market for popular literature, the quality of the supply must as a matter of course be low. The "Penny Cyclopædia" furnished a very sufficient answer to such reasoners.

The calumnies with which I had been personally assailed had not accomplished their object—that of injuring me as a man of business. They did not lessen the regard of my old friends, nor did they cut me off from the confidence which secured me a new and important connexion. Within another year I became associated as Publisher with the great measure of Local Administration that had received the sanction of Parliament.

CHAPTER XVIII.

NEXT to the "Cyclopædia" in the costliness of its production, if not in intrinsic importance, was the "Gallery of Portraits," which I published under the superintendence of the Society. It was issued in monthly numbers at half-a-crown each number, containing three portraits with biographies. The object of the publication was to present likenesses of those eminent men of modern times who have given the greatest impulse to their age. In the selection of subjects for portraiture, the Committee was occupied from the beginning of 1832 (the first number being published in May), to the midsummer of 1834. Their occupation was of a most pleasant and improving kind, for there was scarcely a name suggested that did not involve some discussion upon the merits of those proposed to be represented, or some statement of the sources from which authentic portraits might be obtained. In this latter respect the influence of the Society, or that of its individual members, was most valuable, by securing the admission of copyists to Royal Galleries and private collections. British and Foreign statesmen, warriors, divines, men of science and letters, artists, were thus assigned their due honour in a work, which was essentially different in its plan from the "Portraits of Illustrious Personages of Great Britain," by

Edmund Lodge, Norroy King of Arms. Interesting as much of Mr. Lodge's information was in its genealogical and antiquarian features, the book was not what it professed to be, "A Gallery of the Illustrious Dead"—"A Collection of Portraits and Lives of British Worthies." It was a collection of kings and queens, of noble lords and ladies and officers of state. It was, with very few exceptions, not a gallery of the intellectually illustrious. Of the chief glories of our nation—the poets, historians, philosophers, divines, of the inventors and discoverers in physical and abstract science, of our most distinguished artists, there was not one in this "Gallery of the Illustrious Dead," unless he could claim a place there by some titular or official distinction. Very different was the range of the gallery which I considered it an honour to publish, and the large expenses of which I cheerfully bore until the work became remunerative. The merit of suggesting it, and of most assiduously labouring to carry it worthily forward, is due to Mr. Bellenden Ker. The superintendence of the engravings was confided to Mr. Lupton, a mezzotinto engraver of the first eminence. Mr. Arthur Malkin was the editor of the biographies. These are all distinguished for careful research and an unpretending style. A few of the lives were written by his personal friends, amongst whom was Arthur H. Hallam—the A. H. H. of Tennyson's "In Memoriam"—who died in 1833. From De Quincey I obtained a spirited memoir of Milton; and it was to me a matter of regret, that its length was so out of proportion to the general character of the work, that some curtailment was absolutely necessary.

The 13th of August, 1836, was a remarkable day

in the annals of the press of this country, for on that day two Acts of Parliament received the Royal Assent, which materially influenced all the commercial arrangements for rendering knowledge, political or literary, more accessible to the bulk of the people. The first of these (c. 52), was to reduce the duties on first-class paper from three-pence per pound to three-halfpence, so that the former tax of three-halfpence upon second-class paper should apply to paper of all descriptions. The second of these (c. 76), was to reduce the stamp on newspapers from fourpence to a penny. I have previously mentioned (page 180), a debate in the House of Commons, on the 22nd of May, 1834, upon a motion for the repeal of the newspaper stamp duties. I had at that time learnt something of the desire of several members of the government, including Lord Brougham and Lord Althorp, that these duties should be wholly repealed. Had that been the case, a difficulty would have arisen as to the transmission of unstamped newspapers by post. In a letter to Lord Althorp, I suggested that a penny stamped frank should be issued by the government. Mr. M. D. Hill, in the debate which I have mentioned, described the nature of this suggestion. In the "Companion to the Newspaper," for June the 1st, 1834, there appeared a paper of considerable length "prepared several months ago for the information of some official personages who took a strong interest in the question of the repeal of the stamp duties on newspapers." In that paper it is said, "In order to allow the unstamped papers to pass through the Post-office, it is proposed that franks should be sold (say by the vendors of stamps), at a penny each. It will be necessary to make the postage payable by the person sending the paper; for otherwise, a great many papers, especially the very low-priced ones, would be refused by persons to whom they were addressed. It is obvious that a direct payment to the Post-office, by the transmitter of the paper, would be highly inconvenient, if not impossible. Mr. Knight's plan of a stamped frank obviates the difficulty; and it would facilitate the transmission of all printed sheets under a certain weight." It has always been to me a matter of honest pride that this suggestion contributed, in however small a degree, to the efficient working of the magnificent system of penny-postage. Mr. Rowland Hill, in his celebrated pamphlet on Post-office Reform, published in 1837, says, "A few years ago, when the expediency of entirely abolishing the newspaper stamp, and allowing newspapers to pass through the Post-office for one penny each, was under consideration, it was proposed by Mr. Charles Knight, the publisher, that the postage on newspapers might be collected by selling stamped wrappers at one penny each. Availing myself of this excellent suggestion, I propose the following arrangement:—Let stamped covers and sheets of paper be supplied to the public from the Stamp-office, or Post-office, as may be most convenient, and sold at such a price as to include the postage: letters so stamped, might be put into the letter-box as at present."

In 1836, my views, as to the total repeal of the Stamp Duty on Newspapers, were considerably altered from those of 1834, when, in suggesting a plan for the circulation of unstamped newspapers, I had adopted the opinion that the stamp, except as a postage payment, was injurious. I was apprehensive, as I was before the removal of the stamp in 1855, that cheap newspapers would involve the degradation of journalism. I did not draw sound conclusions from my own experience. I did not believe that Penny Papers would be as innoxious as Penny Magazines and Penny Cyclopædias, and go on making readers, till the great body of those who read would prefer sound nutriment to the garbage which was offered them in the days of high taxation. As in most cases, my own interest gave a colour, I suppose, to my opinions. From the time when William Henry Ord was a contributor to "The Etonian," to the time when he was a Member of Parliament and a Lord of the Treasury, I had some degree of intimacy, almost amounting to friendship, with this amiable and accomplished man. In 1836, in his official position, he had devoted himself to the great measure of the consolidation of the various Stamp Acts. The mass of obscure and confused enactments was to be swept away, and some intelligible fiscal measure was to be substituted. Mr. Ord devoted himself to the herculean task of preparing the way for the proposition which was brought forward by Mr. Spring Rice, then Chancellor of the Exchequer. The labour killed him. In the spring of 1836, I frequently saw him. We had many conversations on the subject of the Newspaper Stamp Duties and the Paper Duty. I fancied that if the government consented to abolish the Newspaper Stamp, they would retain the high Paper Duty. Mr. Ord and I came to the opinion that the safest and the best course would be to lower both imposts. I wrote a pamphlet advocating this policy, which was circulated amongst members of both Houses. Whether it had any effect upon the settlement of the question is not for me to judge. At any rate, the reduction of the Paper Duty was to me a matter of vital importance; and when that boon to the publishers of cheap books came into operation in the autumn, I felt that I had shaken off much of the insupportable weight of the "Old Man of the Sea," and went forward with the words of Milton in my heart:

> "To-morrow to fresh fields and pastures new."

In 1835, Mr. Bellenden Ker having returned from a continental tour, gave me some numbers of a work then publishing in Germany, the "Bilder Bibel." An idea had once been entertained of the Useful Knowledge Society publishing a Bible—an illustrated one; but the notion was given up as impracticable, and not in accordance with the principle upon which the Society was established. Mr. Ker's present revived the project in my mind. Such a publication, in which Art should be employed to delight the young, and learning should not be wanting, offered a strong temptation to my individual enterprise. But the difficulty was to find a fit editor—one who held sound opinions upon the great cardinal points of religion, but who would at the same time content himself with furnishing an ample commentary on such passages as are connected with the History, Geography, Natural History, and Antiquities of the Sacred Scriptures. Thus to limit the objects of the work was to make it acceptable to all denominations of Christians. I had several conversations on this matter with a very learned and liberal divine; but he could not see his course clearly, in avoiding theological questions. I often thought of dividing the labour; and with this view I proposed to Mr. Kitto to furnish notes upon such subjects as had come under his observation during his travels and sojourn in the East. This task he gladly undertook. In a few weeks he came to me and said—in that guttural voice to which I had now become accustomed—"I will undertake it all." We had a little merriment over the boldness of the proposal; but I found that he was perfectly in earnest. As a matter of prudence I proposed that he should complete the book of Genesis, and after that we could determine upon the future course of proceeding. He accomplished this to my complete satisfaction. The enthusiasm with which he entered upon the task was to me an earnest that he could well be trusted to carry it through faithfully. I released him from all other employments; and so, at the beginning of 1836, the first number of "The Pictorial Bible" was issued. In hitting upon the word "Pictorial" I felt that I was rather daring in the employment of a term which the Dictionaries pronounced as "not in use." It has now been rendered familiar by frequent employment. I could not have easily found any other word that would have conveyed the intention to present wood-engravings of the scriptural designs of great painters; of landscape scenes; of costume; of zoology and botany; of the remains of ancient architecture. "The Pictorial Bible" was completed in two years and a half. To me it was profitable, costly as were the wood-cuts. The profit was doubly welcome from the fact, that after having paid Mr. Kitto, during the progress of publication, 250*l.* a-year, I was enabled, upon the completion of the book, to present him with a sum which seemed to him a little fortune. A letter which Mr. Kitto wrote to me, as the work was proceeding, has been published by his biographer: "I cannot begin any observations respecting 'The Pictorial Bible,' without stating how highly I have been gratified and interested in the occupation it has afforded. It has been of infinite advantage as an exercise to my own mind. It has afforded me an opportunity of bringing nearly all my resources into play; my old biblical studies, the observations of travel, and even the very miscellaneous character of my reading, have all been highly useful to me in this undertaking. The venerable character of the work on which I have laboured, the responsibility of annotation, and the extent in which such labour is likely to have influence, are also circumstances which have greatly gratified, in a very definite manner, that desire of usefulness, which has, I may say, been a strong principle of action with me, and which owes its origin, I think, to the desire I was early led to entertain of finding whether the most adverse circumstances (including the privation of intellectual nourishment) must necessarily operate in excluding me from the hope of filling a useful place in society. The question was, whether I should hang a dead weight upon society, or take a place among its active men. I have struggled for the latter alternative, and it will be a proud thing for me if I am enabled to realise it. I venture to hope that I shall: and to you I am, in the most eminent degree, indebted for the opportunities, assistance, and encouragement you have always afforded me in my endeavours after this object." *

* Life of John Kitto, D.D., by John Eadie, D.D., 1857, p. 304.

Of the illustrated books subsequently published, the "Pictorial History of England" occupied seven years in a regular monthly course of publication. It bore upon its title-page that it was produced "By George L. Craik and Charles MacFarlane, assisted by other Contributors." Four out of its eight volumes carried the narrative to the conclusion of the reign of George the Second. The other four volumes comprised only the reign of George the Third. This disproportion was fatal to the success which might have been anticipated if the whole work had been confined within as reasonable limits as the narrative of eighteen centuries, which preceded that of the latter half century. Mr. MacFarlane had undertaken the larger department of civil and military history. The history of religion, of literature, and of commerce, could not have been better confided than to Mr. Craik. In his history of the constitution he was occasionally assisted by Mr. Andrew Bisset, who has recently given an evidence that his characteristic views upon historical questions are unchanged. Sir Henry Ellis, my old and valued friend, lent some aid to the literature of the Saxon Period. The subject of the Arts was in the hands of an eminent architect, Mr. Edward Poynter, whose various accomplishments extended beyond the range of his own profession. Mr. Weir, who subsequently became the Editor of the "Daily News," wrote some graphic chapters on manners in the time of the third George. But upon Mr. MacFarlane rested the chief burden of this elaborate work. In the early half of its chronological divisions the subsidiary chapters rendered the historical narrative less difficult for one writer to manage. For the work, like that of Dr. Henry, was broken up into separate divisions. I came subsequently to the conviction that this was not the true plan upon which a history of England ought to be conducted. "It may be convenient to a writer to treat of a period under distinct heads, such as those adopted by Dr. Henry—Civil and Military; Ecclesiastical; Constitution; Learning; Arts; Commerce; Manners;—but such an arrangement necessarily involves a large amount of prolixity and repetition. The intervals, also, at which the several divisions occur in works so conducted are much too long; for, in a century and a half, or two centuries, social changes are usually so great, that the Laws, Learning, Arts, and Customs at the beginning of such a period have little in common with those of its conclusion." * What was convenient to one writer was a far greater convenience in a history upon which many writers were employed. The plan worked well to the end of the fourth volume. Mr. MacFarlane had a considerable power of narration. He dealt more with military than with civil history, and in this his merit was conspicuous, for, by nature or by study, he had acquired a very competent notion of the military art. Upon paper he "could set an army in the field," and "the division of a battle" well understood. But in other respects he had not the prime quality of the historian, impartiality. He was essentially a partizan. He did not run riot upon vexed questions of past times. He was moderate in his estimate of the virtues of Charles the First,

* "Popular History of England." By Charles Knight. Vol. I. Introduction.

and would not have broken a lance in maintaining the purity of Mary Queen of Scots. But when he came to the French Revolution, then he was for "whole volumes in folio," that he might dwell upon its countless abominations, and say no word about the mighty changes which it was destined to produce upon the condition of the mass of society. He was a most agreeable companion, and an affectionate though not a safe friend. Had I been less attached to him I might, at all risks, have stopped the publication after the disproportion of the latter volumes had been manifested. But it is difficult for a publisher to adopt such a course in a serial work, even if his interest called upon him to be despotic. He is in the hands of others; and he must assent to their completion of the task which they had begun. To go on is dangerous; but to halt midway would be destruction.

CHAPTER XIX.

WHEN I had entered upon the publication of pictorial works, which had become a marked feature of my business, I was naturally led, as one serial approached its completion, to look around me for its fit successor. The Bible, the History of England, were books of universal interest, in which I could carry out my plan of rendering wood-cuts real illustrations of the text, instead of fanciful devices—true eye-knowledge, sometimes more instructive than words. There was one large subject capable of such treatment. It was once the fashion to illustrate Pennant's "London" with prints of every age and character. There could be no want of authentic materials for such a book as I contemplated.

Many descriptions of the great capital, whose past history is as interesting as its present state, had appeared at various periods. In the age of Elizabeth, John Stow published his "Survey of London, conteyning the originall, antiquity, increase, moderne estate and description of that citie." The worthy citizen of London has been fortunate in the eulogy of his modern editor, William J. Thoms, who to the learning of the antiquary unites the graces of the accomplished writer. Well has he said in his introductory notice, "If it were given to the reader to wield for a brief space the staff of Prospero, with power to conjure up a vision of London as it existed in some former period, there can be little doubt but that he would so employ his art that the London of Shakspeare should stand revealed before him. Happily, although Prospero's staff is broken, the conjurations of the mighty magic necessary to call up this busy pageant were lodged in the untiring pen of honest John Stow." In the latter years of the Commonwealth, James Howell published his "Londinopolis; Historical Discourse and Perlustration of London." This is the city in which Milton had dwelt, as a boy, beneath his father's roof in Bread Street, to the time of his death in 1674, a blind old man. Then came laborious antiquaries to delve amongst registers and tomb-stones, with a taste far inferior to the historians who had gone before them. There was a field open to the light essayist; and Leigh Hunt made a very pleasant but very imperfect book of literary gossip about authors and players. As a subject for a pictorial book of some extent, I decided upon publishing "London" in weekly numbers. It was commenced in 1841; it was finished in 1844. I undertook the general conduct of the work. I had valuable contributors in Mr. Craik, Mr. Saunders, Mr. Weir, Mr. Platt, Mr. Dodd, Mr. Planché, and Mr. Fairholt. I adopted the plan of giving the names of the authors of each paper in a table of contents of the several volumes. The proportions in which each contributed to a work extending to two thousand five hundred pages will thus be seen.

In 1837 I began to look about me for artistic materials adapted to a Pictorial Edition of Shakspere. At first view, the existing stores of illustrations seemed almost boundless. There were embellishments to various editions from the time of Rowe, chiefly of a theatrical character, and, for the most part, thoroughly unnatural. The grand historical pictures of the Shakspere Gallery were not in a very much higher taste, furnishing a remarkable example how painters of the highest rank in their day had contrived to make the characters of Shakspere little more than vehicles for the display of false costume. There were a few valuable antiquarian illustrations, such as those given by Mr. Douce. Altogether, it became necessary for me to look carefully at the plays, to see whether the aid of art might not be called in to add both to the information and enjoyment of the reader of Shakspere, by representing the Realities upon which the imagination of the poet must have rested. There were the localities of the various scenes, whether English or foreign; the portraits of the real personages of the historical plays; the objects of natural history, so constantly occurring; accurate costume in all its rich variety. Whilst engaged in my search after such pictorial illustrations, a gentleman, who has since distinguished himself by his antiquarian knowledge, lent me his note-book, in which he had jotted down a somewhat large list of archæological subjects. This kindness of Mr. William Fairholt was of essential use to me. I very early put myself in communication with Mr. Poynter, who made for me a series of the most beautiful architectural drawings, which imparted a character of truthfulness to many scenes, which upon the stage had in general been merely fanciful creations of the painter. Mr. Harvey undertook to produce a series of frontispieces, which, embodying the realities of costume and other accessaries, would have enough of an imaginative character to render them pleasing.

The foundations of my edition as an illustrated work of art being thus laid, I diligently applied myself to a critical examination of the text to be adopted. I procured a copy of the first folio, which was read aloud to me whilst I marked upon a copy of the common *trade edition*, all the variations that presented themselves. I found that no book could be more incorrectly printed than this booksellers' stereotyped volume. I subsequently expressed my belief that the text of Shakspere had not been compared with the originals carefully and systematically for half a century. Not only had words been changed by printers, but whole lines had been omitted. The punctuation of the received text was in the most confused state. Thus far, my way was clear to produce a pictorial edition with a more correct text, even if I absolutely relied upon the authority of the first folio compared with the quartos. Of these scarce morsels I could avail myself in Steevens' very accurate reprint. This accuracy I had tested by having the several plays which he thus reproduced, collated with originals in the British Museum. But then, a new difficulty arose. The conjectural emendations of the variorum editors were so numerous, that it was necessary that I should make up my mind as to their adoption or rejection. I had to decide upon many disputed readings; and for this it was essential to consult the great mass of separate commentary that had been published by the learned, the dull, and the conceited, during the century in which the critical study of Shakspere's text had been pursued by many competent and incompetent writers. There was one man of my acquaintance, for whom I had a high regard—Mr. Thomas Rodd, the well-known bookseller of Great Newport Street —whose knowledge of the works which he sold went far beyond their title-pages. He enabled me to form a considerable collection of commentaries on Shakspere, ranging from Rymer and Dennis to Hazlitt and Coleridge. As I advanced in my Shaksperian studies, I found that my labours would not cease with the acquirement of a more intimate knowledge of all that had been written about the text, but that I must carefully examine the various opinions as to the order in which the plays of Shakspere were produced, unless I were implicitly to adopt the theories advocated in Malone's "Essay" on that very difficult subject. I was satisfied that much depended in coming to something like accurate conclusions as to the plays which belonged respectively to the poet's earlier period, his middle period, and his later period. The historical plays would necessarily follow in the order of the events of which they were the subject. But for the comedies and tragedies, I determined to print them in the order which I believed to be at least an approximation to the period of their composition.

After a year of preparation I issued my prospectus, in which I boldly declared that Shakspere demanded a rational edition of his performançes, that should address itself to the popular understanding in a spirit of love, and not of captious and presumptuous cavilling. In the first number of my edition, containing the "Two Gentlemen of Verona," I made a distinct profession of faith in Shakspere, with a perfect knowledge that I should be assailed on many sides, but that I should call up hosts of friends ready to shake off their allegiance to "the dwarfish commentators who are for ever cutting him down to their own size." I thus wrote in my introductory notice to this play: "We believe the time is past when it can afford any satisfaction to an Englishman to hear the greatest of our poets perpetually held up to ridicule as a sort of inspired barbarian, who worked without method, and wholly without learning. But before Shakspere can be properly understood, the popular mind must be led in an opposite direction; and we must learn to regard him, as he really was, as the most consummate of artists, who had a complete and absolute control over all the materials and instruments of his art, without any subordination to mere impulses and caprices,—with entire self-possession and perfect knowledge."

It was natural for many who had been bred in a reverence for the old school of criticism to consider me presumptuous in declaring my scepticism as to the authority of Steevens and of Malone. Probably, my new-born enthusiasm carried me somewhat too far. I accepted as a seasonable admonition a friendly letter from Mr. Rodd: "Notwithstanding all their squabbles among themselves and abuse of each other, the dulness of some and wildness of others, I consider them as a whole as a body of men who have rendered singular service to English literature. In their readings for illustration of his text, they have thrown great light upon our national history, antiquities and language, and been the means of calling into notice several good authors who had fallen into unmerited obscurity. Let me beg of you to tread more lightly over their ashes in future." But I was not likely, although I might modify my future expressions, to be diverted from my convictions that I had chosen the right path, however perplexed it might be. I had abundant encouragement in my course. Henry Nelson Coleridge wrote to me upon the appearance of my opening number: "It is at once a beautiful and instructive edition; indeed, the first in the country conceived in a right spirit." Mrs. Jameson, in a most welcome letter, expressed her entire sympathy with my opinions: "I thought I had well studied Shakspere myself, but your edition has opened fresh sources of reflection and information." My old friend, Sir Henry Ellis, proffered his assistance, and sent me a genuine slice of the mulberry-tree which he received from the Rev. Mr. Becket, and saw it cut from the block upon which Garrick had himself placed his seal. From Leigh Hunt I received a letter, from which I give an extract, very characteristic of the writer: "It rejoices me to see you in a task like this, because it enables you to live in a world which belongs to you besides the world of business, and which will do you as much good as I believe it will give pleasure and profit to the reader. To live with Shakspere, is to breathe at once the sweetest and most universal air of humanity." I could multiply these testimonies of kindness, were it not distasteful to me to appear like my own eulogist.

Offers of literary assistance in my undertaking reached me from various quarters. I had originally hoped for much direct aid, and had thought that my task would be lightened by having several persons engaged upon various departments. I found this idea, with two exceptions—music and costume—impossible of execution, even if I had not become enamoured of my work, and had derived from it a solace amidst many cares. The labour had not wearied me when I had completed three-fourths of my undertaking. In a postscript to my sixth volume, I thus expressed my feelings: "It is now somewhat more than three years since I commenced the publication of 'The Pictorial Edition of Shakspere,' in Monthly Parts; and during that period I have produced a Part on the first day of each month, with one single exception. The task of editing this work has been to me a most agreeable one. It has been absorbing enough to require my daily attention,—to occupy my habitual thoughts,—to shut out dark forebodings,—to lighten the pressure of instant evils. It has furnished me a useful and honourable occupation, which has not been less zealously pursued because it was associated with the discharge of duties not so pleasurable. I have worked at this task with a full consciousness of the responsibility which lay upon me; but as I have worked in the spirit of love, that consciousness has never been painful."

The Two Gentlemen of Verona was printed for the first time in the folio of 1623. That volume also contained eight other comedies, three histories, and six tragedies, of which no previous edition is known. In addition to these eighteen plays, four other comedies were there first printed in a perfect shape. I had, therefore, ample reason for considering that first folio as standing with regard to half of Shakspere's plays in the same relation to the text as the one manuscript of an ancient author. It was the only accredited *complete* copy of four more of his choicest works. I, therefore, from the first, held that for three-fifths of Shakspere's plays that folio was the only authority, however the quartos might be advantageously compared with its text with regard to the other two-fifths. I did not place an exclusive reliance, as I have often been accused of doing, upon the text of that folio, but I did not rely by preference upon those rare quarto morsels which the editors of the first folio had described as stolen and surreptitious copies. Within a week after the appearance of my first number, I had a letter from Mr. John Wilson Croker, which went to confirm me in my views with regard to the text. He says, "Let me tell you that many years ago (near forty I fear) I wrote a great many pages to establish the principle that you have adopted—the paramount authority of the first folio; and, as well as I can recollect, I went through the whole of Macbeth to prove my position. I know not whether my MS. is in existence, I rather fear not, as I have not seen it for near thirty years, but it may be in some boxes of old papers which are in a lumber room, and I will have it looked for. If I find it, and that it contains anything worth copying, you shall have it. Perhaps, also, I may be able now and then to give you some hints which may be worth your consideration." My old friend, Dr. Maginn, in a letter of the 15th of November, showed that he held the first folio in the same respect as I did myself, but was inclined to treat that and all other authorities with a licence that appeared to me somewhat dangerous: "I have not any Shakespeare collections by me, though I once made a considerable number of notes with a view of giving an edition, not of the kind you are publishing, but merely critical with reference principally to the state of the text. I consider with you the first folio to be in the nature of a

MS., and therefore to be kept always primarily in view, not of course neglecting the second folio, and the quartos; but having been reared in a school of criticism in which even MSS. themselves are used, not worshipped, I have no objection to wielding the hook in a manner which you would perhaps consider as slashing as that of Bentley himself."

Having thus taken up my position with regard to the text, I went on fearlessly and consistently. I preferred perhaps a little too exclusively the authority of the folio. I often adopted the text of a reliable quarto, always pointing out the discrepancies of the two editions. But I utterly rejected the principle of making a hash out of two texts, which had been the common practice of the variorum editors. To decide amidst various readings was really a much more difficult task a quarter of a century ago than it would be now, did the text remain precisely in the state in which it was when I began my labours. There did not then exist such a perfect, I might almost say such a wonderful help to memory as Mrs. Cowden Clarke's Concordance. Ayscough's Index was exceedingly imperfect and ill-arranged. The "Verbal Index" of Twiss—two rare volumes, which cost me three or four guineas—was a book that was to me a perpetual source of perplexity, for the references of a single word to a hundred different places, without the slightest key to its use and significance, led me into a labyrinth whose darkness it was impossible to penetrate. Honoured be the untiring industry and correct judgment of that lady, who came too late to assist me in my first edition, but who has ever since been my reliable aid whenever I was engaged in a critical study of Shakspere.

My continuous work had sometimes relief when questions arose which were of a more novel and exciting character than textual commentary or even æsthetical criticism. The Merry Wives of Windsor took me back into the old scenes of my childhood, which I retraced in companionship with one whose mind was as natural and genial as his landscapes are pure and truthful. Thomas Creswick and his wife spent a few weeks with us in a cottage at Salt Hill. A short walk took the painter with his sketch book, and the editor, with his unwritten knowledge of old familiar haunts, into Windsor, and there we might trace the misfortunes of Falstaff, as he was carried "in the name of foul clothes to Datchet Lane," and thence "slighted into the river where the shore was shelvy and narrow." "About the fields through Frogmore" suggested a stroll in another direction, to find a fit locality for the farm-house where Ann Page was "a feasting." The Windsor town of mediæval architecture was to be imagined, but the position of its streets with reference to the Castle could be well defined. Mr. Creswick's charming designs made the Merry Wives of Windsor the gem of the comedies in my edition. But as if Shakspere, the "gentle Shakspere," was to be always provocative of controversy, I became involved in the discussion of the very doubtful question whether Herne's Oak existed or had been cut down. The subject is stated so fully in my original edition, and, with some additional matter, in the revised issue of the Pictorial Shakspere now publishing, that it is scarcely necessary to add anything to my details of the evidence regarding the controverted points between Mr. Jesse and the "Quarterly Review," beyond printing here an extract of a letter to me from Mr. Croker, of the 13th of January, 1842:—

"Your dissertation on Herne's Oak is conclusive against Mr. Jesse's fable, but there is one point of that fable, of the error of which you cannot be apprised. Mr. Jesse admits that George IV. frequently stated that 'George III. had cut down the tree supposed to be Herne's oak;' but that 'he always added *that it was not so.*' Now I was the person to whom George IV. told the whole story, and I told it, many years ago, to Mr. Jesse, to whom it was then new, and I can assert that George IV. never *added* anything like what Mr. Jesse has stated, but *quite the reverse.* I know not from whom else Mr. Jesse might afterwards have heard the story, nor with what additions; but his statement that George IV. *always* told the story with the addition in question, is assuredly not the fact, for he did not so tell it *me*, and Mr. Jesse first heard the story from me without any such addition. Mr. Jesse asked me to allow him to print my version of the story—not at that time stating that he had heard any other version—but this I refused, out of delicacy to George IV., who, I think, was still alive, and to the rest of the Royal family, for the fact is, that George IV. told me the story as a proof that his father's mental disorder had shown itself earlier than was generally known; and all the circumstances of the anecdote—and they are *very curious*—tended to show that this cutting down of the tree was an act of temporary derangement. So much for my share in Mr. Jesse's story. In 1838 George IV. and even William IV. were dead, and I thought I might, without impropriety, set the substance of the matter right in the 'Quarterly

Review,' which I did in the passage you have quoted."

During my editorial employment upon Twelfth Night, I was led into considerations with regard to Shakspere's domestic character by the perusal of Mr. De Quincey's Life of Shakspere in a Part of the "Encyclopædia Britannica" which had just then appeared. My logical friend had taken up the notion that a passage in Twelfth Night was a pathetic counsel of the poet in his maturest years "against the errors into which his own inexperience had been ensnared." He maintains that when the duke says to the pretended Cesario—

> "Then let thy love be younger than thyself,
> Or thy affection cannot hold the bent,"

Shakspere intends to notice the disparity of years between himself and his wife. Mr. De Quincey's theory that Shakspere's married life was one of unhappiness, was supported by the dictum of Malone in 1780, who first dragged a passage of Shakspere's Will into light, to prove that in this, his last solemn act, the wife of the rich player of Stratford had not wholly escaped his memory; but, as more strongly to mark how little he esteemed her, he had "cut her off, not indeed with a shilling, but with an old bed." Steevens considered the bequest of the second best bed as "a mark of peculiar tenderness," and assumed that she was provided for by a settlement. It certainly occurred to me that such conjectures and inferences were a mere waste of words. I had made what the critical solvers of historical puzzles call a discovery. Well do I remember the glee with which, having written the following paragraph, I showed it to my dear friend, Mr. Thomas Clarke, a sound lawyer, who confirmed my opinion, as fully as did Mr. Long and Mr. Hill, with whom I subsequently discussed the matter. "Shakspere knew the law of England better than his legal commentators. His estates, with the exception of a copyhold tenement, expressly mentioned in his will, were *freehold.* HIS WIFE WAS ENTITLED TO DOWER. She was provided for amply, *by the clear and undeniable operation of the English law.* Of the houses and gardens which Shakspere inherited from his father, she was assured of the life-interest of a third, should she survive her husband, the instant that old John Shakspere died. Of the capital messuage, called New Place, the best house in Stratford, which Shakspere purchased in 1597, she was assured of the same life-interest, from the moment of the conveyance, provided it was a direct conveyance to her husband. That it was so conveyed, we may infer from the terms of the conveyance of the lands in Old Stratford, and other places, which were purchased by Shakspere in 1602, and were then conveyed 'to the onlye proper use and behoofe of the saide William Shakespere, his heires and assignes for ever.' Of a life-interest in a third of those lands also was she assured. The tenement in Blackfriars, purchased in 1614, was conveyed to Shakspere and *three other persons*, and after his death was re-conveyed by those persons to the uses of his will, 'for and in performance of the confidence and trust in them reposed by William Shakespeare deceased.' In this estate, certainly, the widow of our poet had not dower."

In the postscript to Twelfth Night, I had said, adverting to a letter printed by Mr. Collier in his

"New Facts," "There was one who knew Shakspere well—who, illustrious as he was by birth and station, does not hesitate to call *him*, one of the poor players of Blackfriars, 'my especial friend'—who testifies decidedly enough to the public estimation of his domestic conduct." That letter purported to have been written in 1608 by Lord Southampton to Lord Chancellor Ellesmere. I must give another extract from Mr. Croker's correspondence with me on the subject of Shakspere, to show how carefully this friend watched my progress, and with what critical acumen he anticipated the objections of the present day to discoveries of this apocryphal character. "I observe you quote and rely upon the letter signed 'H. S.' discovered among Lord Ellesmere's papers by Mr. Collier. If that letter be genuine I must plead guilty to a great want of critical sagacity, for somehow it smacks to me of modern invention, and all my reconsideration of the subject, and some other circumstances which have since struck me, corroborate my doubts. Mr. Collier is, of course, above all suspicion of having any hand in a fabrication, but it appears that one person at least, and perhaps more, had access to the papers before him, though it would seem that the particular bundle appeared not to have been opened since it was first tied up. In short, I see such strong external evidence of authenticity, and, on the other hand, such internal evidence (in my judgment) of the contrary, that I am puzzled."

In the spring of 1841 I commenced the publication of "Knight's Store of Knowledge for all Readers"—a series of original treatises by various authors. It was issued in weekly numbers at twopence. The first and second numbers were devoted to Shakspere and his writings, and they bore my name as their author. At this period I had finished six volumes of the Pictorial Shakspere, and the seventh, consisting of the doubtful plays and poems, was being printed. I had not yet commenced writing the biography, but I had collected various materials for that object; had visited Stratford, and had inspected several documents preserved there. I was thus prepared to write the papers in the "Store of Knowledge," with many new materials, and a tolerably complete acquaintance with whatever had been published of this very obscure life. That this unpretending production of mine had supplied a want, I was assured in a letter which I have before me from John Sterling, written in February, 1842, when he was staying at Falmouth. He thanks me for the pleasure and instruction furnished by the first volume of my new edition of Shakspere—"The Library Edition," published on the 1st of January, 1842,—and he then adds, "I had previously read with great delight your convincing and comprehensive Life of the Poet in the 'Store of Knowledge.' I was charmed to find so much external evidence for a view which the study of his style—so richly *composite*—must have more or less obscurely suggested to all intelligent readers." The praise of such a man furnished ample encouragement to me to devote my best exertions to the completion of the "Biography" which I had announced. The outline in the "Store of Knowledge" embodied, with slight variations, the general view which I subsequently elaborated. As those papers have probably passed into oblivion, I shall here attempt a very brief analysis of the portions in which I expressed my strong objections, or grave doubts, as to much that had been previously given to the world as the authentic facts of Shakspere's life. My discovery as to his wife's dower, had perhaps made me a little too sceptical—perhaps a little too rash, in regard to many of the stories embodied in the elaborate "Life of William Shakspeare," by Edmund Malone, which occupies nearly three hundred pages of the edition of 1821. I had carried that volume with me to Stratford in my first visit just noticed; and during my few days' sojourn there, had made many marginal notes, for the most part recording my first doubts of the received biographies. At the head of the section in which it is attempted to prove that Shakspere's father was an impoverished and dishonoured man, I find written, "It appears to me that all this may be pounded into nothing."

About six months afterwards, I published in my Pictorial Edition, an "Illustration of the Sonnets." In this elaborate analysis I worked out my theory that the poems of Shakspere, which Meres had, in 1598, termed his "sugared sonnets," amongst his private friends, when published as "never before imprinted," in 1609, "were a collection of 'Sibylline leaves' rescued from the perishableness of their written state, by some person who had access to the high and brilliant circle in which Shakspere was esteemed; and that this person's scrap-book, necessarily imperfect and pretending to no order, found its way to the hands of a bookseller, who was too happy to give to that age what its most distinguished man had written at various periods, for his own amusement, and for the gratification of his 'private friends.'"

I commenced the composition of "William Shakspere, a Biography," at Stratford-upon-Avon, in the summer of 1842. The first book, comprising about half the volume, was published in November of that year. This portion embraces the scanty materials for a life of Shakspere properly so called, up to the period when he left Stratford to enter upon his dramatic career in London. But I endeavoured to associate Shakspere with the circumstances around him, in a manner which might fix them in the mind of the reader by exciting his interest. I might have accomplished the same end by somewhat extending the notice in the "Store of Knowledge," accompanied by a History of Manners and Customs, a History of the Stage, &c., &c. The form of my biography might appear fanciful. It has been called by a prosaic critic a burlesque. But the narrative essentially rested upon facts, and if criticism required me to move in the old tramway, I was content to have chosen a byway more circuitous, but probably more pleasing.

CHAPTER XX.

THE "Penny Cyclopædia" was finished in twenty-seven volumes, in the spring of 1844. The notion of a Supplement had not then been matured. The work was deemed complete, as far as the efforts of the editor and his contributors could keep pace with the rapid march of invention, the improvements of legislation, and the onward rush of every department of knowledge. It is in the very nature of such works that they must be to some extent imperfect. Not Argus with his hundred eyes could note down all the metamorphoses of Time, the great magician, as *he* calls them into life.

Soon after the close of this labour of eleven years, I received an honour upon which I look back as one of my unalloyed "Pleasures of Memory." It comes before me now with the vagueness of an agreeable dream. To give some precision to my recollections, a friend transcribed for me, from the vast file of newspapers in the British Museum, some paragraphs from those of June, 1844. I will give one from the "Athenæum" of the 15th of that month: "Change is our order—the order of the nineteenth century; and, in marking progress, we may record here that authors and publishers seem about to 'handy-dandy,'—and that the contributors to the 'Penny Cyclopædia,' and some personal friends, have given Mr. Charles Knight a sumptuous entertainment at the Albion Tavern, on the completion of that work." The word "handy-dandy" may send my readers to their Shakspere :—"Change places, and handy-dandy, which is the justice, which is the thief?" This were an unsavoury allusion to the change indicated above; if there were any meaning intended. But perhaps the "Athenæum" had turned to Todd's "Johnson," and had there found this definition: "A play amongst children, in which something is shaken between two hands, and then a guess is made in which hand it is retained." There was little of the material reward of industry to be retained in my palm had it been ever so "itching;" and this my "authors" knew. But when one individual amongst "publishers" received such an unusual compliment as was bestowed upon me, I trust that I may regard the circumstance in the spirit of the "Athenæum"—as "marking progress" in the relations between two classes that were generally considered natural enemies, but whose interests are identical and ought never to be separated.

Upon reflection, I do not think it would be seemly in me to present my own recollections of the circumstances attending this dinner. Nor could I faithfully do so. I was at once joyous and frightened in my novel position. As to remembering what I said myself, in returning thanks, it comes before me "like a tangled chain." One thing I recollect. I quoted from Joan of Arc's speech in Henry VI.

> "Glory is like a circle in the water,
> Which never ceaseth to enlarge itself,
> Till by broad spreading it disperse to nought."

And then I ejaculated "not so knowledge."

But I must give some relation of this dinner; and I therefore blend portions of the reports of "The Times" and the "Morning Chronicle," without any deviation of phrase.

"On the suggestion of several eminent persons, it was proposed to give an entertainment to Mr. Knight, in celebration of the successful completion of the "Penny Cyclopædia," and to express their sense of the value and usefulness of the literary undertakings in which he has been engaged as editor or publisher. Accordingly a large party met on Wednesday evening at the Albion Tavern.

"The Chair was taken by Lord Brougham; and amongst the company assembled were Lord Wrottesley, the Rev. Mr. Jones the tithe commissioner, Mr. Bellenden Ker, Mr. John Lefevre, Mr. Parkes, Professor Key, Professor Long, Mr. M. D. Hill, Mr. Christie, M. P., Mr. Chadwick, Mr. Porter of the Board of Trade, and a host of literary and scientific gentlemen, as well as influential individuals connected with the publishing world.

"Lord Brougham, in proposing the health of Mr. Knight, dwelt on the various services which, in connection with the Useful Knowledge Society, he had been enabled to render towards the advancement of society in moral as well as intellectual knowledge; pointed out especially the great service he did to the state in writing and publishing his two little works, "The Rights of Industry" and "The Results of Machinery"—two publications which, at a time of great public excitement, were eminently conducive to allaying the reckless spirit which, in 1830, was leading multitudes to destroy property and break up machines. He also pointed out what Mr. Knight had done in editing and illustrating Shakspere; in the projection and carrying on of the 'Penny Magazine;' and the completion of the 'Penny Cyclopædia.'

"Mr. Knight's health was drunk with much enthusiasm, and he returned thanks in a very expressive manner, modestly urging the greater services of Professor Long, the editor, in the completion of the 'Penny Cyclopædia.' The Chairman, after tendering apologies for the absence of Lord Denman, Lord John Russell, and Dr. Lushington, proposed the health of Professor Long, who duly returned thanks, and called on the assembly to thank the contributors whose valuable aid he had received. After a few words from Professor Key, Mr. Weir proposed the Society for the Diffusion of Useful Knowledge, to which Lord Wrottesley responded.

"Some excellent speeches were made during the evening, especially one by Mr. M. D. Hill, who pointed out that the 'Pictorial History of England,' projected by Mr. Knight, had realised a long-cherished idea, that of seeing a history of England which would make the people and the progress of national institutions a prominent feature. To this toast Mr. Craik responded. The Rev. Mr. Jones, who proposed the health of Lord Brougham, was warmly applauded in declaring that neither the Church nor religion had anything to fear from the spread of useful knowledge, but, on the contrary, its diffusion was tributary to the highest and best interests of mankind."

In connection with the paragraph respecting the dinner at the Albion which I have quoted from the "Athenæum," was the following notice:—"We may add, as equally significant of the change that is coming over the spirit of the age, that Her Majesty has been pleased to signify, through Sir Henry Wheatley, her desire that copies of Mr. Knight's forthcoming publications, entitled *Knight's Weekly Volume,* should be supplied to the libraries established at all the palaces."

The "change that is coming over the spirit of the age" had probably some regard to times happily long past, when literature was the toy of a king and his courtesans, or the scorn of another crowned head who hated "Boets and Bainters." There was a period nearer to our own when the great were considered the exclusive patrons of letters. Queen Victoria upheld "the spirit of the age" in her gracious support of a series of books professedly cheaper than any collection that had previously existed. The undertaking had several features of novelty, and of general interest. I was proud of the patronage of the Queen. Perhaps I was equally pleased with the encouragement I received from a distinguished writer, with whom I had not then the happiness of that intimate acquaintance which I have subsequently enjoyed. On the 4th of June, I received a letter from Mr. Charles Dickens, who had seen my Prospectus, and pronounced "the whole scheme full of the highest interest." He adds:—"If I can ever be of the feeblest use in advancing a project so intimately connected with an end on which my heart is set—the liberal education of the people—I shall be sincerely glad. All good wishes and success attend you."

The prospectus to which Mr. Dickens refers was entitled "Book-Clubs for all Readers." It set forth that one of the first attempts, and it was a successful one, to establish a cheap Book-Club was made by

Robert Burns. He had founded a Society at Tarbolton, called the Bachelors' Club, which met monthly for the purposes of discussion and conversation. But this was a club without books; for the fines levied upon the members were spent in conviviality. Having changed his residence to Mauchline, a similar club was established there, but with one important alteration:—the fines were set apart for the purchase of books, and the first work bought was "The Mirror," by Henry Mackenzie. The prospectus went on to notice that, in 1825, Mr. Brougham, in his "Practical Observations upon the Education of the People," had maintained that Book-Clubs or Reading Societies might be established by small numbers of contributors, and would require only an inconsiderable fund. He says—having mentioned a few works which were then in existence—"I would here remark the great effect of combination upon such plans, in making the money of individuals go far. Three-halfpence a week, laid by in a whole family, will enable it to purchase in a year one of the cheap volumes of which I have spoken above; and a penny a week would be sufficient, were the publications made as cheap as possible. Now, let only a few neighbours join, say ten or twelve, and lend each other the books bought, and it is evident that, for a price so small as to be within the reach of the poorest labourer, all may have full as many books in the course of the year as it is possible for them to read, even supposing that the books bought by every one are not such as all the others desire to have."

The publications which I proposed to make "as cheap as possible," would enable a family to purchase four separate books at the end of a year by laying by a penny a week. But if twelve neighbours, or twelve fellow-workmen, or twelve apprentices, or twelve school boys, were to form a book-club to which each should contribute a penny a week, the association would find itself at the end of the year in possession of fifty-two of "Knight's Weekly Volumes," to be preserved as a Joint-Stock Library, or sold to the highest bidder, according to the plan of expensive Book-Clubs. The first "Weekly Volume" was published on the 29th of June, 1844.

The series of the "Weekly Volume" was commenced with a book written by myself, "William Caxton, the first English Printer, a Biography." During the course of two years, one hundred and five volumes were issued regularly, the weekly publication not having been omitted in a single instance. The subjects had always been selected upon a plan which had (in the course of this time) attained a certain completeness; and a little library having been formed, equally suited to Book Clubs and private purchasers, it was unnecessary to continue the publication at the rapid rate which had been previously thought desirable. The "Weekly Volume" then became the "Shilling Volume." In the monthly issue it was continued for two more years. I shall have occasion briefly to refer to the series in the next epoch of my "Working Life," for some books of original value were comprised in it, and their writers merit especial mention. The editorial conduct of the Series was to me a labour of love. The success, and the reputation which it acquired, compensated me for the falling off in the demand for the "Penny Magazine," for which there were many causes; particularly the extended sale of newspapers, and the application of wood-engravings to their illustration. To close the story of my literary connection with the Society for the Diffusion of Useful Knowledge, I will here advert to the last days of the popular miscellany upon which I had laboured for fourteen years.

The "Penny Magazine" of the Society for the Diffusion of Useful Knowledge terminated on the 27th of December, 1845. In 1841, after the publication of nine volumes of the original form and character, a second series was issued, which is comprised in five volumes. I may truly say that the object of the change was to present to a public which had been advancing in education, a Miscellany of a higher character than the first series. The engravings were superior; the writing was less "ramble-scramble." There were a series of articles on the great Italian painters, by Mrs. Jameson. During three years the factories of London and the country were visited by Mr. Dodd and a competent artist, to provide descriptions of all our great manufactories. Mr. Thorne wrote papers of a topographical nature, which indicated the talent and knowledge which he would subsequently display in "Rambles by Rivers." Mr. Saunders wrote a series of clever articles on "The Canterbury Tales." And yet the sale fell off. The superintendence of the Society had merged in my individual responsibility as editor when I announced a new "Penny Magazine." It was thenceforth to be chiefly a magazine of reading; woodcuts no longer continuing to be the prominent feature in the work. I took a zealous interest in this little Miscellany. In the first number I republished one of Praed's charming Enigmas, with an illustration by Harvey. I also then commenced a series entitled "The Caricaturist's Portrait Gallery." John Wilkes, by Hogarth; Charles Churchill, by Hogarth; Lord North, as the State-Coachman asleep; Burke throwing down the Dagger—these, with brief biographical notices, constituted a novel feature, which I would recommend some weekly or monthly provider of light literature to take up. Of Praed's Enigmas I published fourteen. In the desire to prevent the memory of my early friend from falling into oblivion amongst a new generation, I gave "Some Specimens" of his writings in addition, with a brief memoir. In 1839 this extraordinary genius died in the prime of life.

"Knight's Penny Magazine," as the miscellany which commenced in January, 1846, was called, had a short existence. In the sixth monthly part, I thus announced its discontinuance: "The present Series of the 'Penny Magazine' is closed after an experiment of only six months. The Editor has no reason to complain of the want of public encouragement, for the sale of this Series has exceeded that of its predecessor in 1845. But the sale, such as it is, is scarcely remunerating; and there are indications that it may decline rather than increase. This is a hint which cannot be mistaken. It shall not be said of his humble efforts to continue, upon an equality with the best of his contemporaries, a publication which once had a decided pre-eminence, that

'Superfluous lags the veteran on the stage."

He leaves this portion of popular literature to be cultivated by those whose new energy may be worth more than his old experience. The 'Penny Magazine' shall begin and end with him. It shall not pass into other hands."

Three months before I had thus put an end to my participation in the good or the evil of the Penny Press, the Committee of the Society for the Diffusion of Useful Knowledge announced the suspension of their operations. Their "Address," dated March 11, 1846, offered an explanation of their motives for this step. The circumstances attending the publication of the "Biographical Dictionary" had led to this determination. The Society had undertaken this great work at its own risk. It now felt what it was to engage in a serial publication that was not likely to be concluded during ten or more years, and to find the public support altogether inadequate to defray its literary expenditure. A Society can do what an individual can not dare to achieve. It could leave the battle-field. It was not so with me, when the "Penny Cyclopædia" was dragging me down. The Society had a charter, and might some day renew its active life :

> "He that fights and runs away,
> May live to fight another day."

Had I not fought on to the end of my perilous commercial enterprise, I should have been disgraced. Individual members of the Committee subscribed liberally to keep on their "Biographical Dictionary," and no one more generously than Earl Spencer. Had his death not occurred during the struggle to meet the loss of this bold commercial undertaking, it is probable that the Society would not have thus sung its requiem :—

"Though the Committee always counted upon a loss, or at the best upon a deficiency which could not be made good until long after the completion of the work, neither they, nor others more conversant with the chances of the bookselling-trade, were at all prepared to expect so large a deficiency as appeared by the time the letter A was completed. On these seven half-volumes the excess of expenditure above receipts amounts to nearly 5000*l.* Of this loss, more than half, it appears, has been sustained by the Society, and the remainder of the subscriptions and donations which have been announced from time to time. Though the first sale of the work was encouraging, as giving some reason to hope that it would shortly rise to such a point as might enable the Committee to proceed steadily to the end, yet it was found that the average rate of sale of the seven half-volumes produced the defalcation above alluded to. And careful estimates showed that, under existing circumstances, an additional sum of at least 15,000*l.* must be sunk. A work commenced in parts ought to be continued to the full extent which the capital of the undertaker will allow. The Society has obeyed this reasonable rule, and has exhausted its resources."

The Committee with perfect justice turn away from the contemplation of one failure to rejoice over a long continued success: "The Society's work is done, for its greatest object is achieved—fully, fairly, and permanently. The public is supplied with *cheap* and *good* literature to an extent which the most sanguine friend of human improvement could not in 1826, have hoped to have witnessed in twenty years."

But there was a temporary evil to counterbalance this permanent success. *All* the cheap literature was not good at the period of this triumphant retrospect. This was a circumstance that was sufficiently mortifying to those who, like myself, had formed an over sanguine estimate of the benefit that was likely to result from the general diffusion of the ability to read. The "Penny Magazine" and "Chambers's Journal" had, in 1832, driven the greater number of noxious publications out of the field. The great body of the people appeared satisfied with good solid food, without any inordinate craving for stale pastry, and with an utter disrelish of offal. But a taste for garbage, cooked up for the satisfaction of the lowest appetite, seemed to have returned. I made no lamentation over the cheapness which had become excessive. I did not regret that there was a competition going on in cheap weekly publications which was wholly unprecedented. In 1846, fourteen penny and penny-halfpenny Magazines, twelve Economical and Social Journals, and thirty-seven weekly sheets, forming separate books, were to be found in the shops of many regular booksellers, and on the counters of all the small dealers in periodicals that had started up throughout the country. The cheapness was accomplished in some by pilfering from every copyright work that came in their way. There were very few of these publications whose writers were paid for original articles upon a scale as liberal as that of the best reviews and magazines. There were some of a character to render the principle of cheapness dangerous and disgusting. In the concluding address of "Knight's Penny Magazine," I said: "The editor rejoices that there are many in the field, and some who have come at the eleventh hour, who deserve the wages of zealous and faithful labourers. But there are others who are carrying out the principle of cheap weekly sheets, to the disgrace of the system, and who appear to have got some considerable hold upon the less-informed of the working people, and especially upon the young. There are manufactories in London whence hundreds of reams of vile paper and printing issue weekly; where large bodies of children are employed to arrange types, at the wages of shirt-makers, from copy furnished by the most ignorant, at the wages of scavengers. In truth, such writers, if they deserve the name of writers, *are* scavengers. All the garbage that belongs to the history of crime and misery is raked together, to diffuse a moral miasma through the land, in the shape of the most vulgar and brutal fiction. 'Penny Magazines,' and 'Edinburgh Journals,' and 'Weekly Instructors,' and 'People's Journals,' have little chance of circulation *amongst the least-informed class*, who most require sound knowledge, while the cheap booksellers' shops are filled with such things as 'Newgate, a Romance,' 'The Black Mantle, or the Murder at the old Jewry,' 'The Spectre of the Hall,' 'The Love-Child,' 'The Feast of Blood,' 'The Convict,' and twenty others, all of the same exciting character to the young and ignorant. But the detrimental exercise of the printing-press is only to be met by its wholesome employment. He has no fear for the righteous cause of cheap literature."

My conviction that the cheap press would purify itself was realised in another decade. I had given a name to the wholesome literature for the people,

"The Fountain"—the noxious I had called "The Sewer." But I contended, as I had ever done, that the Paper Duty was an insurmountable barrier to the diffusion of publications that should combine the qualities of literary excellence and extreme cheapness. I maintained that to thrust out the noxious publications, the supply of the higher class must be abundant; the quality of the writing must be of the best, for to write well for the people is the rarest of literary qualifications; lastly, the price must as nearly as possible approach to the cost of the mischievous production. Whatever interferes with the circulation of the higher periodicals by increasing their price—whatever tends to render a false economy necessary, by lowering their payment for the best literary labour—interferes with one of the most important instruments of National Education, using the term in its highest sense. Such were the injurious consequences of the Paper Duty. That long disputed question has now been settled. The total repeal of this impost took place after my commercial career was in a great degree closed. How this tax weighed me down in the production of the "Penny Cyclopædia," I have related in a pamphlet of 1850, which was often quoted in Parliament, and which has some interest as a matter of literary history. I give the most material passage as a Note to this Chapter.

NOTE TO CHAPTER XX.

EXTRACT FROM "THE STRUGGLES OF A BOOK AGAINST EXCESSIVE TAXATION." BY CHARLES KNIGHT. 1850.

ON the 1st of January, 1833, I commenced the publication of THE PENNY CYCLOPÆDIA, in Numbers and Monthly Parts.

This work was entirely original. It was projected by myself, and published under the Superintendence of the Society for the Diffusion of Useful Knowledge. But the entire cost and risk were borne by me. The total cost for Literature and Engravings was 42,000*l.*

The Penny Cyclopædia and its Supplement were completed in 1846. The two works contain 15,764 pages, and the quantity of Paper required to produce a single copy is 2 Reams, each weighing 35 lbs. At the period of its completion, the *entire quantity of Paper* consumed in the work was FIFTY THOUSAND REAMS, the *total weight* of which amounted to ONE MILLION SEVEN HUNDRED AND FIFTY THOUSAND POUNDS. Of this weight 20,000 Reams, or 700,000 lbs., paid the Excise Duty of *Threepence* per lb., amounting to 8750*l.* ; and the remaining 30,000 Reams paid the reduced Duty of *Three-halfpence* per lb. (commencing in 1837) upon 1,050,000 lbs., amounting to 6562*l.* The total Duty paid up to the completion of the Cyclopædia, in 1846, was 15,312*l.* Since that period 2000 Reams of Paper have been used in reprinting, to correct the inequalities of the Stock, making an addition of 70,000 lbs., excised at 437*l.* But further, the Wrappers for the Monthly Parts have used 1500 Reams of Paper, taxed at 500*l.*, and the Milled Boards employed in binding the Volumes have been also taxed about 300*l.* THE TOTAL PAYMENT TO THE

EXCISE BY THE PENNY CYCLOPÆDIA HAS BEEN SIXTEEN THOUSAND FIVE HUNDRED POUNDS.

I propose to show,—

1. That this excessive burthen upon the great work to which I have devoted seventeen years of toil and anxiety, has been the primary cause that the enterprise has not yet been remunerative.
2. That the continuance of the Paper Duty, at the present rate of Three-halfpence per lb., prevents me undertaking the publication of a new and improved edition, *upon its first plan of a continuous alphabetical arrangement.*

1. The positive burthen of Sixteen thousand five hundred Pounds imposed by the State upon the publication of one book, is far from representing the difficulty and loss which that payment has entailed upon the undertaking.

It is well known that the amount of a duty upon raw material by no means represents the amount of the charge which it entails upon the manufacturer. Mr. MacCulloch and Mr. Porter rightly state that the price for a ream of one particular sort of printing paper was in 1831, twenty-four shillings,—in 1843, fifteen shillings and sixpence. From 1833 to 1837, the price of a Ream of Penny Cyclopædia Paper was thirty-three shillings ; from 1838 to 1846, it was twenty-four shillings. The difference in price was nine shillings per ream ; the amount of reduced duty was four shillings and fourpence halfpenny. The paper-makers and the stationers doubled the tax.* But even at the reduced rate it has been satisfactorily shown by my fellow-labourers, the Messrs. Chambers, that the Duty enters one-third into price. Unquestionably, if the Duty were now removed, I could buy a Ream of similar paper for seventeen shillings. The tax, preventing competition, and giving

* "Whatever renders a larger capital necessary in any trade or business, limits the competition in that business ; and by giving something like a monopoly to a few dealers, enables them to keep up the price beyond what would afford the ordinary rate of profit." —John Mill, *Principles of Political Economy*, vol. ii. p. 388. If the tax annihilates profits in a secondary process, such as the conversion of paper into books, it is easy to understand how the monopoly becomes complete.

undue advantages to capitalists, had the effect of making me pay for my Paper, from 1833 to 1837, sixteen shillings a Ream more than the price of untaxed Paper would be, or Sixteen thousand Pounds upon 20,000 Reams ; and from 1838 to 1846, seven shillings per Ream more than I should otherwise have paid, which upon 30,000 Reams amounts to Ten thousand five hundred Pounds. *The tax therefore operated as a burthen upon my publication to the extent of* TWENTY-SIX THOUSAND FIVE HUNDRED POUNDS, during its long and difficult progress to completion. The paper since used for Reprints, and the paper for Wrappers, has been raised in price 2500*l.* by the same process.

The Struggles of one Book against excessive Taxation are, up to this point, to be measured by a burthen of TWENTY-NINE THOUSAND POUNDS.

But I have not yet done. The tax has been working against the Penny Cyclopædia for seventeen years, in the chronic form of interest and compound interest.

It was very long before the periodical sale settled into a regular quantity. The work became too extensive for the great bulk of purchasers. For the first few months of the publication the sale was double what it was at the end of the first year. The sale of the first year doubled that of the fourth year. The sale of the fourth year doubled that of the eighth year,—and then it found its level and became steady to the end, reduced from 55,000 at the commencement, to 20,000 at the conclusion. Every publisher of a periodical work knows the accumulation of Stock that must inevitably take place with a falling demand. There never was a period after the third year at which I had less than Five thousand Reams of the Penny Cyclopædia in my Warehouse ; upon which Duty had been paid, for some portion at the high duty, and for some at the low, averaging 1500*l.* In 1841 there were in my Warehouse 1200 Reams upon which the high duty, expiring in 1837, had been paid. I consider the accumulating interest in this investment, in actually paid Duty, upon dead Stock, to have amounted, in the seventeen years during which I have been labouring to sell that Stock, to 1500*l.*, and including the interest upon the extra price charged by the paper-manufacturer upon the Duty, to 3000*l.*

And here, then, will the usual conclusion arise, that the

Publisher has not borne this load of *Thirty-two thousand Pounds* imposed by the State upon the Penny Cyclopædia, but the purchasers of the Penny Cyclopædia. My answer is very direct. Had that sum of 32,000*l*. been actually saved to me, I should not have been a pound richer by the publication of the Penny Cyclopædia. But with the saving I should not have been to that amount poorer. The outlay was so great, that it could never pay its expenses under a sale of 36,000 copies with the high duty. In the first five years that average number was printed; but the accumulation of Stock locked up 10,000*l*. Under the low duty it paid its expenses at 30,000 copies. The actual average sale during the nine years of that duty was 20,000. It would have required that there should have been no Paper Duty at all to have paid its expenses on a sale of 20,000. Had the Duty not been reduced by one-half at the end of 1836, I could not by any possibility have carried on the work. As it was, I struggled to the end.

2. The reduced Paper Duty, as I have undertaken to show, prevents me making the best use of the valuable Copyright which remains to me,—now that the accumulated Stock is in great part exhausted.

I was advised to propose a Subscription for an entirely new Edition. The highest Personage in the realm accorded me Her support, and so did Her admirable Consort, who is doing for Science and Industry what is worth far more than any money value. Some of the most eminent in the walks of intellect also came forward to aid me. Of the support of the Members of the Legislature which taxed me during fourteen years, I have not much to boast. I have given up the design. Upon a sale that would have merely returned my new outlay, the Paper Duty would have burthened the work to the extent of 3000*l*. Its abandonment would have lightened my risk to the extent of making the work yield me as high a profit from 3000 subscribers, as from 4000 subscribers with the Duty continued. With this encouragement I should have gone on.

There is a steady demand for the existing edition of the Penny Cyclopædia, to the extent of 250 Sets annually. The Paper Duty prevents me meeting this demand with any moderate commercial profit. The technical explanation is not difficult to be understood:—If I print 250 Copies only

—I use 500 Reams of Paper, of which the Duty is 4*s.* 6*d.* each, and the necessary increase of manufacturer's price 2*s.* 6*d.*, making a charge, arising out of the Duty, of 7*s.* per Ream, or 175*l.* upon 250 Copies. But in printing only 250 Copies I have to pay for the Presswork, as high as 15*s.* per Ream; whereas if I printed 500, I should only pay 10*s.* As the number of a book first printed increases, the cost of Presswork, or Machine-work, diminishes; and for this reason a tax upon the raw material of a book, Paper, increasing the risk of printing a large impression, compels a smaller impression, at a higher cost. But if there were no Paper Duty, I should print 500 Copies, by which I should save 350*l.* in the price of Paper, and 250*l.* in the price of Presswork; making a saving of 600*l.* This outlay of 600*l.* is imposed upon me absolutely by the existence of the Paper Duty; and that fact will possibly compel me to give up reprinting a Book which has done more for the advancement of sound knowledge and general education in these kingdoms, than any work ever produced in any country. That 600*l.* saved would afford me an income which would allow me to invest capital in such a Reprint. Printing only 250 Copies at the present price of Paper, a set of this book would cost me 1000*l.* My net profit upon that outlay would not be 10 per cent.

And with all this danger and difficulty—with "this lion in my path"—I am not yet beaten. I have my valuable copyright of the Penny Cyclopædia remaining to me; and I have passed many an anxious hour in seeing how I can best turn it to account. I am about to publish a *Series of separate Cyclopædias,* with large improvements, and I begin with a 'Cyclopædia of British Geography,' and a 'Cyclopædia of Arts and Industry.' Let me show the exact track which "the lion in my path" drives me to seek; and then some of those legislators who find that a fashionable novel, sold at a guinea and a half, pays about fourpence Paper Duty, and thence conclude that it is the lightest of taxes, and by all means should be preserved—especially as books, as they hold, are not necessaries of life—some of those who

"Hate not learning worse than toad or asp,"

may know what it is to maintain a tax upon knowledge,

struggling to preserve its high rank and its useful extension amidst the widest competition of cheapness.

Upon these four volumes, estimated to contain about 3000 pages, I shall expend 1500*l.* upon new editorial labour. I shall further expend about 1000*l.* upon new plates and maps. The printer's charge for setting up the types will be 800*l.* ; and the cost of stereotyping will be 500*l.* Add for advertising 200*l.* ; and I have thus to expend 4000*l.* as a first outlay, whether I sell 500 copies or 5000. At the present cost of paper, 3000 copies (the least number I could print with advantage) will amount to 1500*l.* ; the Presswork will cost 500*l.* : total 6000*l.* The 3000 copies, produced upon this scale, will exactly cover my outlay, without a shilling profit. But let us see how the account would stand with the price of paper reduced one-third by the abolition of the duty. My course would then be to print 4000 copies, and not stereotype, which process is chiefly employed to save the outlay of capital in taxed paper. The first outlay is therefore 3500*l.* ; the Paper for 4000 Copies, at the lower untaxed price, would cost me 1333*l.* ; the Presswork 600*l.* (reduced per ream on account of the larger number). I produce, therefore, 4000 copies for 5433*l.*, instead of 3000 copies for 6000*l.* I expend less by 567*l.*, and I have 1000 copies left to sell for my profit. I could sell 4000 copies, under these circumstances, more easily than 3000 as I now stand, for I could afford to advertise more freely, and to offer higher inducements to retailers. This is something different from a fourpenny tax upon a fashionable novel.

PASSAGES OF A WORKING LIFE.

The Third Epoch.

CHAPTER XXI.

THE greater portion of my Second Epoch was written at Ventnor, in the Isle of Wight. I had spent the winter there with my family, and quitted it when the spring seemed at once passing into summer, and there was such an outburst of leaf and blossom as I had rarely witnessed in the early days of May. What a region of beauty is the Undercliff in all seasons. Winter rarely touches it with an icy finger. When "yellow leaves, or none, or few" hang upon the boughs that mingle with fallen crags, their bareness is hidden by the glossy ivy. In March it is a land of evergreens; in June a land of "flowers of all hues." It is scarcely a place in which to pass "a working life;" but it is a place in which it is good to look back upon the turmoil of such a life—its vain cares, its disappointed hopes,—and to see what was once deemed the highest good fading into nothingness, and the instant evil melting into a twilight in which good and evil wear the same passionless and almost shapeless features. We unwillingly left the Undercliff, which had long been to me a spot sacred to friendship, when the friend was a perennial source of delight to all who had the happiness to know him. It has become to me even more sacred, now that he lies in the most beautiful of churchyards, that of his long-loved Bonchurch.

We moved for the summer to a very different scene, but one, to my mind, equally attractive. I commence the story of my Third Epoch on the banks of the Thames, above Kingston. We are the tenants of an artist, whose spacious and quaint studio where I write is fitted by its seclusion for calling up the most abstracted memories of the Past. The river flows rapidly beneath my window, under the shadow of lofty elms which have flourished for a century, and by gay villas which proclaim the changes which have marked the era of rapid communication. And yet the Present is constantly in view, in the continuous stream of human life, which appears to move on as if it were always " a sunshine holiday."

There was no lack of abundant materials for the new series, in copyrights in which I had an interest. Some might be reprinted without alteration, others could be adapted by their writers. Lord Brougham's Statesmen of the Time of George the Third; his Dialogues on Instinct, and his edition of Paley's Natural Theology, were of this character. Mr. Lane's Modern Egyptians, and Sir John Davis's Manners and Customs of the Chinese, were in the same way valuable works, expensive in their original form, now brought down to the lowest cost. Mr. Craik, out of the extension of his chapters on Literature in the Pictorial History of England, produced six valuable little volumes, which have since been reprinted, as they well deserve to be, in a more costly shape for the library. One of the most original and important works in this series was the Biographical History of Ancient and Modern Philosophy by Mr. G. H. Lewes. In this series I included several summaries of great writers, such as Spenser and Bacon, by Mr. Craik; Molière and Racine, by

Madame Blaz de Bury; Chaucer, by Mr. John Saunders; Hudibras, by Mr. Ramsay. The small comparative sale of such volumes was to me a tolerably satisfactory proof that abridgments and analyses of standard authors are not likely to be successful. Unless important works are inaccessible from their rarity or their bulk, the greater number of readers—and these perhaps are the more judicious—are ill-content with hashes and essences.

Amongst the original works was one which was an exception to the general character of the books in my series, which for the most part carried the recommendation of popular names as their authors. This was "Memoirs of a Working Man." It was writen by a tailor of the name of Carter. He was the author of one of the little books published by Knight and Co., called the "Guide to Trade," and had been recommended to me in 1840 as a highly deserving man, carrying on a little business for himself, with a dependent family, and struggling with the severest ill health. In the introduction which I wrote to the "Memoirs of a Working Man," I stated that when the author brought to me his manuscript, which he wished to be published by subscription, I carefully read his simple record of an uneventful life, advised him to curtail such particulars as could only be interesting to himself and his family, but on no account to suppress what would be interesting to all—the history of the formation of his habits of thought, and thence of his system of conduct—the development of his intellectual and moral life. In conclusion I said: "Upon receiving the Manuscript thus altered and completed, I proposed to publish it in the Weekly Volume. This is the extent of my editorial duty. I have not added, nor have I altered, a single word. The purity of its style is one of the most remarkable characteristics of this little book."

The series of the Weekly Volume, although it did not involve any considerable loss, was certainly not a commercial success. "Why Mr. Knight did not profit largely by the speculation, is a problem yet to be solved," said the writer of a paper on "Literature for the People." The solution was that the people did not sufficiently buy the series. There were not twenty volumes that reached a sale of ten thousand, and the average sale was scarcely five thousand. Although very generally welcomed by many who were anxious for the enlightenment of the humbler classes, the humbler classes themselves did not find in them the mental aliment for which they hungered. They wanted fiction, and the half dozen historical novelets of the series were not of the exciting kind which in a few years became the staple product of the cheap press. It was perhaps as useless as it was unwise to battle against this growing taste, which was not limited to hard-handed mechanics and their families. In 1854, when I was inclined to think too harshly of the popular appetite for fiction, which was stimulated by the coarsely seasoned food of such publications as the 'London Journal,' Mr. Dickens remonstrated with me in the most earnest and affectionate spirit. I extract from a letter of his, marked by his accustomed good sense, a passage which deserves the serious consideration of those who look too severely upon the exuberance of this species of popular literature. "The English are, so far as I know, the hardest worked people on whom the sun shines. Be content if in their wretched intervals of leisure they read for amusement and do no worse. They are born at the oar, and they live and die at it. Good God, what would we have of them!"

At the time of the issue of the Weekly Volume, the sale of books at railway stations was unknown. Seven years afterwards it had become universal. Then, in the vicinity of great towns where there was a railway station, the shelves of the newspaper vender were filled with shilling volumes known as the 'Parlour Library,' 'The Popular Library,' 'The Railway Library,' 'The Shilling Series.' In their bulk of thin paper and close printing they would appear to be twice as cheap as my volumes, but, except in very rare instances, they had involved no expense of copyright. In a few years, a most remarkable development of cheapness in books, especially in works of fiction, was accomplished without "the great damage of the circulating libraries." Wonderful organizations of the circulating library system presented a far greater encouragement to original authorship than at the period when the few rich purchased books for their sole use. The day of furniture books was almost past. When the circulating libraries had done their work of "the season," then came the cheap reprint. This was the crucial test of an author's popularity. My work as a publisher was finished before these times arrived, which are certainly more favourable for publishing enterprise than those of my own commercial experience.

Somewhat before the commencement of the Weekly Volume, I was engaged for several years in the publication of a series of popular books which had a very large sale, but were little known to the general reading public. They were picture books, especially adapted for sale, in the neighbourhood of the great manufacturing towns and other populous districts, by the class of book-hawkers known as canvassers. There were four books, forming seven volumes in folio, which I included under the generic name of "The New Orbis Pictus," in imitation of that work of Comenius, which, after the lapse of two centuries, still holds its place amongst the educational books of continental Europe. That work, which was once amongst the most popular of books, originally contained several hundred rude wood cuts with appropriate descriptions. My series comprised the following separate books: "Pictorial Museum of Animated Nature:" "Pictorial Sunday-Book:" "Old England:" "Pictorial Gallery of Arts." I told the public that what the Orbis Pictus had imperfectly accomplished was fully carried out in this series, in which was accumulated the largest body of eye-knowledge that had ever been brought together, consisting in the whole of twelve thousand engravings. It is satisfactory to me to think that these books may have presented to some portions of the population—who without the canvasser's importunity would never have expended a monthly shilling upon literature—sources of instruction and amusement as various and extensive as my general title implies—The Pictorial World. Of this series I was necessarily the editor. The descriptions in each book were for the most part confided to persons of literary habits and competent knowledge—these were, Mr. William C. L. Martin for Natural History, Dr. Kitto for Sacred History, Mr. Dodd for the Useful Arts, Mr. Wornum for the Fine Arts, and Mr. John Saunders for our National Antiquities. I must mention, however, that the first Book of "Old England" and part of the second, were written by myself. At the period of its publication there was an awakening feeling for the preservation of our historical monuments. The barbarous neglect which had permitted so many druidical remains, such as Abury, to be in great part destroyed; so many traces of the Roman occupation to be buried; and so many of the noble ecclesiastical edifices of the Norman era to be defaced; this ignorant apathy was rapidly giving place to a just reverence for the past.

CHAPTER XXII.

N 1847 I commenced editing and publishing, in monthly parts, a work which furnished me with a really delightful occupation for fifty-two weeks. "Half-Hours with the Best Authors, Selected and Arranged, with Short Biographical and Critical Notices," has had, and still has, so large a circulation that it is unnecessary for me to describe the character of a book so universally known. The complete work contains specimens of three hundred various writers, of which number about forty were living at the period of its publication. From many of these, his contemporaries, the editor received permission to borrow some connected extracts from their writings which would occupy about half an hour's ordinary reading. Judging from the warm expressions of the greater number of these writers, even the most eminent felt something of satisfaction in being included amongst the standard authors who have built up the greatest literature of the modern world. In a postscript I thus spoke of my "short biographical notices;"—"Their brevity must necessarily render them incomplete and unsatisfactory; but they have not been written without serious thought and an earnest desire to be just. There are many who will differ from the Editor in his estimate of some writers, particularly of the more recent.

Dickens I described as "one who came to fill up the void which Scott had left." Of Tennyson, who at the present day has sent Byron into the shade, I wrote in 1848—"He has not published much, he does not live upon the breath of popular applause, but he has more ardent admirers than any living poet, with the exception of Wordsworth."

As I open the four volumes of Half-Hours and review the short notices of contemporaries, I find amongst them many with whom I have had the transient pleasure of an occasional acquaintance or the happiness of a continued friendly intercourse. Let me mention a few of each class, taking the names, for the most part, in the order in which they present themselves in "Half-Hours."

I have met Walter Savage Landor at the table of a common friend. Although he was then a septuagenarian (I read his Count Julian when I was a boy), he was in the full vigour of his understanding. The variety and richness of his knowledge were as manifest in his real as in his "Imaginary Conversations." He could sustain a literary discussion with wonderful acuteness and felicity of illustration. Sometimes indeed with a leaven of those paradoxical opinions, in which he seemed to delight with a wilfulness of exaggeration. Whilst I write this, his death is recorded at the age of ninety. Dickens has painted him, with scarcely any exaggeration, in his "Boycroft." Leigh Hunt could have known nothing of the early friend of Southey when, in the "Feast of the Poets," he termed him, "one Mr. Landor," and made his name rhyme with "gander."

Samuel Taylor Coleridge, I never saw but once. It was about the time when he first went to dwell with Mr. Gillman at Highgate. To me, then a very young man, the outpourings of his mighty volume of words seemed something more than eloquence; and I went away half crazed by his expositions of the power of the human will in producing such effects upon matter as were once ascribed to magic. We are more familiar in the present day with wonders such as some of those he had seen or heard of in Germany; but his belief that the magnetic needle would follow the finger of a bared hand and arm, did not perhaps demand so great an exercise of faith as the stately walks of dining tables and the nimble dances of arm chairs. The Cagliostros of the human race have ever been a thriving family. Coleridge died in 1834. I went to live at Highgate the year after. During a few years' friendly intercourse with Mr. Gillman and his most amiable and intelligent wife, I was deeply impressed with the ascendancy which a man of the highest genius can obtain over those with whom he is brought into daily contact. Their tastes were in some respects essentially different from his. His irregular habits must often have been exceedingly annoying. But this was a remarkable case of hero-worship, in which the devotion was as enthusiastic as in any instance of the few heroes whom the universal consent of mankind has placed upon the loftiest pedestal. I was always enamoured of Coleridge as a poet, and had become convinced, when I wrote my notice of him in the Half-Hours, that there was "no man of our own times who has incidentally, as well as directly, contributed more to produce that revolution in opinion, which has led us from the hard and barren paths of a miscalled utility, to expatiate in the boundless luxuriance of those regions of thought which belong to the spiritual part of our nature, and have something in them higher than a money value." I often thought of Coleridge as I rambled where he had mused for many a year—the pleasant meadows and green lanes near Caen Wood. I used sometimes to think that if it had been my fortune to have dwelt at Highgate at an earlier period, I might have ventured to accost him as the boy Keats did, to crave the honour of shaking hands (although I could not say "I too am a poet") with one who had so largely filled my mind with images of beauty and lessons of wisdom.

I have incidently mentioned my friend Dr. Arnott in these "Passages." In extracting for the Half-Hours the account of the Barometer from his "Elements of Physics" I said, "When we consider that this excellent book can only be completed at the rare intervals of leisure in a most arduous professional life—that at the moments when the physician is not removing or mitigating the sufferings of individuals, he is labouring for the benefit of all by such noble inventions as the Hydrostatic Bed—we can only hope that the well-earned repose which wise men look to in the evening of their day, will give opportunity for perfecting one of the books best calculated to advance the education of the people that the world has seen." Amidst his engagements as a physician and his devotion to science, Dr. Arnott had still leisure for social enjoyment, as every studious man who does not wish to become an ascetic must seek with moderation. There are many who may remember with the same delight as myself the pleasant Thursday dinners at his house in Bedford Square. Here was no ostentatious display, but the warmest welcome. Here was no oppression of great talkers, but men of very various pursuits and acquirements contributed each in his degree to the amusement of a small listening circle. Of science there was no engrossing parade. Our genial host seemed to say, in the words of Milton to Cyriack Skinner:

> "To day deep thoughts resolve with me to drench
> In mirth that, after, no repenting draws;
> Let Euclid rest, and Archimedes pause."

In the wide range of Dr. Arnott's acquaintance, curiously assorted guests would sometimes be found at his board. Of such was the philosophic Brahmin, Rammohun Roy, who was enabled to reconcile the best principles of his native faith with the religion of Christians, and Robert Owen, who had proclaimed the negation of all religious belief as essential to the establishment of his co-operative system of universal love. There was much in the real benevolence of these two men, so different in education and habits, which drew them together with something like a cordial sympathy. But once, when we were in the drawing-room, a quiet talk between them upon the principle of co-operation suddenly broke out into a loud discussion to which we all listened with surpassing interest. The Rajah held his ground with great ability, and with no common knowledge of political economy, against Owen's doctrine, that in the competitive principle were to be found all the crimes and miseries of society. The persevering logician with his common sense was too strong for the kind hearted visionary. Owen, worn out with objections, at length exclaimed, "*Roger, Roger,* you are not a practical man!" The reproach from such lips, and the peculiar pronunciation of the Hindu title, were too much for the gravity of any of us. Robert Owen was a man too respectable to provoke laughter except on such a rare occasion as this—even from those who would smile at his enthusiasm.

Of Wordsworth in the Half-Hours I thus wrote:—"The greatest name in the literature of our own age is William Wordsworth. He has at last influenced the world more enduringly than any of his contemporaries, although his power has been slowly won." I was diligently reading Wordsworth fifty years ago in spite of the sneers of Jeffrey. I can read him now without feeling, as younger men may feel, that he is tedious. The universality of Wordsworth has sent his poetry into the homes of the poor and lowly, and that vital quality will keep him fresh and green for the few, and possibly for the many, of coming ages. During the long course of years in which Wordsworth was to me as it were a household presence, I never saw him until 1849. I was then visiting Miss Martineau at Ambleside. Early on a bright morning, a tall man, not bowed by age but having the deep furrows of many winters on his massive face, entered the house. I knew at once that it was the great poet, for no ordinary Dalesman with his stout staff and his clouted shoon would present a countenance so remarkable in its majestic simplicity. He was then in his seventy-ninth year. After a pleasant chat with my hostess and myself, he asked me to walk with him to his house at Rydal Mount. As we passed along the road the cottagers and the children saluted him with a familiar and yet respectful greeting. He was their old friend, who had lived amongst them from the beginning of the century; who had interested himself in their feelings and habits; and who, in this constant and affectionate intercourse, was not likely to be moved by the exhortations of an Edinburgh Reviewer. He would not be likely to alter his way of life at the bidding of Mr. Jeffrey, and "condescend to mingle a little more with the people who were to read and judge of his poems, instead of confining himself almost entirely to the society of the Dalesmen, and cottagers, and little children, who formed their subjects." When I spent this pleasant morning with the great Lake poet, he had a little condescended to move out of his seclusion from the gay world to go to court in his capacity of Poet Laureate. He laughed a little at the idea of his state costume, and I really thought that the home-spun suit of Wonderful Robert Walker would have been quite as becoming. Yet Wordsworth was a thorough gentleman. He shewed me his favourite books and the antique heir-looms of his study, with the grace of an unaffected desire to bestow pleasure on a chance visitor; he pointed out the most exquisite points of view from his own garden; he sat with me for half an hour on the somewhat dilapidated seat that overlooks the Lower Fall at Rydal. He talked with a deep tenderness of Hartley Coleridge, the gifted and the unfortunate, who had died in the winter before. I was surprised at the very slight acquaintance with the more eminent writers of the previous ten or twenty years which he manifested. Of the novelists he appeared to know nothing. Of the poets he might be excused for not giving an opinion. He has been reproached with wilfully ignoring the merits of his contemporaries. I doubt whether it might with justice be attributed either to envy or to affectation when he told me that he felt no interest in any modern book except in Mr. Layard's Nineveh, which had then been recently published. I was fortunate in the opportunity of seeing this great man in that mountain home where he was best seen. This was only a year before he was laid in Grasmere churchyard. They say that the lowly mounds beneath which rest with him the remains of his wife and his sister—close by which honoured graves Hartley Coleridge was buried—are trampled down by rude visitors—tourists perhaps, but without the reverence that belongs to those who come to look upon such scenes of beauty, even were there no higher motive for reverence in all the associations of this holy ground.

In 1847 the literary reputation of Macaulay, then famous as an orator, was built upon his "Lays of Ancient Rome," and his "Essays" from the Edinburgh Review. I described these essays as having attained a success far higher than any other contributions to the periodical works of our day. Their success, indeed, gave an impulse to this somewhat novel mode of investing the ephemeral productions of the Reviewer with a separate dignity befitting them for a permanent position in a library. The commercial importance of this system was sufficiently ascertained when Mr. Macaulay inserted in Lord Mahon's Copyright Bill that clause which rendered the consent of the author necessary to the re-publication, in a separate shape, of his contributions to a Review or Magazine. This was a salutary arrangement for Letters and literary men. But Macaulay was to attain a far higher reputation than that of the brilliant essayist. The first and second volumes of his History of England were published in 1849. The third and fourth volumes in 1855. The fifth volume was a posthumous fragment. When the youthful contributor to the Quarterly Magazine of 1824 had taken his position in the political world, our once friendly intercourse was necessarily suspended. He took no part, and probably felt no interest, in the Useful Knowledge Society, although many of his intimate friends were active members. After his return from India, I had often a cordial greeting from him if we accidentally met, but I never had the opportunity of listening, during his maturer years, to that wonderful affluence of conversation for which the Scholar of Trinity was as remarkable as the Cabinet Minister. I saw him laid in his last resting place in Poet's Corner on a raw December day of 1859. He had lived twenty years longer than his youthful friend and colleague, Praed. There was time for Macaulay's fame to culminate, but it must always be a matter of regret that his great historical work has not given to the grand epic of the Revolution a certain completeness, by bringing up the splendid narrative to the accession of the House of Brunswick. We cannot

> "call up him that left half-told
> The story."

No one else is fitted to tell it.

Amongst the "Best Authors" are some of whom the traces of our intimacy are indicated with more or less fullness in my previous volumes. Leigh Hunt, John Wilson, Thomas De Quincey, Thomas Hood, are of this number. I may glean a few sentences from the Half-Hours to mark my opinion of their literary excellence. "Mr. Hunt," I said, "who has borne much adversity with a cheerfulness beyond all praise, writes as freshly and brilliantly as ever." I added "Long may those unfailing spirits which are the delight of his social and family circle, be the sunshine of his old age." These unfailing spirits made the great charm of his conversation. The stream flowed gently on, always clear, often sparkling. His vivacity frequently approached to wit, and if there were the slightest touch of satire in his opinions of books or men, it was so subtle and delicate that it was more like the fencing with foils of Congreve's fine gentlemen, than the sword thrusts of one who in his time was foremost in the lists of bold public writers. John Wilson's prose writings, as collected in "The Recreations of Christopher North," are mentioned by me with a warmth of admiration that to many must appear somewhat extravagant. "It would be difficult to point to three volumes of our own times that have an equal chance of becoming immortal." I might have spoken with more moderation had I anticipated that the political partisanship, so fierce and so unscrupulous, of the "Noctes" would have been reproduced in a permanent form, to make us think less of the wit, the fancy, the genial criticism, and the unaffected pathos of their principal writer. Of De Quincey I expressed a deep regret that the unfortunate habit which forms the subject of his "Confessions" should have prevented him from producing "any great continuous book, worthy of his surpassing powers." But whoever carefully reads the fifteen volumes of his collected works will scarcely join in this regret. In his case, as in that of a few other persons, his death was necessary to place him in the rank of a great classic. Thomas Hood had been dead three years when I published the Half-Hours, and there said of him—"He was brought up an engraver; he became a writer of 'Whims and Oddities,'—and he grew into a poet of great and original power. The slight partition which divides humour and pathos was remarkably exemplified in Hood. Misfortune and feeble health made him doubly sensitive to the ills of his fellow-creatures." On several occasions we had corresponded; I had met him a few times in general society, but I had never the opportunity of cultivating a closer acquaintance. I have heard one who was well fitted by his intimacy to judge of Hood's social qualities, speak of the beauty of his domestic life. We had a mutual admiration of his humour and his pathos, and above all could appreciate that exquisite sensibility which made Hood touch the sore places of the wretched with such a tender and delicate hand. That one was Douglas Jerrold.

Although my close intercourse and unbroken friendship with Jerrold was a source of happiness to me for ten years, it was not until 1845 that I even knew his person. In November of that year I had a special invitation to a great Soirée of the Manchester Athenæum, to be held in the Free Trade Hall. I was the guest of Mr. James Heywood, who subsequently represented North Lancashire. As I was better pleased to stay in the pleasant country house of my host than go much into the smoky metropolis of cotton, I was not thrown into the society of the contributors to "Punch," who were assembled there, and might read their names in enormous placards advertised as the great stars of the coming meeting. "Punch," out of a not very promising commencement in 1841, had in four years risen into an unequalled popularity. Jerrold was, however, one of its earliest contributors, a paper of his appearing in the second number. As the publication went on we may every now and then trace some of those flashes of merriment, that biting satire, and those pleadings for the wretched, which characterized his avowed writings. "The Story of a Feather" which commenced in 1843, and "Mrs. Caudle's Curtain Lectures" with which the volume for 1845 opened, raised the reputation of "Punch" to a height which showed how, in a periodical work, the happy direction and the peculiar genius of one man may carry it far beyond the reach of ordinary competition. I described in "Half Hours" the "Caudle Lectures" as "admirable examples of the skill with which character can be preserved in every possible variety of circumstances." It was almost universally known who was the author of this remarkable series, so that when Douglas Jerrold rose in the Free Trade Hall to address an assembly of three thousand people, the shouts were so continuous that the coolest platform-orator might have lost for a moment his presence of mind. I looked upon a slight figure bending again and again, as each gust of applause seemed to overpower him and make him shrink into himself. Mr. Serjeant Talfourd was in the Chair, and had delivered an eloquent address which the local reporters called "massive," and which by some might have been deemed "heavy." The audience was perhaps somewhat impatient even of the florid language of the author of "Ion," for they wanted to hear the great wit who sat on the edge of the platform, and whose brilliant eye appeared as if endeavouring to penetrate the obscure distance of that vast hall, the extremity of which he might possibly have calculated his somewhat feeble voice would be unable to reach. When the moment had at last arrived in which he was called upon to give utterance to his thoughts, he hesitated, rambled into unconnected sentences, laboured to string together some platitudes about education, and was really disappointing, even to common expectations, until the genius of the man attained the ascendancy. Apostrophising the enemies of education, he exclaimed—"Let them come here and we will serve them as Luther served the Devil—we will throw inkstands at their heads." The effect was marvellous, not only upon his hearers but upon the speaker. He recovered his self-possession and succeeded in making a very tolerable speech. A few nights afterwards, I had to take the Chair at the "City of London Literary and Scientific Institution," in Aldersgate Street, and I said there what I have never ceased to feel. I find it reported that I said, "I had just returned from attending the splendid soirée of the Athenæum at Manchester. I had felt that it was a rare, and perhaps unequalled, spectacle—that of three or four thousand ladies and gentlemen comfortably seated in a vast hall glittering with light, to listen to the addresses of popular writers. But, at the same time, I could not avoid feeling that there was something in this display which would not bear the test of sober examination. I ventured to think that it was a mistake to tempt authors out of their proper sphere to come forward as orators—to ask them to play upon an instrument to which they were unaccustomed—and, of necessity, to feel a proportionate disappointment when some one, who had afforded unmixed delight in his own vocation, was found, as a speaker, not to drop all pearls and rubies from his mouth, like the princess in the fairy tale." If it be replied to this argument that Mr. Dickens is the most effective speaker at a public dinner that was ever listened to with general admiration, I will answer, that at the opening of the Manchester Free Library in 1852, I heard one of the greatest masters of the English language utterly break down in addressing a large audience, and take his seat in hopeless despair of being able to complete the sentence which he had begun. That speaker was the autho of "Vanity Fair."

In the "Half Hours" I have described the first great novel of William Makepeace Thackeray as "a masterly production—the work of an acute observer—sound in principle, manly in its contempt of the miserable conventionalities that make our social life such a cold and barren thing for too many. Never was the absurd desire for display, which is the bane of so much real happiness, better exposed than in the writings of Mr. Thackeray. He is the very antagonism of that heartless pretence to exclusiveness and gentility which acquired for its advocates and expositors the name of 'the silver-fork school.' Such authors as this produce incalculable benefit, and will do much to bring us back to that old English simplicity—the parent of real taste and refinement—which sees nothing truly to be ashamed of but profligacy and meanness." Of the private character and conversation of the author of the series of fictions—which will most probably hold their place till some great revolution of opinion sends a new generation to seek for delight in writers of a different school from this great master—I know too little to speak with any authority. In saying here what I did observe in Thackeray, I hope not to be considered as going out of my way to add my voice to the general accord of panegyric which has naturally followed the sudden deprivation we have recently endured. My conviction was, that beneath an occasional affectation of cynicism, there was a tenderness of heart which he was more eager to repress than to exhibit; that he was no idolater of rank in the sense in which Moore was said dearly to love a lord, but had his best pleasures in the society of those of his own social position—men of letters and artists; and that, however fond of "the full flow of London talk," his own home was the centre of his affections. He was a sensitive man, as I have seen on more than one occasion. One, I cannot forbear mentioning. We were dining at the table of Mr. M. D. Hill, on the 9th of April, 1848, the evening before the expected outbreak of Chartism in London. The cloth had scarcely been removed, when he suddenly started up and said, "Pray excuse me, I must go. I left my children in terror that something dreadful was about to happen. I am unfit for society. Good night."

Of our other great novelist, I wrote in "Half Hours"—"Dickens, as well as every writer of enduring fiction, must be judged by his power of producing a complete work of Art, in which all the parts have a mutual relation. Tested by this severe principle, some of his creations may be held imperfect,—written for periodical issue and not published entire,—hurried occasionally, and wanting in proportion. But from the 'Pickwick' of 1837 to the 'Dombey' of 1848, there has been no failing of interest and effect; his characters are 'familiar in our mouths as household words;' his faults are for the critical eye."

Mr. Forster had in 1840 attained a high reputation as the author of "Statesmen of the Commonwealth." It is scarcely necessary here to point out with what mastery of original materials he has improved these biographies into works of permanent historical value. When I published my "Half Hours," he had just achieved a wide popularity as the author of "Oliver Goldsmith, a Biography." Of this charming book I thus wrote:—"Mr. Forster has lighted up the authentic narrative of a literary life with the brilliant hues of taste and imagination; and, what is a higher thing, he has told the story of the errors, the sorrows, the endurance, and the success, of one of the most delightful of our 'best authors,' with an earnest vindication of simplicity of character, and a deep sympathy with the struggles of talent, which ought to make every reader of this life more just, tolerant, and loving to his fellows." As was the case with Mr. Dickens, Mr. Forster and I became more intimately associated about the middle of the century. In his chambers in Lincoln's Inn he frequently gathered around him a small circle of men of Letters. Those who sat at his hospitable board were seldom too few or too many for general conversation.

There I first met Tennyson, and there Carlyle. Some other hand will perhaps complete my imperfect selection from the Best Authors, by a copious addition of names of recent writers, and by supplementing my biographical notices of those there given. He will have to trace the maturity of Tennyson's powers in "The Princess," in the "In Memoriam," in "Maud," in "The Idylls of the King," and in "Enoch Arden." What an influence the poems of Tennyson have had upon the tastes of the present age can scarcely be appreciated, except by a contrast with the fiery stimulus of the feast which Byron prepared half a century ago. There must be pauses in the excitement of these days—in which "onward," the motto of one of the railway companies, may apply to all the movements of social life—when the most busy and the most pleasure-seeking may relish a poet who, with a perfect mastery of harmonious numbers, fills the mind with tranquil images and natural thoughts, drawn out of his intimate acquaintance with the human heart. In familiar intercourse, such as that of Mr. Forster's table, Mr. Tennyson was cordial and unaffected, exhibiting, as in his writings, the simplicity of a manly character, and feeling perfectly safe from his chief aversion, the "digito monstrari," was quite at his ease. Of Mr. Carlyle's conversation I cannot call up a more accurate idea than by describing his talk as of the same character as his writings. Always forcible, often quaint and peculiar; felicitous in his occasional touches of fancy; not unfrequently sarcastic. When I edited the "Half Hours," his "French Revolution" was his chief work, and I could justly say of that book, as I might say of his "Cromwell" and his "Frederick the Great"—"In graphic power of description, whether of scenes or of characters, he has not a living equal."

CHAPTER XXIII.

THE LAND WE LIVE IN, a monthly illustrated publication, was commenced by me in 1847. It had, to a certain extent, the same object as "Old England," of describing monuments of the past, but those notices were always in connection with the aspects of our latest civilization.

Previous to the commencement of the publication of "The Land we Live in," I had availed myself of every opportunity to visit our great seats of industry, chiefly with a view to observe the progress of Education and to inquire into the general condition of the people. For several years I had contemplated a literary undertaking, the materials for which could not be wholly obtained from books. I aspired to write "The History of England during the Thirty Years' Peace, 1815—1845." The publication of this work was commenced in 1846, and a portion of it, embracing the annals of 1816-17, was written by me. The illness of my partner, and his consequent withdrawal from our business, in which he attended to the financial part, rendered it necessary for me to devote myself almost entirely to my commercial responsibilities. The "History of the Peace" was suspended for some months; and I then was fortunate in finding one of the few persons adequately qualified, not only by the power of writing agreeably, but by unwearied industry and a long course of observation upon the social affairs of the country, to produce a book of permanent value. The composition of this History of Thirty Years was resumed by Miss Martineau, and was completed by her with a success that I might have been unable to attain.

In the Session of 1854, a Committee of the House of Commons was sitting to examine witnesses upon that question of the abolition of the Newspaper Stamp, which had occupied the attention of the Legislature twenty years before. After the Meeting of Parliament in 1855, a very general opinion prevailed that the then Penny-stamp would be entirely abolished, except for the purpose of transmitting a newspaper by post. The Chancellor of the Exchequer, Sir George Cornewall Lewis, through his private Secretary, Sir Alexander Duff Gordon, requested me to inform him what was the greatest circulation of each number of the Penny Magazine at any time. In giving this information I referred him to a little book which Mr. Murray had just published for me—"The Old Printer and the Modern Press,"—in which I had taken a rapid view of the circulation and character of penny periodicals at the beginning of 1854. I had stated that of four of these a million sheets were then sold weekly. In my letter, I thought it right to convey fully my opinion upon the question of the abolition of the Stamp, and in support of that opinion I mentioned that Dr. Arnold was strongly impressed with the notion that a Newspaper was the best vehicle for communicating knowledge to the people; the events of the day, he maintained, were a definite subject to which instruction could be attached in the best possible manner. An extract from the letter thus written by me may fitly introduce the general subject of the extension of the Newspaper Press during the last eight or nine years, upon which I propose to treat in this chapter. "The change in the character of the Penny Periodicals during the last five or six years, from the lowest ribaldry and positive indecency to a certain propriety—and of which frivolity is the chief blemish—is an assurance to me that the cheapening of Newspapers by the removal of the Stamp will not let in that flood of sedition and blasphemy which some appear to dread. The character of the mass of readers is improved. In my little book I have opposed the removal of the Stamp, chiefly on the ground that a quantity of local papers would start up, that would be devoted to mere parish politics, and sectarian squabbles, instead of being national in their objects; and that would huddle together the worst of criminal trials and police cases, without attempting to suggest any sound principles of politics, or furnish any useful information. To provide a corrective to this, I have devised the plan detailed in the circular, which I left with you. I sent out an intelligent traveller into the Midland districts last week, confidentially to explain this plan to active printers in towns that had no local paper; and his report shows that the principle will be eagerly adopted."

The plan which I had devised was founded upon my old newspaper experience, during which, for several years, three-fourths of the local Paper of Berkshire and Buckinghamshire were printed at the

"Express" Office at Windsor, and one-fourth at a branch office at Aylesbury. In connection with a highly respectable printing firm, I commenced the publication of the "Town and Country Newspaper" immediately upon the repeal of the Stamp-duty in 1855. There were many elements of success in this plan, but it was defeated by the complex and expensive organization necessary to supply small adventurers into the new world of journalism with the very few impressions each required at first to meet his local demand. Nor was my belief that this sort of publication might be made the vehicle for combining, not only a well digested body of news, but sound practical information upon many subjects of public interest, destined to be realized. The readers in very small towns, in which the one printer was generally the first to make the experiment which I proposed, did not very anxiously desire to see the newspaper made an instrument of education, or for the advancement of objects of public improvement. The undertaking was not remunerative, and I had no desire to press upon my partners the continuance of a scheme that did not pay as quickly as was expected. The plan became very extensively adopted after the establishment of penny local Journals had created a demand, and they were found to supply a public want. Four hundred such provincial Papers are said to be now partly printed in London; but I am informed by a friend, who is perfectly well-acquainted with the curious facts connected with the present state of local and other Newspapers, that the plan of printing one side of a weekly sheet in London is now going out of use. There is another mode adopted, of making the same information, and the same labour of setting up the types, available for many papers, which is a striking example of the effect of new combinations of industrial art and science, for the diminution of expense of production. There is an enterprising proprietor of a local newspaper in one of our large manufacturing towns, who has a stereotyping office in London, and supplies small journals throughout the country with stereotyped matter at a low rate per column, of which he will send any number of columns up to twenty-four. The plan is so simple and so convenient that his customers are very numerous, and he is considered to be making a much better profit out of his stereotype plates, than by his well-circulated Journal. This system is one of the many instances, with which we are becoming more and more familiar, of co-operation for Production. Perhaps a more striking example is furnished in the economical management of some *daily* papers in England and Scotland, published out of London, of which number there are now nearly forty. Several of the proprietors of these large local journals have associated for the establishment of an office in London, with a literary staff, compositors, and stereotype-founders. There are five or more papers which participate in this arrangement. Each paper belonging to this league uses the stereotypes according to its especial wants and convenience, sometimes all that is dispatched; more frequently a selection is made. I have before me a Provincial Daily Paper, of October 20th, 1864,—a large well printed sheet, price 1*d.* My friend has marked for my information the matter which has been thus transmitted to this journal, as to others, by express trains, generally leaving London at 5 p.m., and reaching places two hundred miles distant by 11 p.m. The matter which I thus find in this paper comprises eight folio columns, and necessarily contains the very latest news and comment. What a power do the Managers of this journalistic Confederacy possess for the direction of public opinion, and how real a matter of congratulation it is that the time is past when the influence of the Newspaper Press was too frequently inimical to quiet and good government! Dr. Arnold wrote to the Archbishop of Dublin in 1833, "I think that a newspaper alone can help to cure the evil which newspapers have done and are doing."

In considering the feasibility of carrying forward upon a large scale, the plan of printing the general portion of a newspaper in London, to be completed by the publisher in a country town, I was careful to inform myself of the exact number of Local Journals in every county. The materials were to be collected from a very useful publication, "The Newspaper Press Directory," by C. Mitchell, which had then been established nine or ten years. It is continued annually at the present time; and a comparison merely of the quantity of printed matter in the volume for 1855, and that for 1864, will at once point to the vast increase in Journalism. I find amongst my papers a voluminous abstract of the state of the Local Newspaper Press, which I drew out six months before the abolition of the Stamp. In the forty English counties there were 120 cities and towns, omitting London, in which Newspapers were then published. But in these there were 261 papers, the more important places having, in many instances, more than one such organ of intelligence. To my abstract I appended the number of inhabitants of each town. The result of my examination was, that there were 350 populous towns *without any Local Paper*, viz.—

99	Towns with population above	2000—	under	3000.
106	,, ,, ,,	3000—	,,	5000.
63	,, ,, ,,	5000—	,,	7000.
82	,, ,, ,,	7000 and upwards.		

These were statistical facts of deep significance.

The amount of the change which has been produced in eight years by the abolition of the Newspaper Stamp and the Advertisement Duty—in some degree also by the repeal of the tax upon paper—is sufficiently indicated by the following figures:—There were published in England, at the commencement of the present year, 919 journals. Of these 240 belonged to London; and these included 13 daily morning papers, 7 evening, and 220 published during the week and at intervals. But these London Journals, not daily, comprise the purely literary and scientific papers—the legal and medical, and more numerous than all, the religious journals. Further, since I made my abstract of Local Papers, there have started into flourishing existence no less than 32 *district* journals of the Metropolis and its suburbs. Taking these 240 metropolitan and suburban papers from the total 919 published in England, I find that there are now 679 *Country* Newspapers, instead of the 261 which I found existing in 1855. I may infer, therefore, without going into a minute examination of the matter, that the 350 populous places which, at that time, had no newspaper of their own, are now not left without a vehicle for the publication of their local affairs, whether important or frivolous, whether affecting a nation or a parish. To finish this summary, I may add that Wales has 37 journals; Scotland 140; Ireland 140; the British Isles 14; making up for the United Kingdom a total of 1250. Of the aggregate circulation of these Journals, it is impossible to arrive at any accurate estimate. At the beginning of the century, the annual circulation of newspapers in England and Wales was 15 millions. In 1853, as was shown by the Stamp-Office returns, the annual circulation of England and Wales was 72 millions, and of Scotland and Ireland, each 8 millions. Even the circulation in 1853 was an astounding fact, and I then wrote, "Visit, if you can, the interior of that marvellous human machine the General Post Office, on a Friday evening from half-past five to six o'clock. Look with awe upon the tons of newspapers that are crowding in to be distributed through the habitable globe. Think silently how potent a power is this for good or for evil. You turn to one of the boxes of the letter-sorters, and your guide will tell you, 'this work occupies not half the time it formerly did, for everybody writes better.'" Some of the elder country newspapers and some that have started into life since the repeal of the Stamp, have a circulation that is to be numbered by thousands. But if we only assign a sale of 1000 each to the 679 country papers in England, we have a total annual circulation of 235 millions. The Scotch and Irish Journals will probably swell the aggregate annual circulation of the United Kingdom to 250 millions. Taking the entire population at 30 millions, this estimate would give eight newspapers in the course of the year to every person: and assuming that every newspaper has six readers, there is no present want in these Kingdoms of the literary means of keeping the entire mass of the people informed upon every current event and topic. But there may be other wants to be met besides those which are supplied by the vast increase of journalism before the newspaper can be within the reach of the whole of the adult population. There are thousands growing into men and women who, during the last decade, when newspapers have been rising up for an almost universal use, have acquired the ability to read. The numbers of those wholly uninstructed must be very few in populous districts compared with the days when the newspaper was the most highly taxed article of necessity or luxury. Now that it has become one of the cheapest of inventions for the supply of a general want, it may be well to inquire into the causes which interfere with an universal supply.

An ingenious and instructive "Newspaper Map of the United Kingdom," accompanies Mitchell's Newspaper Press Directory. It is suggestive of several important facts in our social condition, which we are apt to pass over in looking at its multifarious details. The several districts of the kingdom are indicated by different colours, not only as manufacturing, mining, and agricultural, but by other colours, where two or more of these large classes of occupation are combined. When we glance at the Agricultural Counties, twenty-three in number, extending from Somersetshire to Lincolnshire, and bounded by the inland Manufacturing and Agricultural Counties, five in number, we feel something like wonder that amongst these agricultural communities there should appear so great a number of towns having one or more newspapers. It is no matter of surprise that the Manufacturing and Mining Counties, with their enormous populations, should be dotted with a circular mark, indicating the publication of one paper, or with a square mark, indicating more than one. Nor are we surprised that where there is a mixed population, in which farms, and factories, and underground operations, supply the funds for the maintenance of labour, the newspapers should be as numerous as in the seats of the Woollen and Cotton Manufacture, and in the great ports associated with them. A minuter investigation into this map will show how the purely Agricultural Districts so abound with Local Newspapers. The places in which they are published are, with scarcely an exception, situated on the lines of railway. The Railway and the Local Newspaper seem to have sprung up together into an extension which, even ten years ago, it would have required some effort of the imagination to consider possible. How is it, then, that the agricultural labouring population must be held as very imperfectly supplied with the same means of information as the residents in towns? Look at this Newspaper Map, and observe what large blank spaces lie between every thread of the great network of railways. In the North Riding of Yorkshire, which is almost purely agricultural, these blanks are as remarkable as those of Wales when we get away from the Mining Districts, or Scotland, when we have passed from the seats of manufactures and commerce into the mountainous districts. In the blank spaces thus indicated, where dwell the great food-producing population, in small villages and hamlets, the newspaper never comes except by the post. The extension, of late years, of the operations of the Post-office, has rendered the number of those partially excluded from communication with the outer world, much less than it was long after the introduction of Penny Postage. But, with the extension of the Post, the delivery of newspapers by special messengers from the towns has almost ceased. Bearing in mind the cost of communication, whether by direct delivery or by a postage stamp, we need not be surprised that the newspaper, London or provincial, is not often to be found in the labourer's cottage.

CHAPTER XXIV.

THE narrative of my publishing enterprises was, in Chapter XXIII., brought up to 1855; with the exception of the two most important works of my later years, the "English Cyclopædia" and the "Popular History of England." In these undertakings I had a proprietary interest, although, as I stated in the Preface to the present book, "I had to become more a writer and an editor than a publisher." I have reserved a brief account of these works until I should arrive, in the natural sequence of these 'Passages,' at the periods of their completion. The eight years that were occupied by the superintendence of the Cyclopædia — during seven of which I was also occupied in writing the History— bring me to the termination of the Half Century of my Working Life.

One of the most interesting novels of Sir Edward Bulwer Lytton is entitled "What will he do with it?" When, in 1848, after the completion of the "Penny Cyclopædia," I had parted with the stock and stereotype plates, the copyright remained in my hands. It had cost a large sum of money; of its literary value no one doubted; but its commercial value remained to be tested. "What will he do with it?" said the Trade. I turned it to account in an abridgment entitled the "National Cyclopædia." In this the original work was melted down to one-fourth of its dimensions. It was a useful book, but it was far from satisfying the requirements of those who sought in a Cyclopædia to supply the place of a small library. From this "National Cyclopædia" of too scanty dimensions, I turned my attention towards producing one of larger proportions even than the original work. The "Imperial Cyclopædia," of which a Prospectus was largely circulated, was proposed to be divided into eight or ten great compartments, each of which was to be prefaced by a treatise by some eminent writer. It would have been a large undertaking, but I had assurances of support from persons of influence, encouraging enough, but not sufficiently numerous to lead me onward to a great risk. Some of the letters of these supporters are before me. One of them is so characteristic of a nobleman who had an hereditary love of science, and a natural devotion to literature, that I may be pardoned the egotism of its insertion. Lord Ellesmere writes to me on the 19th of June, 1850:—"I shall direct my bookseller to furnish the volumes as they come out, as I look upon your professional labours as among the best exertions of the day for fighting the devil and all his works." Lord Ellesmere's cordial letter to me was his answer to my proposal to publish by subscription. This plan, by which authors and publishers took hostages against evil fortune, was in general use during the first half of the eighteenth century. Like most other human things it was subject to abuse; but it was founded upon a true estimate of the peculiar risks of publishing. It is manifest that, if a certain number of persons unite in agreement to purchase a book which is about to be printed, the author may be at ease with regard to the issue of the enterprise; and the subscribers ought to receive what they want, at a lower cost than when risk enters into price. For more than half a century nearly all the great books were published by subscription; and the highest in literature felt no degradation in themselves canvassing with their subscription receipts. The plan which, upon the face of it, was a just one for all parties—a fair exchange between seller and buyer—came in process of time to be regarded with suspicion. The practice of soliciting subscriptions which, in Pope, and Steele, and Johnson, and fifty other eminent authors, was legitimate and honourable, was in the next century either treated with cold neglect, or regarded with the same suspicion as the devices of the begging-letter writer. I quickly found out my mistake, and united myself with a publishing house who had the means of largely circulating a serial work throughout the kingdom.

I have already devoted two Chapters to the history of the "Penny Cyclopædia." I have there described the labours of the various Contributors, and have recorded some characteristic traits of the eminent persons who were associated in this work. It was completed in 1844. In the nine years that elapsed between that period and the commencement of the "English Cyclopædia," knowledge of all kinds had been accumulating at a rate of marvellous rapidity.

The geographical descriptions, for example, of the "Penny Cyclopædia," had stopped short of the wonderful development of the Australian colonies. The new Cyclopædia was arranged in four divisions,

Geography, Natural History, Biography, Arts and Sciences. The two first of these Divisions were proceeding at the same time, and were each completed in two years and a half. What a store of new materials had been gathering together, for the use of the Geographer and the Naturalist, that required to be set forth in the remodelled Cyclopædia! These two Divisions were succeeded by that of Biography. If no other additions had been required than the introduction of names of living persons, the new literary labour would have been of no small amount—sufficient indeed to form a separate book, not so large but essentially as complete as the 'Biographie des Contemporains.' This Biographical Division, in six volumes, was completed in 1858. The Division of Arts and Sciences included a great amount of miscellaneous subjects, not capable of being introduced into the more precise arrangement of the three previous departments. It was completed in eight volumes in 1861. In my Introduction to the eighth volume, I said—"it has been produced the last in the series, that nothing of new invention and discovery in Science—nothing of progressive improvement in the Arts—might be omitted."

In the conduct of this work I adopted two principles; first that not an article, not a page, not a line, should be reprinted without revision; secondly, that every new Contributor should be so reliable in his talents and his acquirements, that his articles might be safely adopted without undergoing that superintendence which the Useful Knowledge Society professed to undertake for the "Penny Cyclopædia," and which was often very judiciously exerted. Noticing the Contributors to the earlier work, when I was writing these "Passages" in 1863, I was looking back twenty years. There was a sort of historical interest attached to many of these names, and I could speak of them unreservedly and without any invidious distinction. It is not so with the Contributors to a work which was only completed three years before the time when I am now writing. My own duties in the conduct of the work involved little more than a general superintendence. In the Preface to the Natural History Division I acknowledged my obligations to Dr. Edwin Lankester, who had brought the original articles into a more systematic shape; who had removed much that was obsolete; and who, having access to the opinions, and securing the assistance, of the best living authorities, had neglected no new materials that were at that time available. I had further, at the close of the work, to thank my fellow-labourers during many years—Mr. A. Ramsay and Mr. J. Thorne—for the active and intelligent share they had taken in its management, by which the regularity of publication, and the correctness of the text, had been mainly secured.

I might probably have been induced to say more of the plan and conduct of this book—which, without arrogance, I may call a great book,—had I not been able to refer for further details to one of the most learned and interesting articles that ever appeared in a critical work—"The History of Cyclopædias," in the "Quarterly Review" for April, 1863. Of the commendation of this writer I have just cause to be proud, for it is founded upon an acquaintance, little less than extraordinary, with the Cyclopædias of all countries and languages, of far-removed or of recent times. I am satisfied that he speaks from an honest conviction alone, when he says—"the 'English Cyclopædia' is a work that as a whole has no superior and very few equals of its kind; that, taken by itself, supplies the place of a small library; and, used in a large library, is found to present many points of information that are sought in vain in any other cyclopædia in the English language." The "Quarterly Review" is chiefly addressed to those who have leisure and abundant means; but there is another class to whom the "English Cyclopædia" is strongly recommended as a book for those who labour with their hands, and have little time for systematic study. In the "Working Men's College Magazine" for November, 1861, there is an article signed V. Lushington, for which I have abstained from offering my thanks, for I feel that to express personal gratitude to a critic is to imply that other considerations than those of truth and justice may have suggested his praise. I cannot probably, however, better conclude my notice of a work which has brought me abundant honour, than by giving an eloquent passage from this notice. It will be seen that Mr. Lushington is not one of those who think it necessary to write down to the comprehension of working men:—

"Perhaps the first sensation of the reader on opening these massive volumes will be one of bewilderment, and unwillingness to traverse any such mountain of knowledge. But on better consideration he will feel two things; first, that kind of reverence which the spectacle of any great human labour cannot but call forth; and secondly, that this (or indeed any) Cyclopædia is a witness to the inexhaustible interest of reality and simple truth. He will see that it is in fact a record of a thousand thousand conquests over thick night, won in many generations by far-reaching industry, and patient intelligence, in many cases even—say the discovery of America—by downright unmistakeable valour: and so gazing on these columns, there may come flashing through his mind something of the exultation with which a people greets a victorious army returning homeward. At least he cannot but observe how the age in which we live is assiduously minding and doing her business; everywhere extending and consolidating positive knowledge; with honest sober eyes scrutinising the past of human history, studying the starry heavens, the solid earth, and all living things, tracking everywhere the dominion of stedfast laws, then recording what is found, for ourselves and for those who come after. A Cyclopædia witnesses that all these things are being done."

In 1854 I was instigated by an article in "The Times" seriously to contemplate the task of writing a general history of England. Lord John Russell had delivered an address at Bristol on the study of history, and the leading journal took up the subject of the noble speaker's complaint "that we have no other history of England than Hume's"—that "when a young man of eighteen asks for a history of England, there is no resource but to give him Hume." I had published "The Pictorial History of England" some years before—in many respects a valuable history, but one whose limits had gone far beyond what, as its projector, I had originally contemplated. I altogether rejected the idea of making an abridgment of that history. Many materials for a *History of the People* had been collected by me without any immediate object of publication. The remarks of "The Times" led me to depart from my original design of writing a Domestic History of England apart from its Public History. Upon a more extended plan, I would endeavour to trace through our long continued annals the essential connection between our political history and our social. To accomplish this, I would not keep the People in the background, as in many histories, and I would call my work "The Popular History of England."

For more than a year I was gradually preparing for my task, and was ready to begin the printing at the end of 1855. It was to be published in monthly parts. My publishers desiring that the first part should contain an introduction, setting forth the objects of a new history of England, I was induced to explain my motives for undertaking it, with a sincerity which perhaps may be deemed imprudent. It may be as imprudent for the historian as for the statesman to make any general profession of principles at the onset of his career. The succession of events in either case might modify his past convictions. But I have no reason to depart in letter or spirit from what I wrote: "The People, if I understand the term rightly, means the Commons of these realms, and not any distinct class or section of the population. Ninety years ago, Goldsmith called the 'middle order of mankind' the 'People,' and those below them the 'Rabble.' We have outlived all this. A century of thought and action has widened and deepened the foundations of the State. This People, then, want to find, in the history of their country, something more than a series of annals, either of policy or war. In connection with a faithful narrative of public affairs, they want to learn their own history—how they have grown out of slavery, out of feudal wrong, out of regal despotism,—into constitutional liberty, and the position of the greatest estate of the realm."

In the summer of 1858 I had completed four volumes of my history, reaching the period of the Revolution of 1688. In the postscript to the fourth volume I endeavoured to illustrate the principle, so well defined by my friend Mr. Samuel Lucas in a Lecture on Social Progress, that the history of every nation "has been in the main sequential"—that each of its phases has been "the consequence of some prior phase, and the natural prelude of that which succeeded it." I pointed out that the early history of the Anglican Church was to be traced in all the subsequent elements of our ecclesiastical condition; that upon the Roman and Saxon civilization were founded many of the principles of government which still preserved their vitality; that the Norman despotism was absorbed by the Anglo-Saxon freedom; and that the recognition of the equal rights of all men before the Law was the only mode by which feudality could maintain itself. "From the deposition of Richard the Second to the abdication of James the Second, every act of national resistance was accomplished by the union of classes, and was founded upon some principle of legal right for which there was legal precedent. Out of the traditional and almost instinctive assertion of the popular privileges, have come new developments of particular reforms, each adapted to its own age, but all springing out of that historical experience which we recognise as Constitutional."

In November, 1862, I completed the book upon which I had been employed unremittingly for a seventh part of my working life. I then stated in a postscript that, with the exception of three chapters on the Fine Arts, "The Popular History" had been wholly written by myself. Being the production of one mind, I trusted that the due proportions of the narrative, from the first chapter to the last, had been maintained. I again set forth the principles which had enabled me to carry it through with a consistent purpose. "Feeling my responsibilities to be increased by the fact that my duty was to impart knowledge and not to battle for opinions, my desire has been to cherish that love of liberty which is best founded upon a sufficient acquaintance with its gradual development and final establishment amongst us; to look with a tolerant judgment even upon those who have sought to govern securely by governing absolutely; to trace with calmness the efforts of those who have imperilled our national independence by foreign assault or domestic treason, but never to forget that a just love of country is consistent with historical truth; to carry forward, as far as within the power of one who has watched joyfully and hopefully the great changes of a generation, that spirit of improvement, which has been more extensively and permanently called forth in the times of which this concluding volume treats than in the whole previous period from the Revolution of 1688."

"The Popular History of England" to the period of the Revolution embraced a class of subjects that was once considered extraneous to history—the progress of manufactures and commerce—the developments of literature and the arts—the aspects of manners and of common life. The same principle was constantly kept in view in the succeeding four volumes, which brought up the history to 1849—an epoch marked by the final extinction of the Corn Laws. This large class of subjects, so essentially connected with our civil, military, and religious annals, was treated by me, "not in set dissertations under distinct heads, separated from the course of events by long intervals, but in frequent notices, either in special chapters at periods marked by characteristics of progress, or occurring as incidental illustrations of the political narrative." The experience of the present generation may be sufficient to trace the connection between the progress of good government, following the gradual discomfiture of corrupt or ignorant government, and the progress of industry, art, and letters, maintaining and carrying forward the power and influence of political improvement.

The proportions of those chapters of my Popular History of England which have reference to the national Industry and the progress of the Arts, as compared with the chapters on our Civil, Military, and Religious History, scarcely warrant me in accepting the title which has been conferred upon me,—that of "The Boswell of Birmingham." It is a very pretty piece of alliteration, and has the true ring of that small wit which goes a good way towards the making of a periodical critic of the insolent order. In the four first volumes, which bring the history down to the Revolution, one-tenth only of the whole matter is occupied with the subjects of Commerce and Manufactures, of Science and Art, of Literature, of the Condition of the People. In the second half of the work about one-fifth of the whole text is devoted to these subjects. Of the eight volumes, comprising four thousand pages, an amount equal to one volume is devoted to these various manifestations of the progress of a people. Such details were once considered extraneous to history proper; and even now, some who think, or affect to think, that history should confine itself to the concerns of Courts and Cabinets, regard them as vulgar. Such, especially, is their opinion about Commerce and Manufactures. Modern statesmanship has a different creed. It has been compelled to guide its course of political action by a broad view of the social condition of the entire population, rather than by the interests or prejudices of a party or a class. Never in our own country, and to a certain extent in other countries, had the claims of industry—not upon patronage, not upon protection, not upon bounties, but simply to be left free to work out its own good—been more regarded in the highest places, as the one great foundation of national prosperity. The slightest glance at the early history of England will show that with the prosperity of industry, and that security of property, which was necessary for its more general distribution, gradually came internal tranquillity, in spite of disputed successions and constant attempts to put the neck of one class under the heel of another. The "hostile armies" were, in every succeeding generation, becoming reduced in numbers, and more and more open to the reconciliation of their conflicting pretensions. As the mediæval castles gradually became mansions; as the privileges of a caste were put away, like "unscoured armour hung by the wall;" as there grew, out of feudal exclusiveness, an aristocracy not alien to the commonalty; the yeoman, the merchant, the artisan, and last of all the peasant, came to be regarded as integral portions of the state. Then, and not till then, was society secure in the established reign of law and order. Then, and not till then, could those who did not labour with their hands sit secure in their homes, even should an occasional demagogue attempt to re-kindle the lights and fires of the fourteenth century to the tune of—

> "When Adam delved and Eve span,
> Who was then the gentleman?"

I might run over every era of our modern history to show how, with the development of Industry and the accumulation of Wealth, those who have been seeking "to diminish or destroy oppressive and tyrannous privileges and customs" have been constrained to employ other weapons than physical force. There was a time when "resistance was an ordinary remedy for political distempers—a remedy which was always at hand, and which, though doubtless sharp at the moment, produced no deep or lasting ill effects." The historian marks the difference of our own times; when "resistance must be regarded as a cure more desperate than almost any malady that can afflict the state." But there is something better than the sword, if occasion should arise for uttering again the ancient demand for "redress of grievances;" and Macaulay shows us the alternative: "As we cannot, without the risk of evils from which the imagination recoils, employ physical force as a check on misgovernment, it is evidently our wisdom to keep all the constitutional checks on misgovernment in the highest state of efficiency; to watch with jealousy the first beginnings of encroachment, and never to suffer irregularities, even when harmless in themselves, to pass unchallenged."* The old army of resistance has become a Constabulary Force, equipped only with the staff that is the symbol of Law and Order.

Here, strictly speaking, terminates the narrative of my labour and my observation during half a century. This Chapter records the principal employment of my time, to the end of 1862. I regard the chief part of that occupation, during seven years, as having been to me a source of happiness. Removed, in a great degree, from commercial labours and anxieties, that continuous direction of my mind to a subject so interesting and engrossing as a General History of England, had a tranquillizing influence; and prepared me to look back upon my past career with something like a philosophical estimate of its good and evil fortune.

Until the Septuagenarian shall hear "kind Nature's signal to retreat," Rest and Retrospection properly succeed the excitements of "a Working Life." The task of writing these "Passages" has been at once Rest and Retrospection. It has involved no laborious research; it has compelled no violent suppression of natural egotism to forbear speaking of personal matters that could have no interest for others; it has demanded little more than an accurate memory of former events, and a candid and charitable estimate of my contemporaries. Taken altogether, this also has been a pleasurable task;

* Macaulay, "History of England," 1st. ed., Vol. I., p. 36.

and, to compare small things with great, the "sober melancholy" which Gibbon felt when he wrote "the last lines of the last page" of his immortal History, comes over me, as I contemplate taking a final leave "of an old and agreeable companion."

The fiftieth anniversary of my marriage has just passed. Half a century of congenial wedlock is a blessing accorded to few. It brought with it the further blessing of a family united in love; of a home where cheerful faces ever welcomed me. During forty years I had known no great sorrow. I had not been bereft of any one of those who were the joy of my manhood, and the comfort of my age. A dark cloud has cast its solemn shadow over my Golden Bridal; but I feel that our griefs, and the consolations which should come with them, are for ourselves, and not for the outer world. Taken as a whole, my life has been a happy one.

During the progress of these "Passages," I have, as far as I could, steadily resisted the temptation of entering upon any details of my private circumstances or domestic relations. If, in closing this narrative, I have stepped for an instant across the boundary line which I prescribed to myself, and if I look not beyond my own home for one to whom I can offer a concluding tribute of affection, I must be forgiven, in the consideration that "out of the abundance of the heart the mouth speaketh:"

TO MY WIFE;

TO HER WHO HAS BEEN THE BEST FRIEND,

THE ADVISER, THE SYMPATHIZER, THE CONSOLER,

DURING HALF A CENTURY OF MY WORKING LIFE,

I INSCRIBE THIS RECORD,

WITH A GRATEFUL HEART TO THE GIVER OF ALL GOOD.

January 16, 1865.

"AND HERE WILL I MAKE AN END. AND IF I HAVE DONE WELL, AND AS IS FITTING THE STORY, IT IS THAT WHICH I DESIRED; BUT IF SLENDERLY AND MEANLY, IT IS THAT WHICH I COULD ATTAIN UNTO."—*II. Maccabees*, XV., 37, 38.

INDEX OF PERSONS

MENTIONED AS CONTEMPORARIES OF THE AUTHOR.

NEW PUBLICATIONS

OF

G. P. PUTNAM'S SONS.

I.

ENGLAND: POLITICAL AND SOCIAL.

By AUGUSTE LAUGEL, author of "Studies in Science," "The United States during the War of 1861–65," &c., &c. Translated by Prof. J. M. HART.

CONTENTS:

I. The Characteristics of the English Race. II. Characteristics of Protestantism. III. English Nobility. IV. The Chamber of Commons. V. The Formation of Political Habits. VI. The People and Social Questions. VII. Colonial Policy.

12mo, cloth.

II.

THE PHILOSOPHY OF ENGLISH LITERATURE.

Lectures delivered before the Lowell Institute, Boston. By Professor JOHN BASCOM, of Williams College. 12mo, cloth, $1.75.

III.

THE EDUCATION OF AMERICAN GIRLS.

Edited by ANNA C. BRACKETT, formerly Principal of the Normal School of St. Louis.

CONTENTS:

1. Introduction, Anna C. Brackett. 2. A Fair Chance, L. H. Stone. 3. The Other Side, Caroline H. Dall. 4. A Mother's Thought, Edna D. Cheney. 5. English and American Girls, Mary E. Beedy. 6. Mental Action and Physical Strength, Dr. Mary Putnam Jacobi. 7. Michigan University, Sarah Dix Hamlin. 8. Mt. Holyoke Seminary, Mary O. Nutting 9. Oberlin College, A. A. F. Johnston. 10. Vassar College, Dr. Alida C. Avery. 11. Antioch College. 12. Review of "Sex in Education."

12mo., cloth, $1.75.

IV.

THE LIFE OF GEORGE DASHIELL BAYARD.

Late Captain U. S. A. and Brigadier-General of Volunteers, Killed in the Battle of Fredericksburg, December, 1862.

By SAMUEL J. BAYARD.

This Biography of one of the most heroic and daring generals of the war, comprises descriptions of West Point life, experiences on the frontier, and a narrative of his brief but brilliant career in the campaigns in Virginia during 1861–62: also a genealogical history of the Bayard family in America. The volume is illustrated with a portrait, engraved on steel by Hall, an etching of the monument at Princeton, and a map 12mo, cloth extra, $1.75. Half calf, $3.75.

V.

HAMPTON AND ITS STUDENTS. By Two of its Teachers: Mrs. M. F. ARMSTRONG and HELEN W. LUDLOW.

Containing a sketch of the history of the settlement of Hampton; a full record of the founding and development of the Normal College there, biographical sketches of the most interesting of the students, and pictures of life among the slaves and freedmen. It also includes some eighty pages of original Negro Songs, with the words in dialect and the music.

8vo, cloth, with sixteen illustrations, drawn on wood, $1,50.

VI.

SKETCHES OF ILLUSTRIOUS SOLDIERS. By JAMES GRANT WILSON.

CONTENTS:

Gonsalvo of Cordova, Chevalier Bayard, Constable Bourbon, William the Silent, Duke of Parma, Prince Wallenstein, Gustavus Adolphus, Oliver Cromwell, Marshal Turenne, The Great Condé, Prince Eugene, Charles XII, of Sweden, Marshal Saxe, Frederick the Great, Marshal Suwarrow, General Washington, Napoleon Bonaparte, Duke of Wellington, General Scott, Lord Clyde, Marshal von Moltke, Duke of Marlborough, General Lee, General Sherman, General Grant.

Illustrated with Four Portraits, engraved on steel, and fac-similes of Autographs. 12mo, cloth extra, $2.50.

VII.

PASSAGES FROM THE LIFE OF CHARLES KNIGHT, Publisher, Author and Leader in the Work of Popular Education;

Editor of the "Penny Encyclopædia," "The Libraries of Useful and Entertaining Knowledge" and "The Popular History of England." Revised and Abridged from the English Edition. Large 12mo, about 450 pp. With Portrait.

The life of a man like Charles Knight, who may be said to have founded that system of Popular Education which brings the highest literature of the language within the reach of the lowest of the people, should possess a special interest for readers in a nation at the basis of whose institutions such a system must lie. The publication of the "Penny Encyclopædia" and "The Library of Useful Knowledge" completely revolutionized the whole method of teaching the English people. Mr. Knight was, perhaps, the first to perceive that text-books alone could not supply all that was necessary to the development of popular intelligence. What was required to supplement the text-books had hitherto been accessible only to the wealthier classes, but in the admirable series of works planned by Mr. Knight, the clearest scientific information on the one hand, and on the other a knowledge of the higher literature, were placed within the reach of every member of the poorer and working classes.

Apart from this work, Mr. Knight's life was interesting from his association during a most important half century with nearly all classes of the leading and thinking men of Great Britain. The story of his labors is simply and dramatically told in his own language, which has been left unchanged as far as was consistent with the slight abridgement that it has been considered advisable to make from the more voluminous English edition.

‡ **BRISTED. Five Years in an English University.** By Charles Astor Bristed, late Foundation Scholar of Trinity College, Cambridge. Fourth edition. Revised and amended by the author. 12mo, cloth, extra, $2.50.

A new edition of this standard work, for some years out of print, has long been called for. With its facts and statistics corrected, and brought down to recent date, the volume conveys to the college graduate or undergraduate information of special value and importance, while the vivid and attractive record of a personal experience contains much to interest the general reader.

"It is characterized by most excellent taste, and contains a great deal of most novel and interesting information."—*Philadelphia Inquirer.*

BRYANT. Letters of a Traveller. By William Cullen Bryant. With steel portrait. New edition. 12mo, cloth, $2.

—— **Letters From the East.** Notes of a Visit to Egypt and Palestine. 12mo, cloth, $1.50.

—— The Same. Illustrated edition. With fine engravings on steel. 12mo, cloth extra, $2.50.

—— **Orations and Addresses.** Including those delivered on Irving, Cooper, Cole, Verplanck, Shakespeare, Morse, Scott, etc. 12mo, cloth $2.

BEST READING, THE. A Classified Bibliography for Easy Reference. With Hints on the Selection of Books; on the Formation of Libraries, Public and Private; on Courses of Reading, etc.; a Guide for the Librarian, Bookbuyer, and Bookseller. The Classified Lists, arranged under about 500 subject headings, include all the most desirable books now to be obtained either in Great Britain or the United States, with the published prices annexed. Revised Edition. 12mo, paper, $1.00. Cloth, $1.50,

"The best work of the kind we have seen."—*College Courant.*

"We know of no manual that can take its place as a guide to the selection of a library."—*N. Y. Independent.*

† **BLACKWELL. Studies in General Science.** By Antoinette Brown Blackwell. 12mo (uniform with Child's "Benedicite"). Cloth extra, $2.25.

"The writer evinces admirable gifts both as a student and thinker. She brings a sincere and earnest mind to the investigation of truth."—*N. Y. Tribune.*

"The idea of the work is an excellent one, and it is ably developed."—*Boston Transcript.*

† **BLAKE. The Production of the Precious Metals; or, Statistical Notices of the Principal Gold and Silver Producing Regions of the World.** With a chapter upon the Unification of Gold and Silver Coinage. By Wm. P. Blake, Commissioner from the State of California to the Paris Exposition of 1867. One volume, 8vo, cloth extra, $2.50.

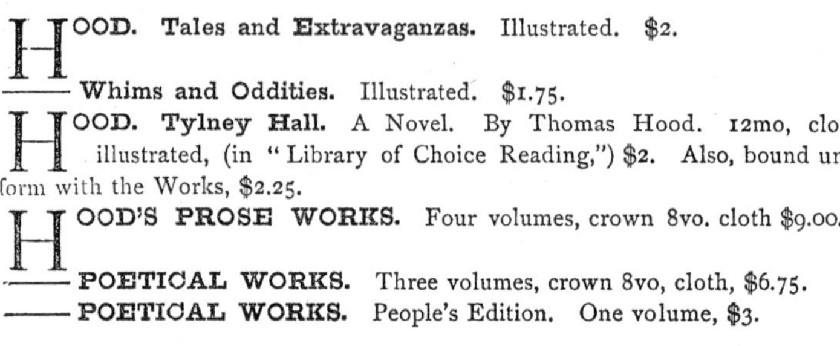

HOOD. **Tales and Extravaganzas.** Illustrated. $2.

—— **Whims and Oddities.** Illustrated. $1.75.

HOOD. **Tylney Hall.** A Novel. By Thomas Hood. 12mo, cloth illustrated, (in "Library of Choice Reading,") $2. Also, bound uniform with the Works, $2.25.

HOOD'S **PROSE WORKS.** Four volumes, crown 8vo. cloth $9.00.

—— **POETICAL WORKS.** Three volumes, crown 8vo, cloth, $6.75.

—— **POETICAL WORKS.** People's Edition. One volume, $3.

—— **PROSE AND POETICAL WORKS.** People's Edition. Two volumes. Cloth, in box, $6.

"Hood's name will be a household word to all who speak the English language." – *London Quarterly Review.*

—— **POEMS.** Illustrated (Wanstead) edition. The Poems of Thomas Hood. Artist's edition. With illustrations by Darley, Eytinge, Gustave Doré Secombe, Birket Foster, and the Etching Club. The letter-press handsomely printed on tinted paper, with red lines. Small quarto, uniform with the Artist's edition of the Sketch Book. Cloth extra, with handsome stamp, gilt edges, $5. morocco, $10.

HOPE. **Till the Doctor Comes, and how to Help Him.** A Manual for Emergencies, Accidents, etc. By George A. Hope, M.D. Revised with additions, by a New York Physician. 12mo, cloth, 60 cts.

"A very readable, as well as useful, little book; one that will keep people from useless tinkering, and guide them correctly till medical aid can be called"—*Scientific American.*

HYACINTHE. **The Family.** A Series of Discourses by Father Hyacinthe. To which are added The Education of the Working Classes; The Church—Six Conferences; Speeches and Addresses With an Historical Introduction. By Hon. John Bigelow. 12mo, $1.50.

N. B.—Both books are published under Father Hyacinthe's sanction, and he receives a copyright on the sales.

—— **Life, Speeches, and Discourses of Pere Hyacinthe.** Edited by Rev. L. W. Bacon. One volume, 12mo, cloth, $1.25.

"We are quite sure that these Discourses will increase Father Hyacinthe's reputation among us as a man of rare intellectual power, genuine eloquence, ripe scholarship, and most generous sympathies."—*National Baptist, Philadelphia.*

"The Discourses will be found fully up to the high expectations formed from the great priest's protest against the trammels of Romish dogmatism."—*Rochester Democrat.*

LOSSING. **A History of England, from the Earliest Period to the Present Time.** With special reference to the Progress of the People in Civilization, Literature, and the Arts. By Benson J. Lossing, author of "Pictorial Field Book of American Revolution," etc. With three maps, large 12mo, cloth, extra, $2.50; half calf, extra, $4.50.

"This work, in one handsome volume of about 600 pages, has been carefully prepared by the editor for popular use. It is a very comprehensive outline of the History of England from the time of the Ancient Britons to the year 1870, and contains every leading fact in that history essential to a general understanding of the progress of the country from its barbarian state to its present condition of highest civilization."

"We know of no compendium of English History so full and complete, so methodized and reliable, and at the same time so attractively and powerfully written.'—*College Courant.*

† MACAULAY. **The Complete Works of Lord Macaulay.** From the last edition, edited by his sister, Lady Trevelyan. Elegantly printed on tinted paper at the Riverside Press, and containing the History of England, Essays, Poems, and Speeches. Sixteen vols., crown 8vo, extra cloth, cut or uncut, $36; half calf, gilt or antique, $64.

‡ —— **Critical, Historical, and Miscellaneous Essays.** With a Memoir, Index, and Portrait. Riverside Edition. Six vols., crown 8vo, extra cloth, cut or uncut, $13.50; half calf, gilt or antique, $24.

—— **History of England.** By Lord Macaulay. Student's Edition. Four vols. 12mo, with a new portrait of Macaulay. Extra cloth, cut, $7; half calf, gilt, or antique, $16.

MEMOIRS OF A HUGUENOT FAMILY. A veritable History of permanent interest. Translated from the original Autobiography of Rev. James Fontaine. By Ann Maury. With a translation of the Edict of Nantes, now first printed in English. 12mo, pp. 508, cloth, extra, $1.75.

"The History of the Huguenot cause has a profound significance and value to all earn est souls."—*Liberal Christian.*

"It is a good book."—*Nation, N. Y.*

MAITLAND. **Higher Law. A Romance.** By Edward Maitland, author of "The Pilgrim and the Shrine." 12mo, cloth, $1.75.

"There is no novel, in short, which can be compared to it for its width of view, its cultivation, its poetry, and its deep human interest, . . . except 'Romola.'"—*Westminster Review.*

"Its careful study of character, and the ingenuity and independence of its speculations, will commend it to the admiration even of those who differ from its conclusions most gravely."—*British Quarterly Review.*

—— **The Pilgrim and the Shrine.** By Edward Maitland. Third edition. 12mo, cloth, $1.50.

"One of the wisest and most charming of books."—*Westminster Review.*

MAYO. Kaloolah: The Autobiography of Jonathan Romer of Nantucket. Edited by W. S. Mayo, M.D. 12mo, cloth extra $1.75.

Some 20,000 copies of this celebrated work have been sold, and it is justly entitled to enduring popularity.

"One of the most admirable pictures ever produced in this country."—*Washington Irving.*

"The most singular and captivating romance since Robinson Crusoe."—*Home Journal.*

"By far the most fascinating and entertaining book we have read since we were bewitched by the graceful inventions of the Arabian Nights."—*Democratic Review.*

——— **Never Again.** A new work by the author of "Kaloolah." Illustrated with numerous engravings, designed and engraved by Gaston Fay. In one volume, over 700 pages, uniform with "Kaloolah." $2.

"Puts its author in the front rank of novelists."----*London Athenæum.*

"A wholesome book; one that really holds up the mirror to American society."----*N. Y. Evening Post.*

"The first real novel of American society. . . . It will be read from cover to cover." ----*N. Y. Times.*

——— **The Berber: A Romance of Morocco.** By W. S. Mayo, M.D., author of "Kaloolah," "Never Again," etc. 12mo, cloth, uniform with "Kaloolah." $1.75.

"A Romance of the highest class, replete with character, plot and incident, and occupying ground entirely new."—*Home Journal.*

The very great favor with which Dr. Mayo's last work, "Never Again," has been received, has induced the publishers to believe that new editions of his earlier books, which had also attained great popularity, would be welcomed by the reading public. Although it is twenty years since the publication of "The Berber," its narrative will be found as fresh, its characterization as vivid, and its pictures of life as accurate to-day as they were shown to be then.

MAYHEW. Benjamin Franklin. The Printer's Boy, the Philosopher, and the Statesman. A Biography for Boys. By Henry Mayhew. Illustrated. 18mo, cloth extra, $1.50

MEMORABLE WOMEN. By Mrs. Newton Crossland. With eight illustrations by Birket Foster. One vol., 18mo, cloth extra, $1.50.

‡ **MILMAN. The History of Christianity; from the Birth of Christ to the Abolition of Paganism in the Roman Empire.** By the Rev. H. H. Milman, Dean of St. Paul's, etc. New edition, three vols., extra cloth, $5.25; half calf, $10.50.

‡ ——— **The History of Latin Christianity; including that of the Popes to the Pontificate of Nicholas V.** By Dean Milman. Eight vols. crown 8vo, extra cloth, $14; half calf, $28.

‡ ——— **The History of the Jews. From the Earliest Period down to Modern Times.** By Dean Milman. A new edition, three volumes crown 8vo, extra cloth, $5.25; half calf, $10.50.

MOLLOY. Geology and Revelation; or, The Ancient History of the Earth, considered in the Light of Geological Facts and Revealed Religion. With illustrations. By the Rev. Gerald Molloy, D.D. With an Introduction to the American Edition by an eminent Geologist, and an Appendix containing Prof. Dana's Chapter on Cosmogony. 12mo, cloth extra, $2.

"We have rarely found such an amount and variety of specific information brought together with more fulness and force."—*Boston Transcript.*

NATIONAL GALLERY OF AMERICAN LANDSCAPE. With twenty-four superb engravings on steel, engraved in the best manner, from paintings by eminent American artists, with descriptions. Atlas folio, half morocco, gilt edges, $50.

——— The same, in portfolio, $40.

——— The same, proofs on India, half morocco, $75.

——— The same, Artists' proofs, $100.

NEW MERCANTILE MAP OF THE WORLD, ON MERCATOR'S PROJECTION. For Merchants, Shippers, Ship Owners etc. Size 55 inches by 40 inches.

The following are the leading features of this Map—

All the States, Kingdoms, and Empires of the World are exhibited, by the aid of Color Printing, in a clear and distinct manner, with their Sea-ports and Principal Towns, showing the most recent changes of Boundaries, and also the latest Geographical Discoveries.

The recognized steam and sailing Routes to and from the principal Ports of the World, with the distances and average time clearly laid down.

The principal Overland Telegraphs, Submarine Cables, and main lines of Railways.

The Currents of the Ocean, with arrows showing their Course, are brought out distinctly, but not obtrusively, by means of Coloring. Warm and Cold Currents are distinguished by a simple sign.

The Northern and Southern limits of Icebergs and Drift Ice are also distinctly defined.

The Northern and Southern limits of permanent human habitation is also clearly shown.

The whole forming not only a compendium of most useful information for all parties engaged in Commerce, but also an ornament alike for the Counting Room and the Library.

Price to Subscribers, mounted on cloth and Rollers, or in cloth case for Library, $10.

O'CONNOR, W. D. Nettie Renton; or, The Ghost. A Christmas Story. 16mo. Illustrated by Nast. $1.

ON THE EDGE OF THE STORM. By the author of "Mademoiselle Mori." 12mo, cloth, with Frontispiece, $1.50; gilt extra, $2.

"This is a charming story. The sympathy which the author evinces towards all her personages, and the justice she does to their different modes of thought and opinion, are the main charm of the book."—*London Athenæum.*

"This book is altogether a delightful one, showing great knowledge, a rare power of writing, and a far rarer artistic mastery over form and detail."—*Pall Mall Gazette.*

Putnams' Series of Popular Manuals.

HALF-HOURS WITH THE MICROSCOPE.
By EDWIN LANKESTER, M.D., F.R.S. Illustrated by 250 Drawings from Nature. 12mo, cloth, $1.25.

"This beautiful little volume is a very complete manual for the amateur microscopist. * * * The 'Half-Hours' are filled with clear and agreeable descriptions, whilst eight plates, executed with the most beautiful minuteness and sharpness, exhibit no less than 250 objects with the utmost attainable distinctness."—*Critic.*

HALF-HOURS WITH THE TELESCOPE:
Being a popular Guide to the Use of the Telescope as a means of Amusement and Instruction. Adapted to inexpensive instruments. By R. A. PROCTOR, B.A., F.R.A.S. 12mo, cloth, with illustrations on stone and wood. Price, $1.25.

"It is crammed with starry plates on wood and stone, and among the celestial phenomena described or figured, by far the larger number may be profitably examined with small telescopes."—*Illustrated Times.*

HALF-HOURS WITH THE STARS:
A Plain and Easy Guide to the Knowledge of the Constellations, showing in 12 Maps, the Position of the Principal Star-Groups Night after Night throughout the Year, with introduction and a separate explanation of each Map. True for every Year. By RICHARD A. PROCTOR, B.A., F.R.A.S. Demy 4to. Price, $2.25.

"Nothing so well calculated to give a rapid and thorough knowledge of the position of the stars in the firmament has ever been designed or published hitherto. Mr. Proctor's 'Half-Hours with the Stars' will become a text-book in all schools, and an invaluable aid to all teachers of the young."—*Weekly Times.*

MANUAL OF POPULAR PHYSIOLOGY:
Being an Attempt to Explain the Science of Life in Untechnical Language. By HENRY LAWSON, M.D. 18mo, with 90 Illustrations. Price, $1.25.

Man's Mechanism, Life, Force, Food, Digestion, Respiration, Heat, the Skin, the Kidneys, Nervous System, Organs of Sense, &c., &c., &c.

"Dr Lawson has succeeded in rendering his manual amusing as well as instructive. All the great facts in human physiology are presented to the reader successively; and either for private reading or for classes, this manual will be found well adapted for initiating the uninformed into the mysteries of the structure and function of their own bodies."—*Athenæum.*

A DICTIONARY OF DERIVATIONS
Of the English Language, in which each word is traced to its primary root. Forming a Text-Book of Etymology, with Definitions and the Pronunciation of each word. 16mo, $1.00.

A HAND-BOOK OF SYNONYMS
Of the English Language, with Definitions, &c. 16mo, cloth. $1.00.

*** These two Manuals are very comprehensive in a small compass.

www.ingramcontent.com/pod-product-compliance
Lightning Source LLC
LaVergne TN
LVHW021321110826
845150LV00003B/636

9781425556624